THE BULL MOOSE YEARS

THE
BULL MOOSE YEARS

Theodore Roosevelt
and the
Progressive Party

JOHN   ALLEN   GABLE

National University Publications
KENNIKAT PRESS   //   1978
Port Washington, N. Y.   //   London

Kennikat Press
National University Publications
Series in American Studies

Manufactured in the United States of America

Published by
Kennikat Press Corp.
Port Washington, N.Y./London

Library of Congress Cataloging in Publication Data

Gable, John A
　　The Bull Moose years.

　　(National university publications: Series in American studies)
　　Bibliography: p.
　　Includes index.
　　1. United States—Politics and government—1913–1921. 2. Roosevelt, Theodore, Pres. U. S., 1858–1919. 3. Progressive Party (Founded 1912) 4. Progressivism (United States politics) I. Title.
E766.G3　　　　　　329'.892　　　　　78-1540
ISBN 0-8046-9187-8

This book is dedicated to my parents,
Allen H. Gable and Mary Jane Gable,
and to the memory of Ethel Roosevelt Derby.

The publication of this book was made possible, in part, by a grant from the Theodore Roosevelt Association. The Theodore Roosevelt Association, founded in 1919 and chartered by Congress in 1920, is a nonprofit national historical society with offices in New York City and Oyster Bay, New York.

CONTENTS

PREFACE

Theodore Roosevelt described the work of the final phase of his career as being "in the prophet business." He had been legislator, bureaucrat, governor, president; in the last decade of his life he was "prophet." Of course, for Roosevelt the roles of politician and officeholder and of prophet were by no means completely separate. Throughout his long career, T.R. always tried to combine the calling of professional politician and officeholder with that of reform prophet. The officeholder often played the role of prophet (the White House, he said, was a "bully pulpit"), and the prophet of the Bull Moose and World War years always played politics. Rather it was a question of emphasis.

The officeholder's business was largely one of brokerage, meeting immediate needs, and producing compromise legislation and policy. The "prophet business" involved taking more risks, and charting long-term goals on behalf of holistic visions. A life and a career have their times and seasons, and Roosevelt always had a keen sense of who and where he was. Custom and circumstance dictated the role of "elder statesman" for former Presidents of the United States. T.R. chose to give new meaning to this tradition and position by becoming, in the years 1912-16, an activist prophet for political and social reform. This book is the story of those years.

Some historians, seeing that the "Republican Roosevelt" could be a clever and compromising politician from the time he entered politics in the 1880s through the White House years, and aware of the high ideals he habitually preached, have concluded that T.R. was little more than a "flim-flam" man whose words and deeds contrasted to the point of hypocrisy—in short, that he was "just another politician." For such historians the Bull Moose years are but another chapter in a crafty careerist's life. Other historians, those with a greater understanding of and respect for the calling of politician and officeholder, see in the "Republican Roosevelt" a *realpolitiker* of practical and worthwhile accomplishment. For these historians the Bull Moose Roosevelt may appear a beserker, a man who lost touch with political reality. This study presents an alternative to these two viewpoints.

The Bull Moose Roosevelt saw an aged party system, largely stagnant since his youth, that did not reflect in partisanship the realities of the great ideological division in the nation between conservatives and progressives; that for the most part was oligarchic in structure and undemocratic in conduct; and that was slow and negligent in addressing issues and implementing needed policies. He had worked as best he could within this party system for thirty years. Nor would he abandon it without first seeing a clear alternative. In 1912, with the progressive movement at high tide, and a legion of supporters ready to follow him, Roosevelt saw an alternative, and formed a new party. The Progressive Party was an attempt to combine the needs of reform with the necessities of professional politics, a fight to re-make the American party system. At the same time, the new party served as an agency for social education to advance solutions to the pressing problems of the industrial and urban America of the twentieth century. In the end, Roosevelt failed to re-shape partisan politics. He did, however, succeed in promoting and publicizing reform measures which have since become the substance of law and national policy. His hopes for a new party were smashed on the rocks of American pluralism and social conservatism, the foundations of the traditional party system, but his blueprints for social and economic reform were crucial in building the America that was to come.

So much for Roosevelt. What of those men and women who followed him into the Progressive Party? Their story has sometimes been viewed as a tragic tale of blighted careers, lost opportunities, wasted energy, and even damage to the cause of reform. The record does not bear out this view. Much practical and immediate good in terms of reform was accomplished by the Progressive Party during its short life. The party proved to be one of the most effective pressure groups in American history, as well as the source for many reforms in later decades. Moreover, most of the Progressives lived on to work and fight another day under other banners. The list of successful political leaders with a Bull Moose past is indeed a long one. This book is the account not only of T.R. in the years 1912-16, but also, equally, of the men and women who fought with him at "Armageddon." The politicians, social workers, reformers, white collar professionals, and academics who joined the new party had somewhat different and sometimes conflicting reasons for choosing the Progressive path. But all saw the Progressive Party as a chance to accomplish more than they had been able to achieve in nonpartisan callings or under the old party system. An examination of the Progressives reveals much about the history of American reform, ideas, and society in the twentieth century.

Finally, this book is also a case study of a political party. Viewed from the perspective of the history of American "third parties," the Progressives uniquely combined the usual third party functions of protest, pressure, and publicity for reform with the methods, organizational structures, and purposes usually associated with the "major parties." Seen from the larger perspective of the history of American political parties in general, the Progressive Party represents an experiment in partisan structure and operation, as seen in the Progressive Service and other components of the party's national organization. Studied from the standpoint of the history of American political reform, the Progressive Party was the most advanced phase of the progressive movement of 1890-1920 and the attempt to bring about substantive changes within the fold of capitalism and constitutional democracy. Ideologically, Roosevelt and the Progressive Party stood for a synthesis of the nationalist and reform traditions in American thought and politics, the "New Nationalism" of the means of the Hamiltonian state for the ends of Jeffersonian democracy; and also, particularly after 1912, for a reconciliation between pluralism and nationalism. In short, the Progressives sought to make a new mosaic out of the myriad pieces of the American experience. The pattern did not set, but parts of their design are still evident in the picture that is the America of a later day.

A scholar accumulates many personal debts in the course of his work. I thank Professor John L. Thomas, teacher and mentor, who directed this study in its earlier stage as a doctoral dissertation at Brown University. I thank my late maternal grandparents, Sidney D. Kirkpatrick and Bonnie Jean Hardesty Kirkpatrick, and my parents, Allen H. Gable and Mary Jane Kirkpatrick Gable, for financial assistance and moral support through the years of this labor. I pay tribute to the memory of the late Hermann Hagedorn, Roosevelt's friend and biographer, who early stimulated my interest in T.R. I thank Theodore Roosevelt's daughters, Alice Roosevelt Longworth and particularly the late Ethel Roosevelt Derby, and his kinsman P. James Roosevelt, former President of the Theodore Roosevelt Association, for help, encouragement, and inspiration. I am grateful to the officers and members of the Theodore Roosevelt Association for providing a generous grant to support the publication of this book. Others who have assisted this work at various stages and who deserve special mention include Professor Elmer E. Cronwell of Brown University, Josiah Bunting, III, Professor Barry Karl of the University of Chicago, Professor Paul Douglas Casdorph of West Virginia State College, Cornell Jaray and the people at Kennikat Press, Professor James Patterson of Brown University, Dr. Stephen R. Fox, Professor Hoyt Landon Warner of Kenyon College, Winifred R. Barton, Karen L. Mota, Elizabeth Roosevelt, Mrs. Harold Kraft, William D. Johnston, and Curator Wallace Finley Dailey and former Curator Gregory C. Wilson fo the Theodore Roosevelt Collection at Harvard, and others too numerous to name here. Finally, it should be obvious from a glance at the notes and references that this study would not have been possible without the wealth of historical literature produced on the progressive era in the last forty years. I owe a great debt to the scholars who have preceded me in the field of progressive era studies. Many people share in whatever merit this study may have. I alone am responsible for any errors of fact or judgement.

John Allen Gable

THE BULL MOOSE YEARS

ABOUT THE AUTHOR

John Allen Gable has been Executive Director of the Theodore Roosevelt Association since 1974. He is also Adjunct Associate Professor of History at C. W. Post College of Long Island University. He received his M.A. and Ph.D. degrees from Brown University and taught there previously.

CHAPTER ONE

THE ROAD TO ARMAGEDDON

You know, Charley, that 1912 really represented merely the goal of thought for which I had always been heading.

T.R.

This swift culmination was the inevitable outcome of long-maturing causes. The present party alignment was certain, sooner or later, to be broken.

Herbert Knox Smith

The climax to the tumultuous fifteenth Republican National Convention came on Saturday morning, June 22, 1912, when the Kansas editor Henry J. Allen, progressive Republican spokesman for former President Theodore Roosevelt, read a message from Roosevelt condemning President William Howard Taft and his conservative supporters. "Under the direction, and with the encouragement of Mr. Taft, the majority of the national committee, by the so-called 'steam-roller' methods . . . stole eighty or ninety delegates, putting on the temporary roll-call a sufficient number of fraudulent delegates to defeat the legally expressed will of the people and to substitute a dishonest for an honest majority." T.R. therefore requested "that the men elected as Roosevelt delegates will now decline to vote on any matter before the convention."

There was a perfunctory and dispirited air about the remaining proceedings as the conservatives' platform was adopted and President Taft and Vice President James S. Sherman were renominated. The galleries and floor slowly began to empty after the reading of Roosevelt's message; for the first time in the fiery five-day convention, hundreds of vacant seats were apparent in Chicago's

Coliseum. Warren G. Harding, a leading "standpatter" from the president's home state of Ohio, presented Taft's name. The vote was Taft 561, Roosevelt 107, Robert M. La Follette 41, others 19. Three hundred forty-four delegates refused to vote.

It was evening when the balloting for president began, and at the same time, elsewhere in Chicago, crowds swarmed along Michigan Avenue outside Orchestra Hall in anticipation of an announced rump convention of Roosevelt delegates. All was confusion, excitement, and enthusiasm inside Orchestra Hall. Reporters at long tables talked to the newspapers and wire services through hurriedly installed telephones, while the galleries applauded the arrival of leaders and delegates from the Roosevelt camp, and chanted, "We want Teddy!"

Although hastily assembled, those gathering on the platform and floor made up a cross section of the progressive movement, the reform wave which in 1912 appeared to be reaching high tide. There were municipal reformers like Francis J. Heney, the pugnacious, red-headed San Francisco graft prosecutor, and Comptroller William A. Prendergast of New York City. Present, too, was Judge Ben Lindsey of Denver, "little Ben" the "kids' judge," who was founder of the juvenile court system, and personified the social worker element in progressivism as well as the movement to "clean up" city government. Dean William Draper Lewis of the law school of the University of Pennsylvania took a prominent part in the Orchestra Hall meeting, representative of the entry of academics and other trained professionals into government and politics through the progressive movement. Reporters noted the presence of the dapper millionaire George W. Perkins, finance chairman of the Roosevelt campaign, a man who was suspect among western progressives because of his Wall Street connections. Perkins, however, was at odds with his former partner J. P. Morgan, a Taft supporter, and was typical of those businessmen for whom ethics, efficiency, and the salvation of capitalism dictated an alignment with progressivism for the reform of American business. Reform governors, like the militant Hiram W. Johnson of California and young Robert Perkins Bass of New Hampshire, were also present in the hall, witnesses to the vitality of the progressive movement on the state level. The delegates recognized James R. Garfield, commissioner of corporations and then secretary of the interior under T.R., and lanky Gifford Pinchot, T.R.'s chief forester, who had been fired by President Taft in a dispute over conservation, leaders who were symbols of the progressive legacy of the Roosevelt administration and the reform movement's work on the national level. Senator Moses E. Clapp, the "black eagle" of Minnesota, and Roosevelt's campaign manager Senator Joseph M. Dixon of Montana, leading Republican insurgents and veterans of the battle in Washington since 1909 against the conservative G.O.P. Congressional leadership and the Taft White House, stood on the platform as the meeting got under way. All these men and more like them assembled in Orchestra Hall that hot summer night under a huge portrait of Theodore Roosevelt.

Governor Johnson presided at the rump convention, condemning the "theft" of the Republican nomination and exhorting bolting delegates to courage and righteousness. Senator Clapp read a resolution attacking the G.O.P. convention and pledging continued support for Roosevelt's candidacy. Next Comptroller Prendergast, who had been scheduled to nominate T.R. at the Republican convention, proposed the former president as candidate of a new party. Dean Lewis and others seconded the nomination. Then the crowd roared and hats flew into the air as Roosevelt appeared.

Reviewing the progressive principles at stake in the battle between Taft and himself, and the actions of the national committee in denying progressives their claimed majority at the Republican convention, Roosevelt declared that "this has now become a contest which cannot be settled merely along the old party lines."

I, therefore, ask you to go to your several homes to find out the sentiment of the people . . . and then again come together, I suggest by mass convention, to nominate a Progressive on a Progressive platform that will enable us to appeal to Northerner and Southerner, Easterner and Westerner, Republican and Democrat alike in the name of our common American citizenship. If you wish me to make the fight, I will make it. . . .

That night the Indiana progressive George Ade finished his article for *Collier's* on the events in Chicago during the preceding week. "It is all over. In other words, it has just begun," wrote Ade. But precisely what was over? And what was beginning?

2

The progressive movement, a many-faceted and general wave of reform, came into being in the last decade of the nineteenth and the first decade of the twentieth centuries as a response to the social, economic, and political conditions brought about by industrialization and urbanization. By the second decade of the twentieth century, the movement had reached a political and ideological crossroads. Within reform ranks the years of the Taft administration witnessed the convergence of the progressive movement on the state and national levels, and the beginning of an examination of progressive political options. Ideologically, these years also marked the emergence of a nationalist philosophy of reform which corresponded to political developments and needs, and which at the same time affected the ways political problems were perceived and approached. The birth of the new party at Orchestra Hall was the direct result of this political and ideological situation.

During the progressive era, as throughout most of American history, three political options were open to reformers: the nonpartisan, factional partisan, and reform party strategies or approaches. Many reformers, like the early proponents of the abolition of slavery and the Mugwumps of the Gilded Age, had chosen the nonpartisan path of working outside the political parties, forming groups and committees for purposes of pressure, lobbying, and social education.

Other reformers, however, had preferred to work within the structure of the major parties, playing factional politics to gain office, partisan power, and the adoption of their proposals and principles by party and government. Finding the major parties often hostile to reform, and factionalism either futile or wasteful of time and energy, still other reformers, like the Free-Soilers before the Civil War, the Greenbackers of the 1870s and 1880s, and the Populists of the 1890s, had organized new parties. These reform parties were similar to the old parties in form and mechanism, but were different in being primarily dedicated to principles rather than political survival, to social education rather than winning office. Each of these three reform political options or strategies had advantages and each had disadvantages.

The nonpartisan political option has often been used to promote a cause or issue like women's suffrage or the needs of a particular interest group such as labor. During the progressive era nonpartisan reform organizations like the National Municipal League, National Conservation Association, and National Child Labor Committee proliferated, representing a wide spectrum of issues and concerns. While these organizations scored many gains for reform, and were probably the most effective vehicles for serving the needs of specific interest groups like the farmers, their approach to reform was piecemeal, confined to separate problems rather than concerned with a holistic view of society. Yet social, economic, and political problems tended to be interrelated, and hence the various nonpartisan reform groups were limited in approach and effectiveness. Moreover, not directly involved in partisan politics, the nonpartisan reformers were severely restricted in power and influence, and sooner or later were forced to go hat-in-hand to the partisan politicians who actually controlled government. Isolated from political power, convinced of the need for a comprehensive approach to social problems, by 1912 many progressives like the social workers Jane Addams, Raymond Robins, and Frances Kellor, and the municipal reformer Edward P. Costigan, not previously involved in partisan politics, were ready for the new party. It seemed time to abandon what the social expert Paul U. Kellogg of *Survey* magazine called "the strategy of a detached position." In part, the nonpartisan path had reflected the distaste of some reformers for the machinations, necessities, and compromises of traditional partisan politics, but the progressive movement seemed to be calling forth a new kind of politics based on principles and substantive issues. The nonpartisan reformers, however, carried their prejudices against professional politics and politicians with them into the new party along with their ideas of public service and social education.

Factionalism is, of course, inevitable in the conduct of politics and endemic to political parties. The goal of a faction is to win control of partisan and corresponding governmental machinery on some level or levels of local, state, and national government. Factionalism has often involved merely divisions between established and aspiring groups within a party, between "ins" and "outs," but has also frequently reflected and been mainly concerned with intrapartisan splits over issues and ideologies. During the progressive era partisan factionalism was acutely developed, reaching major proportions as progressive and conservative factions contended for power in the Democratic and Republican parties in national, state, and district organizations, Congress, many cities, and most states. As Gifford Pinchot observed in 1910, "Differences of purpose and belief between political parties today are vastly less than the differences within the parties."

The advantage of the factional partisan reform option was obvious: progressives directly involved in the partisan and governmental process could translate reform goals into platforms, legislation, and policy through winning office and whole or partial control of party organizations. The work of such urban reformers as Democratic Mayor Tom Johnson of Cleveland and reform governors like the Republican Robert M. La Follette of Wisconsin was witness to the effectiveness if not the complete success of the factional partisan approach. Yet, while the successes of the progressive factions were numerous and well publicized, many of them were half-loaves or far less, and throughout the first two decades of the twentieth century the party organizations in Congress and most cities and states remained largely in the hands of the conservatives. Moreover, as the issues in contention between reformers and conservatives became more numerous and the lines of opposition were hardened by time, the coexistence of the two factions within each major party became increasingly difficult. The clash came to a head during the years of the Taft administration.

The years of the Taft administration marked the convergence of the progressive movement in the states with the reform movement on the national level. By 1910 progressive Republicans everywhere recognized that the individual fights for reform in the various states—from Hiram Johnson's in California to Robert Perkins Bass's in New Hampshire—the revolt of the Congressional insurgents against the Old Guard leadership, and the wide-ranging debate between the upholders of the legacy of the Roosevelt administration and the supporters of the Taft policies, were all part of the same whole. Likewise, progressive Democrats, growing in numbers since William Jennings Bryan's nomination in 1896, viewed the factional struggles within their own party in a similar light. Progressive Democrats, however, generally saw the contest for the Democratic nomination in 1912 as the opportune time for final confrontation. But in 1910 progressive Republicans faced a nationwide fight for survival because the Old Guard brought on a major encounter which could not be avoided.

In 1910 the unity of the progressive Republicans nationally was more apparent than real, ideological rather than organizational. Conservative Republican unity, however, was already powerfully manifest. The White House and the congressional and national party machinery as well as the party organizations in many states were in the hands of the conservatives. This conservative domination of most of the superstructure of the G.O.P. asserted itself and was clearly revealed in 1910 when President Taft, Speaker of the House Joseph G. Cannon, Senate Majority Leader Nelson W. Aldrich, and other Old Guard leaders directed a campaign to purge the progressives from the party. The conservative response to the progressives, and the revolt of the Old Guard leaders in Congress against

T.R.'s legislative and executive legacy, had reached full maturity. Using federal patronage dispensed by Taft, funds raised by Senator Aldrich, the services of administration spokesmen like Vice President Sherman, the influences of the Republican Congressional Campaign Committee, and the resources of local standpat organizations, the conservatives went to work to defeat progressives for nomination or renomination in New Hampshire, New York, Indiana, Wisconsin, Iowa, and other states.

When Roosevelt left the White House in 1909, the future looked bright for the progressive Republicans in spite of continued Old Guard opposition. Roosevelt left an impressive legislative and administrative record in the areas of corporation control and regulation, conservation, and labor welfare reform. Progressive strength was growing in the states, and T.R.'s chosen successor, Taft, was in the presidency. Soon, however, Taft, who had served T.R. mainly in the fields of foreign and military affairs, revealed himself as a congenital conservative and an ally of the Old Guard. First in the fight over "Uncle Joe" Cannon's leadership in the House, and then on tariff revision, conservation, and other issues, Taft had sided with the conservatives. He had campaigned and been elected to carry out Roosevelt's policies. He had, said the progressives, but "on a shutter." The conservative drift of the administration's policies and the attempted purge of 1910 led directly to a "back from Elba" movement to return Roosevelt to the White House.

The campaign for Roosevelt's nomination in 1912, which began in 1910 and 1911 on the state level long before T.R. himself consented to run, was an attempt to capture the national machinery of the G.O.P. for the progressive movement. Conservatives and progressives alike realized that much more was at stake than the political fortunes of Taft and Roosevelt, much more than a nomination. Progressives had decided that nothing less than a national party organization would serve the movement's needs and purposes on all levels of government. As Herbert Knox Smith, appointed federal commissioner of corporations by T.R. to succeed James R. Garfield, wrote in 1912: "By 1910 the split in the Republican Party had reached such proportions, taken with the open hostility of President Taft toward the Progressives, that the Progressives had to fight—and fight effectively—or die; had to forge the Progressive sentiment into an enduring political weapon, or lose the advance of a decade." In short, one way or another, progressives needed to find a secure partisan home. Hence, in 1910 there was premature but prophetic discussion of forming a new party.

On June 11, 1910, Gifford Pinchot, recently fired as chief forester, and James R. Garfield, both veterans of the Roosevelt administration and promoters of its legacy, addressed a banquet of the Roosevelt Club of St. Paul, Minnesota, a group of enthusiastic progressive Republicans. Pinchot and Garfield spoke in general terms about the importance of translating progressivism into partisan politics, but the club's president, attorney Hugh T. Halbert, went further and predicted the emergence of "a new party" with T.R., Pinchot, and Garfield among its leaders. The resulting flurry of discussion in the press demonstrated that Halbert was not alone in his thoughts. "Unquestionably a new political party is maturing in this country," declared the *Atlanta Journal.* The *Kansas City Star,* owned by the influential progressive Republican William Rockhill Nelson, asked in a special front-page editorial: "Is not this the logical time to look forward to a new party which shall include progressive Democrats and Republicans—a party dedicated to the square deal and led by Theodore Roosevelt?" Yet the formation of a new party hardly seemed practical as long as there was a good chance of capturing the "grand old" one. As the *Boston Transcript* put it: "Third-party talk is rife, but not ripe."

Roosevelt himself in 1910 and 1911 avoided and discouraged talk of a new party, believing that progressive Republicans should play out their hand in the factional politics of the G.O.P. before considering other alternatives. He encouraged progressives in their struggles with the Old Guard by personally entering the factional fight in his home state of New York, where he was elected chairman of the 1910 state convention over Vice President Sherman, and by giving voice and definition to the progressive philosophy through articles and speeches, most notably in a fourteen-state speaking tour in August and September, 1910.

Roosevelt's speeches on this tour set forth a progressive philosophy and program, the "New Nationalism," which consisted of a synthesis combining the concepts and issues he had fought for as president, like federal regulation of corporations and natural resources, with further proposals and ideas, such as direct primaries and welfare legislation, commonly being discussed by progressive politicians, intellectuals, and social workers. The climactic address of the tour was the famous New Nationalism speech at Osawatomie, Kansas, on August 31. Although T.R. had expressed most of the principles of the New Nationalism as president, never before had he used such striking and unequivocal language, and never before had he given his philosophy of progressivism such complete and coherent formulation. But Roosevelt's New Nationalism, which proclaimed that the time had come to "work in a spirit of broad and far-reaching nationalism," was not only the product of the maturation of T.R.'s thought. It was also the ideological statement of the political fact of the convergence of progressivism on the state and national levels.

The term "New Nationalism" had been coined in 1909 by the writer Herbert Croly in his book *The Promise of American Life.* Paralleling many passages in earlier writings by Roosevelt, Croly argued for the use of "Hamiltonian" means for "Jeffersonian" ends. That is, he advocated the use of a strong central government to fulfill the needs of the states and the masses of the people. Roosevelt read the book, became friends with Croly, and adopted the term. But the substance of the New Nationalism was not just the sum of the thought of two individuals. It was also the result and expression of the evolution of the progressive movement from local interests, compartmentalized concerns in terms of issues, and half-way measures to a more comprehensive and nationalist view of American society. Nationalism at once, then, served as the symbol of larger concerns and the promise of effective political action.

In the Osawatomie speech Roosevelt called for substantive change in American society. "I stand for the square deal," he declared, repeating the phrase he had made famous as president. "But when I say that I am for the square deal," he continued, "I mean not merely that I stand for fair play under the present rules of the game, but that I stand for having those rules changed so as to work for a more substantial equality of opportunity and of reward for equally good service." He called for a long list of reforms, including graduated income and inheritance taxes, comprehensive workmen's compensation, conservation, regulation of the working conditions of labor, and extension of federal powers

ONE OF THE KIND YOU CAN'T SHUT OFF

and agencies to regulate business. A New Nationalism, he insisted, was necessary in approaching these issues, for "the betterment which we seek must be accomplished . . . mainly through the National Government." Problems which were national in scope should be solved through national action. Setting national priorities, Roosevelt quoted Lincoln: "Labor is prior to, and independent of, capital. Capital is only the fruit of labor, and could never have existed if labor had not first existed. Labor is the superior of capital and deserves much the higher consideration." T.R. explained to the crowd: "If that remark was original with me, I should be even more strongly denounced as a Communist agitator than I shall be anyhow." But then, later in the speech, Roosevelt proclaimed his own twentieth-century version of the Lincoln doctrine: "The man who wrongly holds that every human right is secondary to his profit must now give way to the advocate of human welfare, who rightly maintains that every man holds his property subject to the general right of the community to regulate its use to whatever degree the public welfare may require it."

The response to Roosevelt's tour was accurately summed up by the *Boston Traveler,* which reported that the former president's speeches "have roused his followers to enthusiasm and his enemies to frenzy." Western progressives hailed "the Colonel," as he was popularly called, as the next president, and in Nebraska a conference was called to organize for Roosevelt's nomination in 1912. The conservative *New York Commercial,* however, fulfilling T.R.'s own prediction, spoke of "our peripatetic revolutionist" and his "firebrand's triumphal march": "His new doctrine is more and worse than rank Socialism—it is communism at the limit." And the *New York Herald* also accused T.R. of what it called "waving the red flag."

Roosevelt's tour had its intended effect, and the progressive cause was given a shot in the arm. Taft's purge totally failed, and progressive Republicans captured party nominations in nearly every state where a serious effort had been mounted. In November the progressive Republicans were generally victorious, but the rest of the G.O.P. was buried under a Democratic landslide. Across the country voters seemed to uphold the progressive Republicans while rebuking the Taft administration and the standpatters.

The Republican Party was clearly polarized and close to schism. Republican insurgents in Congress were refusing to abide by the decisions of the G.O.P. caucus and leadership, while at the same time the various state Republican groups, like California's League of Lincoln-Roosevelt Clubs and the Progressive-Republican League of Illinois, were beginning to act more like separate parties than factional organizations. In Wyoming in 1910 the progressive Joseph M. Carey, former Republican senator, was elected governor with Democratic and progressive Republican support over the regular Republican nominee. And in 1911 New Mexico's Republican Progressive League endorsed the winning Democratic gubernatorial candidate against a conservative Republican. That same year in Denver the reformers Ben Lindsey, Edward P. Costigan, and their supporters founded the Citizens' Party, which carried the city elections in May, 1912, against the Republicans and the Democrats. It seemed clear to political observers that unless the progressive factions captured both major parties in 1912 there would be a major shift in partisan alignments or the creation of a third party, and more and more the option of a new reform party seemed to appear on the horizon. Factional partisan reform was reaching the crisis point. The stage was set for 1912.

3

In January, 1912, a Roosevelt National Committee was announced to promote T.R.'s candidacy, and on February 10 a conference of the Colonel's supporters met in Chicago to form a nationwide campaign organization. Senator Joseph M. Dixon of Montana was named chairman of the executive committee, and the newspaper publisher and former Rough Rider Frank Knox, Republican state chairman of Michigan, was chosen vice chairman. A public letter, prearranged by T.R. and Knox, calling on Roosevelt to run was issued, signed by seven Republican governors: William E. Glasscock of West Virginia, Chester H. Aldrich of Nebraska, Robert Perkins Bass of New Hampshire, Joseph M. Carey of Wyoming, Chase S. Osborn of Michigan, Walter R. Stubbs of Kansas, and Herbert S. Hadley of Missouri. Governors Johnson of California and Robert S. Vessey of South Dakota soon endorsed the appeal too. And on February 21 Roosevelt declared: "My hat is in the ring!" A phrase as well as a candidacy was born.

Senator Robert M. La Follette of Wisconsin had announced his candidacy in 1911, but a La Follette boom failed to materialize. The Wisconsin senator was unable to attract wide popular support and could not unify the opposition to Taft. By late 1911 it was evident to most political observers that La Follette's candidacy was doomed. Even among many of his announced supporters he was decidedly a second choice after Roosevelt, and several of the most prominent quickly shifted to Roosevelt when the Colonel launched his drive for the G.O.P. nomination.

During the campaign for the Republican nomination, it became evident that Roosevelt's New Nationalism was in the process of evolution. T.R. presented a platform consisting of the unfinished business of the Roosevelt administration: reform measures needed in the fields of corporation control and regulation, conservation, and labor and welfare. But he also emphasized the need for "direct democracy" reforms in the states, reforms long advocated by many progressives, particularly in the West: direct primaries, initiative and referendum, women's suffrage, direct election of senators, and recall of judicial decisions and elected officials. Since 1910 Roosevelt had been identified as the champion of the primary system, but in the Osawatomie address and other speeches in 1910 he had mainly stressed what government, especially the federal government, should do to advance social change and reform. In 1912 he also spoke of what democracy, what the voters, could and should do to bring about better political and economic conditions. In short, reform was for the people, and it also had to be by the people. After promoting the primary system in 1910 in New York and other states, in 1911 Roosevelt began to defend other direct democracy measures like the referendum as providing useful political machinery for obtaining progressive reforms. He did not view them as panaceas, but as "merely means to ends," necessary tactics for the times in light of the power of the conservative political machines and courts.

Roosevelt's long-standing quarrel with the conservatism of the courts, a quarrel which predated his presidency, led him in an address before the Ohio

Constitutional Convention at Columbus on February 21, 1912, to espouse the popular recall of judicial decisions on the state level. This proved to be a serious blunder. The proposal seemed to strike at the heart of the judicial system and provided ammunition for the conservatives, who had long charged T.R. with wanting to overthrow constitutional government. Moreover, the recall of judicial decisions was widely and easily misunderstood. Roosevelt only meant it to apply in state supreme court cases where state legislation was declared unconstitutional, in effect providing a method for popularly amending a state constitution. Roosevelt specifically said in the Columbus address that the recall

ANOTHER HIDE STRETCHED

should not apply to the federal Supreme Court or in any ordinary civil or criminal cases. But his words were twisted by his opponents, and for the next four years he was forced to explain again and again what he had meant.

Although his support of the recall hurt Roosevelt, his long-time advocacy of the primary system helped him greatly. Taft controlled federal patronage and was supported by most of the G.O.P. state machines, and thus T.R.'s only chance for the nomination lay in winning the presidential primaries being adopted in many states. In fact, 1912 was the first presidential election in which primaries played a role. Since patronage and the Old Guard machines formed the backbone of Taft's support, T.R.'s campaign for the nomination became in effect a fight for the "rule of the people." Thus, Roosevelt was able to transform his candidacy itself into an issue. In a speech entitled "The Right of the People to Rule," delivered at Carnegie Hall in March, T.R. said: "The great fundamental issue now before the Republican Party and before our people can be stated briefly. It is, Are the American people fit to govern themselves, to rule themselves, to control themselves? I believe they are. My opponents do not."

The decision of the primaries was clear. There were twelve northern, border, and western states with direct primaries. La Follette won North Dakota and uncontested Wisconsin. Taft won Massachusetts by a small margin. Roosevelt won the primaries in California, Illinois, Maryland, Nebraska, Oregon, South Dakota, Ohio, Pennsylvania, and New Jersey. All but Maryland were landslides. The Colonel carried California over Taft by a margin of almost two to one; Illinois by more than two to one; South Dakota and Nebraska by more than three to one. In Taft's home state of Ohio the vote was La Follette 15,570; Taft 118,362; T.R. 165,809. La Follette won a total of 36 delegates in the primaries, the president 48, and T.R. 278. The total vote cast in the primaries was La Follette 351,043; Taft 761,716; Roosevelt 1,157,397. The voters had spoken—that is, where they had been allowed to do so.

There were a total of 1,078 delegates to the Republican national convention, with 540 needed to nominate. The rest of the delegates were chosen by district conventions, caucuses, state conventions, or some combinations of methods which did not allow the voters direct expression on the candidates for the nomination. The president's greatest strength was in the South, where federal patronage controlled "rotten borough" Republican organizations which commanded many delegates to the convention but few votes in November. After a series of bitter contests Taft was able to garner a majority of the nonprimary delegates. But even with an army of postmasters, machine myrmidons, and federal officials the Old Guard leaders had not found the task easy. The campaign was marked by roughhouse and name calling, and violence and near riot conditions were common in the district and state conventions. State troops were called out to keep the peace at the Michigan convention. They failed.

In the end 254 delegate seats to the convention were contested. The disputes were decided by the Republican National Committee, which convened in Chicago on June 7 before the convention opened. The National Committee had been selected and ratified by the 1908 convention, and was composed mainly of Taft men. Of the 53 members 15 had failed to be chosen as delegates to the 1912 convention, including Chairman Victor Rosewater of Nebraska, Senator Boies Penrose of Pennsylvania, and Senator W. Murray Crane of Massachusetts, conservatives all. Of the other members, 4 came from United States territorial possessions and 10 from "rotten borough" southern states. These three groups accounted for 29 members of the National Committee—a majority. The outcome of the contests was predestined, but few expected it would be so flagrantly unjust. Of the 254 contested seats, Taft was awarded 235 and Roosevelt 19. It was evident that in many contests in the South Roosevelt supporters had no real case, but in many others outside observers agreed that the National Committee had followed neither justice or logic.

According to the committee, a primary held in Indiana was marked by many irregularities, but since the president had received what the committee considered a clear majority it declined to question the results. Yet in the state of Washington where Roosevelt had won some county primaries by landslides, the committee declared that because of irregularities it would seat the Taft delegates chosen by the state committee. In California two delegates were thrown out, although legally elected for Roosevelt, because the committee held that the state law conflicted with party rules. In Texas the regular G.O.P. organization was controlled by Roosevelt supporters. Roosevelt delegates had been chosen according to party rules—it was impossible even to argue with that—but the committee decided in favor of the Taft contestants because it said that boss rule should be removed from the Texas party.

Those who have studied the contests both then and since have generally concluded that according to party rules and accepted standards of adjudication, Roosevelt was certainly entitled to more delegates than the committee awarded him. T.R.'s own estimate was "eighty or ninety" more. Governor Herbert S. Hadley of Missouri and Senator William E. Borah of Idaho, who represented Roosevelt at the committee sessions, estimated that T.R. should have received a total of about fifty of the contested seats. This figure is in line with the analysis published by the prominent La Follette supporter Gilbert E. Roe in *La Follette's Weekly,* a publication decidedly hostile to T.R. The historian George E. Mowry, who has made the most scholarly study of the matter, agrees with the figure fifty as well.

These fifty delegates would have given the Roosevelt forces control of the convention and probably the nomination. Elihu Root, the Taft candidate, was elected chairman of the convention by a vote of 558 to 502 over Roosevelt's candidate. A motion to deny the contested delegates the right to vote on the matter of seating was defeated 567 to 507. Taft was nominated with 561 votes. A loss of 22 votes would have denied him the nomination on the first ballot. The conclusion seemed obvious to the Roosevelt supporters, and to much of the public at large. The *Chicago Tribune* printed a banner headline: "THOU SHALT NOT STEAL."

Roosevelt had probably hoped to force the Old Guard to surrender and acquiesce in his nomination by demonstrating to them beyond a shadow of a doubt that the price of renominating Taft would be too high to pay. He made a major miscalculation in this assessment, for the Old Guard much preferred defeat with Taft to a Republican victory with Roosevelt. As Senator Penrose put it, it was better to lose the election than lose the party. Taft himself summed up the conservative position in a letter to William Barnes, Jr., the G.O.P. boss of New York:

I quite agree with you that the victory in November is by no means the most important purpose before us. It should be to retain the party and the principles of the party, so as to keep in a condition of activity and discipline a united force to strike when the blow will become effective for the retention of conservative government and conservative institutions. . . . It is the Republican Party with its old principles that we must labor to maintain and keep vitalized and active. If victory comes in November, well and good; if it does not we shall know that in June we accomplished a great victory and that we are merely holding our forces in line for victories in the future. . . .

ROOSEVELT AND TAFT: THE TWO PLATFORMS

Roosevelt had no intention of being "counted out." By early June he had determined to bolt if he lost the nomination because of delegate "theft." Progressive Republicans all over the country likewise prepared for a final and decisive confrontation with the Old Guard. On June 9, before leaving for Chicago, Hiram Johnson telegraphed his fellow California progressive Meyer Lissner: "I THINK WE MAY PRESIDE AT THE HISTORIC BIRTH OF THE PROGRESSIVE PARTY."

The night before the Republican convention opened, Roosevelt addressed a massive rally in the Chicago Auditorium. He reviewed the issues of the campaign and the cases of the contested delegates. "We who are in this fight are not feeble, and we intend to carry the fight to the end," he threatened. He would not permit, he declared, the "overthrow in the interests of certain bosses and the beneficiaries of privilege the clearly and deliberately expressed judgment of the plain citizens who make up the rank and file of the Republican Party." He eloquently concluded with ringing phrases:

Friends, here in Chicago at this time you have a great task before you. I wish you to realize deep in your hearts that you are not merely facing a crisis in the history of a party. You are facing a crisis in the history of a nation. . . . We fight in honorable fashion for the good of mankind; fearless of the future; unheeding of our individual fates; with unflinching hearts and undimmed eyes; we stand at Armageddon, and we battle for the Lord.

The convention opened on June 18. The proceedings were anything but orderly. Tempers flared; insults were hurled; demonstrations constantly broke out on the floor and in the galleries. The streets and hotels were a blur of banners and noise. By June 20, after the election of Root as chairman and the defeat of the motion to bar contested delegates from voting on seating, it was

THE VERY IDEA OF TRYING TO
KICK THAT HAT OUT OF THE RING!

evident that the president and the Old Guard had won. Late into that night and on to dawn a conference was held at Roosevelt headquarters. Governors Stubbs, Aldrich, Hadley, and Glasscock were opposed to a bolt. As officeholders they had much to lose, and were impressed with the difficulties of organizing a new party. Yet other officeholders like Governors Johnson, Carey, and Vessey favored a bolt. Hiram Johnson was particularly decided on the point: "We are frittering away our time. We are frittering away our opportunity. And, what is worse, we are frittering away Theodore Roosevelt."

Those in favor of bolting were more numerous than those opposed. The publisher Frank A. Munsey and the financier George W. Perkins, both millionaires, dramatically pledged their fortunes to the cause, saying, "Colonel, we will see you through." Gifford Pinchot, Garfield, most of the younger Roosevelt men like Medill McCormick of Illinois, and the majority of the Roosevelt delegates wanted to bolt. The decision was finally made. On June 21 Roosevelt announced his willingness to accept the nomination of progressives forming a new party, and the next day Roosevelt delegates withdrew from the G.O.P. convention and met in Orchestra Hall.

4

Writing some months later, Herbert Knox Smith, who resigned as federal commissioner of corporations to organize the new party in Connecticut, insisted that the delegate disputes and the events of the Republican convention were "a proximate, not an ultimate cause" for founding the Progressive Party. The convention "simply furnished the climax and raised the floodgates." Likewise, former Senator Albert J. Beveridge of Indiana argued that "for years this party has been forming." "For the Progressive Party comes from the grass roots. It has grown from the soil of the people's hard necessities. . . ."

Smith and Beveridge overstated the case, but there was a large element of truth in their analysis. Roosevelt's supporters quickly found that the issue of the "theft" of the Republican nomination was the one with the lowest common denominator for the general public, because it involved moral and democratic fundamentals. Furthermore, the events in Chicago provided an essential catalyst for translating G.O.P. progressive factionalism into a new reform party. But for a significant segment of the progressive movement the results of the Republican convention did not really change the direction of their evolution. Many non-partisan reformers had come to see the need for partisan organization. And partisan factionalist progressives had come to believe that nothing less than a party completely dedicated to reform could adequately serve the progressive movement at the various levels of government. The G.O.P. convention proved to many progressives that the only sure way to have a reform party was to make one. Looking back, the new party Progressives saw the outcome as logical and inevitable, and partisan factionalism as futile and counterproductive. Weren't both old parties, as T.R. put it, "boss-ridden and privilege-controlled, each a jumble of incongruous elements"? Yet as the new party founders left Orchestra Hall, a question seemed to hang in the air. Had they backed into a blind alley, or had they turned the corner to a new politics and a better America?

CHAPTER TWO

FORMING THE RANKS AT ARMAGEDDON

> *Will the new party born in Chicago on June 22 die of malnutrition or other infantile disease, as the scoffers predict, or will it, as the most sanguine of its friends declare, grow so rapidly to man's estate as to be able to defeat the Goliaths of Republicanism and Democracy . . . ?*
>
> Literary Digest

The Orchestra Hall rump convention was held on June 22, 1912. The next day Roosevelt conferred with the bolting delegates and their leaders. On June 24 an organizational committee, with Senator Joseph M. Dixon of Montana as chairman, was announced to the press. The new party, formally named the National Progressive Party, nicknamed the "Bull Moose Party" by the newspapers because T.R. had remarked that he felt as fit as a bull moose, set up national headquarters in New York City. Senator Dixon released the "call" for the new party on July 7, signed by sixty-three leaders representing forty states. The national convention was set to open in Chicago on August 5.

Now that the corner had been turned and the third party option chosen, the Progressives faced a host of organizational problems related to the founding of a new party. The complexity of twentieth-century partisan politics made the tasks of organization both Herculean and vital—and there was little time at hand before the fall campaign. A myriad of details demanded attention. Potential leaders had to be contacted and sized up; offices and headquarters rented all over the country; state and local committees formed; publicity and financing organized; county chairmen and district and precinct captains recruited. The results of this organizational effort would provide a crucial measure of the Progressive Party's political strength, character, and significance.

What groups and individuals joined the new party? Who were its leaders, and was the party's leadership politically viable? Where were the party's organizational strengths and weaknesses on the state and national levels? The Progressives also faced major problems dealing with the new party's definition and form within the political and partisan situation in the states and nation.

What was the new party's relationship to the old parties? How did the strategy of a third party relate to political conditions in the various states?

The most important of these problems of definition was out of the Progressives' hands—the course of the Democrats in the campaign. In his speech at Orchestra Hall Roosevelt had called for a new party composed of Democrats as well as Republicans. If the Democrats nominated a conservative as they had in 1904, when their vote fell to a record low, there was a good chance that

THE POLITICAL STORK

progressive Democrats, that large and growing body nurtured by William Jennings Bryan since 1896, might repair to the Bull Moose standard. There might even be a formal split in the Democracy as there had been in the G.O.P. As the opening of the Democratic convention approached, the leading contenders for the nomination were Speaker of the House Champ Clark of Missouri and Governor Woodrow Wilson of New Jersey, followed by Governor Judson Harmon of Ohio and Congressman Oscar W. Underwood of Alabama. Harmon and Underwood were conservatives, and it was difficult for most observers to see the lackluster party stalwart Clark as a reformer. Wilson, long an opponent of the Bryan wing of the party, had however been identified as a progressive since his election as governor of New Jersey in 1910. If Wilson were stopped, the future of the Progressive Party would be bright. Not only would the rejection of Wilson make converts of many Democrats, but it would leave the independent and La Follette voters with no place to go but the Socialists or Roosevelt. B. F. Harris wrote his fellow Illinois Progressive Medill McCormick on June 28: "I'm praying that the Democrats will have a non-progressive platform and candidate."

Another major problem facing Roosevelt and his followers was to win as many Republican leaders and voters as possible away from the G.O.P. to the new party. This was complicated by the problems of presidential electors and state tickets. Many of the electors chosen in the primaries and by those state conventions controlled by the progressive Republicans were Roosevelt supporters. Ordinarily there would have been no question that Republican electors would support any Republican nominee, but since T.R. charged that Taft had been nominated by "fraud" and "theft," many electors saw Roosevelt as the rightful heir to their votes in the electoral college. Certainly, Roosevelt's chances for victory would be greatly enhanced if in many states he instead of Taft were placed on the Republican ticket.

The related question of state tickets was one of the most complicated, difficult, and important to answer. From the standpoints of both practicality and principle, there were numerous considerations. If the Progressives ran only presidential and vice-presidential candidates, the new party could be accused of being nothing but a personal vehicle for T.R., it could not be permanent, and its impact in the states and Congress would be nil. Moreover, straight ticket voting was a widespread American habit. If the Progressives ran only a slate of electors, a "bob-tailed" ticket as Senator Dixon called it, Roosevelt supporters would be forced to vote a split ticket. If Roosevelt ran on the Republican ticket wherever possible, or if a third ticket were composed of Roosevelt together with the various Republican candidates, Democratic support and voters would be lost, and T.R. would probably be placed in the position of running in tandem with some G.O.P. standpatters. But of course Republican support and votes would be lost if in some states a third ticket were composed of Democratic candidates, and doubtless many of the Democratic candidates would be conservatives. It was unlikely, except for minor offices, that very many candidates could or would consent to running on a mixed ticket of Republican and Democratic nominees. Yet if the Progressives ran their own full third tickets, Republicans and Democrats supporting various candidates of the old parties could be antagonized and lost.

Still, it was relatively easy to decide to run full third tickets in states like New York where the Old Guard controlled the G.O.P. and the Democrats offered no real progressive alternative. But if the Progressives ran full third tickets in states where progressive Republicans had captured the state G.O.P., progressive Republicans leaving their old party would lose their hard-won organizations to the conservatives, and the careers of progressive Republican officeholders would be threatened. Such a situation would make it difficult to get the support of Republican incumbents and party officials, would put progressive principles in peril, and alienate many voters. On the other hand, to a large extent the Progressive Party had been founded as an outgrowth of the progressive movement in the states and cities, and if the party meant nothing distinct and new on the state and local level, its status in and utility to the progressive movement and the nation would be severely limited. Progressives pondered and debated these questions and problems as they met in state conventions to bring the new party into existence and select delegates for the Chicago convention.

2

After the rump convention Roosevelt said publicly that he would continue in the race regardless of the outcome of the Democratic convention. A decision had had to be made at the Republican convention, and Roosevelt had committed himself to the bolters. He would not go back on that commitment. The *Washington Star* observed: "Roosevelt will keep on running. He is a study in momentum." While the Democratic convention was in session, he wrote the Indiana civil service reformer William Dudley Foulke:

In strict confidence, my feeling is that the Democrats will probably win if they nominate a progressive. But of course there is no use of my getting into a fight in a halfhearted fashion and I could not expect Republicans to follow me out if they were merely to endorse the Democratic convention. So I hoisted the flag and will win or fall under it.

Roosevelt wrote friends that he was sure the vast majority of his supporters would go back to Taft and the Republicans or decline to vote and quit politics rather than back any Democratic nominee.

Almost all the leaders in the Roosevelt camp, like the Colonel himself, had spent their lives in the Republican Party. To them as to Roosevelt the Democrats were the party of states rights and the Confederacy; free trade, free silver, and other economic vagaries; Tammany Hall and the urban bosses; the depression of the 1890s; and the untutored agrarian radicalism exemplified by men like Bryan as well as the reactionary old-line Cleveland Democracy of leaders like Judson Harmon and the 1904 nominee Alton B. Parker. Young Walter Lippmann spoke for many of his fellow Progressives when he wrote in 1914:

I was a child of four during the panic of '93, and Cleveland has always been a sinister figure to me. His name was uttered with monstrous dread in the household. Then came Bryan, an ogre from the West, and a waiting for the election returns of 1896 with beating heart. And to this day I find myself with a subtle prejudice against Democrats that goes deeper than what we call political conviction.

As Lippmann confessed, these were more prejudices than reasoned objections to the Democrats. Certainly, the Republican progressives had found the G.O.P. boss-ridden, unresponsive to economic and social needs, and factionalized, but the Roosevelt leaders no less than the Republican standpatters had spent their careers fighting the Democracy for office. The bolters, either as progressive Republicans or Bull Moosers, had not entered the political wars in order to let the Democrats take the prizes by default. Moreover, few Progressives believed that the Democrats, who had spent much of the time since the Civil War wandering in the political wilderness, were even capable of governing and administering the nation.

The Democratic national convention opened in Baltimore on June 25. The factionalism within the party was quickly revealed. The Democratic National Committee had chosen Judge Alton B. Parker for convention chairman, but Bryan opposed the 1904 nominee, calling the New Yorker the representative of the reactionary forces in the party. Parker, however, was elected over Bryan by a vote of 579 to 510. But Bryan was not through: he offered a resolution putting the convention on record as refusing to nominate any candidate subservient to the "privilege-hunting and favor-seeking class." The resolution also called for the expulsion of all "Wall Street" delegates. The resolution was passed, but without the provision for the removal of delegates.

The Roosevelt camp watched the proceedings hopefully. Francis J. Heney of California, a former Democrat who had been one of T.R.'s chief lieutenants at Chicago, was sent to Baltimore to confer with Bryan about developments. Letters to T.R. from Progressives and Democrats proposed an alliance with Bryan or Wilson, or the second spot on the ticket for one of them, if the progressive Democrats were defeated at Baltimore. Young Franklin D. Roosevelt, an ardent Wilson supporter, revealed to the press that his cousin Kermit Roosevelt, T.R.'s son, had told him: "Pop's been praying for Clark."

The balloting began on June 28. A two-thirds majority was necessary to nominate. Clark remained in the lead ballot after ballot, followed by Wilson and trailed by Harmon and Underwood. With Tammany's help Clark reached a majority on the tenth ballot. Not since 1844 had a Democrat received a majority and failed to win the nomination. It appeared that Roosevelt's orisons were to be answered. The Wilson delegates, however, stood fast, and the balloting dragged on. Finally, after one of the longest deadlocks in convention history, Roger Sullivan, the unsavory boss of Illinois, and the southern Underwood delegates switched to the New Jersey governor, and on July 2 Wilson was nominated on the forty-sixth ballot. Governor Thomas R. Marshall of Indiana, who described himself as "a progressive with the brakes on," was chosen for vice president. The campaign of the progressive Democrats for the nomination had met with success, unlike the recent parallel progressive Republican effort. Mindful of the Bull Moose threat, the bosses and conservative leaders of the Democracy had chosen to go with a candidate who seemed to promise victory in November.

Roosevelt immediately announced once again that he would continue in the race. And most of the leaders in the Roosevelt camp agreed with the assessment of the New Jersey Progressive Everett Colby.

There are some superficial people who will think that we should support Wilson [Colby wrote Roosevelt], but that is a short-sighted view to take of the situation. Wilson will be checkmated by his party at every move. Within one month after his election, if he is elected, he would find it necessary to begin a fight in the Democratic Party such as you fought within the Republican Party and found to be futile.

Other progressive Republicans, however, particularly those who had backed Senator La Follette for the nomination, saw Wilson as the acceptable and practical alternative to Taft. A Wilson Progressive Republican League was formed with over forty thousand members, among them Rudolph Spreckels and Charles R. Crane, important financial backers of La Follette, and Louis D. Brandeis, the "people's attorney." Although La Follette was widely believed to be for Wilson and his magazine boosted the Democratic nominee's cause, the senator announced that actually he was for no candidate.

The press reported that the most notable defection from Roosevelt to Wilson was Governor Chase S. Osborn of Michigan, one of the signers of the seven governors' letter asking T.R. to run. On June 25 Osborn publicly released a letter to Roosevelt declaring that the former president should not be a candidate if the Democrats nominated a progressive. On July 3 Osborn told the press: "The issue is clearly joined for the people. It is Wall Street *vs.* Wilson." In three private letters the governor urged T.R. not to run because "Woodrow Wilson represents in public life and among the people what you represent." Roosevelt responded that "excellent man though Wilson is individually," his victory would mean the triumph of the Democratic Party, its bosses and policies. Democrats were Democrats.

Eugene Thwing, a prominent magazine editor, angrily wrote Osborn:

Perhaps Woodrow Wilson is a true Progressive. I am not sure. Opinions differ. I am willing to believe he is. But I know that the majority of his party is not. I know that the bosses of the state machines, and the district leaders, and the rank and file of the politicians scurrying eagerly at his heels are not. I know that a party which in many states is as reactionary and corrupt as the Democratic Party is cannot be made progressive by the nomination, still less by the election, of a progressive national ticket on a *partially progressive* and *partially retrogressive platform*. Woodrow Wilson has a respectable name, but his name cannot be made to safely cover such a multitude of sins.

He added in a telegram to Osborn, referring to the leading bosses in both parties: "WHY EXCHANGE BARNES, PENROSE, CRANE AND OTHER REPUBLICAN FREE-BOOTERS FOR MURPHY, TAGGART, SULLIVAN, RYAN AND OTHER DEMOCRATIC FREEBOOTERS...?"

In his June 25 letter and subsequent letters and statements, Osborn had added that he would abide by Roosevelt's decision. Not long after the Democratic convention the governor announced that, after all, he would support Roosevelt in the race, and in the fall he went on the stump for T.R., but his earlier statements had already done their damage.

To the Progressives the platform adopted at Baltimore proved that there were substantive reasons for opposing the Democratic as well as the Republican Party beyond the fact that, as T.R. said, "the bosses are just as powerful in one party as in the other." In an article in the *Outlook* on July 27, Roosevelt examined the Democratic platform in detail.

The Baltimore platform focused on the tariff issue, the staple of Democratic campaign oratory since the 1830s, denouncing the protective tariff in traditional Jeffersonian rhetoric as unconstitutional, "the principal cause of the unequal distribution of wealth," and the bulwark of the trusts. Wilson soon took up this theme in his campaign. The platform also attacked the power of the trusts and called for corrective measures, while insisting that "federal remedies ... shall be added to, and not substituted for, state remedies." The platform condemned the "usurpation" of states rights by the federal government and saw a dangerous tendency to "magnify by indirection the powers of the federal government."

Roosevelt, who in company with many reformers advocated a tariff commission of experts to set or abolish rates on a "scientific" basis, denied that the protective tariff was either wholly harmful or the root of American problems, and pointed out that if the protective tariff were unconstitutional then so too were many federal reforms called for by progressives, like workmen's compensation. The whole Democratic approach to the economic problems of the country, Roosevelt charged, was characterized by professions of progressivism made with "much sound and fury" but accompanied by "weasel phrases" which sucked the meat out of the progressive promises. True, the Democrats condemned the power of the trusts.

But farther on in the platform comes the weasel phrase for this statement, ... for in connection with the antitrust law occurs the further statement that the platform denounces any attempt to enlarge or magnify by indirection the powers of the federal government, and insists that federal remedies ... shall ... not be substituted for ... state remedies. ... Every trust magnate in the country can rest in safety if he can have the law relegated to the states instead of the nation. All danger to him will vanish forthwith. ... The states are powerless in this matter. The nation must act.

Most importantly, the Democrats' strict construction of the constitution as shown in their stands on the tariff and trusts "would at once reduce us to impotence in dealing with nine-tenths of the serious social and industrial problems which now confront us." In short, the Democrats did not measure up when judged by the yardsticks of nationalism and progressivism. On July 13 Roosevelt wrote Herbert Knox Smith: "The Democratic platform shows that the Democratic Party now is as stupid, bourbon and reactionary as ever before. They are adhering to the outworn policy of states rights and narrow construction and literally no reform of any kind worth having can come save under a progressive policy which represents national needs and requires national action and enlarged federal activity."

Roosevelt and the Progressives thus found substantive differences between their nationalist progressivism and the Democratic philosophy of government, and therefore principle as well as prejudice against the Democrats seemed to dictate going ahead with the work of building a third party. Yet was the third

"THIS IS THE LIVE ONE, COLONEL!"

party course practical in light of Wilson's nomination? Victory in November was still possible, but now it did not seem likely. ". . . Of course while this must not be said publicly, I am leading rather a forlorn hope this year," T.R. confessed in a letter on July 10 to a friend in London. But the Progressive strategy was long-term in conception, directed to a partisan realignment along progressive and conservative lines. Progressives believed, as Everett Colby had put it, that if elected Wilson would soon find it necessary—assuming of course that he was a reformer in earnest—to begin a fight within the Democratic Party against the conservatives such as had taken place in the G.O.P. In an article in the October *Yale Review,* Herbert Knox Smith candidly outlined the Progressive position: "We Progressives believe that in the election next November our party will become, if not the first, at least the second party, leaving the Republicans a bad third. In my view, that outcome, at least, is now certain." Because of their overwhelming defeat, the G.O.P. would then disappear "shortly after November, 1912." "There will remain by 1914," Smith continued, "only two great national parties, Progressives and Democrats. While the Democrats probably will not be by that time avowedly the conservative party, the rise of their opponents, the Progressives, will tend to force them toward that position. More strongly still, however, will the basic states rights doctrine work in that direction." The trust magnates and other "special interests" would naturally turn to the Democrats, finding states rights and limited federal power their bulwark of defense. Then the realignment would be complete, and "the results for political advance will be almost incalculable." Issues could be honestly discussed and clear progressive and conservative alternatives presented; "politics will become intellectually honest. . . ." Smith concluded by predicting that the Progressive Party would be in power within the next eight years.

The goals of a permanent new party and partisan realignment were foremost in the minds of many who became leaders in the Progressive Party, as was illustrated by the case of Albert J. Beveridge of Indiana, who had hesitated for some weeks before announcing his adherence to the new party. The handsome and perennially youthful Beveridge had been a senator from Indiana for two terms, 1899–1911, and then was defeated for reelection as the result of the bitter conservative-progressive schism in the Hoosier G.O.P. and the Democratic landslide of 1910. Beginning his career as the champion of conventional Gilded Age Republicans like McKinley, Beveridge had gone on to become one of the Senate's leading progressives, author of the Meat Inspection Act of 1906, advocate of the federal abolition of child labor, insurgent opponent of Senator Aldrich, and sharp critic of the Taft administration. He had campaigned effectively for his friend Roosevelt in the primary campaign, but when the bolt came he held back and declined to have his name put on the call for the new party. He refused to support Taft, and he could never join the Democrats, for he was an ardent nationalist and detested Jeffersonian states rights. But with Wilson in the field he told friends that he doubted T.R. could win in 1912, and he wondered if the new party could survive after the presidential campaign. If the Progressive Party were to be a flash in the pan, bolting made no sense to Beveridge. Then, after receiving assurances from Progressive leaders that the party intended to continue the fight regardless of the outcome in 1912, Beveridge made his decision, declaring in a public letter to the *Indianapolis Star* on July 25 that the time had come for progressives of all parties to "act together through an organization of their own. . . ." The next day Senator Dixon announced that Beveridge would deliver the keynote address and chair the Progressive national convention.

Yet beyond the analyses of specific issues like the trusts and long-term partisan considerations dealing with the political future of the progressive movement, Roosevelt and the Progressives felt an emotional commitment to the course chosen at Chicago in June, a commitment that involved their deepest moral and political beliefs, and which would fix the new party's ideological character. "I have been careful to try to bring with me only the men of the crusading temperament, . . ." Roosevelt cautioned a group of Washington bureaucrats who asked his advice about resigning from the government to help the Progressive cause. "If I could have consistently drawn out of the race," the Colonel wrote the Maryland Progressive W. F. Cochran on July 16, "I would most gladly have done so. . . . But I just did not see how I could conscientiously get out of this fight. . . . I think the issues on which the parties are now divided are false. I think it eminently desirable that we should eliminate from our political life the men who cannot well be eliminated unless both of the old parties are sent down to defeat."

Roosevelt was in a sense saying that he and his followers were prisoners of their own momentum. The logic of their campaign for the Republican nomination compelled them to continue the fight when they were rejected by the bosses and not the people. When Roosevelt entered the race, he accepted a commission from the people to seek the presidency in order to transform America according to progressive precepts. Under these circumstances, he could not honorably retire from the field unless the people retired him. Nor could his followers honorably desert their Colonel at Armageddon. ". . . I enlisted for the war," Hiram Johnson said, explaining his bolt from the G.O.P. It did not matter that Roosevelt's original commission in February, 1912, had been self-proclaimed, though there were of course many indications of popular support, for the primaries—the new element in presidential politics—had validated that commission. And just as T.R. had said that a political decision was beyond the rights of a judge, so "recall" was the prerogative and option not of the G.O.P. politicians, not of the man who lived at Sagamore Hill, but of the people. Furthermore, the issues and rhetoric Roosevelt and his supporters had employed in the primary campaign lifted the cause above ordinary politics. "The right of the people to rule" and "social and industrial justice" were concepts that not only were emotionally potent, they also placed moral obligations upon Roosevelt and his followers. Roosevelt had said that he believed the bosses and parties were thwarting the will of the people for reform, the yearning of the people for social justice and a humane way of life. To then surrender this cause would have been not only craven and self-serving; it would have been to admit that campaigning was just a game, that the issues had been tactical slogans and nothing more, that in fact Roosevelt had lied when he said he had faith in the American people's capacity to choose the right path, to be uplifted by a reform nationalism and humanitarianism. Shortly after the Republican convention he wrote the British author H. Rider Haggard:

I suppose that as we grow older we naturally lose the natural feeling of young men to take an interest in politics just for the sake of strife—the same kind of interest one takes in big game hunting, or football, the kind of interest quite compatible with doing excellent work but which cannot inspire the highest kind of work. As we get older, if we think seriously at all, and if we escape falling into the permanent Palmerstonian jauntiness of attitude, we cannot avoid becoming deeply and indeed painfully impressed with the tremendous problems of our social and industrial life. To me politics and applied ethics ought to be interchangeable terms, and my interest in the former arises chiefly from my interest in the latter. If the whole game is one of mere sound and fury, without any sincerity back of it, any real purpose of achievement, then it is all of as little importance as a contest between the blues and the greens in the Byzantine circus. I am, I hope and believe, a practical man, and I abhor mere sentimentality; but I abhor at least as much the kind of so-called practical man who uses the word "practical" to indicate mere materialistic baseness, and who fails to see that while we of course must have a material and economic foundation for every successful civilization, yet that the fabric cannot be lasting unless a warp of lofty disinterestedness and power of community feeling is not shot through the woof of individualistic materialism. . . . I do not know whether we will be able to succeed in the great movement for social and industrial reform, . . . but I do know that the alternative is a general smashup of our civilization; and succeed or fail, I hold it to be the duty of every decent man to fight to avoid such a smash. . . . It is a fight that must be made, and is worth making; and the event lies on the knees of the gods.

3

Winning Republican voters was mainly work for the fall campaign, but before the Progressive convention met, the new party had to enlist as many Republican leaders and party workers as possible so that the Progressive Party could be effectively organized. One measure of the success of the new party in lining up Republican leaders, a yardstick frequently used by the press, was the positions of the signers of the seven governors' letter of February 10, 1912. At least five of the seven governors continued to endorse Roosevelt's candidacy after the bolt: Bass of New Hampshire, reluctant Osborn of Michigan, Stubbs of Kansas, Aldrich of Nebraska, and Carey of Wyoming. Vessey of South Dakota and Johnson of California, the two governors who had announced their adherence to the February appeal, also continued to support T.R. after the Republican convention. The position of Glasscock of West Virginia was uncertain throughout the campaign, but of the original seven only Hadley of Missouri ultimately endorsed Taft. Some progressive Republicans like Senator Albert B. Cummins of Iowa endorsed T.R.'s candidacy for president but not the idea of a new party, but of the governors who continued to support Roosevelt all except Osborn also backed the Progressive Party. Aldrich, Bass, Carey, Johnson, Stubbs, and Vessey were among the new party's most important recruits.

In June and July there was much confusion as to where various Republicans stood, and there were many inaccurate reports in the newspapers, because for some time it was unclear how the problems of electors and state tickets would be solved in the different states. Thus, in late June when Governor Stubbs told the press that there would be no third ticket in Kansas this was widely interpreted as meaning that he had defected from the new party. As soon became clear, however, Stubbs had meant that in Kansas the new party would consist of the Republican state organization. Maintaining that Roosevelt and the National Progressive Party, not Taft and the "thieving" G.O.P. national committee, were the rightful heirs to the Republican Party, Kansas Progressives intended that Roosevelt would receive the Republican electors in Kansas and the spot at the head of the official Republican ticket. Rather than defecting from the new party, Kansas Progressives wanted to carry the state Republican Party lock, stock, and electors into the National Progressive Party. Progressives in many states at first agreed with this strategy.

The problems of what to do about electors and state tickets were well illustrated in an exchange of private letters between Roosevelt and Governor Herbert S. Hadley in June and July. Hadley had been Roosevelt's floor leader at the Republican convention. After the Republican convention, however, the governor announced that he would not leave the Republican Party. On June 28 Roosevelt wrote Hadley thanking him for his previous services, but repeated that the bolters felt that no further usefulness could come from the G.O.P. Hadley responded on July 5 that the state Republican Party in Missouri was progressive and that a third party movement would endanger the success of the Missouri Republican ticket. "While there is a strong anti-Taft sentiment within the party, and a strong sentiment for you, there is also a pronounced feeling of regularity in this state which would make the work of organizing a new party at this time a very difficult one." Hadley added that neither he nor the state organization could take any part in organizing T.R.'s electoral ticket, but, he suggested, perhaps Missouri Republican nominees could also be placed on T.R.'s ticket.

In further letters Hadley protested that a third state ticket would only lose votes for T.R. Even if the Republican nominees did not appear under Roosevelt's electoral slate, he said, there need be no controversy between the Republican state ticket and the Roosevelt electors. In fact, Hadley proposed, why not have the same electors for both Taft and Roosevelt? Since there was no direct election for president, electors actually receiving the votes cast for candidates, there could be an understanding that the electoral vote would go to the candidate receiving the higher number of popular votes.

Roosevelt replied that it was possible to put Republican candidates on the new ticket, but only if they were prepared to endorse his candidacy.

...I take the view that Mr. Taft's nomination is fraudulent and that every straight out Republican should support me as the man who was honestly entitled to the nomination at Chicago. It seems to me that unless the Republican state and local nominees are prepared to support my candidacy and run on the same column of the ballot that then we should have nominees.

As for negotiating with Republicans over presidential electors, Roosevelt told Hadley what he had said publicly: "I hold that Mr. Taft stole the nomination, and I do not feel like arbitrating with a pickpocket as to whether or not he shall keep my watch." He added, as he had also said publicly, that he would rely on his local leaders for decisions about state tickets. In the end there was a third state ticket in Missouri, and in October, after assurances from Taft that there would be reforms in the G.O.P. presidential nominating system, Hadley spoke as a progressive Republican for Taft's reelection.

Hadley's plan for presidential electors was the same as that publicly proposed by William Flinn. Flinn, the former Republican boss of Pittsburgh, had directed Roosevelt's successful primary campaign in Pennsylvania against the machine of Senator Boies Penrose. Having nominated Roosevelt electors in the primary, and having won a measure of control over the state party organization, Flinn was loath to throw it all away. He told T.R. that he did not think a third ticket could carry the Keystone State. But as he had informed Hadley, Roosevelt did not like such a plan. It would not be right and it would not look right to make a deal with Taft. "I cannot consent to do anything that looks as if I was joining with him," wrote the Colonel to the Philadelphia publisher E. A. Van Valkenburg. In June and July there were conferences at Sagamore Hill in Oyster Bay, Long Island, the former summer White House and now the Bull Moose mecca, with Flinn and other Pennsylvania leaders. Finally it was agreed that Roosevelt would have separate electors in the Keystone State, but some Republican candidates who did not oppose Roosevelt were also permitted on the Pennsylvania Roosevelt ticket.

Roosevelt, however, was not sure what to do about those Republican electors who announced that since he was the rightful nominee they would vote for him if elected on the Republican ticket. The press reported that about one hundred Republican electors in various states had so declared. On July 12 the Colonel wrote one of them, Joseph R. Baldwin of Maryland, to stay on the G.O.P. electoral slate. "I hold that I am in honor and honesty entitled to the vote of every elector nominated by the people through their primaries, and that Mr. Taft is entitled to the votes of those electors nominated by Barnes, Penrose, Guggenheim and Company. . . ." But this was an impossible position. Taft loyalists threatened court action. If Taft's name were on the ballot, it hardly would be honorable, honest, or democratic to take electors in this case. Roosevelt soon decided that he could not accept any such electoral votes.

In Kansas, Nebraska, Iowa, California, and other midwestern, plains, and western states where progressive Republicanism was strongest, still another plan was considered for presidential electors, as Governor Stubbs had indicated to the press. In those states where the state Republican parties were completely controlled by Roosevelt supporters, it was proposed that the state Republican parties become the local branches of the National Progressive Party. It was legally possible in some states for the duly constituted state party organization to designate its own choice for president and not follow the dictates of the Republican national convention. It was finally decided, however, in all states but South Dakota and California, that the proper course was to run independent slates of Roosevelt electors. Obviously, this decreased Roosevelt's chances of winning, but many saw it as the only moral option. "I never knew a more complicated political situation," Roosevelt wrote his former Attorney General, Charles J. Bonaparte, in July.

South Dakota and California Roosevelt leaders, however, proceeded with their original plan and placed T.R.'s name on the Republican ticket. At the South Dakota Republican convention a proposal to choose Taft electors was defeated almost two to one by the delegates. Taft did not appear on the South Dakota ballot at all. In California the law allowed full tickets only to parties which had polled 3 percent of the vote in the last election, and so there was a question about the legal status of the new party. Governor Johnson later explained that when he was making plans for the Progressives his lawyers advised him that the courts would probably decide against a new ticket on the state ballot. Johnson took no chances. California electors were chosen by party conventions made up of those nominated for state offices in the primaries. Only thirteen Taft supporters were nominated in the entire state in the G.O.P. primaries, and thus Roosevelt men were named the Republican electors. The Taft forces declined to try to get electors on the ballot by petition, and therefore Taft was a write-in candidate in California.

The Taft leaders around the country as well as the Progressives were busy with tactical plans. In Pennsylvania the Penrose machine moved quickly, and legally registered many party titles including "National Progressive," "Progressive," and "Roosevelt," depriving the Roosevelt forces of using their proper name. Thus, the new party in Pennsylvania became the "Washington Party"—Penrose had taken out the patent on "Lincoln" as well as "Roosevelt"—with local tickets entitled "Bull Moose" and "Roosevelt Progressive" being set up in some counties. In Idaho the Republican judges of the state supreme court ruled the Progressive Party off the ballot, upholding a petition based on legal technicalities which was filed by the Republican state committee. Subsequently both the editor and publisher of the Progressive *Boise Capital News* were jailed and fined for contempt of court when they criticized the court's action.

While Progressives set up electoral tickets, they also came to grips with the problems of congressional, state, and local candidates. Democratic and Republican candidates for Congress presented different problems for the new party. Republican candidates for Congress supported by the new party or placed on the Progressive ticket might cooperate and vote with a Bull Moose organization in the House. This was the condition for support proposed by Bill Flinn for Pennsylvania, and it could be generally accepted in states where the Republican organization pledged allegiance to the National Progressive Party. Democratic candidates for the House, however, would be likely to cooperate with their own party since it was probable that the Democrats would retain control of the House and its committees. There would also be federal patronage available if the Democracy won the White House. Moreover, it seemed probable that the Democrats and Progressives would clash in Congress on such issues as the tariff. The same kind of conditions applied to candidates for the legislature. While almost any development was possible within the divided state Republican parties, it was improbable in states where Democratic governors and legislatures were in power, or had a good chance of being elected, that Democratic legislators would help a new party organization.

The situation with statewide candidates was clearer. If the Progressives endorsed a Republican or Democratic candidate for governor, and that candidate supported the election of Taft or Wilson, obviously Roosevelt's candidacy would be hurt and embarrassed, and the whole realignment the Progressives sought in American politics confused and hindered. But in states where the Republican organization endorsed the National Progressive Party and T.R.'s candidacy, Republican candidates for governor and state offices could in turn be endorsed by the National Progressive Party. Indeed, such arrangements could greatly aid the new national party, supplying ready-made building blocks. Roosevelt wrote in July: "Now wherever . . . we can simply take the Republican Party bodily into the progressive movement, why that is the thing to do."

In California, South Dakota, Nebraska, Kansas, West Virginia, and Maine, where state Republicans indicated support for Roosevelt and the new party nationally, no third Congressional, state, or local tickets were organized; and the state Republican parties were thereby designated as the local branches of the National Progressive Party. In other states, such as Michigan and Missouri, though there were strong progressive factions in the Republican parties, there were also very strong conservative factions and numerous standpat officeholders, candidates, and party officials. Since Progressives wanted parties that were exclusively dedicated to reform and completely under Progressive control, in such states third tickets and new state organizations were set up. In some states like Iowa, Minnesota, and Washington, there was room for considerable debate over whether or not the state G.O.P. conformed to the standards of the National Progressive Party. Usually a new ticket and state party were established when there was any doubt about where the Republican Party in a particular state stood. In states like Massachusetts, New York, Ohio, Illinois, Utah, and Colorado where the standpatters were unquestionably in control, the decision to run a third ticket was logical and easy to make.

Thirty-three states elected governors in 1912. Louisiana held a spring election, and the Progressives ran no candidates for governor in the southern states of Arkansas and South Carolina where their organization was weak. In Kansas, Nebraska, South Dakota, West Virginia, and Maine, where the state Republican parties were considered part of the Progressive fold, the G.O.P. gubernatorial nominees were backed by the Bull Moose. In Wisconsin Senator La Follette opposed Roosevelt and the new party, but Governor Francis E. McGovern, running for reelection, backed T.R. and no third state ticket was organized. In the remaining twenty-four states the Progressives ran third party candidates for governor and other statewide offices.

In California, Kansas, Nebraska, South Dakota, West Virginia, and Maine, the Republican congressional nominees were backed by the Bull Moose in return for national support for the new party. In North Dakota, Minnesota, and Wisconsin, all states with strong progressive Republican factions, the G.O.P. congressional candidates were considered friendly to the Progressive cause, and only one district was contested in these states. In addition, some Republican congressional candidates in other states who endorsed Roosevelt and the new party were in turn endorsed by the Progressives, as in the case of Congressman Ira Copley in Illinois's eleventh district, and in a few instances Democratic candidates were backed against Republicans. In the southern states of Arkansas, Georgia, Louisiana, Mississippi, and South Carolina, where the G.O.P. frequently did not contest congressional seats, the third party ran no candidates for the House, nor did Progressives in Nevada, Oklahoma, and Vermont nominate candidates for Congress. In the remaining thirty-one states Progressives ran for the House, in some districts in southern and border states, and in nearly every district in the Northeast, Midwest, and West. The new party was determined to elect at least a phalanx of congressmen who would be the vanguard for future Progressive congressional victories, particularly in 1914. In the same spirit Progressives ran full slates for the legislature in most states outside the South. It was hoped that at the very least the new party would gain the balance of power or a strong minority position in many legislatures, thereby winning the power to influence legislation, the selection of United States senators, and other state matters. County and local tickets were also put into the running wherever possible. In short, Progressives intended that the new party would make its influence felt on every level of government and politics.

The decision to run full tickets was crucial in terms of fixing the Progressives' partisan definition. Basically, both before and after 1912, there have been two kinds of third or minor parties in American history: parties like the Liberal Republicans of 1872 which ran only presidential and vice presidential candidates, and those like the Populists of the 1890s which contested congressional, state, and local offices as well. Parties running only presidential and vice presidential candidates were exclusively concerned with national issues, and were almost predestined to be short-lived by the nature of the federal system with its multiple levels of government. A pyramid cannot stand without a base. Parties contesting offices at all governmental levels have a better chance for survival and growth. Thus, the Progressives had made a wise tactical decision, one consistent with the new party's origins in the reform movement on state and local as well as national levels, and one calculated to make the Progressive Party permanent, far more than merely a vehicle for Roosevelt's White House drive. On the other hand, the tasks of launching and sustaining such a broad-based party were so great that since the Civil War the same two major parties had remained dominant, threatened at times but not replaced. The Progressives, however, counted on the strength of the nationwide reform movement to carry them through to success.

4

By August, as the opening of the Progressive national convention approached, the work of organizing was in full swing and the roster of the new party's leaders was nearly complete. Much was revealed about the Progressive Party's political makeup, strength, character, and significance by looking at its leadership nationally and in the states. The Progressive leaders could be readily divided into a number of different types according to background, occupation, and other social characteristics, although of course some fit simultaneously into more than one category. This makeup of the Progressive leadership indicated the extent of the new party's political viability and its strengths and weaknesses from region to region and state to state. The composition of the Progressive leadership further indicated the motivations behind Progressivism and the ideological character of the new party. To know the leaders was to know the party.

As had been predicted, Wilson's nomination prevented a split in the Democratic Party similar to the one in the G.O.P. The Progressives therefore failed to win the number of Democratic converts hoped for. Yet a surprising number of Democrats became leaders in the new party. Paradoxically, the Progressive Party attracted contingents of both "Popocrats" and "Gold Democrats." The Populists and some Bryan Democrats and the Gold Democrats had a history of minimal allegiance to the Democratic Party, particularly on the national level, the Populists and some Bryan Democrats bolting Cleveland and Parker, the Gold Democrats bolting Bryan.

Some Populists had attempted to keep a national organization going after the People's Party had in effect merged with the Democrats in 1896, while others had backed Bryan and the Democracy. In 1912 the remnant of the People's Party formally disbanded. Former Populists who joined the Progressive Party, like Mary E. Lease, former Senator Marion Butler of North Carolina, and the former Georgia Congressman Thomas E. Watson, Bryan's running mate on the Populist ticket in 1896 and the Populist candidate for president in 1904 and 1908, saw in the new party the fulfillment of their platforms and of their hopes to create a party dedicated solely to reform.

On the other hand, Gold Democrats saw in T.R. a man who had long been an opponent of Bryan and untutored agrarian radicalism, and saw in the new party an alternative to supporting the Republicans. The Massachusetts industrialist Charles Sumner Bird had been a delegate to the Gold Democrats' Indianapolis convention in 1896. Oscar S. Straus of New York, merchant, lawyer, philanthropist, was a Democrat who had been minister to Turkey under Cleveland. Opposing Bryan, Straus had supported McKinley and then Roosevelt. McKinley had again appointed Straus minister to Turkey, and in 1906 Roosevelt made him secretary of commerce. Don M. Dickinson of Michigan, friend of Samuel J. Tilden and prominent supporter of Cleveland, had been postmaster general in Cleveland's first term. Bird, Straus, and Dickinson all joined the Progressive Party.

Finally, there was a group of Bull Moosers who might be termed simply "independent Democrats." Some were dedicated to reform above party; some were ambitious free spirits; some had been more active in social work than in politics; some were perennial bolters. Included in this diverse group were R. F. Pettigrew, W. Bourke Cockran, Lucius F. C. Garvin, John M. Parker, Ben B. Lindsey, and Raymond Robins.

Pettigrew had served in the Senate from South Dakota as a Republican from 1889 to 1901, but had supported Bryan in 1896, 1900, and 1908, and had been a delegate to the Democratic national conventions of 1904 and 1908. He had broken with the G.O.P. over issues like imperialism and the trusts, and hoping to advance reform proposals like government ownership of railroads, telephone, and telegraph, left the Democrats for the Progressives. The eloquent, Irish-born Bourke Cockran, one of the country's most famous orators, was practically a party of one. Since the 1880s he had periodically been a Democratic congressman from New York. In 1896 he supported McKinley because of Bryan's free-silver plank, but in 1900 he backed Bryan because of McKinley's expansionism. Early in his career Cockran had been an anti-Tammany leader. Yet later he served as Grand Sachem of Tammany, from 1905 to 1908. By 1912 he had broken with the Tammany boss Charles F. Murphy and joined the Progressives, becoming an unsuccessful Bull Moose candidate for Congress. Later Cockran returned to Congress as a Democrat.

JUDGE BEN LINDSEY
OF COLORADO

Less erratic than Pettigrew and Cockran were Lucius F. C. Garvin and John M. Parker. Both had labored for reform in their respective states for many years; both saw the Progressive Party as a vehicle to advance reform on the state level. Garvin, a Rhode Island doctor, had been a leader of suffrage and industrial reform in his state. He had been elected to the state house thirteen times, the state senate three times. In the predominantly Republican state he had also been defeated for Congress and governor on the Democratic ticket many times. In 1902 and again in 1903, however, Garvin had been elected governor of Rhode Island. Parker, a New Orleans cotton merchant, had been active in city and state reform against the dominant machine of the Louisiana Democratic Party. He was a leader of the Good Government League of Louisiana in 1912 when he joined the Progressive Party.

"The kids' judge," Ben B. Lindsey, a leader in the movement for juvenile courts and a Denver civic reformer, and Raymond Robins, a minister turned Chicago settlement house director, were both Democrats though they had been more involved in social work than in partisan politics. T.R. had long been an enthusiastic supporter of Lindsey's work and the settlement house movement, and Lindsey and Robins joined the Progressives because they were sure that the new party would stand for social justice as no other party had done or did.

These groups of Popocrats and Democrats played a role in the Progressive Party out of proportion to their numbers. This was in part because the new party wanted to emphasize its claim to being more than just a Republican faction, but more importantly, these groups provided the party with some able leadership. Watson was an influential agrarian spokesman; Bird and Parker proved to be popular and effective state leaders (Parker later served as governor of Louisiana from 1920 to 1924); Straus was a respected statesman; and others brought a variety of assets and useful talents to the new party.

In addition to former Populists like Mary Lease and Tom Watson, the Progressive Party also attracted a number of veterans of other third party movements—Greenbackers, Prohibitionists, and Socialists, who, however varied their beliefs, held in common a hatred of the major parties and of the suppression of substantive issues by partisan rhetoric. For these third party advocates the Progressive Party offered a new opportunity. Thus, for instance, a few "socialists impatient with the futile tactics of their party," as Gifford's brother Amos Pinchot described them, joined the Bull Moose ranks. Young Walter Lippmann, president of the Harvard Socialist Club and then secretary to Socialist Mayor George Lunn in Schenectady, convinced that the Socialist Party was doomed to failure, joined the Progressives, as did the Russian immigrant and socialist Isaac A. Hourwich, an official of the International Ladies' Garment Workers Union who became the Progressive candidate for Congress in a special New York election in 1913. But except for some of the Populists, most such third party veterans added little to the Progressive Party's political strength or respectability. The major source of the new party's political strength was not the Democrats or the third parties of the past but rather the G.O.P. The vast majority of the Progressive Party's leaders had been Republicans before 1912.

Roosevelt himself took a hand in organizing the new party in almost all the states. His political experience was invaluable, and, moreover, although there were many lieutenants and captains in the Progressive Party, there was only one "Colonel." Roosevelt's wide network of friends, acquaintances, and associates served him well and helped the new party greatly. Old friends from his ranching days in the West; associates from New York assembly days like Joe Murray who had started T.R. in politics; men he had known as governor like Elon H. Hooker, his former New York deputy for public works who became national treasurer of the new party; family friends like Bronson Cutting of New Mexico; and many others, served the Progressive Party in various capacities. There were the inevitable Rough Riders of 1898 who came to the aid of their Colonel's new army: Congressman George Curry of New Mexico, Jack Greenway of Arizona, Frank Knox of Michigan, and others. There were relatives: Roosevelt's nephew Theodore Douglas Robinson, who ultimately became state chairman of New York; Joseph W. Alsop of Connecticut, national committeeman and state chairman who was married to T.R.'s niece; and Theodore Roosevelt, Jr., his father's faithful aide on many occasions. Most important of all to the party were the men who had served in the Roosevelt administration in various posts, and who assumed positions of leadership in the new party: the former cabinet members James R. Garfield, Charles J. Bonaparte, and Oscar Straus; Francis J. Heney and Albert D. Nortoni, who had been federal attorneys; former diplomats John Callan O'Laughlin and Paxton Hibben; Herbert Knox Smith,

Gifford Pinchot, and others, all of whom looked for a restoration and the completion of the unfinished business of the Roosevelt administration.

Progressive Republican politicians, however, formed the hard core of the new party's political strength—governors like Robert Perkins Bass of New Hampshire and Hiram Johnson of California, insurgents in Congress like Senator Joseph M. Dixon of Montana and Representative Victor Murdock of Kansas, municipal reformers like Donald Richberg and Harold Ickes of Chicago, and reform leaders in the state legislatures and party organizations like Everett Colby of New Jersey and Meyer Lissner of California. These veterans of state house, legislative halls, and party councils possessed the experience and expertise necessary to run a political party. Frustrated in the factional politics of the G.O.P., the Progressive Party found many such practicing politicians ready for the reform party option. In fact, not since the formation of the Republican Party in the 1850s had a new party attracted and been able to count on so many experienced and able political professionals. Yet, as critics of the new party were quick to point out, not all progressives in the G.O.P. made the exodus to the new party.

Some Republican progressives feared losing state organizations back to the standpatters. Others, like Senator William S. Kenyon of Iowa, up for reelection in 1912, feared losing office. The Republican congressional insurgents seemed particularly impressed with the difficulties and dangers of bolting, and they scattered in different directions as the ranks formed at Armageddon. Wisconsin's La Follette and Senator William E. Borah of Idaho stayed with the Republican Party but declined to back any candidate for president. Kenyon swallowed hard and endorsed Taft. Senator Albert B. Cummins of Iowa endorsed T.R. but not the new party, while Senator Moses Clapp endorsed both Roosevelt and the Progressive Party but held back from taking a hand in third party activities in his native Minnesota. Senator Miles Poindexter of Washington, reluctant at first, decided to join the Progressive Party lock, stock, and political future, as had Dixon of Montana. Insurgents who came from Kansas, Nebraska, South Dakota, and the other states where a union was formed between state Republican organizations and the new national party had the easiest path in 1912. They could support Roosevelt and even the new party while still retaining the Republican label in their bailiwicks. Such was the case for Senator Joseph L. Bristow of Kansas, and Representative George W. Norris running for the Senate in Nebraska.

Observers then and later were confused as to what the insurgent consensus was. Certainly it was incorrect to say, as some did, that the insurgents and the Bull Moose were separate herds, for this assertion ignored the roles played in the Progressive Party by Beveridge, Dixon, Murdock, Poindexter, and others. Yet it was also true that La Follette, Kenyon, Borah, Cummins, and others wanted nothing to do with forming a new party, believing that the G.O.P. could still be won for liberalism. The fact was that there simply was no insurgent consensus, and the varying stands on issues during the following years among the independent and individualistic men who were the original insurgents seemed to show that it had been futile to expect one in 1912. But Roosevelt had no patience with those insurgents who wavered and faltered in the summer of 1912. He was giving his all; lesser mortals could do the same. "What a miserable showing some of the so-called Progressive leaders have made," he wrote Cal O'Laughlin, commenting on the actions of the insurgents. "They represent nothing but mere sound and fury."

Yet if Roosevelt dismissed reformers like La Follette who stayed with the G.O.P. as "so-called" progressives, critics could in turn point to the anomaly of Republican bosses like Timothy Woodruff, William Flinn, and Walter F. Brown who joined the new party, making up a small but important group in the Progressive ranks. "Tiny Tim" Woodruff, as reporters called the portly Republican boss of Brooklyn, and cigar-chewing Bill Flinn, former G.O.P. boss of Pittsburgh, had both lost political power in their states and saw the Progressive Party as a chance for a political comeback. Walter F. Brown, on the other hand, the smooth-mannered Republican boss of Toledo and Ohio state chairman of the G.O.P., was tired of sharing power with others, and decided to get into the new party where there would be less competition. All these merchants in political loaves and fishes had been identified with the conservatives before 1912, but ambition brought about a sudden conversion to the Progressive crusade. Their acceptance by the Progressives into party councils was viewed by some as hypocritical, and so it was, but it also was indicative of the Progressives' determination to beat the old parties at their own game of professional politics.

At the other extreme from the handful of bosses, and more representative of the ideological character of the new party, were the many Social Gospelers like the *Outlook* editor Lyman Abbott, the writer and Columbus, Ohio, pastor Washington Gladden, and the Episcopal clergyman R. Heber Newton, all pioneers of the Social Gospel, who saw the Progressive Party as the political expression of the movement to promote Christian social concern and activism. An official publication of the new party proclaimed:

The churches, as such, by the very nature of their organization and work, cannot provide an opportunity for the exercise of the religious spirit in the sphere of politics. The Progressive movement, broadly humanitarian, representing a splendid idealism in the field of practical achievement, offers a fitting medium through which the fervor, the enthusiasm, the devotion of true religion can utter itself in terms of social justice, civic righteousness and unselfish service.

In this "recrudescence of the religious spirit in American political life," as it was described, Vermont Progressives nominated the Rev. Fraser Metzger as their candidate for governor. Metzger's parish in Randolph, Vermont, formed by a union of local Protestant churches, had a gymnasium, music hall, bowling alley, and other accouterments of a Social Gospel "institutional church." As a founder and leader of the Inter-Church Federation of Vermont, Metzger had called attention to such social problems as the working conditions of women and children. In addition to clergymen like Metzger and Gladden, many of the laymen in the new party, like the novelist Winston Churchill of New Hampshire, were also identified with the Social Gospel movement, and the Social Gospel as much as reform and direct democracy came to characterize the ideology of the Progressive Party. Most Progressives literally believed that, as Roosevelt put it, they stood at Armageddon and battled for the Lord. Nothing like this had been seen in partisan politics since the abolitionist Free-Soil Party of the 1840s and 1850s.

Just as important as the Social Gospelers in forming the Progressive Party's ideological character and partisan uniqueness were the academics, particularly social scientists, and the social workers who enlisted in the new party. Such social workers as Jane Addams and Raymond Robins of Chicago, Frances Kellor and Lillian D. Wald of New York, and Owen Lovejoy of the National Conference of Charities and Corrections joined with academics like Dean George W. Kirchwey of the Columbia Law School, the political scientist Charles E. Merriam,

GEORGE W. KIRCHWEY
COLUMBIA UNIVERSITY LAW SCHOOL

and Dean William Draper Lewis of the University of Pennsylvania's law department in rallying to the Progressive banner. "... The launching of the new third party has been the signal for the political outcropping of social workers," the editor Paul U. Kellogg reported in the *Survey*, the journal of social work. "The libraries and laboratories of the colleges are being rediscovered as assets of value to the common good. Academic learning, the gibe of the professional politician, is being harnessed to the service of the state," declared a Progressive pamphlet. Social workers and academics had for the first time "found a political instrument in sympathy with their aspirations." Abandoning the path of nonpartisan reform, social workers and academics interested in economic and social change turned to Progressive partisanship.

Dean Lewis was named chairman of the platform committee for the August national convention, and in July social workers and academics went to work drawing up planks. The list of those who helped draft the Progressive platform included Addams, Robins, Merriam, Kirchwey, Arthur and Paul Kellogg of the *Survey*, Charles McCarthy of Wisconsin's famed Legislative Reference Bureau, the social theorist Walter Weyl, and Henry Moskowitz of the New York Society for Ethical Culture. Moskowitz enthusiastically wrote Lillian Wald on August 2 that in Roosevelt "social reform has the services of America's first publicity man and our ideas will become common currency." Mary Kingsbury Simkhovitch of New York City's Greenwich House wrote Roosevelt: "My last fourteen years spent in social settlements have forced me to knowledge of our social needs which life alone can give. At last to see these needs recognized & tackled by a political party is to fill me with thanksgiving." Jane Addams and many other social workers echoed Mary Simkhovitch's sentiments of gratitude for Roosevelt and the new party.

Academics who joined the Progressive Party included James A. Woodburn, the Indiana University expert on political parties; Presidents Benjamin Ide Wheeler of Berkeley and Flavel Luther of Trinity College; and George Ray Wicker, who had taught economics at Dartmouth since 1900. Wicker became the Progressive state chairman for New Hampshire. The Yale physiologist Yandell Henderson became a Bull Moose candidate for Congress, while Benjamin Parke DeWitt, who taught English and government at New York University, ran for the New York legislature. Frederick M. Davenport, professor of law and politics at Hamilton and a former state senator, in later years a congressman, became Progressive candidate for lieutenant governor of New York in 1912 and for governor in 1914.

Academics, of course, formed a larger and more diverse group than the social workers, and they did not act with the same degree of unanimity, but an extraordinary number of professors rallied to the Progressive Party. One of the reasons for this was that many professors considered Roosevelt a man of letters essentially in their circle. Roosevelt had been an original member of both the National Institute of Arts and Letters and the American Academy of Arts and Letters; he was the author of many works on history and natural history; he was slated to be the president of the American Historical Association in 1912; and he was the close friend of many academics. Some scholars considered Roosevelt too radical, but many agreed with Edwin R. Seligman, professor of economics at Columbia, who wrote T.R. on July 28: ". . . I do not believe that either Mr. Wilson or President Taft is alive to the fundamental issues of modern political & economic life, as you are." Many saw in Roosevelt's call for social justice and reform the fulfillment of their research and work. This was particularly true of social scientists like Merriam, Davenport, Wicker, and DeWitt, but it was also true of others. William Henry Crawshaw, professor of English and dean of Colgate, wrote T.R.:

As a teacher of English literature, I have been telling my students for the past fifteen years or more that the dominant interest of the age was changing from science to questions of social welfare, and that the early part of the twentieth century was almost surely destined to be a great period of social reform. I have insisted that this was not a movement toward socialism but toward what I have called altruistic individualism. The literature of the past fifty years is full of unconscious prophecy to the man who has ears to hear any prophetic voices at all. Therefore the Progressive movement found me ready and waiting. I did not expect its coming so soon in the field of actual politics; but when it came, I could not have a moment's hesitation as to where I must stand. Neither could I doubt that its early coming was due to your great leadership and fearless initiative.

Some academics who joined the new party were Democrats like Willard Fisher, professor of economics at Wesleyan. Many more were Republicans, like Albert Bushnell Hart, the noted Harvard historian and ardent progressive nationalist, who wrote Roosevelt:

I was loath to break with the Republican Party, into which I was literally born, a few days after the passage of the Kansas-Nebraska bill, of which my father was an original and implacable opponent. But the progress of the last few months makes it evident that a separate third party is the only way. I have enlisted in that party for the war; and propose to wear the uniform, carry the flag, and fire the musket of the Progressive service.

Wars, political and otherwise, have been generally fought by men. But the Progressive ranks and party councils included women like Jane Addams and Frances Kellor. Favoring women's suffrage, Roosevelt and the new party opened the doors to female participation, nationally and in both suffrage and non-suffrage states. As a symbol of this unique partisan policy, Helen J. Scott was named a Progressive elector in Washington, and became the first woman to cast a vote in the electoral college. Women delegates attended state conventions, state committees and party organizations included women members, and the Progressive national convention in August was the first of a major party to admit women delegates. According to party rules, four women were to be members-at-large of the national committee so as to insure female representation. In the equal rights policy, as in other matters, the Progressives were breaking new ground in the field of partisan politics and offering a definite challenge to and contrast with the old parties.

While the Progressives made women a new factor in national partisan politics, the party also brought new men into the political arena. Political leadership was traditionally recruited mainly from among lawyers, newspaper editors, and businessmen, and indeed the bulk of the new party's leaders came from these occupational groups, but in addition the Progressive Party drew into politics members of professions such as social work, teaching, and the arts not usually associated with political leadership. It was unusual to find a professor like Dean Lewis chairman of a platform committee, or to see men like the Connecticut Progressives Gutzon Borglum, the sculptor, and the Yale physiologist Yandell Henderson, as prominent leaders in a party. Moreover, the new party attracted men from all walks of life, many of them young, who had not previously been politically active.

Much was made of the youthful character of the Progressive leadership. "The Progressive Party will be a young man's party, a party of the present and future; not of the past," predicted the *Boston Journal*. Donald Richberg later recalled: "The progressive movement of 1912 was ... a revolt of youth against age; of idealism against materialism. My generation was spoiling for a fight with the ancient enemies of progress...." Young men like New York attorney George Rublee, the intellectuals Walter Weyl and Joel E. Spingarn, the Chicago reformers Richberg and Harold L. Ickes, the socialite Herbert C. Pell, the New York reformer Stanley M. Isaacs, the Denver civic leader Edward P. Costigan, the progressive Republicans Everett Colby of New Jersey and Bronson Cutting of New Mexico, and United States District Judge Learned Hand of New York, all come of age in an era of reform ferment, found in Roosevelt an idol and in the Progressive Party an outlet for youthful enthusiasm and idealism as well as ambition. Learned Hand, typical of the group, wrote T.R. in August: "Rublee told me you said I would flop to Wilson. You see, good sir, you were a poor prophet; I am glad you so often disclaim the art. Nearly all of us are with you heart and soul. Indeed, the greater part of conscience and brains—under forty,—of the country that I see, are fine Bull Moose."

It was true that there was an element of generational conflict involved in the Progressive cause, and there were many young leaders in the party. In 1912 Richberg was 31, Bronson Cutting 26; the Massachusetts state chairman Matthew Hale and the Pennsylvania leader M. Clyde Kelley were both 29; and Ickes, Costigan, and Everett Colby all 38. Yet an overemphasis on the youthful contingent in the party tends to obscure several facts. The historian Norman M. Wilensky has found that nationally Progressive leaders were younger than their conservative Republican opponents, a conclusion confirmed in state studies by E. Daniel Potts for Iowa and Richard B. Sherman for Massachusetts. On the other hand, Potts found the average age of Iowa Bull Moosers and progressive Republicans who stayed with the G.O.P. differed only slightly, while Sherman discovered that Massachusetts Democratic leaders on the average were about the same age as their Progressive rivals. Moreover, across the country many older men held positions of leadership in the new party. In 1912 William Dudley Foulke of Indiana was 64, Governor Carey of Wyoming 67, Lucius F. C. Garvin 71, and Oscar Straus, Pennsylvania's Willis J. Hulings, and the Iowa gubernatorial candidate John L. Stevens were all 62. Actually, and as might be expected, most Progressive leaders were over 40 and under 60. Finally, an overemphasis on the factor of youth tends to obscure the fact that many of the young leaders were experienced in government and politics in spite of their years. Hale, Isaacs, and Pell were politically wet behind the ears, but Colby, Costigan, Richberg, Ickes, and others were already political veterans.

In fact, the whole question of the experience of the Progressive leaders has often been confused. Some newspapers painted the Progressives as politically naive, while others sneered that there were mainly "has-beens" in the party. The party did contain both political neophytes like Matthew Hale, Gutzon Borglum, and Fraser Metzger, and men who were retired from office or reaching the end of their political careers like former Governor Garvin, former Senator Pettigrew, and John L. Stevens. These men at the extremes of the scale of political experience nevertheless were useful to the party in many ways. The older leaders had reputations, contacts, and experience important in organizing the new party, while neophytes often brought useful professional talents to the partisan enterprise, like expertise in financing, law, or social planning. Furthermore, while it was true that in some states like Massachusetts state parties were plagued by a lack of experienced political talent, in most states the parties were mainly directed by seasoned leaders.

Most of the Progressive leaders, young or old, political veterans or neophytes, were "old stock" Americans—northern European in ethnic origin and Protestant in religion—and came from middle or upper class backgrounds which provided educational and professional opportunities. This sociological background was similar to that of their Republican opponents. Progressive leaders, however, seem to have had more formal education than Republican leaders. Studies of Vermont and Iowa Progressives have shown exceptionally high levels of education among the new party's leaders. E. Daniel Potts has determined that 52 percent of the Iowa Bull Moose leaders had gone to college as opposed to 45 percent of the loyalist liberal Republicans and 43 percent of the Iowa standpatters. Moreover, compared to the old parties the leadership of the Progressive Party was strikingly urban. Some farmers like state Senator L. Whitney Watkins of Michigan were leaders in the new party, but even in rural states such as Minnesota, Iowa, and Oregon Progressive leaders tended to come from urban centers. Yet, though urban-oriented, the Progressive Party attracted few labor leaders. In sum, the Progressive leadership was largely composed of old stock, well-educated, white collar Americans, from Republican backgrounds, who lived in cities. These men were the managers and architects of the growing urban and industrial order, confident of their skills and ready to assume political as well as social and economic leadership.

Thus, the mainstream of the leadership of the new party was made up of progressive Republican politicians, Roosevelt worshipers, Social Gospelers, academics, intellectuals, social workers, and civic-minded newcomers to politics drawn from all occupational groups, plus handfuls of disgruntled Democrats, third party crusaders, and erstwhile Republican bosses. Like the bosses, a few of the leaders were camp followers but most had joined the new party believing that the time had come for a new strategy for reform and social change and a new day in partisan politics. Formerly nonpartisan reformers like the social workers now wanted a partisan vehicle to carry them to power and publicize and promote programs, while partisan reformers like the progressive Republicans had decided that the tactic of factionalism was a waste of time, offering less hope for the future than a new party exclusively dedicated to their ideals. Roosevelt's personal following looked for a "return from Elba" and the restoration of the Roosevelt administration. Social Gospelers saw a chance to bring their message into the political arena. Academics and other professionals saw an opportunity for wider influence and the public utilization of their skills and training. Urban dwellers and women found a party responsive to their needs. Some Progressive leaders were men being drawn into politics for the first time, baptized in the spirit of progressive participatory democracy. Others already active in public life and works were drawn into partisanship for the first time, convinced that the political realities demanded more than good government committees and conferences on charity. Still others who were veterans of party warfare believed that what was needed for effective reform action was a realignment of partisanship along the lines of the progressive-conservative factional split in the old parties. All agreed that the new times of the progressive era demanded a new approach to partisan politics.

5

Yet the question remained: was the leadership of the new party politically potent and viable? Further, what was the strength of the party's organization in the different regions and states of the country? The answers were to be found in large measure in a study of the state Progressive parties and their leaders and candidates for office. The nature of the federal system demanded political strength at the state and local levels if a party—even one dedicated to nationalism—were to survive or make an important impact on American politics.

As might be expected, the Progressive Party was weakest in the Democratic "solid South." But new party advocates managed to patch together state parties composed of Republicans like Cecil Lyon, the G.O.P. state chairman of Texas, and Pearl Wight, a Republican national committeeman from Louisiana; Gold and independent Democrats like John M. Parker of Louisiana and Judge Oscar R. Hundley of Alabama; former Populists like Tom Watson of Georgia and Marion Butler of North Carolina; and businessmen and industrialists of the "New South" who had in most cases not previously been active in politics, like the dime-store chain owner Charles W. McClure of Georgia and the cotton mill president T. H. Wannamaker of South Carolina. Except in Louisiana, where Parker directed a vigorous party, in the South as everywhere else in the nation it is probable that the Progressive Party could not have been organized without the help of former Republicans, which meant that the party's appeal to the mass of southern Democrats was severely limited. But although offices were not contested in all southern states, the Progressives entered candidates in four of the six November gubernatorial elections, nominating the wealthy rancher Edward C. Lasater in Texas and attorneys William C. Hodges in Florida, W. F. Poston in Tennessee, and Iredell Meares in North Carolina.

Southern Progressives were convinced that the key to their success lay in creating a "lily-white" party. They believed that the presence of blacks in the councils of the southern Republican parties was the main reason that the Democracy was able to continue its grip on the former Confederacy. White Progressives in Texas, Mississippi, Alabama, Florida, and elsewhere moved quickly in their state conventions to exclude blacks from party positions. Contesting Negro delegations from Mississippi, Alabama, and Florida went to Chicago to place their cases before the Provisional National Progressive Committee, which met in early August before the convention opened. Roosevelt conferred with party leaders as the news arrived from the South. The issue was in the open for all to see, but it would have to wait for the committee hearings to be finally resolved.

In the New England states of Maine, Massachusetts, and Rhode Island the Progressive Party suffered from a lack of politically experienced leadership. In Maine Roosevelt followers endorsed the Republican organization and state ticket, only to find after the September state elections that the G.O.P.'s professions of loyalty to Roosevelt and the new party had been less than whole-hearted. In Massachusetts no really prominent politicians joined the party in 1912. Matthew Hale, the 29-year-old Massachusetts state chairman and national committeeman, was a Boston alderman, but his first real political experience had been gained in Roosevelt's unsuccessful Bay State primary campaign. The industrialist Charles Sumner Bird, Progressive candidate for governor of Massachusetts, proved an effective and popular campaigner, but he had been inactive in politics since the Gold Democratic campaign in 1896. Aside from former Governor Garvin, Rhode Island Progressives also could point to few seasoned state leaders, and Mayor Albert H. Humes of Pawtucket, Bull Moose nominee for governor, found it impossible to mount an effective campaign.

The Progressive political situation was somewhat better in Vermont and Connecticut. In Vermont the able Charles H. Thompson of Brattleboro, a former mayor, and the gubernatorial candidate Fraser Metzger led a vigorous party with strong grass roots support, although few established politicians joined the cause. In Connecticut, though such state leaders as Trinity College's President Flavel Luther and the sculptor Gutzon Borglum were newcomers to politics, state Senator Joseph W. Alsop, the gubernatorial nominee Herbert Knox Smith, active in Connecticut politics before going to Washington and the Bureau of Corporations, and Willard Fisher, Wesleyan economics professor and two-term mayor of Middletown, provided experienced leadership. In New Hampshire the future of the new party looked more promising than anywhere else in New England because of the leadership of Governor Robert Perkins Bass and the novelist Winston Churchill. Churchill, nominated for governor to succeed Bass, was a long-time opponent of the railroad interests that controlled New Hampshire politics, and a veteran of the state legislature whose novels revealed him to be as much a student of contemporary social problems as a weaver of popular romances.

Since New England was a heavily Republican region, the lack of Progressive organizational strength in several of the states threatened the national party's prospects for victory and survival. The main reason that the Progressive Party was not stronger in New England was simple: New England, the land of "steady habits," was a bastion of conservatism. Although there had been attempts at reform in some states, only New Hampshire had experienced a real progressive movement before 1912. The Progressives were breaking new ground in rocky soil. In all the states there were strong standpat Republican organizations, like Murray Crane's in Massachusetts and Nelson Aldrich's in Rhode Island. The new party faced an immense task in challenging the New England G.O.P., and there were aggressive Democratic parties in several states.

The Progressive picture was different in the eastern states of New York, New Jersey, and Pennsylvania, and the old northwestern states of Ohio, Indiana, and Illinois, regions where the Republican Party was strong but not always dominant. In these states Progressive organizations were generally strong, forming a solid belt from the Atlantic to the Mississippi. Bull Moose strength was the result of able leadership, and also of the growing reform sentiment in these areas.

The party in New York State was led by William H. Hotchkiss, a former state insurance commissioner who became state chairman, the New York City Comptroller William A. Prendergast, the professor and politician Frederick M. Davenport, the Brooklyn boss Timothy Woodruff, Roosevelt himself, and others. Former Secretary of Commerce Oscar S. Straus, a member of the Permanent Court of Arbitration at The Hague, was nominated for governor, the first Jew to run for governor of New York, as he had been the first of his religion to hold a cabinet post. The rest of the ticket was also distinguished. Davenport was chosen for lieutenant governor, and Dean Kirchwey of Columbia and Dean Carlos C. Alden of the Buffalo Law School were designated for the state court of appeals. Labor was represented on the ticket by Homer D. Call, secretary and treasurer of the National Association of Butchers and Meat Cutters, nominated for secretary of state. General Horatio C. King, a leader in the G.A.R. and other veterans' groups, was chosen for comptroller, Judge John Palmieri of Brooklyn for attorney general, and Professor O. M. Leland, head of the Cornell engineering department, for state engineer and surveyor.

In neighboring New Jersey the Progressive Party also recruited some outstanding leaders in former Governor John Franklin Fort, George L. Record, and Everett Colby. Fort had been a city, county, and state supreme court judge before being elected governor of the Garden State in 1908. Record had been a successful reformer in Jersey City before becoming the chief theoretician of the "New Idea" Republicans, as the progressive faction was called, in their fights for such reforms as the limitation of public franchises. Colby, born in Wisconsin, joined a New York City law firm, and settled with his wife in the fashionable New Jersey suburb of Llewellyn Park, West Orange. He had led the respectable residents of the Oranges in a revolt against the boss of Essex County, Newark's Major Carl Lentz. Capturing the Essex G.O.P. from Lentz, Colby went on to lead the New Idea Republicans in both houses of the state legislature. By 1910 Fort, Record, and Colby had all reached an impasse with the conservative Republican bosses allied to the powerful corporate interests in New Jersey, the first state to allow holding companies. All three were ready for a new partisan organization.

In Pennsylvania the able Bill Flinn was joined by the newspaper publishers E. A. Van Valkenburg and Alexander P. Moore, Dean Lewis, Gifford Pinchot, and a host of local officeholders and political leaders in building the "Washington Party" in opposition to the G.O.P. machine of Senator Boies Penrose. In Ohio the new party was led by former Secretary of the Interior James R. Garfield, son of President Garfield; Walter F. Brown, chairman of the Republican state committee; and Arthur L. Garford, president of Cleveland and Elyria manufacturing concerns. Funds in Ohio came from Garford, Henry H. Timken of the roller bearing company, and the ambitious and erratic Dan R. Hanna, son of Mark Hanna. Garford was nominated for governor, and was joined on the Bull Moose state ticket by John J. Sullivan, former state senator and United States attorney, who resigned from the Republican ticket as nominee for secretary of state to accept the same position on the Progressive ticket.

Michigan Progressives had trouble recruiting experienced leaders, although state Senator L. Whitney Watkins, farm leader and conservationist, made an attractive candidate for governor. Indiana Progressives, on the other hand, had many experienced leaders, including Albert J. Beveridge; the former Republican state chairman Edwin M. Lee; the veteran reformers Lucius B. Swift and William Dudley Foulke; former Congressman Frederick Landis, novelist and playwright; and numerous others. On the local level the Indiana party had the services of able young leaders like the former diplomat Paxton Hibben. On August 1 1,441 enthusiastic and wildly cheering Hoosier delegates met in Indianapolis and nominated former Senator Beveridge for governor and Landis for lieutenant governor.

FREDERICK LANDIS
OF INDIANA

On August 2 the Illinois Progressive state convention nominated state Senator Frank H. Funk for governor. Funk, whose family produced the well-known Funk corn seed, had been a football star at Yale, and was serving his second term in the state senate. Leadership in Illinois centered around a remarkable Chicago group: Medill McCormick, Raymond Robins, Charles E. Merriam, Donald Richberg, and Harold L. Ickes. The wealthy McCormick was an owner of the *Chicago Tribune,* and Robins had struck it rich in the Klondike before becoming a social worker in Chicago. Robins, the noted political scientist Merriam, and attorneys Richberg and Ickes had all been active in Chicago reform politics. This Cook County contingent was supplemented by Funk, Judge William H. Hinebaugh of Ottawa, Congressman Ira Copely, the bankers B. F. Harris and John L. Hamilton, and others. The Progressive Party in Illinois looked promising, particularly in light of the fact that both old parties in Illinois were widely and publicly discredited as corrupt machines.

Among the border states Maryland and Missouri were well organized, while the right leaders could not seem to be found elsewhere. In Maryland the party was led by the Baltimore patrician reformer and former cabinet member Charles J. Bonaparte, whose political experience dated back to the Liberal Republican Party of 1872. In Delaware the weak state party chose George B. Hynson, lawyer, poet, and newspaper editor, for governor. The new party in Missouri, much to Governor Hadley's dismay, was organized in almost all counties by late July, and Judge Albert D. Nortoni, former United States attorney and judge of the St. Louis court of appeals since 1905, was nominated for governor, with Colonel William R. Nelson, the doughty editor of the *Kansas*

City Star and his young assistant Ralph Stout aiding the Progressive cause.

In South Dakota, Kansas, California, and the other states where the state Republican parties backed the National Progressive Party, there was no need to build new state organizations in 1912, but certain leaders emerged to direct the Roosevelt campaign and help in building the new party nationally. In South Dakota Governor Robert S. Vessey led the state delegation to the national convention, while in Kansas Roosevelt particularly looked to Governor Stubbs, Congressman Victor Murdock, and the newspaper editors Henry J. Allen and William Allen White for leadership and counsel. In California the new party advocates were Francis J. Heney, Chester H. Rowell, Meyer Lissner, and Governor Hiram W. Johnson, and the Republican machinery of the state was probably the single most important political accession to the Progressive Party.

Heney, the red-headed son of immigrant parents, had been expelled from college for fighting, and he had been in one kind of fight or another ever since. He moved from San Francisco to Arizona in the 1880s, where he became a cattleman and then ran an Indian trading post at Fort Apache. Once he killed a man in a street gunfight. Later he served as the Democratic attorney general of the territory. In 1895 Heney returned to San Francisco, and in 1906 became special prosecutor in the graft trials involving the machine of the San Francisco boss Abe Ruef. Ruef ultimately went to prison, but Heney was shot and wounded by gangsters before the trials were over, and was forced to turn the prosecution over to young attorney Hiram Warren Johnson. Johnson and Heney both joined with the League of Lincoln-Roosevelt Republican Clubs, founded in 1907 by Chester H. Rowell, editor and publisher of the *Fresno Republican,* the Los Angeles reformer and attorney Meyer Lissner, and others, to fight the conservative G.O.P. state machine allied with the Southern Pacific Railroad. Johnson was elected governor in 1910 with the League's backing. Heney and Johnson were members of the provisional national committee of the new party, and subsequently Rowell became the California member of the permanent national committee with Lissner serving on the executive committee of the same body.

In those midwestern, plains, and western states where progressive Republicans largely controlled the G.O.P. but the state Republican organizations declined to endorse the Progressive Party, as in Minnesota, Iowa, and Oregon, separate third parties were set up. This competition alienated loyalist liberal Republicans, many of whom supported T.R. for president though they clung to the G.O.P., and thus the new party failed to enlist many of the most prominent progressive Republicans in these states. It was paradoxical, in states like Minnesota and Oregon where Roosevelt and progressive sentiment was strong, that the organization of the Progressive Party was relatively weak.

In Minnesota attorney Hugh T. Halbert, president of the Roosevelt Club of St. Paul, who had been pushing for a new party since 1910, became the Bull Moose leader when more prominent progressive Republicans failed to volunteer for the job, and Paul V. Collins, owner of the widely read *Northwestern Agriculturist,* was nominated as the third party candidate for governor. In North

Dakota, where La Follette had won the primary over T.R. and Taft, the La Follette following made it difficult to organize the Progressive Party, as was also the case in Wisconsin. In Wisconsin Roosevelt supporters backed Republican Governor Francis McGovern for reelection, but in North Dakota, where conservative Congressman Louis B. Hanna had managed to capture the G.O.P. gubernatorial nomination from the insurgents, the Bull Moosers ran Mayor William D. Sweet of Fargo against him. In Iowa, where Senator Cummins endorsed Roosevelt but not the new party and Senator Kenyon backed Taft, the Progressives nominated for governor John L. Stevens, successful businessman and former judge who had been active in politics since the 1870s. In Oregon, where the "Oregon system" of primaries and direct democracy had fostered a breakdown of all partisan organization, Bull Moosers, located mainly in the Portland area, put together a patchwork party led by the long-time Roosevelt supporter Dr. Henry Waldo Coe and the former Populist L. H. McMahan, a crusading reformer and persistent third party advocate, as well as by ambitious newcomers to politics.

In those western states where conservative Republicans were strong or dominant, however, there was not the reason to stay in the G.O.P. that there might be in midwestern states like Iowa or Wisconsin, and thus many progressive Republicans welcomed the new party. But Bull Moose strength varied in such states because of local conditions and because in several of the states the progressive movement itself was weak. Fairly strong Progressive state parties were established in New Mexico, Colorado, Wyoming, Washington, and Montana. The new party organization was weaker, however, in Arizona, Utah, and Idaho, and had little support in Oklahoma and Nevada.

In Oklahoma and Nevada, where the Democratic Party was strong, the Progressive cause seemed hopeless, and in Idaho the new party faced an uphill struggle against both conservative Republicans and the followers of Senator Borah, an insurgent who remained with the G.O.P. Utah, the bastion of the standpatter Senator Reed Smoot, was a stronghold of conservative Republicanism and Taft support. Nevertheless, Progressives in Idaho and Utah ran candidates for governor, nominating attorney G. H. Martin in Idaho and in Utah N. L. Morris, Mormon leader, prominent businessman, and former state legislator.

The Progressive Party in Arizona, mainly directed by Dwight B. Heard and John C. Greenway, lacked seasoned political leadership. Heard, a wealthy cattleman and land developer, had been active in the conservation movement but not partisan politics before 1912, and the former Rough Rider Jack Greenway, copper mine director, also lacked political experience. The situation was better in neighboring New Mexico, where the party was led by Congressman George Curry, another Rough Rider veteran, former Governor Miguel A. Otero, and young Bronson Cutting. Otero had been the first Hispanic governor of the territory, serving from 1897 to 1906. Otero and Cutting, a wealthy New Yorker moved to New Mexico for his health, and other foes of the standpat G.O.P. machine of the state, had formed the Progressive Republican League, which split from the G.O.P. in 1911, backing the Democratic candidate for governor. In 1912 the League joined the Progressive Party, with Otero becoming state chairman and national committeeman and Cutting serving as state treasurer. Cutting, who was at the start of a long political career which would culminate in a Senate seat, purchased three newspapers, including the Spanish language *El Nuevo Mexicano,* to serve as organs of the Progressive cause. The new party in Wyoming had also in effect been started before 1912. Governor Joseph M. Carey, former mayor of Cheyenne, territorial delegate to Congress, and United States senator, had broken with the G.O.P. in 1910 when he was elected with Democratic and progressive Republican support. Carey was an enthusiastic supporter of the new party movement, and his son Robert D. Carey, subsequently also governor and senator, became Wyoming's national committeeman.

The Progressive Party in Colorado, Washington, and Montana was also vigorous and promising. Colorado's Republican Party was run by bosses like "Big Steve" Stephenson, who aided the Taft forces on the national committee during the G.O.P. delegate hearings, and Senator Simon Guggenheim, whose family ran mining interests hated by conservationists and labor leaders. In opposition, Judge Ben Lindsey, the famous promoter of the juvenile court system, the Denver reformer Edward P. Costigan, Republican Attorney General Benjamin Griffith, and other reformers and progressive Republicans established a militant Colorado Progressive Party. Judge Lindsey served on the executive committee of the national party, while Costigan was nominated for governor, and Griffith, who resigned from the G.O.P. ticket, ran for reelection as attorney general. A prominent supporter of Lindsey's juvenile justice system, Austin E. Griffiths of Seattle, Washington, a civic leader active in reform groups, was in many ways typical of the progressive Republicans in western Washington who led the drive for a break with the state G.O.P. The western and Pacific Coast section of the state was the stronghold of conservative Republicanism in Washington, and western progressives were eager for a new party. Republican progressives like Senator Miles Poindexter from the reform-minded eastern area were reluctant at first, many of them holding office and partisan power, but ultimately Poindexter and his supporters went along with the strategy of a new party. Robert T. Hodge, sheriff of King County, was chosen for governor. In Montana Poindexter's fellow insurgent Senator Dixon, Progressive national chairman, led his followers out of the Montana G.O.P. to form the new party, which nominated five-term Mayor Frank J. Edwards of Helena for governor.

Thus, the Progressive Party was well organized in the Middle Atlantic states and most of the old Northwest, as well as in parts of the New England, plains, Rocky Mountain, and Pacific regions, while weak in the South and various states like Wisconsin and Utah elsewhere. The degree of organizational strength was directly proportional not to the strength of the progressive movement in each state, a factor which had a varying effect, but to the number of experienced and able political leaders recruited by the new party. Success in such recruitment usually depended on factors in the local political climate. It was all well and good to bring new people into partisan politics—social workers, academics, women, and others—but unless the party could play professional politics in the same league with the old parties, its chances of effectiveness would be virtually nil.

How strong was the Progressive Party? Although many Progressive leaders like Hale of Massachusetts and Heard of Arizona were political newcomers, the party could point to a substantial number of seasoned men in key states who were qualified for positions of partisan leadership. Certainly Edwin M. Lee, Walter F. Brown, and Cecil Lyon were qualified to be state chairmen: they had been Republican state chairmen of respectively Indiana, Ohio, and Texas. And other Progressive state chairmen such as William H. Hotchkiss of New York and former Governors Fort of New Jersey and Otero of New Mexico were also experienced professionals. Such state organizers for the new party as George L. Record of New Jersey, Bill Flinn of Pennsylvania, and Governor Carey of Wyoming were essentially doing the same kind of work they had been doing for years. Several of the new national committeemen had previously served on the G.O.P. national committee, and the roster of the Progressive national committee included the names of able politicians and reformers like Chester H. Rowell of California, Ben Lindsey of Colorado, and Governor Vessey of South Dakota. Not surprisingly, the Progressive Party had trouble enlisting incumbent officeholders, men with much to lose, but the striking and remarkable fact was that in the end the new party attracted so many officeholders as it did, as well as other men in the prime of their political careers. Local officials like Prendergast of New York City and

WILLIAM FLINN
OF PENNSYLVANIA
WEARING A BULL MOOSE
CAMPAIGN BANDANNA

Mayor Frank J. Edwards of Helena, Montana; state officers and legislators such as Attorney General Griffith of Colorado and state Senator Frank Funk of Illinois; governors like Johnson of California, Carey of Wyoming, Vessey of South Dakota, and Bass of New Hampshire; members of Congress such as Poindexter of Washington, Curry of New Mexico, and Dixon of Montana; and others like them joined the new party. Moreover, the high caliber of the leadership of the new party was revealed in the background and careers of leaders like Herbert Knox Smith, Oscar S. Straus, Everett Colby, Gifford Pinchot, Charles J. Bonaparte, James R. Garfield, Albert J. Beveridge, and Edward P. Costigan.

The Progressives organized down to the county and local level wherever possible. Walter Brown of Ohio brought with him to the new party 10 of the 21 members of the G.O.P. state committee and 17 of the 88 county organizations, while virtually the entire Republican state and local organizations in some states like South Dakota came over, and most counties in the larger states had Bull Moose organizations and committees. Still, in the end, it was impossible in a few short months to parallel completely the organization and experienced personnel of the old parties, particularly on the local level. The Progressives, however, were certainly strong enough to launch a formidable challenge, wage state and national campaigns, and make a promising beginning on the road to permanence. It seemed clear that the Progressives would not be defeated, as so many new parties have been before and since, by a failure to recognize and attend to the practical realities of professional politics.

6

In addition to this general survey of the state Progressive parties, further evidence of the political viability and credibility of the new party is found in a study of samples of Progressive candidates for the United States House and for governorships. The Progressive Party was offering the nation a program of social justice and democracy on all levels of government. This program was translated into planks in the Progressive state platforms of 1912 which spoke to the particular needs and conditions in the various states: the unseating of conservative machines in states like Massachusetts and Pennsylvania; cleaning up corruption in states such as Illinois; democratizing political procedures in states like Rhode Island and New York; curbing corporation influence in the politics of states such as New Hampshire and Colorado; and reforming labor relations in every state. If, however, Progressive candidates for Congress, governor, and other offices, when measured by the usual yardsticks of political experience, background and training, and distinction in politics, business, civic affairs, and the professions, were in fact unqualified for office, as is usually the case with candidates of minor or third parties, then the Progressive Party could have been easily dismissed by the voters. Progressives had to indicate by the quality of their candidates that they had capable personnel as well as relevant proposals. Unless this were done, the Progressives would be merely another "protest party" and not seriously in the running. In most states in 1912 the Progressive Party passed this crucial test of political viability and credibility, just as the party had surmounted most of the problems of organization in state after state.

Albert Shaw's *Review of Reviews,* a magazine friendly to the third party, claimed that the "Progressive candidates for Congress were—typically—men of high standing, brilliancy, and promise,...." although no evidence was offered to prove this assertion. But a random sample of twenty-two Progressive candidates in six states, selected from congressional districts where Bull Moose sentiment was relatively strong and from the better publicized House races, shows that in fact the new party was able to nominate many able and politically credible candidates.

In Washington excellent candidates were nominated for the two positions of congressman-at-large, James Wesley Bryan and Jacob Alexander Falconer. Bryan, a Yale graduate, had been Bremerton city attorney before being elected to two terms in the state senate, and the lumberman Falconer had been mayor of Everett before serving in the state house, where he was speaker, and then in the state senate. In Illinois's twelfth district Judge William H. Hinebaugh, on the La Salle County bench since 1902, a former president of the state association of county judges, was nominated. Charles M. Thomson, an attorney three times elected to the Chicago city council, was chosen to run in one of the Cook County districts. The dentist mayor of Bay City, Michigan, Roy O. Woodruff, began his thirty-four-year career in the House as the Bull Moose candidate in the state's tenth district. In Pennsylvania the new Washington Party selected an outstanding slate of congressional candidates, including the Rev. Henry Willson Temple, Reformed Presbyterian minister, author, and professor of political science and history at Washington and Jefferson College, to begin twenty years service in the House; Willis J. Hulings, brigadier general in the Spanish-American War, former member of both the Pennsylvania house and senate; former Mayor Fred E. Lewis of Allentown; and young M. Clyde Kelley, newspaper editor and

OSCAR S. STRAUS
OF NEW YORK

member of the state house, also to serve twenty years in Congress. The Progressive candidate in Roosevelt's home district, New York's first, was former Democratic Congressman W. Bourke Cockran. In New York City Gifford's brother, the reformer Amos Pinchot, and Lindon Bates, Jr., who had been a leading Republican insurgent in the state assembly, were among the Bull Moose nominees. In Connecticut state Senator Joseph W. Alsop ran in the first district and Professor Yandell Henderson of Yale in the third. In sum, the *Review of Reviews* appears to have been correct in its assessment: the Progressive candidates for the House in the random sample of twenty-two from six states were "men of high standing, brilliancy, and promise...."

Thirty-two states elected governors in the fall of 1912. In six states the new party backed the Republican candidates, and in two southern states did not contest the elections. Progressive gubernatorial candidates on third party tickets entered the contests in the other twenty-four states, and in nearly every case the new party was able to field qualified and politically viable and credible candidates. Even hostile newspapers joined in praising Progressive nominees for governor like Albert J. Beveridge of Indiana, Winston Churchill of New Hampshire, and Oscar S. Straus of New York. The Republican *New York Tribune* said that the nomination of Straus "will everywhere be regarded as creditable," the Democratic *World* admitted that the former secretary of commerce "fully measures up to the governorship," and Woodrow Wilson told the press that the nomination would put Democrats "on our mettle." Judged by the normal yardsticks of experience, background, and professional distinction, it could be fairly said that only three of the twenty-four Progressive candidates were probably not qualified for governor. William C. Hodges of Florida had apparently not held public office before, while G. H. Martin of Idaho and Robert T. Hodge of Washington had held relatively minor posts, and none of the three seemed otherwise sufficiently distinguished in business, professional, or civic affairs to make them credible candidates.

Of the other twenty-one candidates for governor, at least fourteen had previously held public office. Iredell Meares of North Carolina had been only a minor official, but his prominence in the Tarheel State as lawyer, writer, public speaker, and descendant of a distinguished family made him an attractive candidate. The rest of the fourteen had impressive records of public service. Herbert Knox Smith of Connecticut, Churchill of New Hampshire, L. Whitney Watkins of Michigan, W. F. Poston of Tennessee, Funk of Illinois, and N. L. Morris of Utah had all been state legislators. Smith had also been on the Hartford common council, and was federal commissioner of corporations when he resigned to join the new party. John L. Stevens of Iowa had been a district attorney and judge, as well as a commissioner to the Department of the Interior, and in 1911 he had helped draw up Iowa's employers' liability and workmen's compensation law. Albert H. Humes of Rhode Island, William D. Sweet of North Dakota, and Frank J. Edwards of Montana were mayors of important cities in their states. Albert D. Nortoni of Missouri had been a city attorney and United States attorney before being elected a judge in St. Louis in 1904. Straus, of course, was a former cabinet member and a distinguished diplomat, and Beveridge was one of the best-known political figures in the nation.

Of the candidates who had not held public office, seven out of the eight qualified as credible gubernatorial nominees by their prominence in business and the professions: George B. Hynson of Delaware, Paul V. Collins of Minnesota, Arthur L. Garford of Ohio, Charles Sumner Bird of Massachusetts, Edward C. Lasater of Texas, Fraser Metzger of Vermont, and Edward P. Costigan of Colorado. Hynson and Collins as publishers and writers were well-known observers of public affairs; Garford and Bird were among the leading industrialists of their states; Lasater was a wealthy stockman, president of the Texas and Southwestern Cattle Raisers Association; Metzger's many civic and religious activities gave him a respected name; Costigan's numerous civic endeavors included service as attorney for the Honest Election League of Denver, the Law Enforcement League, and the Anti-Saloon League, and as an organizer of the Citizens Party of Denver.

Most of the candidates had taken a leading role in various charitable, fraternal, religious, and service activities. N. L. Morris was a leader of the Salt Lake Stake of the Mormon church; Nortoni was active in many St. Louis clubs; and Straus was a well-known leader in the Jewish community, founder of the American Jewish Historical Society, active in several Jewish welfare organizations. Watkins of Michigan was active in many farm and conservation groups, and had been a member of the state board of agriculture. In an era when a college education was still exceptional, at least thirteen of the candidates had attended college, and several had done graduate work. Churchill, of course, was a best-selling novelist, but a number of the other candidates had also written books. Meares,

Funk, Morris, and Straus came from families long noted in the business and political affairs of their states. Most of the candidates, including those who had been active in politics, were successful in various business enterprises. Charles Sumner Bird owned a chain of paper mills; Arthur L. Garford manufactured an automobile which bore his name; Frank H. Funk had been an officer of the prosperous Funk Brothers Seed Company; N. L. Morris was a bank president and had construction and insurance interests. In short, the lineup of Progressive gubernatorial nominees was impressive from every standpoint. They would have been credible candidates on any party ticket.

Why did these men run for governor? Motivations are usually mixed and complex, but some generalizations can be made about the Progressive candidates. Some were certainly ambitious for the office. Churchill and Garford had previously been candidates for G.O.P. gubernatorial nominations—Churchill in 1906, Garford in 1912—and Beveridge longed for a return to public office. For many of the nominees like the mayors and state legislators a race for governor or some other high office was the next logical step in a political career. Others like Straus, Bird, and Metzger seem to have been motivated simply by the philanthropic and civic-minded spirit that had characterized their previous careers, and agreed to run when duty called. Most of the nominees could see their candidacies as opportunities for larger service to the reform cause they had long served. All could see that they faced an uphill fight against heavy odds and risked future political careers by opposing the old parties. Smith had made a great sacrifice in leaving the federal government and the Republican Party for the uncertainties of third party politics, and men like Funk, Watkins, Edwards, and Nortoni might well have been generously rewarded by the G.O.P. for refusing to bolt. Even those like Garford, Churchill, and Beveridge who had been frustrated in their ambitions by conservative Republican machines might have found more political security by remaining with an established party than by joining a new one. Yet Churchill, Smith, Costigan, and others had always been more interested in promoting reform than in gaining office. Beveridge might still have been in the Senate in 1912 had he not offended conservative Hoosier Republicans. In short, most of the Progressive candidates for governor seem to have been caught up in the fervor of the Progressive cause, willing to sacrifice and work for reform and the restructuring

FRANK H. FUNK

of the party system. One can guess that it must have been the same with many other Progressive candidates for office and new party leaders.

7

Between the meetings of the June Republican and August Progressive conventions, Taft leaders, La Follette's followers, Democratic spokesmen, and the newspapers loyal to the old parties made every effort to discredit Roosevelt and the new party and keep voters and leaders on the old partisan homesteads. Roosevelt's supposed radicalism was attacked by both Republicans and Democrats.

SENATOR JOSEPH M. DIXON,
PROGRESSIVE NATIONAL CHAIRMAN

The flag of the Progressives was the red bandanna, the handkerchief of the common man, which was wildly waved at all rallies. "It may be difficult to distinguish the bandanna from the red flag," warned the *Philadelphia Record.* Conservatives solemnly forecast the demise of constitutional government and the end of private property under the Progressives. President Taft cautioned voters against those who were "sowing dragons' teeth." On the other hand, La Follette told progressive Republicans that T.R. was really a conservative and always had been, a wolf in sheep's clothing trying to break into the progressive fold.

The difficult problem that the Progressives faced in trying to decide what to do in states where progressive Republicans controlled the state parties was mocked by the opposition press as a case of hypocrisy. There is dignity in a bolt, said the *New York Tribune,* but not in a mere factional fight for control of party machinery. The idea that T.R. might get the Republican electoral votes in several states provoked a rhyme in the *New York Times:*

> Thou Shalt Not Steal!
> That's very true, but then you see,
> The text does not apply to me;
> It's written most explicitly
> *Thou* Shalt Not Steal.

It was widely reported that because of Roosevelt's leadership the new party was a one-man show. The *Chicago Record-American* told its readers: "An anxious correspondent wishes to know whether the plural for bull moose is 'bull mooses' or 'bull meese.' There is no plural for bull moose. There is but one bull moose." Untrue reports that Governors Stubbs and Aldrich had deserted the cause along with Hadley were given extensive circulation. Many observers declared that it did not look as if the new party could make a showing. Any differences between Progressives were interpreted as evidence of impending collapse, while agreements were taken as proof of T.R.'s dictatorial control.

NOW TO VICTORY!

The role of women in the Massachusetts and New York state conventions seemed amusing to the *New York Times,* which had definitely decided by August that the new party was not amounting to much. A *Times* dispatch from Chicago reported on August 4: "Tomorrow at noon there will open in the Coliseum a convention managed by women and has-beens. About everybody here who wears trousers is an ex. There are ex-Senators, ex-Secretaries, and ex-Commissioners galore. Everybody who is not an ex is a woman."

On August 3 Senator Dixon had convened a meeting of the Provisional

National Progressive Committee at Chicago's Congress Hotel. Among those present were such officeholders as Governors Johnson, Carey, and Vessey, and Senator Poindexter. Dixon noted that the call for the new party had been issued less than thirty days before. In that time, he reported, conventions had met in forty-seven states to choose delegates to the national convention and to establish the new party. Some "faint hearts" had doubted that normal delegations could be raised. "As it stands this morning, more than two-thirds of the states in the enthusiasm of the local situations have sent delegations here double, and treble, and quadruple . . . the number of delegates named in the call. . . . The truth is we have been issuing brigadier-generals' commissions galore in order to keep up with the demand." Surveying the rapid progress of organizing the new party, Herbert Knox Smith wrote: "The force was gathered and long ready. Not otherwise could so swift a civic miracle have been wrought." Donald Richberg later recalled: ". . . When T.R. located Armageddon and the band played marching hymns, we put on shining armor and went out to battle for the Lord."

CHAPTER THREE

LILY-WHITE PROGRESSIVISM

One of the really puzzling questions with which I have to do, in connection with this progressive party, is the question of the negro.

T. R.

On August 3, two days before the opening of the Progressive national convention, the Provisional National Progressive Committee met in Chicago under the chairmanship of Senator Dixon. The committee was faced with the task of settling delegate contests from the South, a circumstance reminiscent of the predicament that had confronted the G.O.P. national committee in the same çity in June. As the Progressive Party was being organized in the South, an old issue had arisen as a new factor in the 1912 campaign. Progressive leaders in several southern states had declared that the new party in the South was going to be a white man's party; but many southern Negro Roosevelt supporters had protested, and when the Alabama, Mississippi, and Florida state conventions chose all-white delegations to the national convention black Progressives elected their own contesting delegations. Although it was too late to prevent contests before the national committee, in late July Roosevelt decided to forestall further disputes at Chicago and prepare for the fall campaign by formulating a Progressive position on the "race issue."

White southern Progressives were almost unanimous in urging Roosevelt to come out for lily-white parties in the former Confederate states and drop what a Virginia Progressive termed the "negro incubus." John M. Parker of New Orleans, chief southern strategist of the Progressive Party, wrote Roosevelt: "Nearly every letter I receive urges strongly the importance of having the Progressive Party a White Man's party strictly. Such a plank would be a power throughout the South...." Parker warned that the South "cannot and will not under any circumstances tolerate the negro...." It was fitting, moreover, that the white man should lead the new party in the South, "recognizing the superior ability of the white man and his superior civilization.... The negro has been perfectly content to remain the ignorant savage devoid of pride of ancestry or civic ambition." Roosevelt valued Parker's advice since the New Orleans businessman was a prominent civic and state reformer and one of the most noted southern Democratic converts to the Bull Moose. Hoping to attract Democrats in general and southern Democrats in particular, Roosevelt for a time considered running Parker for vice president in 1912.

The past policies of the Republican Party toward the Negro and the South were much on Roosevelt's mind as he sought to formulate positions for the new party. Roosevelt's own background and experience in fact reflected the history of the G.O.P.'s racial and southern policies. As with most men of his generation, the heritage of the Civil War had made a deep impression on his thinking. His family had been Democrats before the Civil War (the Hyde Park branch of the family still was in 1912), but Theodore Roosevelt, Sr., the future president's father, had become a "Lincoln Republican," and had served the northern cause as an organizer of such groups as the Union League and as one of Lincoln's army allotment commissioners. A Republican "by inheritance and education," as he put it, the younger Theodore had waved the "bloody shirt" in the 1880s, roundly attacking the Democrats as "the party that tried to destroy the Union, that supported slavery. . . ." Like other Republicans, T.R. championed the cause of the Negro oppressed and disenfranchised by the Democrats of the South. "As long as the Democracy depends for success upon the electoral votes of these Southern states being obtained by force or fraud," he said in 1885, "just so long the North should deny it all space in the control of the national government." These were conventional Gilded Age Republican sentiments, conventionally held and expressed by a young politician; but Roosevelt as president had been forced to devise his own policies toward the South and the Negro.

Roosevelt generally subscribed to the views of Booker T. Washington. That is, he believed that many years of educational, vocational, and self-help training for blacks would be needed before the problems facing the Negro could be solved. A competent naturalist well-read in the literature of natural history and evolution, Roosevelt did not think that any race was inherently or biologically inferior or superior to any other. But he was anthropologically and philosophically provincial in his views of culture and "civilization." Thus, he found American blacks as a group "inferior" to American whites as a group, because he did not think that the long oppressed blacks had yet reached as high a degree of education, economic success, and social and cultural achievement as the majority of whites had. Roosevelt tended to believe that white racism would disappear as the mass of blacks became the educational, social, and economic "equals" of the whites. Segregation was, he thought, a local matter to be worked out by black and white "neighbors."

As president, Roosevelt preached equal justice for all and condemned southern persecution of blacks, but he made few moves to extend federal power for the protection of Negro rights in such matters as lynching and suffrage. Under the Roosevelt administration, however, Negroes were given more government jobs in the North than in previous administrations, and were selectively appointed to offices in the South. Southern Democratic racists like Governor

James K. Vardaman of Mississippi and Senator "Pitchfork Ben" Tillman of South Carolina bitterly attacked T.R. for his Negro appointments, and for breaking bread in the White House with black leader Booker T. Washington. On the other hand, most black leaders condemned the president for his handling of the Brownsville affair of 1906, when Roosevelt summarily dismissed from the army Negro troops accused of firing on the town of Brownsville, Texas. Roosevelt defied these criticisms from both sides of the ideological spectrum, defending his black appointments and denying that racial prejudice was involved in his Brownsville decision.

As president, Roosevelt's goal in the South was twofold: he wanted to take control of the southern G.O.P. machinery and at the same time win over southern Democrats to the Republican Party. The former national chairman Mark Hanna, hero of Republican standpatters, had frequently replaced the so-called black and tan leadership of the southern G.O.P. with white leaders loyal to him. Roosevelt in turn replaced Hanna men with black and tan and white politicians loyal to the president. For white appointments T.R. turned to the southern Gold Democrats. Because of his progressive policies, the southern Popocrats might have seemed likely Republican converts, but Bryan was able to keep these southerners within the Democratic fold, and so Roosevelt turned to Bryan's Gold Democratic enemies.

Roosevelt had an obsession with the South: he believed that if his doctrine of political, economic, and cultural nationalism were to succeed it must take root on a truly nationwide basis. Nearly half a century after the Civil War the Republican Party was still a sectional party, and the Democratic Party while national in scope was heavily weighted with sectional biases because it was dependent on southern votes in Congress and the electoral college. The G.O.P. could win Congress and the presidency without the support of the South, but Roosevelt found Republican sectionalism abhorrent to his belief in nationalism. While he appointed some blacks in the South, he usually appointed whites, "three-fourths of them . . . Democrats, for the most part sons or daughters of ex-Confederates, or themselves ex-Confederates." But though the G.O.P. made gains in the South during his administration, as president Roosevelt failed to destroy the Democracy's Dixie hegemony. As he left the White House, he viewed the winning of the South for Republican nationalism as part of the unfinished business of his administration. He failed, however, to see the incongruity of his alliance of Gold Democrats and ex-Confederates with southern Republican Negroes. The Negroes revered the Union cause and the goals of Reconstruction, while conservative Democrats and former Confederates sought to keep alive the white-dominated South which the Republican Party had been founded to oppose.

The questions of the South and the Negro were forcibly brought to Roosevelt's attention again in 1912. The black and tan delegates representing the Republican organizations in the South were crucial to Taft's margin of victory at the June convention—ironically so, since Roosevelt as president had been responsible for forming or perpetuating these southern machines. Arguing that the Negro cause would be better served by Roosevelt than by Taft, some Negro leaders urged blacks to support T.R. Not only was Taft opposed to progressive policies, but he had appointed few Negroes to office. Roosevelt's primary victory in Maryland was largely due to the support of black voters. At Chicago heavy pressures had been put on the Negro delegates, and both sides appear to have offered bribes to these often corrupt veterans of numerous patronage wars. In the end the Negro delegates remained loyal to Taft because their political lives depended on the favor of the administration and the Old Guard bosses. A Negro officeholder in Washington, Ralph W. Tyler, wrote Roosevelt that "the colored delegates at Chicago hesitated betwixt love and duty...." Amos Pinchot recalled: "They loved Massa Roosevelt, but they loved Massa Taft, too."

Some Negroes at first had hopes that the new party would offer blacks a better political future than either of the old parties. W. E. B. Du Bois, a leader of the National Association for the Advancement of Colored People and editor of the organization's magazine the *Crisis,* prepared a plank on Negro rights for the Progressive platform, and a significant faction of the militant black National Independent Political League was friendly to Roosevelt's third party candidacy. Black delegates were elected to the Progressive convention from Rhode Island, New Jersey, Pennsylvania, Ohio, Indiana, Illinois, Delaware, Maryland, West Virginia, Virginia, Kentucky, Tennessee, and Arkansas. Progressives claimed that there were more Negro delegates than there had ever been in the conventions of either of the old parties. Negroes wrote to Roosevelt pledging their support. On July 28 William H. Maxwell, editor of the *Jersey Spokesman* of Newark, reminded the Colonel of the need to speak of "equality of opportunity and justice for the Negro." "The colored people of this country are in dire need of a champion," he wrote; "you have ever been friendly to them, you have ever striven to give them a fair chance and I know that they appreciate it."

Roosevelt replied to Maxwell on July 30 in a letter marked "Private: Not for Publication":

Most certainly I will take up the question of equality of opportunity and justice for the negro. . . . But, my dear Mr. Maxwell, you must not forget that there is another side upon which we must also insist. The Republican Party has been ruined, it has been kept from becoming a progressive party because of the votes of the "rotten borough" Republican delegates from the Southern states where for forty-five years we have striven to get a Republican Party composed almost exclusively of negroes with the result that the negro has not been benefitted, the white men of the South have been kept solid, and finally, the Republican Party has been destroyed. If the negro delegates last month had been willing to stand by the progressive cause, and follow the lead of the great Republican states, the Republican Party would now be the genuine progressive party of the country; but seven-eighths of the negro delegates, and about the same proportion of the white men representing negro districts in the South, went for Mr. Taft. It is a very hard and difficult question. I do not blame the colored men. . . . I know that they simply have not had the chance that the colored men of the

North have had. I want to get them that chance; and at the same time I do not wish to try to get it for them in ways that hurt them, that hurt the white man of the South, and that ruin any national party with which they are connected.

The actions of the southern Negro politicians at Chicago made it easier for Roosevelt to accept the proposal of Parker and others for a lily-white Progressive Party in the South. Even more decisive was his consuming desire to break the solid South. Roosevelt wanted Negroes to participate in the new party in the North, for he was not and never had been in favor of a general suppression of the Negro, but he came to believe that the peculiar conditions in the South justified a "Jim Crow" party from the standpoints of both political expediency and the long-term interests of southern blacks. At first the Colonel sought to avoid taking any public position on the policy of Parker and the white southern Progressives. Delegate disputes and local party policies, he told the press, were purely state matters. The publicity and controversy arising from the delegate disputes, however, soon made it necessary for him to take an open stand on the principles involved. By the time he wrote Maxwell, Roosevelt had already decided what that stand would be.

On July 24 Roosevelt rehearsed his arguments in a confidential letter to the Rev. Bradley Gilman, a white Massachusetts Unitarian long interested in the race problem. In the North, wrote T.R., the situation was "simple." Justice demanded that northerners "give the negroes who dwell among us an absolutely fair show. . . ." The Negro had been "only a small element in debauching" the Republican Party in the North, and it was possible "to take him in on the same terms with the white man." In the southern states, however, conditions were "totally different." "In these states if we are wise we will deal not with any theory but with the existing and melancholy facts." The effort of the G.O.P. to build a party in the South with the Negro as "a big element" had been a disaster. Southern whites had been kept united within the Democratic Party; the G.O.P. had remained "a negligible quantity" in the South; blacks had attained no influence in southern government and had been oppressed; and finally, of course, the Republican Party on the national level had been brought to its present state. "The new progressive party must not repeat the capital error which had led to these disasters." Hopefully, southern whites could be persuaded "gradually" to give the Negro the same rights the race had in the North, but in the meantime it would be "worse than foolish" to try to form a new party in the South with Negroes in positions of leadership.

Literally worse than nothing would be accomplished by building up another futile vicious little black and tan organization in the ex-Confederate states, duplicating the present Republican organization there, and exposing the whole movement to derision, and making it simply noxious as far as the South is concerned. The only alternative is to try to make up our party in the South from among the men of real power, leadership and principle, and that means to try to organize it among the white people.

On August 1 Roosevelt outlined his policy on the Negro in a public letter to Julian LaRose Harris of Georgia, editor of *Uncle Remus's Home Magazine* and son of Joel Chandler Harris. Roosevelt tried to show that his position was the moderate one. He said that he had received letters from the North urging him to secure black delegates from the South, and from the South asking him to "declare that the new party shall be a white man's party." He was, he declared, unable to agree with either proposition. In the North political and social conditions were such that the Negro could be welcomed into the movement, but, on the other hand, he argued that nothing could be accomplished for either race in the South by the old Republican policy of basing party support on the Negro.

Progress among Negroes in the South, he claimed, was the result of "effort along industrial and educational lines," not G.O.P. political policies. In fact, "by trafficking in negro votes," the Republican Party had divided blacks from whites, and yet it was only through the help of his white neighbors that the Negro could be effectively aided. The situation had been deleterious for southern whites as well, because it kept them "solidified in an unhealthy and unnatural political bond, to their great detriment and to the detriment of the whole Union. . . ." But the Progressive Party would learn from the lessons of the past. "I earnestly believe that by appealing to the best white men in the South, . . . and by frankly putting the movement in their hands from the outset we shall create a situation by which the colored men of the South will ultimately get justice as it is not possible for them to get justice if we are to continue and perpetuate the present conditions."

Reaction to the Harris letter was divided. Most Negro leaders both inside and outside the new party strongly protested. Booker T. Washington and many of his followers had already declared for Taft, but the Harris letter further lessened the possibility of a mass exodus of Negro leadership from the G.O.P. Jane Addams, Joel E. Spingarn, Henry Moskowitz, and other white Progressives active in the Negro cause took issue with Roosevelt and determined to take their case to the national convention, while the contesting black Progressive delegates from the South remained unmoved by the Colonel's position. President Luther of Trinity College admitted to Roosevelt that the reasoning of the Harris letter was correct, but protested that it grated on his boyhood memories of the Civil War. On the other hand, Albert Shaw, editor of the *Review of Reviews,* and such new party leaders as Senator Dixon and Medill McCormick of Illinois, supported the new southern strategy, while white southern Progressives hailed the new policy as a triumph of statesmanship. Julian Harris replied to Roosevelt on August 3: "For the South you have opened a path, that, if followed, will prove the way by which it may return permanently to the exalted position it had once as a birthright, and which by virtue of statesmanship it held until the results of the Civil War forced on it an unnatural and artificial party solidarity."

In the last analysis, Roosevelt's position on the southern Negro was riddled with contradictions and paradoxes. He was trying to bring the South back into the Union with a policy based on the very causes of the Civil War—the South's peculiar institutions and social practices. He wanted to establish the New Nationalism on a nationwide basis by using a sectionalist approach; he sought to bring an end to racism by a racist strategy. He did not believe the Negro inherently or biologically inferior, and indeed hoped for full racial equality in American society ultimately, but he played into the hands of his old enemies the white supremacist Democrats like Vardaman and Tillman with the implied endorsement of their ideas carried by the adoption of their modus operandi. Roosevelt wrote Harris that "in this country we cannot permanently succeed except upon the basis of treating each man on his worth as a man," and yet he punished all southern Negroes because of the actions of less than a hundred black Republican delegates. Roosevelt's distinction between southern and northern Negroes was in part based on the supposed superiority of northern blacks, who he claimed were more fit for responsibility than their southern brothers, but he applied no such tests of social and political fitness to any other citizens of the nation.

Roosevelt's position on the race issue and the Progressive Party in the South revealed at the very beginning of the new party the difficulties inherent in the New Nationalism within the context of American pluralism and sectionalism. Caught in a trap of his own nationalist rhetoric, Roosevelt was faced with the alternatives of compromising with pluralism and sectionalism by supporting a lily-white organization in the South, or of calling for an integrated party, and thereby in effect making the Progressive Party as sectionalist as the G.O.P. by confining its strength to the North. He had to choose between preserving the ideological integrity of the New Nationalism with a racially integrated southern party and the chance of establishing the new party politically throughout the country by making concessions to southern sectionalism. He took the time-honored American path of sacrificing racial equality for the supposed good of the white majority. Yet the Progressive Party's dilemma in the South had further significance than as a part of the American pattern of racism: it was indicative of the many difficulties ahead for the new party in its nationalist challenge to prevailing American patterns of pluralism and sectionalism.

Roosevelt's position, of course, made some sense from the standpoint of political expediency. Robert Minor, Jr., of the *St. Louis Post-Dispatch* drew a cartoon depicting the southern lily-white policy, showing a poker-playing T.R. deliberately and dispassionately discarding the ace of spades. But Roosevelt would never admit in public and seldom could admit to himself in private that he was ever motivated solely by political considerations. Roosevelt actually was willing to compromise on the race issue because it was not an issue that concerned him deeply in the way that social welfare and conservation did. He wrote Professor Brander Matthews of Columbia in 1913: "Ugh! There is not any more puzzling problem in this country than the problem of color. It is not as urgent, or as menacing, as other problems, but it seems more utterly insoluble." The fact was that Roosevelt desperately needed all the electoral votes he could possibly garner in 1912, while at the same time he fervently wanted to reunite the divided nation by ending the partisan insularity of the South. Here was the real juncture of his principles and political needs: the solid South had to be broken if the country were to be one and nationalist, and he could not afford to leave any stone unturned in his search for support for the new party. He wrote Parker on July 15: "Really if I could carry one of the eleven ex-Confederate states, I feel as though I could die happy." But as the Progressives assembled in Chicago it remained to be seen if any purpose at all would be served by Roosevelt's new southern strategy.

DISCARDING THE ACE OF SPADES

2

Senator Dixon convened the Provisional National Progressive Committee in Chicago's Congress Hotel on August 3. All the forty-eight states except South Carolina were represented by one or more committeemen; among them were such leaders of the new party as Francis J. Heney, John M. Parker, Senator Poindexter, Bill Flinn, Matthew Hale, and Governors Johnson, Vessey, and

Carey. The committee sessions opened with a pointed reminder of the policy of Roosevelt and the lily-white southern Progressives as Senator Dixon explained that South Carolina would go unrepresented at the convention because the "right men" had not been found to organize a Palmetto State party. Without authority from Progressive headquarters in New York, a group of South Carolina Negroes had tried to call a state convention to elect delegates. "We knew that meant suicide," said Dixon, who had wired a disavowal of the blacks' call. Yet it soon became apparent that while most of the members agreed with the principles of Roosevelt's letter to Julian Harris, the committee was determined to give the contesting delegates a fair hearing and decide the cases strictly according to proper standards of adjudication. The committee had no intention of being a rubberstamp, making the new party liable to the charges of boss rule and injustice that had split the G.O.P. The cases would be decided on their own merits, not on the basis of pronouncements made by Roosevelt or Dixon.

Chairman Dixon, John M. Parker, and others maintained that all three southern contests simply rested on the question of whether or not southern Progressives were to have lily-white leadership, a question which, they reminded the committee, Roosevelt had already answered for the party in his letter to Harris. The majority of the committee members, however, viewed the cases in an entirely different light. While they were willing to accept white supremacy in the South—some reluctantly, others with enthusiasm—the majority insisted that this principle could only be instituted through accepted and legal political procedures. Not only was this seen as the only moral and constitutional course, but members frequently pointed out that it was the only politically safe path to follow. Unless "the public conscience of the North" were "satisfied," declared California's Heney, "we will lose ten votes in the North to every one we get in the South." Moreover, the committee majority held that each of the three state disputes involved different legal and procedural issues and questions which could not be fairly resolved by any blanket judgment.

In Alabama the state convention had selected an all-white delegation over the protests of a small group of black Progressives, who then held a rump caucus and chose a contesting delegation. In Florida, however, the state chairman and national committeeman H. L. Anderson had arranged for a separate black convention to meet in St. Augustine on the same day that a white Progressive convention met in Ocala. Objecting to the policy of political segregation, a contingent of black Progressives had insisted on attending the white convention, and when denied admittance had held a rump conclave in another hall. Learning that the St. Augustine convention of blacks was not to be permitted to elect any delegates to Chicago, the Ocala rump and the St. Augustine convention, in contact by telegraph, agreed on their own slate of delegates, one white and five black men. In Mississippi the national committeeman B. F. Fridge had made no provision at all for any black participation in his state's party. Fridge had issued a call for a lily-white convention and informed the press: "It should be borne in mind, first of all, that this is strictly a white man's party. The movement is led by white men and we expect only white men in our organization."

Maintaining that Fridge had "exceeded his powers and authority as the agent of this party" when "he disfranchised us with one stroke of his pen," and therefore that Fridge's convention call was "null and void," Negro attorney Perry W. Howard and other blacks and whites had called a convention which elected a racially mixed delegation to challenge the seats of the Fridge delegates.

The case for the regular Alabama delegation was presented by Judge Oscar R. Hundley of Birmingham, the state's national committeeman. Hundley testified that he had issued a call for a state convention open to all and had welcomed blacks into the party, in spite of protests from white Democrats joining the Progressive ranks. The spokesman for the contesting delegation agreed that this indeed had been the judge's policy. Hundley said that he was opposed to "discrimination against a man because of his color or religion," and had unsuccessfully tried to have a black included in the regular delegation. But he insisted that the issue at stake in the Alabama contest was one of majority rule. The national committee agreed and voted to seat the regular Alabama delegation. There was little argument among members because the case seemed open and shut. As Governor Carey put it, "The minority protested simply because there were no colored men named." Testimony showed that white supremacists had dominated the state convention, but they had done their work in a legal manner. Hundley had refused to call for a lily-white party in Alabama, but one had emerged anyway.

There was, however, considerable debate among committee members over the Florida and Mississippi contests. Matthew Hale of Massachusetts opened the debate on the Florida dispute by insisting that "it does not involve the race question only. . . ." Rather, "It involves the question of common honesty." Hale accused the state leader H. L. Anderson of subterfuge in his dealings with the blacks. Anderson had called two conventions, and a letter was produced by the protesting blacks in which Anderson had assured them both conventions would have the same "object." Furthermore, testimony and press clippings pointed to the conclusion that it had been widely understood that the purpose of both Florida conventions was to elect delegates to Chicago. If the Anderson delegation were seated, argued Hale, the committee would thus be endorsing "a plain, open fraud." On the other hand, Hale did not see how the committee could seat the St. Augustine and rump convention delegates since they had been elected without proper partisan or legal authority. Hale therefore opposed seating either Florida delegation. Chairman Dixon and Julian Harris argued for seating the Anderson delegation on the principle of lily-white rule, but Anderson, alternately unctuous and threatening in his pleadings, was roundly condemned for fraud by Francis J. Heney and other committee members. Finally, a resolution proposed by Judge Hundley of Alabama was adopted, stating that "whereas, it appears that an error was committed in the call of two conventions," neither Florida delegation would be seated, although Anderson would be allowed to continue in his party posts.

The committee considered three different proposals for dealing with the Mississippi contest. Chairman Dixon wanted the regular delegation seated, and protested that "there is no question of fraud in Mississippi." But there was strong sentiment on the committee for throwing out the regulars because it was argued that B. F. Fridge's lily-white convention call was neither constitutional nor authorized by any terms in the original national convention call. Thomas Lee Moore of Virginia proposed a compromise, which the committee finally adopted by a vote of 22 to 12, seating the Mississippi regulars but publicly reprimanding Fridge's exclusionist convention call.

The committee then moved quickly to finish its business. There had been an additional dispute over the Georgia delegation, but since the contestants from Georgia failed to appear at the committee hearings, it was voted to seat the regular delegation. In the final minutes before adjourning on August 5, two motions were unanimously adopted without debate: one proposed by Heney stating that henceforth the election of delegates would be purely a local matter to be settled by the laws of each state, and one offered by George W. Perkins endorsing Roosevelt's public letter to Harris.

Thus, the committee seated the regular Alabama delegation, threw out both contesting delegations from Florida, and admitted the Mississippi regulars with a reprimand. The Alabama case was easily decided, for regardless of any possible moral issues involved, the black delegation clearly had no legal or partisan title to the national convention seats. The Florida case was decided fairly, though perhaps there was some justification for seating some members of both delegations, and Anderson's rebuke for "fraud" seemed well deserved. The Fridge call had violated the principles of the federal Constitution and in fact had gone further than Mississippi's racial restrictions on voting and citizenship. Still, the rump convention was held without the proper sanction of state or national party officers, while the Fridge convention had partisan authority behind it. A case could be made for throwing out both Mississippi delegations, but there were also grounds for admitting the Fridge delegation. In short, the committee's decisions in the three contests were fair when measured by the yardsticks of the political rules accepted by the old parties. Certainly, all sides had a fair hearing and the decisions were based on the evidence presented.

The committee had also refused to be dominated or bossed by Chairman Dixon, and declined to turn to Roosevelt for imposed solutions. At the beginning of the sessions the committee quickly asserted its independence by rejecting a proposal by Dixon to grant convention votes to delegates from the United States territories and possessions. As Heney pointed out, such "rotten borough" representatives were pawns for the bosses in Republican and Democratic conventions and national committees. Dixon had also been defeated in his attempt to seat the Florida regulars. At one point, while arguing against the Hundley motion to throw out both Florida delegations, Dixon had invoked Roosevelt's name. "Now, gentlemen, I don't want to bring Colonel Roosevelt into this contest," the chairman said. "He is upstairs in 1248. I went up and submitted the case, giving all the details as to everything." Dixon did not quote his leader further than to say that Roosevelt was in sympathy with organizing the party in the South with white leadership (which of course was already known), but without actually saying so, the mention of the conference in room 1248 seemed to imply that T.R. and Dixon were in agreement about what should be done. But Francis Heney, speaking for the committee majority, declared that if the tainted Anderson delegation were seated, "I tell you right now that we will regret it every day from now until election . . . , and I don't care whether Colonel Roosevelt himself says to do it." Subsequently the committee defeated a motion offered by Matthew Hale requesting Roosevelt to personally work out a settlement to the Mississippi dispute. In short, to the extent that the committee reached fair judgments according to accepted procedures of adjudication, and showed that the Progressive Party was not merely the puppet of Roosevelt or a few leaders, the hearings were successful. It was, however, predetermined that the hearings could only be a limited success, for there was no way the committee could have pleased alike southerners and northerners, white racists and defenders of Negro rights.

Yet far more significant in the long run than the merits of the contests or the justice of the proceedings were several facts that became evident in the course of the hearings. First, there can be no doubt that racism was pervasive among these representative Progressive leaders who made up the national committee. The remarks of Progressives from California, Pennsylvania, Massachusetts, and other northern and western states had been as racist as those of southerners like Parker, Anderson, and Fridge. California's Heney and Pennsylvania leader Bill Flinn both said they favored white supremacy in the South, and the committee was in general agreement about this proposition. Hale of Massachusetts declared:

We of the North, our fathers and grandfathers fought for the negroes, and now for the first time we are saying publicly and openly that our fathers and grandfathers were wrong and have been wrong since the Civil War. This is a mighty serious thing that we men from the North are doing. We are saying to you people in the South, "Your attitude on the negro problem is right, and ours is wrong." . . . Now . . . all we ask from you people in the South, when we surrender our views on this negro problem . . . , is the same courtesy and the same generosity from you that Grant granted Lee at Appomattox.

Second, the fact of the matter was that Roosevelt's concept of leadership by southern whites meant in practice the total elimination of southern blacks from the new party, a partisan disenfranchisement from politics. When asked if he favored white leadership, Negro attorney Perry W. Howard of Mississippi, in later years a deputy federal attorney general, replied: "I think you beg the question when you say . . . white leadership. We confess we are willing, we want white leadership, we are not leading you now. . . ." Howard and the other black contestants merely asked for a place in the new party, but in Alabama, Florida, and Mississippi there had been no distinction between a party led by whites alone and a party composed of whites alone. The most a black might contribute was his vote, if he had one. But while the committee was willing to sacrifice Negro rights for political gain, it insisted on so doing only by legal adjudication, because propriety was good politics after the G.O.P. debacle. Finally, it became clear that though humanitarian and comparatively radical on other social issues, in company with most of their fellow Americans the Progressive leaders were retrogressive on Negro rights, with northerners even willing to admit "that our fathers and grandfathers were wrong and have been wrong since the Civil War." The Negro was simply not really important in the Progressives' political, intellectual, and moral scheme of things. It was a tragic paradox that on the Negro question most Progressive leaders approached the issues from the states rights, legalistic, and strict constructionist viewpoint that was typical of their conservative Republican and southern Democratic opponents.

3

Shortly after Roosevelt arrived in Chicago for the convention, he met privately with Joel E. Spingarn, Professor Alfred Hayes of the Cornell Law School, and Dr. Henry Moskowitz of the Ethical Culture Society, three Progressives interested in the Negro cause. Spingarn, a wealthy New Yorker who devoted his time to reform causes and writing, was a leader in the N.A.A.C.P., and as a delegate to the Progressive convention he brought a plank on Negro rights for inclusion in the new party's platform. The original draft had been prepared by the militant W. E. B. Du Bois, but Spingarn showed Roosevelt a much watered-down version. In private the Colonel warned Spingarn that Du Bois was a "dangerous person," but the press reported that Roosevelt approved the plank, which read in part:

The National Progressive Party recognizes that distinctions of race and class in political life have no place in a democracy.... The National Progressive Party, therefore, assures the American of African descent of its deep interest in his welfare, and in the gradual recognition by North and South of the principle that the colored man who has the same qualifications that are held to entitle the white man to political representation shall receive the same treatment.

Spingarn unsuccessfully tried to get an endorsement of the plank in the caucus of the New York delegation, and the plank was also rejected by the convention's platform committee. Introduced to the platform committee by Hugh T. Halbert of Minnesota and strongly supported by Jane Addams, it was opposed by Charles McCarthy of the University of Wisconsin and others, and the committee—probably with Roosevelt's approval—discarded it. The Progressive platform was completely silent on the Negro question.

On August 6 the convention endorsed the decisions of the national committee on the delegate contests, and heard Roosevelt in the course of his "Confession of Faith" address defend his position on the Negro in response to a question from the gallery. "I hold that we are standing against the brutality of the Democracy and the hypocrisy of the Republicans," he declared. Nearly all the black delegates to the convention stayed with the Progressive Party and signed a statement endorsing Roosevelt's stand on the race question. A "National Progressive Party of Colored Men" met and adopted a resolution proposed by Bishop J. M. Conner of Little Rock backing Roosevelt. James H. Hayes, who had organized the National Negro Suffrage League in 1902 to fight disenfranchisement, became the director of the "Colored Bureau" of the party, and an active campaign was conducted to win the Negro vote in the North. A Negro was chosen a Progressive elector in Illinois, four blacks were named to the New York state committee, and groups like the "Cuyahoga County Afro-American Progressive League" in Ohio were formed. Jane Addams, much to the shock of some of her reformer friends, swallowed her defeat on the platform committee and defended the party in the pages of the N.A.A.C.P. *Crisis.* She wrote that like other N.A.A.C.P. members she had found it inconsistent for the party to pledge relief to the oppressed workingman "while leaving the colored man to struggle unaided with his difficult situation. . . ." She had agonized over whether her abolitionist father would have "remained in any political convention in which the colored men had been treated slightingly," but had finally concluded that the new party, in spite of its lily-white policy in the South, ultimately offered blacks the best hope. The Republicans had paid but lip service to the Negro cause, while the Democrats really offered nothing. The Progressive Party, on the other hand, aimed to become not just a sectional party like the G.O.P. but a truly national party dedicated to reform. When the party was established on a national basis and the solid South broken, then, she affirmed, the new party was "bound to lift this question of the races, as all other questions, out of the grip of the past and into a new era of solution."

The Progressive logic, however, appealed to relatively few black leaders. The black militant William Monroe Trotter wired Jane Addams at the Progressive convention: "WOMEN SUFFRAGE WILL BE STAINED WITH NEGRO BLOOD UNLESS WOMEN REFUSE ALLIANCE WITH ROOSEVELT." Trotter, Du Bois, J. Milton Waldron, and other black militants endorsed Wilson's candidacy on the basis of vague assurances from the Democratic candidate that Negroes would be fairly treated under his administration. Wilson's New York campaign office spent over $50,000 to win the black vote, and after the election his supporters claimed that over 100,000 blacks had voted for Wilson, the first significant black defection in history from the Republican Party. Yet the majority of black voters either followed tradition and the lead of Booker T. Washington and voted for Taft, or bolted to Roosevelt with James H. Hayes and other black northern Progressives. After the election Wilson forgot his promises to the blacks and instituted segregation in various government departments. Du Bois, Trotter, and other black leaders bitterly protested, but to no avail since the southern-born Wilson had believed all along in segregation and the inferiority of the Negro race. Thus, there was a pathetic quality to the support of Wilson in 1912 by blacks like Du Bois and Trotter. It was a gauge of the Negro's desperate political situation. The Republicans offered platitudes, while the Progressives presented a face of open if selective racism and Wilson gave vague and insincere assurances.

While reaction of blacks to the Progressive Party was mixed, the southern white press was almost unanimous in its condemnation of Roosevelt and the new party. Roosevelt's call for a lily-white party in the South did not impress most southern editors, who reminded their readers of T.R.'s Negro appointments as president. The Progressive Party made a distinction between southern and northern blacks, but the *News* of Birmingham, Alabama, pointed out that white southerners did not. Josephus Daniels, editor of the *Raleigh News and Observer,* agreed, proclaiming that the South sought not just a sectional race policy but a national one as well. Roosevelt, Daniels admonished, should recognize that "the subjugation of the negro, politically, and the separation of the negro, socially, are paramount to all other considerations in the South, short of the preservation of the Republic itself." When Roosevelt dined with two Negro Progressives in Providence, Rhode Island, in August, southerners pointed to this as final proof that the Colonel had not mended his ways since the days of the meal with Booker T. Washington in the White House. In response to a poll in August, thirty-two Southern editors and leaders wired the *New York Times* that there was virtually no support for the new party in the South. Dixie conservatives, of course, also objected to Roosevelt's reform views. Furthermore, southerners generally rejoiced at the nomination of a son of the South by the Democracy, and longed for partisan patronage after years in the political wilderness. "Democrats will surely support the party when the prospects of success are better than they have ever known . . . ," predicted the editor of the *Columbia* (South Carolina) *State.* The prediction was correct, and Roosevelt fared worse in the South than had several Republican presidential candidates in the preceding elections. Taft outpolled T.R. in Tennessee, Texas, and Virginia, while the new party won less than 20 percent of the total vote in Alabama, Arkansas, Georgia, Louisiana, and Virginia, and less than 10 percent in Florida, Mississippi, and Texas. Roosevelt had compromised himself for a mess of pottage. The ideological integrity of the New Nationalism had been sacrificed for nothing.

If Roosevelt and the Progressive Party were to be judged solely on the basis of their attitudes on race, the verdict would be grim indeed, but, as Jane Addams noted, the party's racial policies flatly contradicted the Progressive stand for social justice on other issues. Roosevelt and his followers had a blind spot in regard to race. Racism, of course, has been a constant theme in American life and politics, and yet the Progressives cannot be judged simply as part of the white mainstream. Their responsibility and guilt were all the greater because they had pledged themselves to a quest for a nationalist America liberated from the forms, prejudices, and slogans of the old order.

CHAPTER FOUR

CONSECRATION IN THE COLISEUM

> *Never doubt that we will solve in righteousness and*
> *wisdom every perplexing problem. Never doubt that*
> *in the end the hand from above that leads us upward*
> *will prevail over the hand from below that drags us*
> *downward. Never doubt that we are indeed a nation*
> *whose God is the Lord. And so, never doubt that a*
> *braver, a fairer, cleaner America will surely come,*
> *that a better and brighter life for all beneath the flag*
> *surely will be achieved. Those who now scoff soon*
> *will pray. Those who now doubt soon will believe.*
>
> Albert J. Beveridge

At 12:42 P.M. on Monday, August 5, Chairman Joseph M. Dixon called the first National Convention of the Progressive Party to order in Chicago's Coliseum, scene of the June Republican convention. From the moment of the Lutheran Pastor T. F. Dornblazer's invocation, punctuated "continuously" with "amen's," all observers noted the convention's religious tenor. "It was not a convention at all," reported the *New York Times.* "It was an assemblage of religious enthusiasts. It was such a convention as Peter the Hermit held. It was a Methodist camp meeting done over into political terms." Richard Harding Davis wrote of the convention in *Collier's:* "There was in it something inspired, spiritual, almost uncanny. It caught one by the throat. It was what Stevenson calls 'a brutal assault upon the feelings.' 'This is not dancing, Margaret, it is religion.'" The delegates sang hymns like "Onward Christian Soldiers" and "The Battle Hymn of the Republic"; keynoter Beveridge and other speakers made frequent biblical references; Roosevelt's address to the convention was entitled "A Confession of Faith"; numerous stories circulated about reporters sent to the convention by their papers to "scoff" remaining to "pray"; the revival hymn "Follow, Follow, We Will Follow Jesus" became:

Follow, follow, we will follow Roosevelt,
Anywhere, everywhere, we will follow him.

Observers also noted that the Progressive delegates were of different types from the professional politicians, patronage hacks, and officeholders who attended Republican and Democratic conventions. William Menkel, writing in the *Review of Reviews,* saw the "plain American businessman, clean-cut and successful looking," ministers, and "uplifters" among the delegates. Davis saw "young men with the look of the Pilgrim Fathers and Cromwell's army; their faces showed that they still possessed illusions, still held to high ideals." Amos Pinchot recalled, among others, social workers, professors, "restless sentimentalists," schoolteachers, "liberal-minded clergy," and "radical thinkers who believed in old-fashioned American ideals and objected to the inroads of plutocracy." Women seemed to be everywhere in this first major national convention to permit women delegates. The Kansas editor William Allen White later wrote: "We were, of course, for woman suffrage, and we invited women delegates and had plenty of them. They were our own kind, too—women doctors, women lawyers, women teachers, college professors, middle-aged leaders of civic movements, or rich young girls who had gone in for settlement work." The delegates were mainly political amateurs, observers agreed, but they were not the kind usually associated with third party movements. White remembered:

I had seen many a protest convention. As a boy I had watched the Greenbackers. As a young man I had reported many a Populist convention. Those agrarian movements too often appealed to the ne'er-do-wells, the misfits—farmers who had failed, lawyers and doctors who were not orthodox, teachers who could not make the grade, and neurotics full of hates and ebullient, evanescent enthusiasms. I knew that crowd well. But when the Progressive convention assembled at Chicago I looked down upon it from the reporters' stand and saw that here was another crowd. Here were the successful middle-class country-town citizens, the farmer whose barn was painted, the well paid railroad engineer, and the country editor. It was a well-dressed crowd. . . . Proletarian and plutocrat were absent. . . .

It was true that compared to the conventions of the old parties the Progressive convention was unique in its moralistic, religious tenor and the types represented among its delegates, but these facts tend to obscure equally important though less colorful and dramatic aspects of the convention. While the conclave was marked by fervor, enthusiasm, and piety, which could be twisted by hostile newspapers into the claim that it was, in the words of the *New York Times,* "a convention of fanatics," the content of the Progressives' political faith as presented by convention speakers and the platform was as reasoned, detailed, and coherent as it was idealistic. The Progressive "faith," of course, was not born in the heat of convention passion or the exigencies of the moment. The analyses and solutions set forth in speeches and platform were the culmination of decades of research by social scientists like Charles E. Merriam and William Draper Lewis, and the experience of social workers like Jane Addams and Raymond Robins and practicing politicians like Roosevelt, Beveridge, and Johnson. Like all political gatherings the Progressives' employed bombast and banners; unlike most there was substance behind the rhetoric and pageant.

And while many of the delegates were neophytes in the political arena, many others were veteran campaigners. Though critics scornfully noted the presence of Bill Flinn and Tim Woodruff as anomalous in a gathering of reformers, few noted that the rank and file of the leaders at the convention were tested progressive politicians like Everett Colby, George L. Record, Lucius F. C. Garvin, William Dudley Foulke, Robert S. Vessey, Joseph M. Carey, Chester H. Rowell, and Miles Poindexter. In short, as the work of organization in the states had already revealed, the Progressives were not only "Christian soldiers marching as to war," they were also mature believers of their "faith" led in most cases by men tried in battle. The Progressive Party was a crusade, but it was not a children's crusade.

THE BIG FOUR AT THE
TWO CHICAGO CONVENTIONS

2

After the invocation Senator Dixon introduced Albert J. Beveridge of Indiana as keynoter and convention chairman. Beveridge, slim, well-dressed, earnest yet boyish, handsome as a matinee idol, began an address observers called the best in his career of oratorical triumphs. He began:

We stand for a nobler America. We stand for an undivided nation. We stand for a broader liberty, a fuller justice. We stand for social brotherhood as against savage individualism. We stand for an intelligent cooperation instead of a reckless competition. We stand for mutual helpfulness instead of mutual hatred. We stand for equal rights as a fact of life instead of a catch-word of politics. We stand for the rule of the people as a practical truth instead of a meaningless pretense. We stand for a representative government that represents the people. Ours is a battle for the actual rights of man.

These lofty principles, Beveridge continued, were to be translated into "a plain program of constructive reform," and it was for this purpose that the new party had been formed. In a sense, the people were really the founders of the party:

For the Progressive Party comes from the grass roots. It has grown from the soil of the people's hard necessities. . . . For years this party has been forming. Parties exist for the people, not the people for the parties. Yet for years the politicians have made the people do the work of the parties instead of the parties doing the work of the people. And the politicians have owned the parties. The people vote for one party and find their hopes turned to ashes on their lips; and then, to punish the party, they vote for the other party. So it is that American political victories have come to be merely the people's vengeance; and always the secret powers have played the hidden game.

This condition, the former senator explained, was the result of the artificiality of the party system. Most Americans were either progressives or conservatives, and yet "neither of the old parties is either wholly progressive or wholly reactionary." "So there is no nation-wide unity of principle in either party, no stability of purpose, no clear-cut and sincere program of an opposing party." This situation helped foster the boss system, which controlled both old parties, and made it "impossible most of the time, and hard at any time," to enact reform policies. The boss system also made it easy for economic "special interests" to subvert politics by buying the bosses:

These special interests which suck the people's substance are bi-partisan. They use both parties. They are the invisible government behind our visible government. Democratic and Republican bosses alike are brother officers of this hidden power. No matter how fiercely they pretend to fight one another before election, they work together after election. And, so acting, this political conspiracy is able to delay, mutilate or defeat sound and needed laws. . . .

Thus, the root of the problem in securing a progressive program was that the government and the old parties were no longer responsive to the people. "And so the first purpose of this Progressive Party is to make sure the rule of the people." This required direct election of senators, initiative, referendum, recall, and direct primaries for all nominations. With the rule of the people would come the solution of the people's problems.

What were these problems? "Today these problems concern the living of the people." It was as basic as that. Workers found it difficult to make a living wage; children were forced into factories; business was uncertain, subject to cyclical reverses and poorly drawn laws; no provisions were made for the unemployed, sick, or aged; working conditions were often unhealthy and brutal. Yet since the nation was blessed with abundant natural resources and human and industrial potential, "there ought not to be in this republic a single day of bad business, a single unemployed workingman, a single unfed child." "Hunger should never

HERE HE IS, CHILDREN OF THE REPUBLIC—FOR YOU!

walk in these thinly peopled gardens of plenty." His sentences punctuated by applause, Beveridge reached one of the several crescendoes of his address:

The Progressive Party proposes to remedy these conditions. We mean not only to make prosperity steady, but to give to the many who earn it a just share of that prosperity.... The Progressive motto is: "Pass prosperity around." To make human living easier, to free the hands of honest business, to make trade and commerce sound and steady, to protect womanhood, save childhood and restore dignity of manhood—these are the tasks we must do.

To accomplish these goals, Beveridge declared, "the first work before us is the revival of honest business." The Sherman Antitrust Act as it stood was virtually useless: trusts continued to flourish while business conditions were rendered uncertain by arbitrary suits and changing court rulings. Beveridge, who believed "trust busting" futile and against the interests of the economy, argued that businesses should not be attacked simply because of size. But anti-social practices, many of which led to monopolies, should be clearly defined and outlawed, with offenders sent to prison rather than fined. Moreover, the tariff should be taken out of politics and administered by a nonpartisan commission of experts.

Next Beveridge turned to "other questions as important and pressing" as the reform of business. Child labor should be abolished, and federal legislation was the only way to secure uniform regulations on this matter. Beveridge, who had proposed child labor legislation in the Senate, declared that "children workers at the looms in South Carolina means bayonets at the breasts of men and women workers in Massachusetts who strike for a living wage." Furthermore, wages for women should be set by a minimum federal standard and equalized with those for men, and to enable women to obtain social justice they should have the vote. Measures should also be passed for all workers providing for the care of the aged and those injured in industry. Of course, the "public spokesmen for the invisible government" said that many of these reforms were unconstitutional. Beveridge answered that the general welfare clause of the Constitution meant that the federal government could perform those tasks necessary for the people as a whole. "The Progressive Party believes that the Constitution is a living thing, growing with the people's growth, strengthening with the people's strength, aiding the people in their struggle for life, liberty and the pursuit of happiness, permitting the people to meet all their needs as conditions change."

His high, starched white collar wilted from the August heat, looking out at men who were like himself risking career and reputation by joining the new party, the Hoosier orator concluded his hour-and-a-half speech:

Knowing the price we must pay, the sacrifices we must make, the burdens we must carry, the assaults we must endure—knowing full well the cost, yet we enlist and we enlist for the war; for we know the justice of our cause and we know too the certain triumphs. Not reluctantly, then, but eagerly; not with faint heart but strong, do we now advance upon the enemies of the people. For the call that comes to us today is the call that came to our fathers, and as they responded, so shall we.

Beveridge recited a verse of "The Battle Hymn of the Republic": "He hath sounded forth a trumpet that shall never call retreat.... Our God is marching on!" As the delegates cheered, tears were seen on many faces. The crowd began to sing the old Civil War hymn. "It reminded me of the psalm singing of the Boers before the battle of Sand River," wrote Richard Harding Davis.

3

The next day, Tuesday, August 6, Beveridge called the convention to order at 12:35 P.M. The Coliseum was packed beyond its 12,500-seat capacity as he announced simply: "...The hour and the man, Theodore Roosevelt." As Roosevelt appeared on the platform and took his place before a giant sounding

LAYING THE FOUNDATIONS

board under portraits of Washington, Jefferson, and Lincoln, the crowd roared its approval. A sea of waving red bandannas covered the floor and galleries; delegations marched in the aisles; the Colonel shook hands with Progressive leaders who mounted the platform, bowed, grinned, and waved; delegates tossed hats into imaginary rings for the man who had coined the phrase "My hat's in the ring"; some delegates sang while most just yelled. The demonstration lasted nearly an hour. Then Roosevelt began his "Confession of Faith," a voluminous address running to some twenty thousand words, interrupted by applause 145 times according to the count of Ernest Hamlin Abbott of the *Outlook*.

The familiar figure standing before the crowd had grown stocky with the years, heavy about the waist; gray now flecked the stiff, closely cropped hair; but the old energy and platform magic were stronger than ever. Glinting pince-nez sat on a large nose; the drooping mustache framed dazzling white teeth which snapped for emphasis; head and thick neck thrust forward from muscular shoulders and barrel chest as he spoke, broad jaw with flexing muscles, fists decisively cutting the air, a voice that was high-pitched and piercing, no mellowness in the tone, words pronounced with each syllable distinct, and a broad Harvard *a,* words that seemed hurled out like projectiles—this was the leader of the Progressives as he spelled out the articles of his creed to an adoring multitude.

Roosevelt began by justifying the existence of the new party. "The old parties are husks," he declared, "with no real soul within either, divided on false lines, boss-ridden and privilege-controlled, each a jumble of incongruous elements, and neither daring to speak out wisely and fearlessly what should be said on the vital issues of the day." It did not matter whether Taft or Wilson were elected, because both old parties were controlled by bosses and special interests: "... the real danger to privilege comes from the new party, and from the new party alone." "... Scant indeed would be the use of exchanging the whips of Messrs. Barnes, Penrose, and Guggenheim for the scorpions of Messrs. Murphy, Taggart, and Sullivan." The Progressives, on the other hand, proposed to make their platform a "contract with the people" which would offer solutions to the problems of modern industrial society based on the principle that the government should be used "as an efficient agency for the practical betterment of social and economic conditions throughout this land."

"The first essential in the Progressive program is the right of the people to rule," Roosevelt continued, echoing Beveridge. The "rule of the people" required national adoption of presidential primaries, direct election of senators, women's suffrage, the short ballot, and corrupt practices acts. On the state level, Roosevelt said, "I do not attempt to dogmatize as to the machinery by which this end should be achieved." The initiative, referendum, and recall of officials and judicial decisions were not the "ordinary" and "normal" avenues of governmental process, but they could be useful "instrumentalities" in states where "representative government has in actual fact become non-representative. . . ." The courts in many states, for example, continually frustrated the will of the people by striking down laws for social justice. "I have not come to this way of thinking from closet study, or as a matter of mere theory; I have been forced to it by a long experience with the actual conditions of our political life."

Roosevelt's analysis of the political situation was similar to that of Beveridge, though the former president was more qualified in his support of direct democracy reforms, but his examination of social and industrial problems was more detailed and wide-ranging than Beveridge's. Industrial conditions, Roosevelt said, necessitated many federal reforms: minimum wage commissions and levels, mine and factory inspection standards, workmen's compensation laws, the strengthening of the pure food law, a commission to inquire into the cost of living, the revival of the Country Life Commission, and the creation of a department of public health. With the exceptions of the new fact-finding commission and new federal department, Roosevelt had called for all these measures in one form or another in the previous decade. Now he went further and called for the creation of a full welfare state by advocating social security insurance to cope with the "hazards of sickness, accident, invalidism, involuntary unemployment, and old age. . . ."

Then Roosevelt turned to the problems of business regulation. Mindful of the debate between those who saw the solution to the nation's economic ills in a restoration of competition through stringent trust busting, and those who believed economic concentration inevitable and desirable and in need of regulation, he attempted to straddle. On the one hand, he declared that "the antitrust law should be kept on the statute-books and strengthened so as to make it genuinely and thoroughly effective against every big concern tending to monopoly or guilty of antisocial practices," and that "wherever it is practicable we propose to preserve competition. . . ." On the other hand, he noted that in some cases "modern conditions" had eliminated real competition beyond restoration, and he quoted the University of Wisconsin President Charles R. Van Hise's assertion in *Concentration and Control* that "through cooperation we may eliminate the wastes of the competitive system." Thus, he paid homage to competition and the antitrust tradition, while at the same time he embraced the new corporate and industrial order. Roosevelt had performed the same balancing act often since becoming president in 1901, and after much thought he still declined to resolve the contradictions of his position. Also as in the past, however, he made it clear that by itself the hoary Sherman Antitrust Act of 1890 was inadequate: "It is utterly hopeless to attempt to control the trusts merely by the antitrust law, or by any law the same in principle. . . . These great corporations cannot possibly be controlled merely by a succession of lawsuits. The administrative branch of the government must exercise such control."

Roosevelt's solution was the creation of a "national industrial commission." He had said this before, but now he proceeded to spell out in detail what he meant. The commission "should have complete power to regulate all the great industrial concerns engaged in interstate commerce—which practically means all of them in the country." The commission would supervise corporate securities to make capitalization honest and prevent stock watering, and "have free access to the books of each corporation and power to find out exactly how it treats its employees, its rivals, and the general public." ". . . The artificial raising of prices, the artificial restriction on productivity," and "the elimination of competition by unfair or predatory practices" should be prohibited. The commission would issue orders to corporations on these matters. If a corporation refused to obey commission directives, then it should be prosecuted under an expanded antitrust law.

Roosevelt in effect was saying that the question of monopoly versus competition was largely irrelevant, except in cases where monopoly was achieved or maintained through antisocial practices. The main issue was rather one of public versus private control, and this could not be solved by the antitrust policies of the past or any new Wilsonian variation thereof. Roosevelt's "national industrial commission," of course, would have performed functions which were later assigned to the Federal Trade Commission, Securities and Exchange Commission, and other federal regulatory agencies created after 1912.

Roosevelt also viewed the revision of the tariff as a part of needed business reforms. Like Beveridge and other Progressives he called for "a permanent commission of non-partisan experts" to replace the "old crooked, log-rolling method of tariff-making." While defending the theory of protection attacked by the Democrats, T.R., unlike the Republican protectionists, placed the emphasis on the wage earner rather than the manufacturer: ". . . There is no warrant for protection unless a legitimate share of the benefits gets into the pay-envelope of the wage-worker." Other necessary business measures included currency reform to prevent "manipulation by Wall Street or the large interests," and inheritance taxes.

Roosevelt devoted other sections of the "Confession" to the need for help for the farmers, a strong army and navy, and conservation of natural resources. "There can be no greater issue than that of conservation . . . ," he insisted characteristically. Water power sites should not be sold; grazing lands, forests, and soil and mineral resources must be preserved. Alaska provided an opportunity for social experimentation: the government should tax unused land and unearned profits from land (a nod to single-taxers in the new party like George L. Record); construct, own, and operate railroads and telegraph lines; and protect coal fields. A complete development of the lower Mississippi River should be undertaken for flood control and commercial traffic, utilizing the machinery and "human experience" which would be "left free by the completion of the Panama Canal. . . ."

Throughout the speech Roosevelt roundly condemned both the Republican and Democratic platforms. The Colonel took particular pains to demonstrate that the states rights, antitrust, and free trade proposals of the Democrats could not meet current needs:

There is no more curious delusion than that the Democratic platform is a progressive platform. The Democratic platform, representing the best thought of the acknowledged Democratic leaders at Baltimore, is purely retrogressive and reactionary. There is no progress in it. It represents an effort to go back; to put this nation of a hundred millions, existing under modern conditions, back to where it was as a nation of twenty-five millions in the days of the stagecoach and canal-boat. Such an attitude is Toryism not Progressivism.

Concluding his "Confession of Faith," Roosevelt exhorted:

Surely there was never a fight better worth making than the one in which we are engaged. It little matters what befalls any one of us who for the time being stands in the forefront of the battle. I hope we shall win, and I believe that if we can wake the people to what the fight really means we shall win. But, win or lose, we shall not falter. Whatever fate may at the moment overtake any of us, the movement itself will not stop. Our cause is based on the eternal principle of righteousness; and even though we who now lead may for the time fail, in the end the cause itself shall triumph. Six weeks ago, here in Chicago, I spoke to the honest representatives of a convention which was not dominated by honest men; a convention wherein sat . . . a majority of men who, with sneering indifference to every principle of right, so acted as to bring to a shameful end a party which had been founded over a half-century ago by men in whose souls burned the fire of lofty endeavor. Now to you men, who, in your turn, have come together to spend and be spent in the endless crusade against wrong, to you who face the future resolute and confident, to you who strive in a spirit of brotherhood for the betterment of our nation, to you who gird yourselves for this great new fight in the never-ending warfare for the good of mankind, I say in closing what in that speech I said in closing: We stand at Armageddon, and we battle for the Lord.

4

Roosevelt did not stand at Armageddon and battle for the Lord, said the Wilson-supporting *New York Times* in an editorial the next day. "He stood at Chicago and preached Socialism and Revolution, contempt for law, and doctrines that lead to destruction." Many observers agreed that what the Colonel had "confessed" was indeed socialism. The *New York Press* added that it was socialism as recognized and declared by avowed socialists; and in fact the socialists Victor Berger and Eugene Debs agreed with the conservatives that Roosevelt had taken over much of the Socialist Party platform. The *New York Sun,* calling the speech "a manifesto of revolution," concluded that "the sum, tendency, and purpose of his proposals is nothing less than the destruction of the American polity as it is under the Constitution and the creation of a monstrous socialist despotic state, a state whose supreme law is the fitful occasional plebiscite." Said the *Times:*

It is unmistakable. Mr. Roosevelt has planned, and in that speech he outlines, a vast system of State Socialism, a vast Government of men unrestrained by laws. . . . His is a program of extreme paternalism that is, in many respects, frankly Socialistic, and it so unmistakably tends toward Socialism in all its fullness and all its emptiness that the adoption of these Progressive principles would beyond doubt, and within measurable time, make this a Socialist Republic.

Progressives, of course, did not agree that their leader was preaching socialism. General Horatio C. King of New York, a leader of the G.A.R. and the Society of the Army of the Potomac, declared that the new party had been founded to stop the country's drift towards socialism. Albert Bushnell Hart of Harvard warned that if the Socialist Party continued at its then current growth rate a Socialist would eventually be elected president. "There is only one way to head off the danger, and that is the formation of a party which will take over

the reasonable part of the Socialist program. . . . The Progressive Party must
. . . become the bulwark of the Nation by satisfying the just demands of the
people before they go over to Socialism as the only remedy that they see."
Roosevelt himself had said in the "Confession":

I am well aware that every upholder of privilege, every hired agent or beneficiary
of the special interests, including many well-meaning parlor reformers, will
denounce all this as "Socialism" or "anarchy"–the same terms they used in the
past in denouncing the movements to control the railways and to control public
utilities. As a matter of fact, the propositions I make constitute neither anarchy
nor Socialism, but, on the contrary, a corrective to Socialism and an antidote
to anarchy.

Was the Progressive program then counterrevolutionary? Students of a later
period might view it as such, as well as see in it tendencies toward fascism.
The Progressive program did co-opt socialist welfare state measures, and thus
viewed from a Marxist perspective was counterrevolutionary. Certainly, most
Progressives, like General King and Professor Hart, hoped to stem the then
rising ride of American socialism. But the primary reason for the parallels between the Progressive and socialist welfare programs was that the Progressives and socialists alike faced a common enemy–laissez-faire capitalism
and the social and political conditions which it had spawned. Roosevelt
explained the situation in a speech at Hartford in September:

I am opposed to some of the socialists, to those who preach hatred, but there
are many who see existing evils and who are trying to find a solution for them.
Their trouble is that they are trying to take about 200 steps at once. I am in
favor of taking two or three now [,] and then . . . perhaps we shall see our way
clear to taking two or three more when we can meet the next needs.

The comparison between fascism and the Progressive program breaks down
at several points, particularly in light of the Progressive advocacy of direct
democracy reforms. Parallel with the government agencies and increased federal
power the Progressive program called for, was the promotion of popular control
and participatory democracy. Furthermore, the Progressives did not seek the
abolition of civil liberties or the end of legislative power. Yet in some respects
the Progressive program did squint towards, on the one hand, Mussolini's corporate fascism, and on the other towards the kind of socialistic welfare state
later developed in Sweden and Britain. But the most fruitful approach to understanding the meaning of the Progressive program is to view it in the context of
the Progressive "faith" of which it was an expression, rather than in comparisons
with ideologies essentially alien to it.

What then was the Progressive "faith"? The convention addresses of
Beveridge and Roosevelt, the speeches and writings of party leaders, and the
Progressive platform, the "contract with the people" adopted by the conven-
tion on August 7, made clear the basic outlines of a core of beliefs held by
Progressives–an ideology which as much as their partisan label distinguished

members of the new party from progressives and conservatives in the old parties. The Progressive faith, of which Roosevelt's New Nationalism was the most complete and coherent formulation, revolved around the key concepts of nationalism, democracy, the "engineering mentality," "modernism," the welfare state, the "new politics," and the Social Gospel. Since first proclaimed at Osawatomie in 1910, Roosevelt's New Nationalism had evolved from a general philosophical outline of nationalist and reform principles and issues to the comprehensive Progressive "Confession" delivered at the new party convention. After Osawatomie, and particularly during the 1912 primary campaign, the New Nationalism had been expanded to include a greater reliance and emphasis on direct democracy. And after the bolt from the G.O.P. Roosevelt had fully embraced the concepts of a new partisanship and "new politics" with the goal of a welfare state brought about through engineering and consonant with "modernism" and the Social Gospel.

The New Nationalism, envisioning a country "one and indivisible," was based on an organic view of society, a commonwealth or general interest theory which held that every citizen, section, ethnic group, and economic component was vitally interrelated by common material interests and the bonds of Christian brotherhood. "None of us can really prosper permanently if masses of our fellows are debased and degraded. . . . We believe that this country will not be a permanently good place for any of us to live in unless we make it a reasonably good place for all of us to live in," Roosevelt said in his Armageddon speech in June. Senator Miles Poindexter in the *North American Review,* explaining "Why I Am for Roosevelt," wrote: "More and more by the inevitable law of nature and by our own inventions we have been drawn together as one organism. We are but as a hive of bees, each dependent on the community. What affects a part affects the whole."

Nationalism and the federal government provided the logical framework and instrumentality for the realization of an American commonwealth because they were at once the heritage of the past and the promise of the future. The Federalist bias of Roosevelt, the biographer of Gouverneur Morris, and Beveridge, soon to be the biographer of John Marshall, blended naturally with the Republican and Union tradition in which most Progressives had been nurtured. At the same time, the nationalization of industry, markets, transportation, and communication seemed to point the way to a nationalist approach to social and economic problems. This nationalist approach clearly differentiated the new party Progressives from the progressive Democrats who, like Wilson, held to their party's traditional beliefs in states rights and a strict construction of the Constitution, as well as from all reformers who believed in limited government, laissez-faire, and the other doctrines of classical liberalism.

Nationalism, however, was not unique to the new party. Progressives shared the nationalist philosophy with many conservative Republicans like T.R.'s estranged friends Elihu Root and Henry Cabot Lodge, both articulate spokesmen for conservative nationalism. The G.O.P., of course, had always stood for nationalism, and traditional Republican arguments for the protective tariff were based on a broad construction of the Constitution and a general interest theory of society. Conservative nationalists, however, held a pessimistic view of the nature of man, and saw the social order as essentially static and hierarchical. Moreover, conservative nationalists mistrusted democracy—"republican" and "representative" were their favorite words in describing the ideal polity—and since the days of Hamilton and the Federalists nationalism had in part been seen as a bulwark against Jefferson's mob. In contrast, Progressives held a dynamic view of society, and were optimistic about the nature of man and the possibilities for democracy and social engineering to create a just and classless society. ". . . The Progressive Movement assumes the innate decency of man. . . . We believe that the spirit of fair play is dominant in the hearts of most of us, and will awaken to new strength under conditions designed to stimulate it and make it easier of operation," T.R. wrote in 1913. Furthermore, Progressives sought to end the traditional dichotomy between Hamiltonian nationalism and Jeffersonian democracy. Progressives stood for a marriage between nationalism and democracy in order to build what Roosevelt called "an American commonwealth which in its social and economic structure shall be four square with democracy."

According to the Progressive analysis of American history, cogently expressed by Herbert Croly in *The Promise of American Life,* in the past, democracy and the individual self-fulfillment it implied and championed had been associated with states rights and the limitation of governmental power. New conditions, however, had meant that individualism and democracy run riot had given rise to "robber barons" in business and politics, those whom T.R. called the "malefactors of great wealth," comparable to the autonomous European bandit barons before the advent of the nation state. This had brought about what Beveridge termed the "invisible government" that towered over and controlled the visible political structures. At the same time, as the young Progressive Paxton Hibben put it, "sinister forces . . . have been able . . . to skulk behind the falsework of state lines." For Progressives the solution was to harness democracy to nationalism. Nationalism—the New Nationalism—would now serve the ends of democracy because the problems of the people were national in scope, and hence required solution by the federal government and state governments purged of parochialism and pledged to the federal commonweal. Through the weapons of the primary, direct election of senators, women's suffrage, and other measures, democracy would in turn destroy the "invisible government," elect the New Nationalists, and provide plebiscitory mandates for the policies of disinterested government experts. The New Nationalism could then furnish the statutes, governmental structures, and planning necessary to control American society to the end of preserving those cherished goals associated with democracy like equality of opportunity and individual economic security. Herbert Croly was dubious about direct democracy reforms, and Roosevelt had some reservations, but Beveridge, Hiram Johnson, and most Progressive leaders had come to see them as vital to their contest with the old parties, for much of the success of the progressive movement had hitherto depended on popular uprisings and participatory democracy.

Closely related to the development and nationalization of the economy, and the new party's faith in a marriage between nationalism and democracy, were the Progressive beliefs in efficiency, planning, management, bureaucracy, the welfare state, science, and mechanical and other types of modern engineering —a set of beliefs which made up what might be called an "engineering mentality." The rise of industrial and technological efficiency and productivity, mechanical and other kinds of engineering, social planning, and new management techniques

and bureaucratic skills put men's problems in a new light. If a Panama Canal could be built, then surely engineering could transform the Mississippi Valley region and also accomplish the varied tasks of American conservation. If corporations could market goods and services and operate on a national basis, then social services could be provided nationally by utilizing many of the same bureaucratic, technological, and management methods. If "company towns" could be planned and constructed, then planning could rebuild the cities and meet the needs of public housing. Social workers like Jane Addams, academics like Dean Lewis, reform-minded businessmen such as Charles Sumner Bird, and intellectuals like Walter Weyl, caught up in the engineering mentality, saw the possibility of unlimited progress in fields like housing, public health, and social welfare. "What could we not make of the world if we employed its genius!" exclaimed Walter Lippmann.

For the new party the welfare state seemed the next logical step on the road of American progress. ". . . That government is best which provides most," Lippmann wrote. For the first time in history it seemed both possible and practical to solve the problems of human need and suffering. In fact, human suffering seemed no longer efficient or practical, and thus Progressives extended the concept of "conservation" to people as well as natural resources. While invoking humanitarianism and the Social Gospel, Progressives also argued in the name of efficiency that what T.R. called the "human wreckage" of the industrial system was a waste of economic potential and resources as well as a drag on society. Thomas A. Edison, in an interview with Will Irwin explaining why he had joined the new party, expressed sentiments common among Progressives:

You see, getting down to the bottom of things, this is a pretty raw, crude civilization of ours—pretty wasteful, pretty cruel, which often comes to the same thing, doesn't it? . . . Our production, our factory laws, our charities, our relations between capital and labor, our distribution—all wrong, out of gear. We've stumbled along for a while, trying to run a new civilization in old ways, and we've got to start to make this world over.

In "making this world over" the Progressives were guided in part by their belief in what might be termed "modernism," which was the Whig belief in the inevitability of progress combined with a predisposition to see value in something because it was new. Conservatives noted with alarm that the Progressive program called for much experimentation, but Edison replied that his famous achievements were based on experiments, and intellectuals familiar with the philosophical pragmatism of William James and John Dewey viewed experimentation as the only viable way of life for individuals and societies. The Progressives, like most of their fellow Americans, were impressed and even intoxicated by the inventions and gadgets, the skyscrapers and expanding cities, the whole panoply of modern America. This intoxication led to the optimism so characteristic of the Progressives. ("We are none of us progressives when we are worried or tired . . . ," confessed Lippmann.) They felt they were the wave of the future. Just as carriages were being replaced by automobiles like the "Garford" manufactured by the Ohio Bull Moose candidate for governor, and gas lights by Edison's electric bulbs, so it seemed natural to Progressives that the new age required a new party. They were supremely confident as they faced their opponents, because they knew that nothing could stop "progress," at least not for very long.

Many conservatives in the old parties were also impressed by the achievements of modern engineering, industry, and technology, but conservatives believed that these advances should be confined to the private sector. Change in the private economic sphere was welcome and to be encouraged, but government regulation, control, and social welfare planning were anathema because they threatened the sanctity of private property and the "natural" workings of the immutable laws of classical economics. On the other hand, many progressives in the old parties feared large corporations, the process of nationalization in the economy, government bureaus which could be perverted by special interests, and centralized power, whether private or public. Some even cursed urbanism and large-scale industrialism. These progressives, men like the loyalist Republican insurgents and the Wilsonian progressive Democrats, longed for a return to the nineteenth-century world of agrarianism, small companies, regional markets, and local economic and political control. Dismissed by T.R. as "rural Tories," such progressives, whom the historian John Braeman has labeled the "traditionalists" of the reform movement, believed that the economy needed trust busting on a massive scale and the restoration of full competition. President Taft, much to the displeasure of some of his Wall Street patrons, favored trust busting and agreed with much of the "traditionalist" progressive economic analysis, as did some of the old-line conservatives in the G.O.P. and the Democracy. During the fall campaign Roosevelt frequently pointed to this paradoxical alliance of conservatives and "traditionalist" progressives on the trust issue, of men as disparate as La Follette, Taft, and Wilson standing united in favor of trust busting, while in contrast the new party offered the regulation and continuous management of a federal trade commission.

Conservatives and many "traditionalist" progressives were also one in their veneration of "rugged individualism" and opposition to the welfare state. Both feared that a welfare state would sap individual initiative, character, and autonomy. Moreover, classical economics was based on the Malthusian concept of scarcity, "the niggardly hand of nature," and communicants of the old parties believed "Ye have the poor always with you," and that no society could materially afford the luxury of a comprehensive welfare system.

There was a range of differing beliefs on some of these matters among Progressives too, although there was a consensus on the essentials of the new party program. Like Roosevelt, most Progressives were ambivalent about economic competition, recognizing its waste and antisocial character, yet fearing the unknown consequences of its abolition. As would become apparent during the writing of the Progressive platform, some new party leaders like Gifford and Amos Pinchot favored stiff trust busting as well as the rule of a trade commission, while others like Beveridge and George W. Perkins wanted regulation of business but were basically hostile to the old-time system of competition between small-unit corporations. Furthermore, most Progressives put limitations on their philosophy of "modernism," while a few like Lippmann and the poet-journalist George Sylvester Viereck believed that "modernism" and progressivism should extend to every area of life from art to sexual relations. Roosevelt did not like Cubist painting and was opposed to birth control, and he and most Progressives held traditional attitudes about culture and private morals and conventions. But Viereck championed free love, and Lippmann and many of the young new party intellectuals promoted the "new art," "new poetry," and a host of similar progressive movements in arts and letters.

The Progressive call for labor reform and a welfare state was largely the product of the engineering mentality and the humanitarian and Social Gospel faith. But for some Progressives support for these reforms was based primarily on the conviction that a prosperous America, enjoying almost continuous good times since 1896, fecund in goods and food, possessing a large class of millionaires, could well afford to be generous. As Beveridge put it, the time had come to "pass prosperity around," and this became one of the Progressive campaign slogans of 1912. Walter Weyl explained that the country had a "social surplus"—the wealth produced above what was necessary to run commerce and return fair profit, the wasted wealth which built villas in Newport and fueled "conspicuous consumption." The Progressive program proposed corporate, income, and inheritance taxes, as well as minimum wage, workmen's compensation, and social insurance, measures which would regulate and redistribute the social surplus. "This surplus is the legitimate fund of progress," declared Walter Lippmann.

Yet Progressive support of the welfare state was limited by the boundaries of prosperity, the profit system, and pre-Keynesian economic theory. The profit system was the goose that laid the golden egg of Weyl's "social surplus." "It is quite clear that no sane man wishes to attack the economic life of a nation in any way that would make it less productive," wrote Lippmann, explaining that while favoring new taxes he was opposed to tax levels that might "ruin industry." Deficit spending and Keynesian economics were of course unknown to pre-World War I reformers. It is, therefore, not surprising that some Bull Moosers later opposed the deficit spending and taxation policies of the New Deal welfare state of the second President Roosevelt.

Related to the Progressive welfare proposals, spirit of "modernism," and advocacy of a union between nationalism and democracy, was the call for a "new politics," the partisan and political expression of the New Nationalism. Beveridge and T.R. had made clear that the "new politics" was issue-oriented, with a division between the parties based on the ideological cleavage between conservatism and progressivism. Parties were to be controlled by the membership through primaries, and governments were to be continuously responsible to the people through the referendum, recall, and other forms of direct democracy. The "new politics" obviously required a highly civic-spirited, informed, and politically involved electorate. This vision, of course, was at odds with much of American political experience and practice. Substantive issues and ideological divisions had been avoided as part of the reaction to the political battles that preceded the Civil War, and simply as the safest political course. All parties in the past had essentially been run by elites. And one of the main reasons why parties had been controlled by elites, and the government in turn conducted by the parties, was that the American electorate had—not surprisingly—failed to manifest on a constant basis those virtues which the "new politics" assumed it possessed.

The Progressives were aware of these objections to the "new politics," and had answers to them. They argued that the people had never been given a chance to prove themselves as citizens. As Beveridge had noted, the bosses and the machinery of the parties had prevented the people from expressing their will except under the restricted circumstances of an election where the candidates were chosen by the bosses of the parties. "What profiteth it the people if they do only the electing while the invisible government does the nominating?" the Hoosier Progressive asked. Furthermore, the voters could not directly elect senators, and most women did not even have the ballot. Moreover, Progressives insisted, the decisions of the majority at the polls for nominations, and in referendums, or with the recall of judicial decisions, could scarcely be more inimical to the public interest than those made by bosses, legislators, and judges in the service of the "invisible government." Finally, the Progressives had no intention of abandoning the principles of leadership, representative government, or even ruling elites. Their program called for the administration of government by experts as well as direction by plebiscite, and thus differed from the kind of participatory democracy envisioned by the Jacksonians.

The Progressives fully realized that issue-oriented politics and, more particularly, ideological politics were contrary to much of post-Civil War American theory and practice. Indeed, they compared themselves to the Republicans of the 1850s who had refused to bury the issue of slavery, "men in whose souls burned the fire of lofty endeavor," as T.R. put it. The Progressives in fact welcomed polarization as an effective and necessary step in bringing about needed changes in the political and economic system and the realignment of the party division. As Beveridge had said, the people were already divided along progressive-conservative lines, and it was therefore both just and logical that the party division reflect this split. Moreover, for Progressives the whole American system of government had to be judged a failure if substantive issues concerning the "living of the people" could not be debated and decided by citizens through their parties and government mechanisms. The virtues of continuity, stability, and order, commonly associated with the traditional party system, were necessary to the republic, but they could and should not be purchased at the price of avoiding the important problems of the day.

Yet, though the Progressives had considered many of the problems involved in direct democracy, they had not fully faced all the implications of the "new politics." There was to be no intrapartisan factionalism under the "new politics." Progressive Republicans and Democrats joining the Bull Moose herd were sick of the factional divisions and struggles in the old parties, and insisted that no real service to the people could come from a partisan house divided against itself. Since the new party was founded on the reform ideology of the Progressive faith, Progressives assumed that the party would be free of factionalism. But although there was indeed a general consensus among Progressives on the main articles of the Progressive faith, most of the details of the convention platform, and Roosevelt's leadership, factionalism quickly appeared in the new party ranks, proof perhaps that factionalism was endemic to all parties, whatever their nature.

First, there was a division on the platform committee between those who favored trust busting and competition and those who did not. Next, Progressives quarreled over the choice of George W. Perkins for party executive chairman. Both disputes were papered over at the convention and during the campaign, but they emerged again after the election to disrupt the party. Finally, there was a general division among Progressives about the purposes and conduct of a party dedicated to the "new politics," with some leaders emphasizing the necessities of professional politics, and others giving first priority to the task of social education. The division between the political professionals and the social educators was not really revealed in the first months of the party's existence,

THE SUFFRAGISTS PARADED
TO THE CONVENTION HALL

but after 1912 it became a crucial problem for the party's national organization. Moreover, further internal disputes would also cause the party trouble after 1912. Thus, the Progressive Party was not to be free from factionalism. Indeed, these first divisions fit the classic partisan factional types. The trust dispute was based on an issue, the Perkins fight on a particular leader, and the division between the social educators and the political professionals on an ideological division, just as the old party factions had been based on issues, personalities, and philosophies.

Most important in terms of Progressive thought were the differences between the social educators and those who emphasized the problems and needs of professional politics. Social workers, academics, nonpartisan reformers, and intellectuals who joined the Progressive cause tended to view the first function of a party as educational. Just as nonpartisan reform groups, academic organizations, and citizens' committees had worked to inform and educate the public, so parties should use platforms, campaigns, and organizations for the work of education. These Progressives had found the nonpartisan reform strategy frustrating and sterile, and had opted for a reform partisan path which could bring them political influence, power, and control. But in their view social education had first priority because the voters had to be informed, convinced, and converted before the new party could hope to win office. This was in effect a long-term missionary strategy. Professional politicans in the new party, more numerous than the social educators, objected that the Progressive Party had to grow quickly or die. Professional politicians argued that the old parties were strong because of their political organization, and therefore that victory was to be reached through the well-marked path of partisan success—strong political organization from the grass roots up. In short, the social educators believed that public education should have primacy over conventional politics, while the politicians insisted that in playing partisan politics it was necessary to fight fire with fire, to beat the enemy at its own game.

The two groups, however, had much in common, including ultimate reform goals and the communion of the Progressive faith, and during the campaign the social educators and politicians complemented each other more than they conflicted. There was a division of labor with much to do for both groups. The social educators gave the Progressive program substance, detail, and publicity, while the politicians handled the work of organization and administration. Schism would not appear until a later day.

In the final analysis, the new party was not seriously threatened in 1912 by its incipient factionalism or the differing interpretations of some of the articles of the Progressive creed. The organizational strengths of the old parties and the time-tested appeal of traditional laissez-faire conservatism were far greater threats to the Progressive cause. The most crucial political and ideological problem confronting the new party and the Progressive concepts of New Nationalism and a "new politics" was the fact of American pluralism: the pluralism of the sectional, ethnic, religious, racial, economic, and historical divisions of American society. This was a heterogeneity that translated into a politics making Vermont Republican and South Carolina Democratic; Germans in St. Louis Republican and the Boston Irish Democratic; some interest groups follow one party and others follow the opposition; one neighborhood solidly Democratic and another in the same city loyal to the G.O.P. The old parties were deeply rooted in the soil of the American past and present. Could the roots be torn up? The New Nationalism and the "new politics" assumed that Americans could be made to rise above the divisions and see a common, transcendent identity and nationalism. It was no coincidence that Roosevelt always used the metaphors of war, continuously appealing to veterans and pointing to them as examples, for it was perhaps only in wartime that the country had exhibited the spirit of patriotism and nationalism called for by the Progressive Party. The dispute over the southern delegations demonstrated the tenacity of pluralism even within the new party, and Progressive politicians were well aware that interest groups would have to be courted during the fall campaign, particularly on the state and local levels. But there were two hopes for the success of the New Nationalism and the new politics beyond whatever pluralistic adjustments and compromises might be made: the middle class and the heritage of American Christianity.

The middle class had been growing in size and importance throughout American history, and the post-Civil War industrialization and urbanization, while creating a large proletariat, had also strengthened the middle strata in many ways. White collar workers were essential to an urban and industrial society, and opportunities for real if modest social and economic advancement abounded. Suburban enclaves of the middle class began to surround the cities, duplicating in some ways the class's traditional small town bastions; consumer goods were produced largely for the benefit of the middle class; and magazines, newspapers, and cultural institutions began to cater to and depend on this group that seemed to have such a bright future. Sectional, religious, and ethnic differences began to blur among white, native Protestants and some ambitious children of immigrants, creating a new homogeneity bred by similar economic and social conditions. The middle class, of course, had its own special interests and needs, but its size, scope, and character were closest to what writers meant when they spoke of "average Americans." Perceived as the American majority, it was in fact this group that the Progressives had in mind when they spoke of "the people," not ethnic or social minorities. The middle class might be reached by an appeal to nationalism, because its identity seemed to transcend pluralistic divisions, and, as observers following the state and national conventions of the new party noted, the Progressive Party was already drawing its grass roots strength from this class. The middle class was firmly committed to the ethic of self-help and private property, the underpinnings of American conservatism, and in the North and West was for the most part traditionally Republican, but it could be swayed by arguments based on the new spirit of "modernism" and the engineering mentality, programs based on efficiency, management, engineering, and planning, all values which were vital to middle class society. And, too, the middle class might be moved by appeals to Christianity.

The Progressive faith had many components, but its core was the "faith of our fathers." As Roosevelt said, "We battle for the Lord," and the religious aspects of the convention accurately reflected the Protestantism of most of the delegates and their literal belief in Roosevelt's injunction. For all their "modernism," most Progressives believed that the moral principles of the Bible were everlastingly relevant, the "rock of ages" upon which all political, social, and economic institutions and policies should be built. Roosevelt spoke of "the eternal principle of righteousness" in his "Confession," and Edison remarked that "this movement's part reduction of waste and equalization of wealth, and part just plain morals." Indeed, the religious and humanitarian beliefs of the Progressives are crucial to an understanding of the New Nationalism and new politics. The divisions in American society were to be abandoned not in service to a state, but rather for a philosophy of one for all and all for one. The state was to be valued just in so far as it provided for the welfare of every citizen. The pluralism attacked by the Progressives was not that of tolerance and variety, but that born of what Beveridge termed "savage individualism" and "special

THE PROGRESSIONAL

interests." In fact, though most of the Progressive leaders were Protestants, the Progressive faith was really the dispensation of the Social Gospel, a movement not confined to any sect or group of sects. The Social Gospel was broad enough to embrace reform-minded Roman Catholics like Father J. J. Curran, champion of the Pennsylvania coal miners, and some Jews like Oscar Straus. The Social Gospel spirit of brotherhood, "uplift," and social ethics informed and infused much of the Progressive Party's program and campaign. Although Americans were separated from each other by many differences, the Progressives hoped that their fellow countrymen could be called to the paths of brotherhood and humanitarianism by sounding the Gospel trumpet. The middle class, with its roots deep in the Protestant past, was counted on particularly to fill the ranks of the crusade to save modern America from becoming a Tower of Babel.

Was the Progressive faith too narrow? The new party program included many proposals to help the blue collar worker, but the Progressives refused to appeal openly to the "labor vote," because such an interest group approach conflicted with the Progressive general interest theory of society. After all, according to the Progressive analysis, special interests were the enemies of reform and the commonweal. The Social Gospel, though broad in appeal and embracing much of the Judeo-Christian tradition, was most influential among the educated and the Protestant clergy. Might not immigrants detect in the King James vocabulary the accents of northern European stock Protestants representing a world-view alien to the churches of Sicily or Greece and the synagogues of eastern Europe? Progressive social and political theory was familiar to intellectuals and those citizens who read the latest books or the pages of the *Outlook* and other reviews. But what about the less educated? The middle class was large and carried great political weight, but Progressives could hardly afford to ignore the rest of the country. A viable nationalist appeal had to be inclusive rather than exclusive, ecumenical beyond the folds of Protestantism and the liberal intellectual elite. Thus, the ultimate weakness of the Progressive faith was found in the very nature of its monistic missionary appeal.

5

While the convention proceeded, the platform committee under Dean William Draper Lewis was slowly forging the final draft of the "contract with the people." Throughout July conferences on the platform had been held at Sagamore Hill, and letters and visitors arrived at Roosevelt's home from all over the country. Governor McGovern of Wisconsin wrote urging that La Follette's proposed Republican platform be consulted, and James R. Garfield advised T.R. to study Owen Lovejoy's social welfare report to the National Conference of Charities and Corrections. Young Hamilton Fish wrote from London commending British measures like the Shops Act, Old Age Pension Act, and National Insurance Act. Captain William Sims of the Naval War College sent data for use in drawing up a plank favoring the construction of more battleships. Visitors at Sagamore Hill included President Van Hise and Charles McCarthy of the University of Wisconsin, Professor Merriam from Chicago, and leaders of the new party from dozens of states. On July 18 a large conference was held for the purpose of discussing social welfare issues, attended by Dean George W. Kirchwey of Columbia Law School, Raymond Robins, Walter Weyl, Henry Moskowitz, and other social workers and intellectuals. Before the Chicago convention at least six full platform drafts were prepared for consideration, and numerous individual planks were submitted by various Progressives. Deans Kirchwey and Lewis each worked up a separate preliminary draft, as did Charles McCarthy, the Pinchot brothers, Chester H. Rowell of California, and the Kansas editor William Allen White.

Gifford Pinchot, White, and others began work in Chicago several days before the convention, but the platform committee formally convened in the Congress Hotel at 9:00 P.M. Monday, August 5. In an open hearing and then in closed session the committee heard testimony on numerous issues, finally adjourning at 1:30 A.M. Tuesday. That day and through the night a subcommittee of nine, which included Chairman Lewis, White, Senator Dixon, Chester H. Rowell, Dean Kirchwey, and Professor Merriam, labored to produce the platform. Progressive leaders were generally allowed free access to the deliberations, and Beveridge, George W. Perkins, McCarthy, the Pinchot brothers, and others conferred frequently with the subcommittee. Roosevelt was present to give his approval to each plank and reconcile opposing viewpoints. Because of the multiplicity of issues considered and several disputes on particular planks, the platform was not ready on Wednesday morning as scheduled, and the convention was forced to pass on to the nominations. The full committee approved the final draft on Wednesday afternoon, and later that day Lewis presented it to the convention for ratification.

What happened during the deliberations of the platform committee and subcommittee became a matter of public and private debate after the election when Charles McCarthy and Amos Pinchot charged that a paragraph of the platform adopted by the committee dealing with the Sherman Act had been "stolen" and dropped from printed versions of the platform. Subsequently scholars have joined in this debate. It has been said that no records remain of the committee proceedings or the working drafts used at the Congress Hotel. Scholars have therefore relied, as did the Progressives in the months after the election, on the recollections of those involved in making the platform. There exist, however, among the Progressive Party papers now at Harvard, some typed drafts for the platform and individual planks, annotated in handwriting by Roosevelt, Lewis, and others, as well as minutes for the meetings of the full committee. From these papers as well as from the recollections of Progressives it is possible to reconstruct much of what happened.

There were a number of disagreements about specific planks, although there was a general consensus on the major welfare and direct democracy proposals. Jane Addams, it was said, had a hard time "swallowing" the two battleships T.R. called for building every year, and she was distressed at the omission of any reference to Negroes, though this pleased McCarthy and the southerners. A single tax plank supported by George L. Record, which T.R. opposed, was rejected only after considerable debate. Many Progressives were prohibitionists, and the Virginia delegation submitted a plank calling for restrictions on federal liquor licenses. The platform, however, was silent on the liquor issue, though a convention floor fight was averted only at the last minute by Roosevelt's personal intervention. No agreement could be reached on the Philippine question, and so no plank was adopted. A proposal for the recall of senators was rejected; Roosevelt struck out a proposal for amending the Constitution by referendum; and it was decided to omit reference to the recall of judges while devoting a plank to the "popular review of judicial decisions" along the lines of T.R.'s 1912 Columbus address.

The most important dispute was on the regulation of interstate corporations. Surviving drafts show that the platform makers were agreed that an anti-trust law of any sort alone could not provide the answer, and that a federal regulatory trade commission was necessary. "Experience has . . . shown that legislation, enforced by lawsuits, is not sufficient," read the Rowell draft, paralleling T.R.'s frequent assertions. The Pinchot brothers also called for a commission, as did plank drafts revised by Learned Hand, Herbert Croly, and George Rublee. Thus far there was agreement. The dispute centered on the future of the Sherman Act, though of course it also involved the larger questions of competition and monopoly. Well over a dozen drafts of the proposed plank remain. Only one of the surviving drafts was a thorough trust-busting plank, even though Amos Pinchot and others believed in such an approach. This draft (marked "Dean Lewis") stated in part: "We believe that the Sherman Anti-Trust law, and similar laws in the several states, recognizing, as they do, the necessity for the preservation of competitive conditions, are founded on a principle, not only sound, but essential to the prosperity of the country. We pledge the party to an honest and vigorous enforcement of such laws." Other drafts called for the retention and strengthening of the Sherman Act, but also spoke ambiguously of regulating "unavoidable natural monopolies," or of destroying only "monopolies that are found to be oppressive." Still others avoided mentioning the Sherman Act, and lauded the benefits of concentration while endorsing a federal commission, but these too were ambiguous in that they spoke of ending trade practices commonly associated with monopolies and trusts.

In the end, the platform makers fought over two alternative plank drafts. The draft supported by the Pinchots, McCarthy, and others consisted of two paragraphs, one long and one short. The first and long paragraph endorsed a federal commission which, among other things, would regulate stocks and "natural monopolies," and "have regulatory control over the conditions that create and determine monopoly prices." To guard against the "irresponsible use of power" the commissioners "should be subject to recall by Congress." The second paragraph read:

We favor strengthening the Sherman law by prohibiting agreements to divide territory or limit output; refusing to sell to customers who buy from business rivals; to sell below costs in certain areas while maintaining higher prices in other places; using the power of transportation to aid or injure special business concerns; and other unfair trade practices.

The plank supported by Beveridge, Perkins, and others, several versions of which remain, was longer. "The concentration of modern business, in some degree, is both inevitable and necessary for national and international business efficiency," it stated. "But the existing concentration of vast wealth under a corporate system, unguarded and uncontrolled by the nation, has placed in the hands of a few men enormous, secret, irresponsible power over the daily life of the citizen—a power unsufferable in a free government and certain of abuse." This power had been abused in the monopoly of natural resources, "unfair competition and unfair privileges," stock watering, and corrupting the government. The solution was "a strong federal administrative commission of high standing" which would publicize corporate activities, "attack unfair competition and special privilege, and . . . guard and keep open to all the highways of American commerce." There were also some platitudes about the virtue of honest business, but there was no mention of the Sherman Act or statement that legislative approaches had failed. Most versions of this plank ended with a call for reform of the patent laws, ending unjust restrictions.

Roosevelt tried to work out a compromise between the two factions. He attempted to reduce the issue to one of mere detail. The platform was already crowded with specifics, he claimed, and so there was no need to add more on the Sherman Act when he had already stated in the "Confession," and promised to do so again in later speeches, that the Sherman Act should be retained and strengthened. Furthermore, the Colonel argued, the inclusion of some of the practices to be outlawed would imply that these were the only ones, whereas all admitted there were more. The Colonel said he would mention such practices in his speeches, but further legislation should be most concerned with defining the nature of antisocial practices and leave specific details and cases to the courts and the commission. White recalled:

I was sitting on a chair in the hall . . . , working on my newspaper story, and saw the Colonel pendulating between Perkins' room and Pinchot's room. He would toddle out of one room, looking over the top of his glasses, with the contested plank in his hand, and enter another room—maybe Perkins' room; and then in a few moments, like a faithful retriever, would come popping out, panting across the hall to Pinchot's room, still with the papers in his hand, grinning at me like a dog wagging his tail as he tried to compromise the differences between the pinfeather wings of his new party.

At last a plank that Roosevelt hoped would satisfy all was sent downstairs to the committee with Dixon and Beveridge, who spoke for its adoption. Dixon reported back that the plank had been passed. The committee minutes state that "the Colonel's suggestions were all adopted," and on August 11 Lewis wrote Roosevelt: "The substituted business plank went through without opposition; indeed I think practically all were satisfied that it was better than the original."

When Lewis presented the platform to the convention, he read the plank that Perkins had supported plus the short paragraph from the plank backed by the Pinchots. Perkins jumped up from his chair and left the hall in evident distress, saying that a mistake had been made and the Sherman Act paragraph did not belong in the platform. After hurried conferences among Dixon, Beveridge, T.R., Perkins, and Lewis, it was agreed that a mistake had been made. Lewis had been reading from a confused batch of sheets brought from the committee and could easily have made an error. O. K. Davis, the party publicity chairman, was therefore instructed to remove the paragraph from all printed versions of the platform, and he convinced the Associated Press to send out the corrected text. The incident was unknown to the public until after the election. Then most of the committee members recalled that the antitrust paragraph had in fact been included by the committee, and upon further reflection Lewis decided that this had been the case.

What had actually been in the plank finally passed by the committee? How can the mixup be explained? Certainly, Perkins could not have intended to "steal" the lines from the platform since such action was bound to be detected and rebuked. It seems safe to assume that Roosevelt, Dixon, Beveridge, and Lewis also acted in sincerity. It can probably never be known for certain what happened, but the surviving drafts suggest an answer. No one contended that the entire draft plank backed by the Pinchots had been adopted, and no one disputed that all of the plank finally adopted except the antitrust paragraph came from the draft Perkins supported. Most of the platform planks passed by the committee and appearing in the printed versions of the platform are among the surviving drafts and have "adopted" written in hand on them. The draft backed by the Pinchot brothers appears with the first, long paragraph crossed out and "adopted" written under the second, short paragraph which concerns the Sherman Act. No copy of the Perkins-supported plank has "adopted" written on it, but several versions and copies exist with the concluding patents clause crossed out. A patents clause does not appear in any of the printed versions of the business plank. (The clause appears elsewhere in the platform as a separate plank.) Perhaps the committee adopted the Perkins plank omitting the patents clause and substituting the antitrust lines. Perhaps this in fact was the version sent down to the committee by Roosevelt, which would account for the statements of the minutes, the Lewis letter of August 11, and Dixon. Perkins may have thought Roosevelt was only sending his draft alone to the committee. Roosevelt may have forgotten the next day what he actually agreed upon; later he confessed he could not remember for certain what had happened. In any event, the committee had probably passed the Perkins draft with the addition of the Pinchot Sherman Act paragraph.

The imbroglio over the business plank revealed two points of division among the Progressives: first, the split between those who basically favored the restoration of economic competition, and those who saw economic concentration as inevitable and beneficial; and second, the quarrel over the position of Perkins in the new party. To a large extent Roosevelt had managed to paper over the trust dispute. The final platform condemned various unfair trade practices similar to those mentioned in the Pinchots' antitrust paragraph, and did not condone monopoly in any form, while in the "Confession" T.R. had endorsed and called for strengthening the Sherman Act. Though the platform would have been clearer had it explicitly endorsed the Sherman Act, the real source of contention, for which the Pinchots' paragraph served as a symbol, was the differing economic philosophies of Progressives like the Pinchot brothers on one side, and Perkins, Beveridge, and such Progressives as the publisher Frank Munsey on the other.

For Amos Pinchot, the most outspoken of the antitrust Progressives, American economic problems could be solved by restoring competitive capitalism. In addition to the antitrust plank, Amos had prepared a plank on the "cost of living," which stated that monopolies were the "prime" cause of high prices. Roosevelt vetoed Amos's draft, writing "utter folly" on his copy. In an analysis following T.R.'s in the "Confession," the adopted plank on the cost of living stated that inflation and high prices were caused by a variety of factors, and could only be solved in part by regulating corporate pricing. For Amos, however, economic problems were simpler, and could be met by crushing the trusts. To Roosevelt such an attitude was not simple but simplistic, and thus he had joined with Amos's opponents in curbing the trust-busting proposals.

Perkins, Beveridge, Frank Munsey, and other Progressives believed on the other hand that the age of competition was over. "We cannot go back to the old system . . . , with its unstable prices, unwise competition, and greater cost and greater waste," wrote Munsey. They wanted the Sherman Act repealed and antitrust suits replaced by government regulation of a corporate system of large units, nor did they fear monopoly if properly supervised by federal administration. "The great question of the day," Perkins had declared in 1910, "is whether we shall go on with a war between corporations and the people which is certain to do neither any good."

Both the Pinchot and Perkins positions, however, were minority viewpoints in the new party. Although Amos Pinchot has often been seen as a "radical," his economic views in fact followed the "traditionalist" progressive analysis, and were closer to the trust-busting position of the Wilsonian Democrats—and President Taft—than to the New Nationalism. Perkins, Beveridge, and Munsey represented the other extreme, and went much further in embracing the trusts than most Progressives were willing to go. Most Progressives, ranging from Hiram Johnson's California reformers to Herbert Croly and the party's intellectual elite, supported Roosevelt's midway, straddle position.

Roosevelt had come to the position outlined in the "Confession" after much thought. Since his days as president he had rejected the simple dissolution approach of the Sherman Act and advocated a trade commission for business regulation. He saw economic benefits to corporate concentration, but he opposed cutting off competition through trade practices like those enumerated in the Pinchot antitrust paragraph. Trusts, therefore, were "good" unless they were built or behaved in a "bad" manner. But Roosevelt was well aware that many reformers and an as yet uncounted number of voters believed in trust busting and competition in all fields. The "New Freedom" Woodrow Wilson was calling it, while Taft was pointing to his administration's record of many antitrust suits. Senator Joseph L. Bristow of Kansas, a Republican insurgent at first friendly to the new party, had warned T.R. of the dangers ahead because of widely held faith in competition. Do not ask for repeal of the Sherman Act, rather use the word "amend," he wrote Roosevelt on July 15. "I would suggest that you indorse the idea of preserving competition where it is practicable to do so. . . . In this way I think you can hold some of our friends. . . ." He added that he himself had his doubts about Roosevelt's commission proposal, though he was "about ready to admit" that there was probably no other way. "But in this scheme of regulation is there not grave danger that 'big business' will more likely control the government than the government control 'big business'?" Bristow suggested that the solution might be to insure that the government was popular by even further extending the initiative, referendum, and recall. Perhaps federal judges could be elected and perhaps the recall could be extended to the president.

Roosevelt had gone as far as he cared to with direct democracy reforms, which he viewed as mainly tactical weapons for the state level, but Bristow had correctly seen the two major problems with Roosevelt's corporation control plan. Competition was viewed by most Americans as the normal and desirable state of affairs, and government commissions could as in the past become the servants rather than the masters of business. Roosevelt decided that he would have to convince the people that competition while sometimes desirable and possible was an overrated concept in fact impossible of universal realization. Competition in many cases had led to antisocial practices and conditions, and to inefficiency in production and distribution. The history of the Sherman Act proved that in many instances real competition simply could not be restored. This seemed to be the conclusion to be drawn, for example, from Taft's ineffective attempts to break up the oil and tobacco trusts. In short, pre–Civil War capitalism was dead, and Wilson and Taft were being both foolish and demagogic in telling the people otherwise, in declaring that antitrust suits were the solution to corporation regulation and control. On the other hand, Roosevelt could in good conscience advocate prosecution for unfair trade practices and antisocial business conduct, thereby appealing to antitrust and antimonopoly sentiment. This position seemed to meet the needs for regulation and curbing corporate abuses, though it left the question of trusts and monopolies open.

But in building his half-way house Roosevelt invited attacks both from big business and from antitrust enthusiasts, while his failure to resolve the problems of possible commission corruption, and to include specific praise for the Sherman Act in the convention platform, provided fodder for the opposition. For Roosevelt, the problem of seeing that commissioners and officials remained servants of the commonweal would be solved by electing a president who would appoint only the right men—in short, by voting the Progressive ticket! This was no real solution to a problem that would plague twentieth-century liberalism for decades to come.

Roosevelt had, however, made great strides in coming to grips with the problems of modern business. Roosevelt's position on business regulation found general favor among Progressives, with only a few like Amos Pinchot dissenting. The Indiana reformer William Dudley Foulke wrote to the Colonel reporting on a "round table conference" of Progressives attending the Los Angeles convention of the National Municipal League, of which Foulke was president. Albert Bushnell Hart, Meyer Lissner, Chester H. Rowell, the league secretary

Clinton Rogers Woodruff, and about a dozen others had discussed the Progressive program. There were many important issues, Foulke wrote, but he thought that the question of corporation control would probably turn out to be the big issue of the campaign:

After talking with many persons my conviction increases that the trust problem is the crux of the whole situation and the point at which both the Republican and Democratic parties have most completely failed is in aiming to restore competition rather than to regulate big business. . . . Almost unanimously the men I talked with favor your plan—an industrial commission on the lines of the Interstate Commerce Commission with power to determine even prices wherever these are unreasonable. On that point I think your position is invulnerable. Unless this is effectively done republican institutions will finally break down and a plutocracy, followed perhaps by the red terror, will supervene.

Since most Progressives agreed with Roosevelt's position on the trusts, years later William Allen White decided that for the most part the dispute over the wording of the business plank had been an outgrowth of the animosity felt by many Progressives for George W. Perkins. Nurtured on hatred for Wall Street, many reformers saw something sinister in having a former partner of J. P. Morgan high in party councils. Beveridge shared Perkins's views on business, but he was not attacked or resented because he was not, like Perkins, a member of the boards of International Harvester and United States Steel, two much-publicized trusts. The dispute on the platform marked a divergence in Progressive doctrine among a few Progressives, but it was also a harbinger of future quarrels over Perkins.

On August 8, the day after the convention closed, the Progressive National Committee met to choose officers and an executive committee. Senator Dixon was continued as permanent chairman of the national committee. Perkins was Roosevelt's choice for chairman of the executive committee, which meant that he would be in charge of party headquarters in New York City and manage the party's business affairs, functions he had already been essentially performing since June. Dixon was an experienced politician, adept at handling the press and fellow politicians, but he was not skilled in office management and business as Perkins was. After making his fortune on Wall Street, Perkins had retired from active business to devote himself to charity and public service. Roosevelt's finance chairman in the drive for the G.O.P. nomination, he had been put in charge of arrangements for the Bull Moose convention. Perkins had kept convention costs to $17,000, a much smaller sum than the G.O.P. had spent, and by selling tickets the party realized a profit of $2,000 from the convention. Later in the campaign when three million copies of the "Confession of Faith" were set to be printed with photographs of Roosevelt and Hiram Johnson on the covers, publicity man O. K. Davis discovered that the printer had not obtained permission from the photographers, Moffet Studio, for using the pictures, and the copyright law provided a fine of one dollar per copy for violations. Davis rushed to Perkins with the news. Perkins quickly sent a telegram to the studio informing the photographers that the party was using their pictures and this would be great advertisement. How much, Perkins asked, would the studio pay the party for using the photographs? The studio wired back that this had not been done before, but under the circumstances Moffet would pay $250. Such was Perkins's business skill. Of course, his services as "dough moose" were needed just as badly by the Bull Moose Party, and Perkins's contributions in 1912 and later were indeed substantial. The opposition press found Perkins's generosity proof that the trusts controlled the new party, and many Progressives also found Perkins's connections suspect. This was in many ways ironic. The great bulk of big business executives opposed Roosevelt. Moreover, as far as is known all the other officers of both United States Steel and International Harvester backed either Taft or Wilson (Wilson received financial support from Harvester executives), and J. P. Morgan, Jr., tried to force Perkins to resign from the United States Steel board because of his political activities.

At the August 8 meeting a group of Progressives on the national committee tried to block Perkins's election as executive committee chairman. A small band, including Meyer Lissner, Harold Ickes, and William Allen White, spoke out against Perkins and his Wall Street background. A much larger group of members were in sympathy but declined to oppose T.R.'s choice. Matthew Hale suggested that Perkins perform the functions of the executive office but another man hold the title. J. F. Cleveland of Arizona responded: "We believe in toting guns down our way. But we don't carry 'em concealed." Perkins was elected, but the quarrel was hardly ended.

The debates over the business plank and the choice of Perkins, however, were behind closed doors. What the country noted was the content of the platform. Basically, it was a summary of Roosevelt's "Confession of Faith," calling for broad economic, social, and political reform in a detailed yet concise fashion. It has since become a classic, one of the most important political platforms ever adopted. Amos Pinchot, feeling that the only fundamental issues were monopoly and the cost of living, complained that it contained everything "from the shorter catechism to how to build a birchbark canoe," but most observers were impressed by the social welfare demands—proposals over which there had been virtually no disagreement on the platform committee. The novelist Winston Churchill declared: "It is the most concrete and practical program of modern social democracy ever put forward, the result of years of thought of the ablest students of social conditions in the land." In a backhanded tribute the opposition press criticized the fact that, as Churchill said, the platform was "the concrete expression of the thought of the foremost economists and political scientists in America." The *New York Times* sneered:

It was fortunate for the colleges that the Bull Moose convention was held during vacation. Had it occurred in term time, their courses of study would have been seriously interrupted. In the West, those great high schools of Socialism which, out there, they call State Universities, were heavily drawn upon for delegates and doctrine. Here in the East, the Faculties of some of our chief seats of learning have sent a great part of their socialistic membership to Chicago. We observe, though, that one university professor hereabout is still faithful unto Debs.

6

Although the speeches of Beveridge and Roosevelt had provided the convention with stirring crescendoes, there was still much business to conduct. On August 6, after Roosevelt delivered his "Confession," the convention adopted Frank Knox's report from the Committee on Credentials, which upheld the decisions of the national committee on the contested southern seats. On Wednesday, August 7, when Beveridge called the convention to order at 11:30 A.M., Medill McCormick of Illinois presented the report of the Committee on Rules, which reflected the bitter experience of the June Republican convention. In future Progressive conventions each state was to have one delegate and alternate for each congressional representative and senator plus one from each congressional district for every five thousand votes cast for the Progressive presidential candidate in the previous election. This would mean that there could be no "rotten boroughs" in a Progressive convention. All delegates were to be chosen in primaries wherever possible, and no contested delegate had the right to vote until his contest was decided. No person could sit on the national committee who held a federal appointment from the president, and four women were to be members-at-large to insure female representation. The report was greeted with applause and adopted.

After a luncheon recess Henry J. Allen of Kansas announced that the platform was not ready and moved that the rules be suspended and the convention proceed to the nomination of candidates. This voted, Comptroller William A. Prendergast of New York City delivered the nominating speech for Roosevelt he had not been able to give at the G.O.P. convention: "My candidate is more than a citizen; he is a national asset." After a lengthy demonstration Judge Ben Lindsey, representing the Democrats who had joined the new party, gave the first seconding speech. He said that the Democratic bosses had only nominated Wilson to keep in power by appealing to the progressive sentiment among the voters, and declared that the "Baltimore by-product" of Roosevelt's fight was not as good as "the real thing."

Next Jane Addams seconded Roosevelt's nomination, the first woman ever to address the convention of a major political party. As she concluded, she was handed a yellow "Votes for Women" banner, and a demonstration began with delegates marching in the aisles. The former Harvard president Charles W. Eliot, who was backing Wilson, commented to the press on the speech: "It was a very spectacular proceeding, but it was in very bad taste." He explained: "Women have no proper share in a political convention."

Roosevelt's southern strategy and hope for a Progressive union of North and South was apparent in the next four seconding speeches by Alexander T. Hamilton of Georgia, the Union veteran General Horatio C. King, and Confederate veterans Colonel T. P. Lloyd of Florida, and General John H. McDowell of Tennessee. The seconding speeches continued with addresses by Henry J. Allen, former Governor Garvin of Rhode Island, the gubernatorial nominee Paul V. Collins of Minnesota, John J. Sullivan of Ohio, and the congressional candidate Robert S. Fischer of Arizona. The platform now being ready, the convention adopted the "contract with the people" presented by Dean Lewis. Finally, on the motion of Governor Carey of Wyoming, the Progressives nominated Roosevelt by acclamation, and quickly turned to the vice presidential nomination.

John M. Parker and Judge Lindsey had been mentioned and supported for the second spot on the ticket since both were former Democrats and Parker could appeal to the South, but when Parker nominated Governor Hiram W. Johnson of California and Lindsey delivered the first seconding speech, it was clear that Roosevelt had decided on the popular leader of the politically vital western state. Johnson was seconded by a battery of Progressive leaders: C. S. Wheeler of California, James R. Garfield, attorney Bainbridge Colby of New York,

THE AYES APPEAR TO HAVE IT—THE AYES HAVE IT!
WHEN THE COLONEL WAS NOMINATED BY ACCLAMATION

former Congressman Landis of Indiana, Raymond Robins, who called Johnson "the great knight errant of the last frontier," Gifford Pinchot, Governor Vessey of South Dakota, Bill Flinn, and the Negro John R. Gleed of New York. Johnson was also nominated by acclamation, and then Roosevelt and the fiery reform governor were escorted to the platform by the notification committees—the first time nominations had been accepted at a major political convention, something not done again until 1932 with another Roosevelt. As Roosevelt and Johnson acknowledged the cheers of the delegates, a huge banner was unfurled from the rafters inscribed with an altered verse from Kipling:

> Roosevelt and Johnson,
> New York and California,
> Hands across the continent.

> For there is neither east nor west,
> Border nor breed nor birth,
> When two strong men stand face to face
> Though they come from the end of the earth.

The delegates sang to the tune of "Maryland, My Maryland":

> Thou wilt not cower in the dust,
>   Roosevelt, O Roosevelt!
> Thy gleaming sword shall never rust,
>   Roosevelt, O Roosevelt!

The Colonel, obviously affected by emotion, with a tremor in his voice, for once was brief as he said:

... I come forward to thank you from my heart for the honor you have conferred upon me, and to say of course I accept. I am measuring my words, I have been President, I have seen and known much of life, and I hold it by far the greatest honor and the greatest opportunity that has ever come to me, to be called by you to the leadership for the time being of this great movement in the interests of the American people.

Johnson stepped forward to accept: "It is with the utmost solemnity, the deepest obligation, that I come to tell you that I have enlisted for the war." Johnson was described by one observer as never pleasant or smiling on the platform, having a voice that "grates and snarls and pierces, and puts you all on edge," possessing the ability to make men want to fight, and this day he ended his brief speech with a crusader's disregard for the odds: "I would rather go down to defeat with Theodore Roosevelt than to go to victory with any other Presidential candidate." Beveridge declared the first national convention of the Progressive Party adjourned as the delegates burst into the doxology.

The Progressive convention had revealed much about the new party. First, the party had publicly presented to the country an able corps of leaders led by Roosevelt and Johnson. It was clear that Roosevelt and the Progressives could not only staff a party and a campaign with such leaders as Beveridge, Dixon, Vessey, and the others but also a national administration if the voters gave the mandate. Progressive leadership was clearly viable and credible. Second, Roosevelt and the Progressives had offered the country a detailed and rational program percipient of the nation's needs. Unless the old parties dismissed the platform on grounds of principle, claiming that it subverted republicanism or smacked of socialism, the best they could do was misrepresent it or say that it was too utopian to be realized. The Progressives had captured the high ground of the campaign in terms of program. Third, the memorable and colorful conclave in Chicago had given the country the promise of a realignment and restructuring of the American party system. The new party was manifestly more than a rump movement in protest against Taft. Revealed, too, at Chicago was that the new party was not to be free of factionalism. But the public knew nothing yet of Amos Pinchot's bitterness or the widespread opposition to Perkins. What the public saw was that the Progressives could work together, run a convention, resolve delegate disputes, formulate a program, and organize for battle. In short, the convention had in large measure proved that the Progressive Party was indeed a viable alternative to the old parties.

Joel Spingarn wrote on the train returning to New York from Chicago:

> Like the Moslem home from Mecca, we have seen the sacred shrine;
> We have made a pilgrim's journey and bring back the word divine.
> We have tiptoed to the altar, we have opened up the door;
> Oh, the world will never seem to us the world it was before!

CHAPTER FIVE

THE CRUSADE

*The moose has left the wooded hill; his call rings
through the land.*

Progressive campaign song

Roosevelt returned to Sagamore Hill from the convention on August 9, and for the next several days conferred with party leaders. He opened the campaign on August 16 in Providence, Rhode Island, first touring New England, then heading westward and on to the Pacific coast. After speaking in Washington, Oregon, and California, the Colonel moved eastward again, whistle-stopping through Arizona, Colorado, Nebraska, Kansas, and other states, and then undertaking a six-state southern tour. October found Roosevelt returning to the Midwest to begin his final campaign drive. During the sixty days before his campaign was cut short by a would-be assassin, Roosevelt carried the Progressive message to thirty-two states and every section of the country, delivering over 150 speeches. In Rhode Island thousands purchased tickets to hear him; on September 5 the crowd at the state fair grounds in St. Paul, Minnesota, was estimated at fifty thousand; in Portland, Oregon, the path from the train to the waiting automobile was covered with roses; in Los Angeles traffic was halted and stores closed as the Progressive candidate was cheered by 200,000 lining the streets in a parade from the station to the Shrine Auditorium. He spoke from the back of whistle-stop trains, from automobiles, to crowds in city streets and clusters of citizens in small towns, at open fair grounds and in capacious halls, and almost everywhere he was greeted with the enthusiasm reserved for national heroes.

Other Progressive candidates emulated Roosevelt's vigorous campaigning. The vice presidential nominee Hiram Johnson delivered hundreds of speeches in an extensive twenty-two-state tour. Oscar Straus canvassed New York State by whistle-stop train in his bid for the governorship, while Albert J. Beveridge toured Indiana by automobile delivering five or six speeches a day, and other Progressive candidates like gubernatorial nominees Fraser Metzger in Vermont and Frank Funk in Illinois waged similarly active campaigns. Roosevelt and Johnson frequently appeared with state, congressional, and local candidates to emphasize that more was at stake in the election than the contest for the

White House. The Progressive state platforms and campaigns reiterated the national platform's demands for democracy and social justice while also addressing the peculiar needs of the various states, like free school books in Indiana and an end to the antiquated suffrage restrictions of Rhode Island. The new party, in short, was making every effort to translate progressive sentiment into a new partisanship and align state politics with national politics, to weave the varied threads of the pluralistic American polity into the seamless garment of the New Nationalism.

Yet it remained to be seen how effective the Progressive appeal would be. Optimism and fervor marked Bull Moose rallies for Beveridge, Straus, and other Progressive candidates, and Roosevelt was greeted with mass enthusiasm in city after city and state after state. But how many voters would the Progressive candidates lure from their traditional partisan homesteads? And how much of the popular acclaim for and interest in T.R. the colorful hero would be translated into votes for Roosevelt the candidate and the third party tickets? "He will draw crowds, of course—Jack Johnson draws crowds," observed the *Providence Journal* when Roosevelt campaigned in conservative Rhode Island. In the excitement of the campaign Beveridge and other Progressive leaders became confident of victory for the new party at all levels, but in private Roosevelt confided to close associates that the odds were against winning since the G.O.P. was well entrenched and the Democrats were effectively appealing to popular sentiment by proclaiming the Democracy as the party of progressive reform.

2

The Progressive Party was seeking to replace the Republican Party, but early in the campaign when a voice from a crowd asked about Taft, T.R. replied: "I never discuss dead issues." The Republicans indeed seemed moribund. Vice president James S. Sherman was kept from the campaign trail by an illness which resulted in his death before election day, and Taft decided not to campaign but to carry out his presidential duties in a "business-as-usual" fashion. On September 28 the president briefly emerged from seclusion to preach the conservative gospel to Beverly, Massachusetts, Republicans. The G.O.P. stood for the "preservation of institutions of civil liberty as they were handed down to us by our forefathers . . . ," Taft declared, while the Progressive platform contained "every new fad and theory" and was definitely "socialistic." Though it was a three-cornered race, Progressive and Democratic leaders told the press that the president and his party had been virtually eliminated, and thus while flailing the G.O.P. Roosevelt and Wilson reserved their big guns for each other. Taft was the forgotten man of the fall campaign, but in spite of this Progressives privately worried over how many votes the G.O.P. tickets might garner from habitual Republicans and the powerful Republican machines in states like New York and Indiana.

Wilson concentrated on the issues of the tariff and the trusts, pledging to lower the tariff and embark on a trust-busting crusade. His New Freedom program combined traditional Democratic appeals for a low tariff, which he sweepingly promised would both raise wages and lower the cost of living, with a call for the restoration of full-scale competition through destruction of the trusts. After conferring with the "people's attorney" Louis D. Brandeis, Wilson, who had been confused and largely uninformed about the problems of big business, decided that the Democracy should stand for "regulated competition."

ROOSEVELT FAVORED VOTES FOR WOMEN;
WILSON STRADDLED THE ISSUE IN 1912

Unfair trade practices and monopoly would be outlawed and crushed, thereby restoring and maintaining competition and free enterprise. He contrasted the New Freedom for "the men who are on the make" that would be brought about by trust busting with the "legalized monopoly" which would result from Roosevelt's New Nationalism. "This is a second struggle for emancipation," Wilson said in Denver on October 7. ". . . If America is not to have free enterprise, then she can have freedom of no sort whatever." As applied to business regulation, the New Freedom was little more than the old trust-busting approach to be carried out under an expanded antitrust law, but somehow under the magic of Wilson's eloquent rhetoric the old formula took on a new luster.

Although by late September Wilson was "ready to admit that we may have to have special tribunals," he continually charged that the Progressive proposals for tariff and trade commissions would lead to tyranny. Such commissions, he warned, would become captive to big business. Furthermore, the former president of Princeton opposed government by experts. "God forbid that in a democratic country we should resign the task of governing ourselves and give the government over to experts," Wilson declared in a Labor Day address.

Wilson agreed with most of the Progressive direct democracy planks, but insisted that women's suffrage was a question for the individual states. Privately, the Democratic candidate admitted he was undecided about that question. On social welfare and labor reforms the New Freedom was almost completely at odds with the New Nationalism. While Wilson professed sympathy for Roosevelt's goal of social and industrial justice, he took issue with the specific Progressive proposals. The abolition of child labor, the regulation of working hours, and most other labor matters were purely state issues, Wilson maintained, while minimum wage acts would hurt labor by tending to drive all wages down to the minimum level. In general, Wilson found Progressive social welfare and labor measures paternalistic and dictatorial, robbing free men of their right to run their own lives. In a speech to a workers' dinner on September 4 he declared: "No government has ever been beneficent when the attitude of the government was that it could take care of the people. Let me tell you that the only freedom exists where the people take care of the government."

Wilson's general strategy was to attack on the one hand the tyrannical tendencies he found in the Progressive program, and on the other hand to laud the humanitarian and democratic spirit which had led many reformers into the new party. Such reformers were merely misguided, whereas Roosevelt was a "self-appointed divinity" and enemy of the free enterprise system, who sought to sell out the progressive movement to the trusts and make himself a dictator in Washington. In the accents of classical liberalism, he reminded Americans: ". . . The history of liberty is a history of the limitation of governmental power, not the increase of it." Wilson presented himself as a man in the center between the impossibly reactionary Taft and the egotistical berserker Roosevelt. The Democratic nominee seemed to be offering voters progressivism without disturbing or fundamental change, reform without risky innovation, a politically potent appeal in a country where it had taken generations before laissez-faire capitalism and the conservative political hegemony were significantly challenged.

Roosevelt began his campaign in the role of an evangelist for the Progressive faith, invoking humanitarianism and the Social Gospel, presenting the Progressive platform as a noble new covenant which would bring, as he said in a speech in Revere, Massachusetts, on August 17, "a giant republic . . . throned on the seats of righteousness where the voice of the people strives to utter the biddings of divine right and where the soul of the people is bent on realizing the brotherhood of man." The Progressive campaign was to be one of moral uplift and social education, designed to convince Americans of their interdependence in modern society, and therefore of the necessity for a nationalist and general interest approach to economic and social life. With rallies combining elements of revival meetings and lyceum lectures, it was to be a new kind of campaign to promote the new party and the new politics. But before long Roosevelt found himself mired in the polemics of the old politics. Some of his opponents launched a smear campaign against him, and Wilson and Brandeis cleverly and effectively misrepresented and twisted the Progressive program. Thus, Roosevelt was soon placed on the defensive. His long public career made him vulnerable to the kind of attacks from which Wilson's brief career in politics was immune, and while the Republican and Democratic platforms classically straddled most issues, the specificity and detail of the Progressive platform and Roosevelt's speeches invited attacks from every side. The center had always been Roosevelt's favorite preserve in the past, and he sought to maintain this stance again in 1912 by lumping Wilson and the Democrats with the reactionary G.O.P. on the right, and pointing to the fourth candidate, the Socialist Eugene V. Debs, on the left. This equation, however, was unconvincing to many in the light of Wilson's reputation as a progressive and the parallels many newspapers found between T.R. and the Socialists. As the campaign progressed, Roosevelt found himself boxed in by his opponents, pictured as a leftist demagogue secretly serving the trusts. But the Colonel had never lost a battle for lack of self-defense. He hurled himself into the whirlwind of political rhetoric, turning from lectures to the colorful harangues which were the stock in trade of the old politics. Thus, the campaign of moral uplift and social education was soon abandoned in favor of a more conventional campaign. As the wolves closed in around the Bull Moose, it seemed natural to kick back.

3

On August 21, at the beginning of the campaign, Roosevelt journeyed to Wilkes-Barre, Pennsylvania, to take part in the golden jubilee of Father J. J. Curran. Roosevelt had become acquainted with the noted Roman Catholic priest during the coal strike of 1902 when he had relied on the counsel of this champion of the miners. Though the newspapers were skeptical, the trip was billed as strictly nonpolitical. The Colonel was indeed fond of the old priest, but the occasion was tailor-made for the kind of campaign Roosevelt was trying to wage. It gave him an opportunity to demonstrate the brotherhood of general interest and humanitarianism as he, a Protestant of old stock, stood side by side with immigrant coal miners, representatives from the different denominations, and Roman Catholic clergy in paying tribute to a man who had devoted his life to realizing Christian ideals in industrial and community life. Once again the close relationship between the Social Gospel and Progressivism and the transcendence of pluralism through the New Nationalism could be emphasized. The trip, however, was marred because Roosevelt was drawn into controversy with Pennsylvania's Republican boss.

The August issue of *Hearst's Magazine* published letters showing that John D. Archbold of the Standard Oil Company had given $25,000 to Senator Boies Penrose of Pennsylvania during the 1904 campaign when Roosevelt was running for reelection as president. Penrose, Nelson Aldrich's successor as Senate Republican leader, was the hulking, hard-drinking boss of the Keystone State G.O.P., a veteran politician whose career had involved nearly every form of graft known. Self-righteously Penrose explained on the floor of the Senate that the money was part of funds contributed by Standard Oil to the G.O.P. in 1904, and that in effect he had merely been acting on behalf of Roosevelt and the national committee. Both Penrose and Archbold claimed that T.R. knew of the contribution, and indeed had insisted on a larger sum in exchange for immunity from administration prosecution of Standard Oil. But Standard Oil had subsequently been prosecuted, and Penrose and Archbold could furnish no proof that the monies in question had ever been transmitted to the G.O.P. national campaign chest. In an ironic alliance, Penrose and La Follette joined in sponsoring a resolution calling for Senate investigation of campaign contributions in 1904, 1908, and 1912. Senator Moses E. Clapp of Minnesota, a Progressive, was made chairman of the special investigating subcommittee, but the other subcommittee members were hostile to Roosevelt and the new party. Time was found at the end of the Senate session to hear testimony from Penrose and Archbold, but then the subcommittee members propitiously left Washington and Clapp was forced to inform T.R. that his testimony would have to wait until Congress reassembled. Unable to have his day in court until October 4, Roosevelt turned to the platform and the newspapers to respond to the charges.

In Wilkes-Barre Roosevelt denounced Penrose's Senate speech: "Like a cuttle fish Penrose squirted ink at the enemy hoping to escape that way." In a public letter to Senator Clapp on August 28, he reviewed the whole controversy, producing letters from his files to corroborate various points. Roosevelt denied that he had ever solicited a contribution from Standard Oil, and he submitted letters he had sent to the Republican national chairman in October, 1904, stating that he had heard a rumor that Standard had contributed to the campaign fund and that if this were so the money was to be returned. Roosevelt said that he had been assured that no funds had been or would be received from the controversial company. Since no checks or receipts could be produced, the only proof of a contribution to the national fund was the word of Archbold and Penrose. Reviewing his relations as president with Standard Oil, Roosevelt offered his letter files on the subject for public inspection. The real point of the furor caused by the Hearst revelations, T.R. argued, was that both Archbold and Penrose had now publicly confessed to wrongdoing. The Senate Republican leader's testimony before the subcommittee, recounting that he himself told Archbold that Standard Oil would be in trouble unless the company contributed, "embodies a far worse accusation against him than I ever should have dreamed of making," Roosevelt concluded.

Roosevelt and Johnson

"For there is neither East nor West,
Border nor Breed nor Birth,
When two strong men stand face to face
Though they come from the ends of the earth."
—Kipling

1912 Progressive campaign poster:
T.R. and Governor Hiram W. Johnson of California

Theodore Roosevelt Collection, Harvard University

Senator Joseph M. Dixon of Montana,
National Chairman of the Progressive Party
Library of Congress

Governor Robert Perkins Bass of
New Hampshire
Library of Congress

Albert J. Beveridge of Indiana
Library of Congress

Oscar S. Straus of New York
Library of Congress

T.R. on the campaign trail in 1912
Theodore Roosevelt Collection, Harvard University
The Progressive candidate speaks at a country crossroads
Theodore Roosevelt Collection, Harvard University

T.R. voting in Oyster Bay, Long Island, November 5, 1912

Theodore Roosevelt Collection, Harvard University

A Congressional caucus at Progressive headquarters in Washington, D.C.: (left to right) Cong. Fred E. Lewis of Pennsylvania, Cong. William J. MacDonald of Michigan, Cong. Roy O. Woodruff of Michigan, Cong. Victor Murdock of Kansas, Theodore Roosevelt, Cong. William H. Hinebaugh of Illinois, James R. Garfield of Ohio, Senator Moses E. Clapp of Minnesota and Cong. Willis J. Hulings of Pennsylvania.

Theodore Roosevelt Collection, Harvard University

William Allen White of Emporia, Kansas.
The Kansas State Historical Society, Topeka

George W. Perkins, Executive Committee
Chairman of the Progressive Party
Library of Congress

Herbert Knox Smith of Connecticut
Library of Congress

Frances Kellor, Director of the Progressive
Service
Underwood & Underwood

Francis J. Heney of California
Library of Congress

Gifford Pinchot of Pennsylvania
Library of Congress

Edward P. Costigan of Colorado
Library of Congress

Raymond Robins of Illinois
Library of Congress

John M. Parker and T.R. on a bird watching field trip
in Louisiana in 1915
Theodore Roosevelt Collection, Harvard University

Theodore Roosevelt addresses supporters at his home Sagamore Hill
in the spring of 1916
Theodore Roosevelt Collection, Harvard University

T.R. and General Leonard Wood confer on preparedness at
Plattsburgh, New York, August, 1915

Theodore Roosevelt Collection, Harvard University

The Clapp hearings brought into sharp focus the whole question of campaign contributions. In 1904 contributions from corporations were not illegal, as they were by 1912, but the real purpose of the investigation was to smear the leaders of the Progressive Party. Ultimately Roosevelt and Beveridge, whose 1904 senatorial campaign fund was also investigated, were vindicated, but not before the accusations made national headlines. Progressives wondered how many voters subscribed to the theory that where there is smoke there is fire as Democrats and Republicans, taking cues from the Hearst furor, charged that the new

T.R. AND GEORGE W. PERKINS

party was a captive of the Wall Street interests who preferred Roosevelt's regulation plan to trust busting. Wilson maintained that United States Steel and other trusts were behind the Progressive Party. Roosevelt angrily responded that, except for George Perkins, men like Jacob H. Schiff, the noted Republican Wall Street financier who publicly announced his support for Wilson, and the officers of United States Steel, International Harvester, and other trusts were for either Wilson or Taft. This was true; few financiers connected with the major corporations agreed with Perkins's politics. But Schiff, the International Harvester officials Cyrus H. McCormick and Thomas D. and David B. Jones, and Wall Street's Bernard M. Baruch, all Wilson supporters, were not leading figures in the campaign, while Perkins was.

Both the Democratic and Progressive parties made much of their financial support by the average voter. The Democrats launched "dollar drives." "Wanted, 100,000 earnest citizens to contribute each one honest dollar to elect a President of and for the People, no trust money accepted," read the message of a *New York World* cartoon which gave the address of the treasurer of the Democratic National Committee, and showed a man, lunchpail over his arm, reaching into his pocket. Roosevelt admitted that Perkins and others had given large sums, but maintained that "we who fight for the cause of justice and fair dealing . . . have only a few supporters among the very rich." He publicly called attention to the five dollars sent him by an Italian laborer, representing two days wages, the ten dollars young Hermann Hagedorn had donated from the sale of a poem, the dollar from a veteran in an old soldiers' home, and many other such contributions. This propaganda, however, avoided the truth about political campaigns in modern society. Wilson's and Roosevelt's campaigns may both have been popular movements related to a new politics, but parties needed the kind of big money that only a wealthy few or an established political machine could provide, as was evident after the accounts were added up and the books closed.

The Democratic National Committee spent a whopping $1,110,952.25 in 1912. With the scent of victory in the air, the Democracy was not lacking for riders on the bandwagon. Forty major contributors gave more than the total donated by 88,229 small contributors. Schiff gave $12,500; Baruch and the Democratic organization of Kentucky each donated the same sum; while the Jones brothers of Harvester donated $20,000. Taft's campaign fund was reported as totaling $904,828, with Andrew Carnegie donating $35,000 and J. P. Morgan $25,000. The Progressive National Committee spent the more modest sum of $596,405.04. There were seven major contributors: financier August Heckscher gave $25,000, as did philanthropist Alexander Smith Cochran and T.R.'s brother-in-law Douglas Robinson; cousin W. Emlen Roosevelt contributed $50,000; Robert Bacon, secretary of state under T.R., gave $10,000; the National Committee treasurer Elon H. Hooker and his family contributed $12,500; while the publisher Frank A. Munsey donated $135,000 and George W. Perkins $130,000. The sum of $163,657.15 was received from smaller contributions.

The significance of these figures is clear. The old parties could turn to political organizations like the Democratic machine of Kentucky and faithful party patrons, but the new party with its seven major contributors to the Democrats' forty was hard put to compete. It is inconceivable that a new party could have kept so prominently in the running without the connections Roosevelt was able to provide. The sum received from small contributors did not equal the total of the Munsey and Perkins donations. Furthermore, the Roosevelt family gave a total of at least $77,500, adding the contributions of Douglas

Robinson, Emlen Roosevelt, and the smaller sum of $2,500 given by cousin George E. Roosevelt. This meant that not only was a Roosevelt the third largest contributor (Emlen's $50,000), but the total given by the family surpassed the combined donations of all other major contributors except Munsey and Perkins. These figures indicate several facts not only about the Progressive Party, but about reform movements and third parties in general.

First, it is evident that it is next to impossible for a major party to rely solely on popular contributions. The increase in organizational expenses necessary

THE REVOLUTIONIST

to raise larger sums from the public than were garnered in 1912 would probably have had to come from the same sources a party usually depends on. Second, it seems that reform movements and third parties are more likely to be forced to rely on a few large contributors than are established political organizations, particularly since reformers can be expected to alienate many ordinary sources of political income. The difficulty in financing a reform movement was reflected in Roosevelt's solicitude for Perkins's feelings about the trust plank at the convention. The Colonel later said that there would have been a place for

Perkins in his cabinet. Munsey and Perkins did not join the Progressive Party in order to "buy" the party or obtain special favors for their business interests, but Roosevelt was well aware how much he needed their support. Roosevelt's integrity, of course, was not for sale, and in 1913 he broke with Munsey over matters of party policy, but in so far as he could conscientiously do so he tried to give Perkins's and Munsey's opinions every consideration. The leaders of the old parties faced the problems of dealing with the wishes of large contributors too—indeed, T.R. was familiar with this from his years in the White House— but many reformers thought that a party advocating a new politics should be different. Faced with the mundane realities of paying the bills for the new politics, Roosevelt knew better. But he could not admit this truth in public, for he was in a sense a prisoner of progressivism as well as its prophet.

Perkins, the "dough moose," was widely attacked during the campaign, but Bull Moose Roosevelt was the chief target for the opposition guns. The attacks of Archbold and Penrose were just the beginnings of the torrents of abuse. Every aspect of Roosevelt's long career was twisted and smeared. The *New York Sun* predicted that once elected Roosevelt would be president for life: "As the Emperor Sigismund was above grammar, so is Theodore Rex above recall, except that of his promises and his principles." George Harvey, an early Wilson booster, in an editorial in his *North American Review* entitled "Roosevelt or the Republic," stated that "Roosevelt was the first President whose chief personal characteristic was mendacity, the first to glory in duplicity, the first braggart, the first bully, the first betrayer of a friend who ever occupied the White House." Harvey found T.R. "half mad," but Colonel Henry Watterson, the Louisville, Kentucky editor and conservative Democrat, went further. "More than ever the *Courier-Journal* is sure of his insanity," read an August editorial. "If he be not of disordered mind, the record would show him a monster of depravity and turpitude." His election would mean "the end of the Republic and the beginning of a Dictatorship." Old and baseless stories that Roosevelt was a drunkard were revived. The *Iron Ore,* a small Republican newspaper in Michigan, was typical of the depths to which some of T.R.'s enemies descended in 1912 when it proclaimed on October 12: "Roosevelt lies, and curses in a most disgusting way; he gets drunk too, and that not infrequently, and all his intimates know about it." Roosevelt decided to stop the rumor that he was a drunkard once and for all and instituted a libel suit against the newspaper, but most of the attacks and smears stopped short of libel and were not so easily squelched.

Yet more damaging to the Progressive cause than smears were the Democrats' misrepresentations of the new party's program. In an effort to win the labor vote, Louis D. Brandeis attacked the Progressive platform in a speech to the Massachusetts American Federation of Labor on September 17: "Nowhere in that long and comprehensive platform . . . can there be found one word approving the fundamental right of labor to organize, or even recognizing this right. . . ." Wilson repeated this charge to workers in Fall River, Massachusetts, on September 26. Progressives protested that this was simply untrue. The

Progressive platform not only stated that the party favored unions, but pledged the party to prohibiting strike injunctions, providing jury trials in cases of contempt arising from labor disputes, and creating a federal department of labor. But President Samuel Gompers of the A.F.L., who had been converted to Wilson after meeting with him in July, declared that while the new party advocated many needed measures, labor had found it impossible to obtain what it wanted under the Roosevelt administration. Organized labor had decided to invest in the Democratic Party rather than follow the Progressives' siren call. Moreover, there were ethnic factors operative among union members that militated against joining with the Progressives, for in many urban areas immigrant workers had over a period of time become wedded to the dominant Democratic machines. Perhaps, too, workers were alienated by the intellectual and mainly old stock leadership of the new party.

While Wilson stumped the country with the message of the New Freedom, Brandeis found a platform for their views in the pages of *Collier's* magazine. Norman Hapgood, editor of the magazine and an enthusiastic Wilson supporter, invited Brandeis to write articles on the trust question, and Brandeis obliged by contributing two articles which purported to prove that Roosevelt wished to legalize monopoly and that the Democrats offered the only solution to the trust problem. Brandeis also wrote five editorials attacking the new party, which appeared anonymously on Hapgood's editorial pages in September and October. *Collier's* had until this time ardently supported Roosevelt and the Progressive Party, a position reflecting the views of the publisher Robert J. Collier and the associate editor Mark Sullivan. The damage done the Progressive cause by the Brandeis-Hapgood partnership was great. Not only were Wilson's contentions that Roosevelt wanted to legalize monopoly and turn the government over to big business given wide circulation by *Collier's*, but it seemed as if one of the country's most influential magazines had turned against its former hero. After the October 19 issue Collier fired Hapgood and directed *Collier's* back into the Bull Moose camp, but the elections were fast approaching and it was too late to counter Brandeis's work. Not until the November 9 issue were readers informed that the author of the five editorials had been one of Wilson's advisors. "... We were not made aware until recently how frequent a contributor he had been to these pages ... ," *Collier's* lamented.

The political professionals in the Progressive Party countered the Democratic advance by employing all the organizational and publicity techniques of modern electioneering, regardless of their relevance to the new politics of education, issues, and reason. Celebrities were enlisted in the crusade: William Gillette, the handsome "Sherlock Holmes" of the stage, was sent on a speaking tour; Lillian Russell, wife of the Pennsylvania Progressive Alexander P. Moore, was photographed purchasing Bull Moose buttons at New York headquarters; Thomas A. Edison's endorsement of the new party was given wide publicity. The national publicity bureau began publication of the slick and colorfully illustrated *Progressive Bulletin* magazine. Frederick Palmer and Will Irwin organized a syndicate of Progressive writers to supply copy to the newspapers, with Richard Harding Davis, C. P. Connolly, Edna Ferber, William Allen White, Franklin P. Adams, and John T. McCutcheon among the contributors. Ethnic appeals seemed out of place for a party dedicated to the New Nationalism, but Progressive headquarters issued campaign literature in Italian, Yiddish, and other languages. A Danish National Progressive League, Austrian and Hungarian Club of New York, Italo-American Progressive Club in Rhode Island, National German-American Roosevelt League, and other ethnic groups were organized. The poet George Sylvester Viereck wrote to members of the National

DON QUIXOTE

German-American Roosevelt League of their hero, who was of Dutch and English ancestry: "I need hardly point out to you that Colonel Roosevelt is the only candidate in the race in whose veins flows German blood, who has received part of his education in Germany and who refuses to tie this country to the apron-strings of Great Britain."

The main burden of the Progressive counteroffensive, of course, fell on Roosevelt's shoulders. Both old parties were making much of the tariff issue, the G.O.P. boasting of the "full dinner pail" as the party had for decades, the Democrats promising that a low tariff would reduce the cost of living and cure many other economic ills. Roosevelt countered that the tariff was a "red herring" being used by the old parties to divert attention from more basic issues like social justice. The tariff should not be a question of protection versus virtual free trade, he insisted, but rather a problem to be worked out "scientifically" by a comission of economic experts. Facts, not slogans, were needed. Wilson's objections to strong government commissions to regulate the tariff and business, T.R. continued, resembled earlier attacks made by businessmen against the Interstate Commerce Commission and public utility commissions. As for Wilson's opposition to the minimum wage, Roosevelt replied that the Democratic nominee was obviously ignorant of working conditions: a minimum wage would not depress wages, because employers were already paying wages as low as the labor market would allow. Hiram Johnson added that Wilson's stand on the minimum wage showed he was lacking in either "intellect or heart." Wilson found the solution to labor's problems in trust busting. Yet competition, Roosevelt noted, did not necessarily produce good working conditions. Speaking in Colorado, the Progressive candidate pointed out that the Colorado Fuel and Iron Company owned by the Rockefellers was not a trust, and yet its working conditions were among the worst in the industry. The same was true of other major companies in other industries. In short, the economic problems of labor and the public went beyond the suppression of monopoly.

Over and over Roosevelt insisted that the Progressives did not propose to destroy free enterprise and legalize monopoly, as Wilson and Brandeis charged. He too favored retaining and expanding the antitrust law, Roosevelt said, repeating in speeches and statements the long list of unfair trade practices to be outlawed which he had enumerated in his Chicago "Confession." The main point, he argued, was that government regulation and management through a trade commission had to replace ineffective regulation by lawsuit. Roosevelt's defense, however, would have been more convincing if the Progressive platform had specifically endorsed the Sherman Act. And he had no answer to the charge that big business might subvert a trade commission. Moreover, he remained ambiguous about competition while Wilson lauded it as an essential of the New Freedom. In September T.R. declared that "our proposal is to abolish monopoly and restore competition where possible, and where this is not possible, then absolutely to control the monopoly in the interest of the general public." But just before the election he flatly proclaimed in a statement for *Collier's:* "I am not for monopoly. We intend to restore competition. . . ." The voters had reason to be confused. In response to attacks from Wilson and Brandeis, Roosevelt gradually shifted to a stand on competition that resembled the philosophy of progressive Republicans and Democrats, although the crucial distinctions between the regulatory commission and lawsuit approaches remained clear. The shift on competition was a campaign accommodation, and one easily made, for Roosevelt had always been uncertain about competition and monopoly. But if the shift was politically necessary, if expediency dictated paying homage to the American competition totem, then the decision should have come earlier in the campaign before Brandeis and Wilson had a chance to deliver their telling blows.

Behind the differences on specific issues like the minimum wage lay the ideological dichotomy between the New Nationalism and the New Freedom, a split which Roosevelt elaborated in a speech in San Francisco on September 14. Taking as his text Wilson's statement that "the history of liberty is a history of the limitation of governmental power, not the increase of it," Roosevelt proceeded to spell out the differences between the New Nationalism and the

BETTER BE CAREFUL!

New Freedom. Wilson's assertion, he said, was "a bit of outworn academic doctrine which was kept in the schoolroom and the professorial study for a generation after it had been abandoned by all who had experience of actual life." This laissez-faire doctrine, one which Wilson himself was admitting had exceptions, had some relevance in "a primitive community" but none in a modern industrial society.

So long as governmental power existed exclusively for the king and not at all for the people, then the history of liberty was a history of the limitation of governmental power. But now the governmental power rests in the people, and the kings who enjoy privilege are the kings of the financial and industrial world; and what they clamor for is the limitation of governmental power, and what the people sorely need is the extension of governmental power.

Wilson, said T.R., was "fond of asserting his platonic devotion to the purposes of the Progressive Party," but such devotion was "utterly worthless" because "he antagonizes the only means by which those purposes can be made effective," the use of the powers of the federal government. Roosevelt enumerated the social welfare problems facing the nation—occupational disease, factory working conditions, industrial accidents, and general living conditions—all of which required "an extension of government control" on a national basis, and all of which Wilson declared were matters for the states. Wilson's philosophy left the federal government powerless to deal with these problems. Furthermore, the Democracy's traditional concept of the use of the taxing power only to raise revenue made any sort of protective tariff or consumer regulation impossible. "The people of the United States have but one instrument which they can effectively use against the colossal combinations of business—and that instrument is the government of the United States. . . ." Wilson proposed to "throw away" this "one great weapon" of the people. The issue was clearly drawn. Wilson was against "using the power of the government to help the people to whom the government belongs." Roosevelt continued:

We take flat issue with him. We propose to use the government as the most efficient instrument for the uplift of our people as a whole; we propose to give a fair chance to the workers to strengthen their rights. We propose to use the whole power of the government to protect all those who, under Mr. Wilson's laissez-faire system, are trodden down in the ferocious, scrambling rush of an unregulated and purely individualistic industrialism.

4

In October, as Roosevelt returned to campaign in the Midwest, he was still on the defensive. His charges that the Democratic Party in state after state was dominated by bosses like Murphy of Tammany, Taggart of Indiana, and Sullivan of Illinois were accurate, but they had fallen flat because of well-publicized quarrels Wilson had had with the Democratic bosses of New Jersey and New York over the state tickets. The Progressive candidate had appealed for social legislation, but the leaders of the A.F.L. remained in the Democratic camp, and the new party's program had convinced many that Roosevelt was a radical and socialist. As the prophet of the New Nationalism, Roosevelt had scored debater's points against Wilson by showing that the New Freedom was not "new" and stood for "freedom" only in the limited, laissez-faire sense. But this just seemed to put Wilson in the American mainstream and make the New Nationalism appear a risky break with the past rather than the logical development of modern trends and conditions. Wilson was winning popular response on the trust issue, forcing T.R. to explain repetitiously that Progressives did not propose to turn the government over to trust magnates. The chances for Progressive victory, never bright, seemed to be slipping further away as the campaign entered the final stretch.

Roosevelt's voice was hoarse and rasping as he spoke in Chicago on October 12. The months of campaigning since February had taken toll on his throat and strength. The next day he canceled scheduled speeches in Illinois, Indiana, and Wisconsin, but on October 14 insisted on keeping a speaking date in Milwaukee.

Arriving in Milwaukee, Roosevelt went to the Hotel Gilpatrick to rest before the evening's speech. Shortly before eight his party left the hotel and entered a waiting open-topped automobile. Roosevelt stood up in the vehicle to acknowledge the cheers of the crowd. Suddenly from the crowd a pistol fired, and T.R., hit in the chest, slumped to the car seat. Roosevelt's secretary Elbert Martin dove over the side of the car and tackled the would-be assassin, a New York saloonkeeper named John Schrank. Schrank was a deranged anti–third-term fanatic, who had been told in a dream by William McKinley that Roosevelt was his murderer. In the car Roosevelt coughed and put his hand to his mouth to see if there was any blood. There was none, and Roosevelt decided that the bullet had not hit a lung. He therefore determined, with that mixture of calculation, bravery, and showmanship that was characteristically his, to proceed to the auditorium and make his speech. Refusing to go to a hospital, he said: "... This is my big chance, and I am going to make that speech if I die doing it."

Walking out on the stage, the Colonel raised his hand to silence the cheers. He informed his audience that he had just been shot, "but it takes more than that to kill a Bull Moose." The bullet had gone through his metal spectacle case and his folded manuscript, probably saving his life, and he held these up for the audience to see. A stenographer took down his words as he spoke:

First of all, I want to say this about myself: I have altogether too important things to think of to feel any concern over my own death; and now I cannot speak to you insincerely within five minutes of being shot. I am telling you the literal truth when I say that my concern is for many other things. . . . I want you to understand that I am ahead of the game, anyway. No man has had a happier life than I have led; a happier life in every way. . . . I am in this cause with my whole heart and soul. I believe that the Progressive movement is for making life a little easier for all our people; a movement to take the burdens off the men and especially the women and children of this country.

Foolhardy he may have been, but it was his supreme moment. His opponents had said that he was motivated only by ambition in this campaign. Now he could prove definitely—or so he thought—that he cared more for the Progressive movement than for his own life. Roosevelt's credibility had been constantly attacked, but now the people would hear and read what he had to say with new respect. The assassination attempt seemed to elevate him above petty politics. The unifying bond of universal sympathy evoked by the shooting might be converted into the spirit of brotherhood, nationalist vision, and "uplift" which he believed to be necessary for Progressive success. By being shot, Roosevelt had recovered the offensive.

I am telling you the literal truth when I say that my concern is not for my own life.
I am in this cause with my whole heart and soul; I believe in the Progressive movement the betterment of mankind, a movement for making life a little easier for all our people, a movement to take the burden off the man and especially the woman in this country who is most oppressed.

A MESSAGE

He continued his rambling remarks, saying that unless the Progressive movement succeeded the American people would become divided, "have-nots" against "haves," ethnic group against ethnic group. "When that day comes then such incidents as this tonight will be commonplace in our history." He recalled that in his career he had never cared about a man's birthplace or the way he worshiped God, that he had worked in the army and government with Catholics, Protestants, Jews, Germans, Irish, and Poles. Likewise, the Progressive Party appealed to rich and poor, laborer and businessman, to stand together for the common good, "to stand by one another without regard to differences of class or occupation."

Then the Colonel turned his attention to Wilson, returning to the partisan issues of the campaign. He recalled that when he became president the anti-trust law "was practically a dead letter and the interstate commerce law in as poor condition." He had had to "revive" both laws. Now, on the basis of his past experience, he proposed to do more. He did not propound legalized monopoly, but rather the creation of a commission which would force corporations to live up to requirements spelled out in new legislation. Wilson, on the other hand, proposed old remedies, and had done nothing as governor about the trusts in New Jersey, a well-known refuge for such corporations. "The chapter describing what Mr. Wilson has done about the trusts in New Jersey would read precisely like a chapter describing the snakes in Ireland, which ran: 'There are no snakes in Ireland.'" The Democratic platform and candidate were committed to "the old flintlock, muzzle-loaded doctrine of states rights, and I have said distinctly that we are for the people's rights." The Republican bosses had tried to stop the movement but failed. "They did not like me, and the longer they live the less cause they will have to like me. But while they do not like me, they dread you." The Democrats had misrepresented the Progressive program, but their own position was now clear—they opposed laws limiting working hours, the abolition of child labor, a minimum wage, and other needed social reforms. Roosevelt concluded: "I ask you to look at our declaration and hear and read our platform about social and industrial justice and then, friends, vote for the Progressive ticket . . . , for only by voting for that platform can you be true to the cause of progress throughout this Union."

The final weeks of the campaign were dominated by news of Roosevelt's convalescence and recovery from his chest wound. By October 30 he was well enough to speak at a mammoth rally at Madison Square Garden, where he delivered a sermon-like appeal for the Progressive faith. "The doctrines we preach reach back to the Golden Rule and the Sermon on the Mount. They reach back to the commandments delivered at Sinai. All that we are doing is to apply those doctrines in the shape necessary to make them available for meeting the living issues of our own day." It was nonsense, Roosevelt continued, to claim that social welfare measures would destroy the character of the American people:

Our people work hard and faithfully. They do not wish to shirk their work. They must feel pride in the work for the work's sake. But there must be bread for the work. There must be a time for play when the men and women are young. When they grow old there must be the certainty of rest under conditions free from the haunting terror of utter poverty. . . . We must shape conditions so that no one can own the spirit of the man who loves his task and gives the best there is in him to that task. . . . We are striving to meet the needs of all . . . , and to meet them in such fashion that all alike shall feel bound together in the bond of a common brotherhood, where each works hard for himself and for those dearest to him, and yet feels that he must also think of his brother's rights because he is in very truth that brother's keeper.

He concluded:

We, here in America, hold in our hands the hope of the world, the fate of the coming years, and shame and disgrace will be ours if in our eyes the light of high resolve is dimmed, if we trail in the dust the golden hopes of men.

Roosevelt made another appearance in New York City, on November 1, to endorse Straus and the Progressive state ticket; and on November 4, the day before the elections, he toured Long Island and made a final speech in Oyster Bay. The next day the Colonel drove down to the village to cast his vote, and went back to Sagamore Hill to await the returns.

The campaign of 1912 was over at long last. The country had been in almost continual political turmoil since that day in February when Roosevelt tossed his hat into the ring challenging the renomination of President Taft. Since then a new party had been born, transforming the political scene, the Democratic Party had chosen to follow the progressive movement by nominating a reformer, and the nation had witnessed a virtually unprecedented discussion of substantive issues. Women's suffrage, the minimum wage, primaries, child labor, government by commission, and other issues long discussed in civic-minded periodicals, on the state and city level, and by different groups of reformers now had become the stuff of national political debate, clearly indicating that the Progressive Party represented the nationalization of the reform movement and the synthesis of the movement's concerns and programs. For a change it seemed as if as much light as heat had been generated in an election year. Politicians and parties found it hard to avoid taking stands, thereby to some extent fulfilling the Progressive demand for an issue-oriented and ideological new politics. From the Progressive standpoint, therefore, the strategy of a new reform partisanship had already paid dividends before the votes were counted.

Taft's performance throughout the year had been one of ineptitude and blunder, but he had succeeded in clearly presenting the voters with a conservative option. Wilson had waged an effective campaign, capitalizing on progressive sentiment, keeping his party in line by his obeisance to traditional Democratic doctrines on the tariff and states rights, presenting himself as a rational and respectable moderate between the poles of reaction and radicalism. Wilson had, in short, added a center to the equation of partisan ideological polarization the Progressives sought to promote, a development not anticipated by the new party. Roosevelt had proved an eloquent and able spokesman for the advanced wing of the progressive movement, but he had made grave tactical errors in the campaign. His choice of Perkins for party executive chairman brought dissension within his own ranks and left the new party open to the charge of Wall Street influence. His handling of the trust issue was sometimes confusing, as he praised and damned the Sherman Act and wobbled on the question of monopoly. His attempt to build a lily-white party in the South, and his extensive fall campaign tour of the South, were worse than useless—they were counterproductive in terms of the new party's image and wasteful of precious campaign time.

Under heavy attacks from the opposition, Roosevelt had been diverted from his original campaign of proselytizing and social education, and became repetitious and defensive, only recovering momentum in the final weeks of the campaign. The new party had thus been unable to dictate the terms and the ideological configuration of the election debate completely.

Yet, even had Roosevelt been able to stick to his original missionary strategy, or succeeded in bringing about complete ideological polarization between the Progressives and the old parties, he probably could not have expanded his original progressive Republican and middle class base of support. The refusal of some Republican insurgents to join the new party, and Wilson's campaign for the Democrats, demonstrated the resiliency and tenacity of the traditional party system. Equally important, Roosevelt and the Progressives refused to stoop to conquer. Committed to the vision of an organic commonwealth, Roosevelt declined to make interest group appeals, to appeal to labor as labor or the poor as the poor. He was willing to offer salvation, but only to those who would embrace the straight and narrow path of the tenets of the Progressive faith. In 1912 Roosevelt was an innovator, a prophet of change and new strategies for reform, but in order to win the day the New Nationalism required a comprehensive national religion, catholicity, not a new sectarianism.

CHAPTER SIX

COUNTING THE BALLOTS AND CHARTING THE FUTURE

We have fought the good fight, we have kept the faith, and we have nothing to regret. Probably we have put the ideal a little higher then we can expect the people as a whole to take offhand.

T.R.

We are full of spirit for the long pull ahead.

Richard Washburn Child

As most political analysts had predicted, Wilson was elected president as a result of the split in the normal Republican vote. Roosevelt carried Pennsylvania, Michigan, Minnesota, South Dakota, Washington, and 11 of California's 13 electoral votes for a total of 88 electoral votes. Taft carried only Utah and Vermont and 8 electoral votes. Wilson won the rest of the states and 435 electoral votes. The popular vote was Wilson 6,301,254; Roosevelt 4,127,788; and Taft 3,485,831. Though Wilson's victory was an electoral landslide, he polled only 41.8 percent of the popular vote, and was thus a minority president. Moreover, he polled 109,411 fewer votes than Bryan had in 1908, and fewer votes than Bryan won even in 1896 and 1900. Wilson ran behind the Democratic state tickets in Massachusetts, Ohio, Illinois, Missouri, and other states. In short, he had won with a minimal Democratic vote. His was a partisan triumph.

The combined total for Roosevelt and Taft was also below Taft's vote in 1908 and T.R.'s in 1904. The Socialist Eugene V. Debs with 901,255 votes more than doubled his total of 1908, winning votes that had gone to the old parties four years earlier. Some observers considered the Socialist increase and the Progressive vote a measure of the growth of radicalism in the United States. This was probably claiming too much, but the combined Socialist and Bull Moose votes did seem to demonstrate widespread dissatisfaction with and rebellion against the old parties.

Roosevelt's vote was spectacular in many ways. Not only did he carry five states and most of California, but he came close to victory in nine additional states and ran second in twenty-three states. In Kansas 1.77 percent of the total vote separated Wilson from T.R., in Maine 2.03 percent, and in Iowa 3.77 percent. In Pennsylvania, Michigan, South Dakota, and Washington the race was not even close. T.R. carried nearly every county in Michigan and South Dakota, and polled 35.22 percent of the vote in Washington to Wilson's 26.9 percent and Taft's 21.82 percent, while the Keystone State vote was Roosevelt 447,426, Wilson 395,619, and Taft 273,305. Generally, Roosevelt ran well in the cities, carrying Pittsburgh, Detroit, Chicago, Los Angeles, and other urban centers, though his rural vote was high in many states as well. In the East T.R. carried Pennsylvania and ran strongly in Maine, Vermont, and New Jersey, but came in behind Taft in New Hampshire, Massachusetts, Rhode Island, Connecticut, and New York. For all his efforts, Roosevelt made little impression in the South and border states, polling a vote lower than the normal G.O.P. vote and running behind Taft in several states. Roosevelt's strongest showing was in the Midwest and West, the stronghold of the G.O.P. and progressive Republicanism. Nationally, he did well only in those states where the normal Republican vote was high, although he ran poorly in some traditionally Republican states like New Hampshire. All the states he carried were usually found in the G.O.P. column and had a normal Republican vote large enough so that a fraction thereof could win the state. For instance, in 1908 Minnesota cast 195,843 votes for Taft and 109,401 for Bryan; in 1912 the vote was T.R. 125,856, Taft 64,334, and Wilson 106,426. Nationally, Roosevelt failed to garner many Democratic votes, but the majority of the G.O.P.'s normal vote was his by a margin of over half a million.

Placed in the perspective of all the presidential elections before and after 1912, Roosevelt's vote appears even more extraordinary. The Populist Party in 1892 won over one million votes, or 8.5 percent of the total, carrying four states and one vote each from two states for a total of twenty-two electoral votes, whereas T.R. polled 27.4 percent of the total popular vote and eighty-eight electoral votes from six states. In fact, no third party candidate for the presidency before or after 1912 has ever received so large a percentage of the popular vote or as many electoral votes as Roosevelt did. Only La Follette in 1924 and George C. Wallace in 1968 have received even so many popular votes. Moreover, never before or since 1912 has a Republican presidential nominee been so badly defeated or run third in the popular and electoral votes.

Taft's debacle, however, was expected. It was in many ways remarkable that Taft did as well as he did, considering his unpopularity, that he did not campaign much for reelection, and that his renomination was widely viewed as dishonestly won. Taft carried only two states, but he came in second in nineteen states, including Massachusetts, New York, Ohio, and Michigan. The G.O.P. had been able to muster 3,485,831 votes with a candidate who was a liability and with most of the issues working against the party.

In sum, the election figures showed that Wilson won with a minimal Democratic vote, Roosevelt placed second in a strong showing, and Taft ran a poor third but still polled nearly 3.5 million votes. These are what might be termed the surface results of the election. But what did the results signify? Voting figures provide certain obvious conclusions, like the facts that Roosevelt came in second in twenty-three states and Taft in nineteen, but in order to understand the reason for the election results it is necessary to study the political, economic, and social realities behind the ballots. By utilizing the information provided by the U. S. Census of 1910, and examining the political situation in the various states, it is possible to reach a number of probable though tentative conclusions about who voted for Roosevelt and why. Such an analysis, of course, will also shed light on who voted for Wilson and Taft and why.

2

The historian George E. Mowry has noted that Roosevelt generally ran stronger in urban rather than rural areas, though his work presents no detailed analysis of election figures. More recently Alon Jeffrey's study of the Progressive Party in Vermont found that Roosevelt indeed did well in the largest towns in the Green Mountain State (the largest town in Vermont had a population of 20,468), but that he polled his highest percentage of the vote—40.2 percent—in those towns with the highest rate of growth, 31.1 percent. These figures suggest the possible thesis that Roosevelt ran well in urban counties and best in urban and more densely populated counties with high rates of population growth, and conversely that he made a poor showing in counties losing population and those with the lowest density of population. An analysis of the vote in urban counties across the nation, and of the vote in counties in a sample of eleven northern and western states, in fact bears out this thesis. Oklahoma and Idaho, where Roosevelt was not on the ballot, and the traditionally Democratic southern and border states, have been excluded from consideration. Categories such as "city," "major city," "densest in population," and others employed in this analysis are taken directly from the U. S. Census definitions for each state. The eleven states were selected as representative of states where Roosevelt won, placed second, and placed third.

The national rate of population growth in the decade 1900-10 was 21 percent. Fourteen cities in the North and West (excluding Oklahoma and Idaho) of over 25,000 population in 1910 had grown at a rate of over 100 percent in the years 1900-10. Taft carried none of the counties in which these cities were located, Wilson won 4, and Roosevelt won 8 counties in which ten of these cities were located. Except for Schenectady, New York; Huntington, West Virginia; and Flint, Michigan; all of the fastest-growing cities were west of the Mississippi. Roosevelt carried the county where Flint was located but lost the other two to Wilson. Of the 22 northern and western counties of over 25,000 population in 1910 which had grown by over 100 percent in the previous decade, Taft carried 3, Wilson 7, and Roosevelt 12. Roosevelt won 2 of the 3 of these counties east of the Mississippi.

If we look at the sample of eleven states, much the same pattern is found in most states. In New York State Roosevelt came in third, but he placed second in

8 of the 24 counties with the highest density of population, the five boroughs of New York City, and 4 of the 7 counties with a growth rate of over 25 percent in the decade 1900-10. On the other hand, Roosevelt came in third in all 15 counties which had lost population since 1900 and all 13 counties with the lowest density of population. Taft carried 8 of the 15 counties losing population and 8 of the 13 New York counties with the lowest density of population, Wilson winning the remainder. In New Jersey Taft carried no counties, but Roosevelt carried Essex, Passaic, and Cumberland counties. Essex and Passaic were part of greater metropolitan New York City, and contained 5 of the Garden State's 14 major cities and 2 of the 6 cities with a growth rate of over 50 percent. In Pennsylvania Roosevelt won the state and the majority of counties, running strongly in both urban and rural areas. The state rate of growth from 1900 to 1910 was 21.6 percent: of the 16 counties with a growth rate of over 25 percent Roosevelt carried 13 and Wilson 3, while of the 19 counties which had lost population Wilson won 8 and T.R. 11. Roosevelt also won in Michigan, carrying a majority of all counties, 8 of the 9 counties where the largest cities were located, 7 of the 8 counties with densest population, and most of the counties which had grown by over 25 percent since 1900. Taft's and Wilson's support was confined mainly to rural counties. Eight of Wilson's 10 counties had lost population, and 8 of Taft's 11 counties were among the Michigan counties with the lowest density of population. Most of the state's major cities had experienced rapid growth in the decade 1900-10: Detroit 63 percent, Lansing 89.4 percent, Flint 194.2 percent. It is interesting to note that Saginaw, the only major city in Michigan carried by Wilson, had the smallest rate of growth—19.3 percent—and had lost population in the decade 1890-1900. In neighboring Indiana Roosevelt and Taft trailed far behind Wilson, but T.R. carried urban Lake County, which had grown by a phenomenal 118.7 percent from 1900 to 1910, a growth rate more than 60 percent higher than that for any other Hoosier county. Booming East Chicago, Gary, and Hammond were located in this industrially expanding area. Fifty-six, or over half, of the Hoosier counties had lost population in contrast to Michigan's rapid growth. In Illinois the race between Wilson and Roosevelt was close, the Democratic nominee polling 35.34 percent of the vote to T.R.'s 33.72 percent, with Taft left with 22.13 percent. Roosevelt won 2 of the 3 counties which had grown by 50 percent or more since 1900 and 3 of the 10 which had grown 25-50 percent. He also carried 6 of the 12 counties where the largest cities in the state were located. The vote in massive Cook County was Taft 74,875, Wilson 130,702, and Roosevelt 166,061. Of the 14 counties with densest population, T.R. won 8, Wilson 5, and Taft 1; whereas of the 50 counties which lost population, T.R. won 11, Wilson 34, and Taft 5. Taft carried 11 Illinois counties in all, 5 of which had lost population and only 2 of which had grown by over 15 percent since 1900. In Iowa the race between Roosevelt and Wilson had also been close, with Wilson winning 37.64 percent of the vote, T.R. 32.87 percent, and Taft 24.33 percent. Roosevelt won 5 of the 6 counties which had grown by over 15 percent, 3 of the 8 counties where the largest cities were located, and about half of the

counties with densest population. The three cities won by Roosevelt had by far the highest rates of growth: Des Moines 39 percent, Sioux City 44.4 percent, Waterloo 112.2 percent. Waterloo, population 26,693, was one of the fastest-growing cities in the nation, but Iowa as a whole had lost .3 percent population in the preceding decade, with 71 counties decreasing in population and 28 increasing. Roosevelt carried 14 of the counties gaining population, Wilson 12, and Taft 2. Of those losing population, Wilson carried 39, T.R. 25, and Taft 7. Taft carried only 9 counties in all.

The most sparsely populated regions of the country were in the West, and yet the decade 1900-10 had witnessed a boom in western urban growth, making the section increasingly important politically. In Montana Wilson polled 35 percent of the vote, Roosevelt 28.13 percent, and Taft 23.19 percent. The state had grown in population by 54.5 percent from 1900 to 1910. Only 2 counties had lost population; Wilson carried both. Most Montana counties had grown dramatically. Roosevelt and Wilson were tied among those with a growth rate over 50 percent, each winning 6, with Taft taking 2. Roosevelt carried 2 of the 6 counties where the largest cities were located, and these two cities had by far the highest rates of growth—Billings 211.4 percent and Missoula 194.8 percent. The next highest growth rate was Butte's 28.5 percent, while Great Falls had actually decreased in population. On the Pacific Coast Roosevelt carried Washington with 35.22 percent of the vote to Wilson's 26.9 percent and Taft's 21.82 percent; the Roosevelt and Wilson percentages were almost exactly reversed in Oregon; and in California the Roosevelt-Johnson ticket narrowly defeated the Democrats by less than two hundred votes. In Washington the majority of counties had increased in population by over 50 percent, and Roosevelt carried a majority of these, as well as all the counties where the six major cities were located. All these six cities had grown dramatically, from Everett's 216.6 percent to Walla Walla's 92.7 percent. Seattle, the largest city, had a population of 237,194 and had grown by 194 percent since 1900. Only 1 county had lost population, and Wilson carried it. Thirteen counties had a population density of less than six per square mile; T.R. carried 4, Taft 2, and Wilson 7. In Oregon the rate of population increase for the state as a whole was 62.7 percent compared with Washington's 120.4 percent, and the state had only two cities of over ten thousand population while its northern neighbor had six. Wilson carried most of the counties in Oregon and Taft won more than T.R., but the Progressive candidate came in second in the state's vote because all the G.O.P. counties were among those with the lowest density of population, while Roosevelt ran strongly in the more populous areas.

California is an interesting state to study, because Taft was not on the ballot and Wilson and Roosevelt were almost tied in the popular vote: T.R. 283,610, Wilson 283,436. The state had experienced a population increase of 60.1 percent in the decade 1900-10. Eighteen of the 58 counties had grown by over 50 percent, and 10 had lost population, while 8 counties had a population density of over forty-five per square mile and 6 less than two per square mile. Roosevelt and Wilson were closely matched in the fastest-growing and most densely populated counties: T.R. won 8 and Wilson 10 of the former, while each won 4 of the latter. But Wilson carried 9 of the 10 counties losing population and 5 of the 6 with less than two persons per square mile. The Census of 1910 designated eight major cities. Roosevelt captured the counties where five of the eight were located, including the two cities with the highest rate of growth—Pasadena 232.2 percent and Los Angeles 211.5 percent. Of the three major cities he lost, only one, San Diego, had a growth rate over 100 percent. San Francisco, carried by Wilson, had the lowest growth rate among the state's major cities—21.6 percent—just .6 percent above the national population increase. It was southern California which had experienced the greatest growth in the state, while all counties losing population were in the north, and it was in the southern part of the state that Roosevelt found his greatest support, just as Hiram Johnson had in his gubernatorial contest in 1910.

Finally, it is relevant to note the election results in the 10 largest cities in the nation, none of which were located in the West. Roosevelt carried 3: Pittsburgh, Detroit, and Chicago; Taft won Philadelphia; Wilson captured the other 6: New York, Baltimore, Boston, Buffalo, Cleveland, and St. Louis. Wilson came in second in 2 of the 10 cities, Taft in 2, and T.R. in 6. Four of the 10 had grown by over 25 percent since 1900: New York, Cleveland, Detroit, and Chicago, and of course T.R. and Wilson each carried 2. Detroit, in the Progressive column, was by far the fastest-growing of the cities, with a population increase of 63 percent, followed by Cleveland's 46.9 percent and New York's 38.7 percent. Two of Wilson's cities, Baltimore and St. Louis, were located in border states where the Progressives had little chance. New York, Boston, and Philadelphia had been major cities since colonial times, and Philadelphia and 4 of Wilson's cities had shown a growth rate smaller than the national average. Such cities, long major centers of population with a relatively stable growth rate, had voting patterns, social habits, and political organizations established by generations of development and tradition.

In summary, evidence shows that Roosevelt ran strongly in urban areas and best in urban and more populous counties with the highest rates of population growth. And he generally made a poor showing in counties losing population and those least densely populated. What are the implications of these findings? As George E. Mowry has written, Roosevelt's program was essentially "not agrarian but urban in its appeal." The Progressive platform with its call for welfare state measures and continuous intervention and management by government in social and economic life was particularly addressed to the problems of an urban and industrial society. Moreover, the Progressive platform embraced the new urban-industrial order while many liberal and conservative leaders in the old parties looked nostalgically back to the days before urbanization and the corporate colossus. In short, Roosevelt's general urban strength indicates that there may be a correlation between the appeal of the Progressive program and the response of the voters. Yet the further question remains: why did Roosevelt do best in urban areas with the highest rates of growth? The answers seem suggested by the characteristics of such areas provided by the analysis and statistics of the U. S. Census of 1910.

Cities with the highest rates of population growth, like Detroit's 63 percent or Seattle's 194 percent, distinctly differed from cities with growth rates close to or below the national average. The fastest-growing cities had a much higher percentage of the young and early middle aged than other areas both urban and rural. Young men and women were leaving the farms in a continuous stream to the cities in search of jobs and opportunities, leaving the rural counties of Indiana, Iowa, and other states for cities like Gary and Des Moines or, farther west, Spokane and Los Angeles. Others moved from older cities to newer ones. And the young from the farms and cities of Europe came to seek what Herbert Croly called "the promise of American life." Unlike earlier boom towns, the burgeoning twentieth-century cities required many white collar workers to manage and staff stores and companies, trained experts and professionals to do the complex and specialized work of modern industry and society, and skilled as well as unskilled workers. Thus, the new cities had a high percentage of the educated and skilled. Also unlike earlier boom towns, these cities had rising expectations coupled with improved transportation and communication, which meant that the new cities did not have to wait a generation or more for education, professional services, culture, and comforts. The new arrivals in the rapidly growing cities had largely left behind their identifications with the farms, towns, and cities from which they came, those roots that bound people to localism, sectionalism, and tradition. Doubtless, they considered themselves "progressive" and "modern" in spirit and outlook, for they were the ones who had left home— in a sense had left the past—and sought a new life. As Robert H. Wiebe has noted, many of the white collar workers, professionals, and trained specialists found new identities and loyalties as members of their respective professions, and corporately as fellow members of the new professional and managerial elite. These were ties that transcended localism as well as ethnic, traditional, and cultural identities. The forces building for nationalism and a new social structuring were at work in all urban areas, but they were particularly marked and influential in cities where from half to two-thirds of the population had arrived in the previous decade. The high rate of population increase also meant that established political organizations faced greater difficulties in the new cities in commanding the allegiance of voters than did their counterparts in cities with a small growth rate or in other areas with declining or relatively constant population. Finally, it should be noted that nearly all the cities and counties with the highest growth rates were found in the Midwest and West. These regions were by and large traditionally Republican: progressive Republicanism was strongest here and the new party well organized. Furthermore, foreign immigrants to the Midwest were often Canadians, Germans, British, and Scandinavians. Southern and eastern Europeans tended to settle in the eastern cities, while northern Europeans frequently headed westward. By reasons of culture, religion, language, and appearance, northern Europeans were more easily assimilated into the population than immigrants from other countries. This meant that they added less to the social forces making for particularism and division than did many of the immigrants in eastern cities.

The reasons for Roosevelt's voting strength in these modern boom towns seem manifest. People who had left home would probably be more easily attracted to the New Nationalism than those who had stayed behind, subject to the ties of localism, sectionalism, and traditional partisan allegiances. Men and women with loyalties to nationwide professions; white collar workers seeing themselves as part of a managerial elite national in scope; trained specialists cognizant of the contributions their fields could make to society; workers who had left American rural and urban poverty or European poverty for the middle class; educated young people aware of the problems and currents of their times; and people whose lives had been directed by the quest for a new and better life, all could find much that was appealing in the Progressive program with its emphasis on experts, bureaucracies, welfare standards, management, progressivism, "modernism," and the "engineering mentality." In short, the general urban appeal of the Progressive Party was particularly suited to the conditions in the modern boom towns. Moreover, it must have been easier for Republican leaders in Philadelphia, which had one of the oldest urban G.O.P. machines in the country, to carry the city for Taft, and for the venerable Democracy of Boston to muster winning votes for Wilson, both cities having a growth rate lower than the national average, than it was for their fellow partisans to keep voters in line for the old parties in rapidly growing cities like Detroit, Des Moines, and Seattle.

Analysis of the urban vote reveals much about Roosevelt's strength, but further information should be considered in order to determine the sources of Roosevelt's voter support. Roosevelt generally ran strong in the cities, but in addition he had significant rural support in Maine, Michigan, Minnesota, Iowa, Kansas, and other states. What does an examination of the vote show about this rural support? The important factor of ethnic voting patterns also merits and requires consideration. Finally, since the Progressive Party was so markedly influenced by academics and other professionals, and based its appeal on an informed understanding of the issues, any evidence about the educational level of Progressive voters should be assessed.

As has been noted in the survey of voting in eleven states, Roosevelt did poorly in counties losing population and those least densely populated. These facts suggest the possible thesis that T.R.'s rural support came from areas with the most prosperous farms and the best land, areas which because of favorable economic conditions generally would not lose population or be thinly populated. An index to demonstrate the validity of this thesis is a comparison of the value of farm lands in counties carried by the three candidates. For this purpose correlations have been made between the value of farm lands given in the 1910 Census and voting figures in eight midwestern and western states noted for agricultural production: Michigan, Indiana, Illinois, Iowa, Kansas, Washington, Oregon, and California.

There appear to be no significant differences among the values of farm lands in counties carried by the three candidates in Indiana and Kansas, but differences do emerge in the other six states in the sample. Generally, in these states Taft's rural support came from counties with the least-valuable farm lands, strikingly so in Michigan, Illinois, and Oregon. Except in California Wilson's rural support came from counties fairly evenly distributed along the scale of farm land values. In contrast to Taft and Wilson, Roosevelt's rural strength was found disproportionately in counties with high farm land values. For instance, in Illinois, carried by Wilson in a close contest with T.R., the average value of farm land was $95.02 per acre. There were 38 counties with farm land valued at over $100 per acre: Wilson won 19, Roosevelt 16, and Taft 3. Taft carried all 3 counties with the lowest land value in the state, $10–15 per acre, while 8 of his 11 Illinois counties had farm land valued below the state average. Only 1 of Roosevelt's 27 counties had farm land valued below the state average, 9 were in the average $75–100 category of the Census, and 16 had farm lands worth over $100 per acre. Wilson's Illinois counties were more evenly distributed along the value scale than those of the other two candidates. In California, where Taft was not on the ballot, there was a marked difference at the ends of the scale between farm land values of Progressive and Democratic counties. The average value of farm land in the state was $47.16 per acre. Nine counties had farm land valued at over $75 per acre: Wilson carried 3 and Roosevelt 6, T.R.'s counties including the rich lands of Imperial County. Twenty-three California counties had farm lands worth less than $25 per acre: Roosevelt won 3 and Wilson 20.

While the results of this survey are not as striking as the analysis of the urban vote, the evidence does suggest that Roosevelt did best in counties with prosperous farms and high land values. Farmers in such counties generally could afford machinery and the improvements of "scientific farming." In a sense, they were as much a part of the America that was building as were the white collar workers and industrial experts. Perhaps for these farmers there was money enough for education, leisure, and travel: children allowed to finish high school, a son sent to the state university, time for reading and lyceums, trips to the state fair and the big cities. Doubtless, these farmers considered themselves "progressive" and "modern" like their city cousins in Detroit or Los Angeles. Perhaps men with some economic independence were more likely to be politically independent than farmers in poor counties chained to the soil in a fight for survival. Perhaps farmers with greater educational and cultural opportunities were better able to understand the progressive platform than those whose horizons did not extend beyond the boundaries of their farms. At any rate, for whatever reasons, Roosevelt's rural appeal to a large extent seems to have been confined to the more prosperous farming areas.

To study the ethnic factors in the voting, it is instructive to look at the election results in the seven states with 25–35 percent of the population foreign born, those with the highest percentage of immigrants in the nation: Massachusetts, Connecticut, Rhode Island, New York, New Jersey, Minnesota, and North Dakota. Roosevelt came in third in 4 of these 7 states, Massachusetts, Rhode Island, Connecticut, and New York; placed second in 2, New Jersey and North Dakota; and carried only 1, Minnesota. The largest immigrant groups in the 5 eastern and New England states with the highest percentages of foreign born were Irish, Italians, and eastern Europeans as well as French Canadians in Massachusetts and Rhode Island. In 4 of these 5 states, Roosevelt placed third, and his support was weakest in those counties with the highest percentages of foreign born. In Massachusetts, for example, 8 of the 14 counties in the state had immigrant populations of over 25 percent. Of the 8, Taft won 5, Wilson 2, and Roosevelt 1. Six Bay State counties had less than 25 percent foreign born: T.R. carried 3, Taft 2, and Wilson 1. Two of Roosevelt's 4 Massachusetts counties had immigrant populations of less than 15 percent. In Minnesota, which Roosevelt carried, and North Dakota, where T.R. came in second, the ethnic composition of the immigrant population varied considerably from those in the eastern and New England states considered. Scandinavians made up 49.8 percent of the total immigrant population in Minnesota and 41.4 percent in North Dakota, while Germans made up 20.2 percent of the foreign born in Minnesota and 10.6 percent in North Dakota. Roosevelt carried most Minnesota counties, including the 7 with 35-50 percent of the population foreign born. In North Dakota there were 6 counties with 35-50 percent of the population foreign born: Wilson carried the state and 2 of these counties, Taft won 1, and Roosevelt carried 3 and placed second in 3. The results from the 7 states with the highest percentages of foreign born indicate that Roosevelt did not run as strongly as Wilson or Taft in counties with high percentages of immigrants unless the immigrants were largely from northern Europe. This proposition was further tested in 3 additional states across the country: Michigan, carried by T.R.; Montana, won by Wilson; and California, where T.R. and Wilson were almost tied. The results were virtually the same as in the 7 other states: Roosevelt generally did well in counties with a high percentage of immigrants only when those immigrants were northern Europeans.

The results in 10 states thus indicate that unlike Wilson's and Taft's, Roosevelt's immigrant appeal was highly restricted. Lake County, Indiana, carried by T.R., and some of Roosevelt's counties in Pennsylvania contained large numbers of southern and eastern Europeans, but generally Roosevelt seems to have attracted relatively few foreign born unless they were German, British, or Scandinavian. Without a thorough understanding of the English language or of American culture and issues, it would have been difficult for many immigrants to understand the New Nationalism and the Progressive program. Perhaps, on the other hand, some immigrants were repelled by the New Nationalism, seeing in it a possible threat to their ethnic identity. Immigrants in cities like Boston, New York, and Philadelphia found it easier to follow the familiar party leaders in their neighborhoods than to answer the call of the new party. Many ethnic groups had made commitments in various cities and states to one of the old parties. They had been rewarded by favors and jobs, government services, and political office. A new party must have hardly seemed a secure home for immigrants who were largely at the mercy of the dominant and established political and economic interests around them. Northern Europeans, however, were of course more easily assimilated into the American population than immigrants from other countries. Many were farmers who had acquired their own land in the Midwest and West. Others were skilled workers easily finding places in urban centers across the nation. Suffering less from religious and cultural prejudice than other Europeans, many had become men of property and standing whose children could enjoy the benefits of education and enter the professions. The evangelical and Social Gospel rhetoric of the Progressives was probably more likely to appeal to Scandinavian and German Lutherans and British Protestants than to Italian Roman Catholics or Orthodox eastern European Jews. Many Germans and Scandinavians, familiar with socialism and the welfare state, may have found the Progressive platform attractive. Furthermore, Germans in the United States had traditionally been attracted to reform movements. Finding a measure of acceptance in the United States and a culture resembling those of their native lands, northern Europeans may not have found the New Nationalism alien to their thinking. Moreover, many northern Europeans were Republicans and doubtless left the G.O.P. for the same reasons so many other Republicans did. The failure of the Progressive Party, however, to win more immigrants, like the Republican French Canadians in Rhode Island and the Democratic Irish in the big cities, meant that the new party's strength was severely restricted, particularly in the East.

Finally, since the Progressive Party attracted so many academics, professionals, and intellectuals, and presented a sophisticated program, an attempt should be made to assess the educational factor in voting divisions. All contemporary observers noted the high level of education among the new party's leaders and candidates. Alon Jeffrey's study of the Progressive Party in Vermont found that 22 percent of the Progressive members of the state legislature, from 1913 to 1917, had had education beyond secondary school, compared with 17.1 percent of the Republicans and 11 percent of the Democrats. It is difficult, however, to determine the educational level of those who voted for the three parties. The Census of 1910 did not study the educational background of Americans by state, city, or county, but it did compile extensive statistics on illiteracy. Illiteracy was defined as an inability to read any language, but the figures to some extent can also be taken to indicate the general level of education in a given area. Outside the South immigrants made up the bulk of illiterates in most states, but there were many counties in the North and West in which the majority or a high proportion of the illiterates were native whites, and there were counties where blacks formed a high percentage of the illiterates. To see if there was a correlation between illiteracy and the support for the three candidates, 7 states were examined: Massachusetts, New York, Michigan, Illinois, Montana, Washington, and California. Roosevelt carried 3 of these states, placed second in 2, and third in 2. The results of this 7-state survey showed that Roosevelt did poorly in counties with a high rate of illiteracy. Taft and Wilson, on the other hand, ran strongly in such counties, and in some states much of their support came from these counties. Roosevelt's counties in these states generally had illiteracy rates below the state average, and he often carried the counties with the lowest rates of illiteracy. In Massachusetts, Michigan, Illinois, and other states, however, the majority of Taft's counties had illiteracy rates above the state average, while Wilson consistently won much support in counties with above average illiteracy. The figures for Illinois are typical. In Illinois, where Roosevelt and Wilson were closely matched and Taft a poor third, the state illiteracy rate among voting age males was 4.6 percent. Native whites formed a high proportion of those unable to read in many counties, and there were also many immigrant illiterates. Thirty-six counties had illiteracy rates above the state average: Taft won 7, Wilson 24, and T.R. 5. Roosevelt carried none of the 18 counties with rates above 6 percent, Wilson winning 11 and Taft 7. Taft only carried 11 Illinois counties in all.

In part, Roosevelt's lack of support in counties with high illiteracy was a function of his failure to win more immigrant votes than he did, but many of the counties considered also had high percentages of native white and black illiterates. The results of the survey of illiteracy when considered in conjunction with the evidence of Progressive support in urban and prosperous rural areas, areas where educational opportunities were greatest, suggest that Roosevelt's appeal was largely confined to the most educated segments of the population. The conclusion is tentative because of the nature and extent of available evidence, but the thesis seems plausible. That the Progressive Party should appeal to the educated was natural for a party whose platform was written by social scientists and other experts. The illiterate and poorly educated were, of course, those least able to understand the Progressive program and the issues, and were the voters most likely to remain captive to partisan traditions. The failure of the Progressive Party to broaden its appeal beyond the educated is understandable in the days before the propaganda and educational possibilities of radio and television, and in view of the complexity of the Progressive program, but it was a fatal weakness in a mass democracy.

In any election many causal elements are involved in the outcome, and only a few have been examined with the surveys of urban, ethnic, and other voting factors. Roosevelt's victory in Michigan and his low vote in Rhode Island seem in part functions of the different ethnic composition of the two states, but the results were also attributable in some measure to different political conditions. In Michigan the Democratic Party was weak and there had been a strong current of progressive Republicanism for some years, while in Rhode Island the Democracy was vigorous and conservative Republicanism strong. Roosevelt generally did well in states where the progressive movement was strong and in states with high proportions of German and Scandinavian immigrants. Yet Roosevelt placed third behind Taft in Wisconsin, a citadel of progressive Republicanism where there was a large population of Germans and Scandinavians, and in Missouri, where there was a strong progressive movement in the G.O.P. and a significant number of Germans in the population. In both cases T.R.'s poor showing probably resulted from the opposition to the new party by the progressive Republican leaders of the respective states, Senator La Follette in Wisconsin and Governor Herbert S. Hadley in Missouri. Furthermore, while Roosevelt's heavy vote in Minnesota, South Dakota, Kansas, California, and other midwestern and western states was probably related to the phenomenon of the modern boom towns, ethnic factors, and the strength of progressive voter sentiment in these areas, it was also probably attributable to the fact that many leading Republicans in these states endorsed Roosevelt. The strength of the Progressive organization was important too in determining the outcome in most states. In Pennsylvania standpat Republicans had long been dominant, and there were large numbers of eastern and southern European immigrants, but Roosevelt carried the state. The probable cause was the strong Progressive organization formed by Bill Flinn, the former G.O.P. boss of Pittsburgh, with the help of others like the wealthy newspaper publishers E. A. Van Valkenburg and Alexander P. Moore. Roosevelt's high vote in Illinois was also in large measure attributable to a strong state organization, while his low vote in Rhode Island and some other states was the result of weak organization as well as other political and social factors. In a few states like Ohio strong new party organizations had been able to make little headway against vigorous opposing parties, but usually Roosevelt's showing at the polls was directly proportional to the strength of the state Progressive organization.

Issues as well as political conditions also played an important role in determining the outcome of the election. It is axiomatic among politicians that issues count, but, as scholars have recently emphasized, the bulk of voting in most elections appears to follow patterns based on ethnic, historical, and social circumstances rather than divisions that seem based primarily on issues. The election results indicate that Roosevelt attracted mainly Republican voters, either native born or northern Europeans, who lived in cities or prosperous farming areas. Yet Roosevelt did not win all such voters. At the least, it seems logical to conclude that the issues were one of the determinant elements in the voting division among these voters. Moreover, American elections are often decided by a small percentage of the total vote, and according to modern opinion polls issues are the prime factor in deciding a statistically important number of votes. In 1912 only a few percentage points separated Roosevelt from Wilson in Kansas, Illinois, Maine, and other states. In the days before scientific opinion polls, however, the influence of the issues in any election is perhaps the most difficult factor to measure in assessing the outcome, and therefore any conclusions must remain speculative and tentative.

The issues most discussed in 1912 were the tariff, progressivism, the trusts, welfare measures, and the formation of the Progressive Party. Observers attributed Roosevelt's rural support in Maine, Michigan, Minnesota, and other states near the border to Taft's Canadian Reciprocity Treaty—the treaty Paul V. Collins, Bull Moose candidate for governor of Minnesota, called "the crime of 1911." Many Republicans, particularly in the Midwest and West, had also been alienated by the standpat Payne-Aldrich tariff. On the other hand, Taft's identification with the protective tariff and the "full dinner pail" probably kept many workers in the G.O.P. fold in New England and the East. Roosevelt's endorsement of direct democracy reforms probably attracted Republicans in the West and Midwest, where many of the reforms had already been adopted, and alienated Republicans in the East, where Old Guard orators equated them with the French Revolution and the Reign of Terror. The new party, of course, claimed to be the only genuine partisan champion of progressivism, and this appeal clearly won Roosevelt votes in states where progressive Republicanism had taken root, but the refusal of La Follette, Hadley, and some of the other insurgents to leave the Republican Party probably kept the G.O.P. from losing more votes than it did in Wisconsin, North Dakota, Iowa, Missouri, and other states with a strong progressive Republican constituency. George E. Mowry and other historians have maintained that Roosevelt's stand on the trusts lost him more votes than it won. This seems a reasonable conclusion. Wilson and Brandeis had effectively attacked and misrepresented Roosevelt's program, while both Taft's and Wilson's positions were closer to the popular trust-busting and anti-monopoly tradition than was the New Nationalism. The welfare measures advocated by the new party, which Roosevelt considered the most important part of the Progressive program, would have benefited most Americans, but unemployment and old age insurance, the minimum wage, and the other Progressive proposals would have particularly helped blue collar workers, the immigrant masses of the ghettoes, and the poor in general. But the labor unions had not endorsed Roosevelt, preferring the gradualism of Gompers and the promises of the Democrats, while the poor and the immigrants for the most part stuck to the old parties and their established voting patterns. Roosevelt had blunted the impact of his social welfare program by his general interest rhetoric and failure to speak directly to interest groups.

For many Americans Roosevelt himself was a major issue in the campaign. Doubtless, the Progressive total included many "Teddy votes," as William Allen White called them—citizens who voted for the Colonel more out of admiration for the man than for his principles. Others opposed Roosevelt because of agreement with the editors George Harvey and Henry Watterson that he was a demagogue and would-be dictator. The Progressive Party itself, and the reasons for its formation, had also been widely debated. Some progressive Republicans had followed La Follette and refused to vote for Roosevelt, while others like Senator Cummins of Iowa voted for T.R. but declined to join the new party and support Bull Moose state tickets. But, of course, still other progressive Republicans had followed Roosevelt, Johnson, Beveridge, and other reform leaders into the new party. The issue of "honesty" and "bossism"—the "theft" of the Republican nomination and the control of the G.O.P. by bosses like Barnes and Penrose—was probably the issue among all the others in the campaign that worked strongest for the Progressive Party—strongest because it was the easiest to understand. It remained to be seen, however, how many of the Progressive voters of 1912 had made a long-term commitment to the new party.

For various reasons, therefore, the Progressive following was not a majority of the American whole. Widespread differences among the voters over issues like the trusts, the strength of Republican and Democratic political organizations, and local factors had played important roles in the Progressives' failure to win. In the last analysis, however, the most important causes of Roosevelt's defeat were American pluralism and innate social and political conservatism.

Roosevelt and the Progressives, for all their talk of general interest and inveighing against class divisions, had in fact based the campaign largely on an appeal to the middle class. They had seen "middle Americans" as the only hope for the success of a nationalism directed to progressive goals. But in the United States, unlike some other countries, even classes were fragmented and pluralistic. Politically the middle class had been divided between the two old parties. Respectability and tradition dictated a Democratic allegiance in southern and most border states, and in some northern districts, while in much of the North Republicanism was equated with Protestantism and morality. Maude Howe Elliott of Newport, Rhode Island, daughter of Julia Ward Howe, reported to T.R. after the election: ". . . While Mrs. Medill McCormick assures me that it is respectable in Chicago to be a Progressive, but not fashionable, in Rhode Island it has not been respectable. . . ." Progressives in Tuxedo Park, New York, put up election posters at night for fear of being seen and suffering retribution or social ostracism from Republican employers and neighbors. Habits and prejudices die hard, and the Republican and Democratic parties were deeply ingrained in the American way of life. The Federalists had been a dominant party for less than a decade, the Whigs lasted about twenty years, but in 1912 the Grand Old Party was fifty-six years old, and it had been over eighty years since Andrew Jackson called forth the Democrats. The size of Taft's vote was but one indication of the resiliency of the old parties. Wilson's nomination had precluded any mass exodus of progressive and Bryan Democrats to the new party, but even had the Democracy nominated a conservative or lackluster candidate, the party would have certainly retained significant support, especially in the South and urban areas. In many parts of the nation ethnic identification with the parties had become so strong that voting for the opposition was tantamount to rejecting one's parents and friends. Moreover, though it became commonplace to point to Roosevelt's and Wilson's combined vote as proof of the nation's progressivism, many conservative southern Democrats and northern Cleveland Democrats had voted for Wilson, just as some Republican progressives had voted for Taft with Governor Hadley. The two old parties were products and expressions of American tradition and pluralism. They were adapted to the historical, social, and economic divisions the Progressives sought to overcome.

Roosevelt was also defeated because of America's innate social and political conservatism. In contrast to the political divisions in Europe, Americans had always prided themselves on their moderation and refusal to take sudden turns to the right or left. In practice, however, this moderation often worked for the forces of conservatism, as it had in the 1890s against the Populists and the labor movement, because whereas many European countries had traditions of commonwealth and a strong state, the American political tradition was deeply rooted in the doctrines of laissez-faire capitalism, individualism, a weak state, and private property. Wilson's identification as the middle-of-the-road candidate, and therefore of Roosevelt as left of center, had hurt the Progressive Party. Wilson's New Freedom with its emphases on competition, individualism, and liberty seemed closer to the American tradition than did the New Nationalism. Union members seemed to have preferred Gompers's tactic of gradualism to the immediate and sweeping reforms promised by the Progressives, while many businessmen and white collar workers may have feared the costs and regulations involved in social reform. Edward S. Van Zile, a newspaper writer and novelist, wrote T.R. after the election that the new party had failed to win the vote of what he called the "tired business man," who seemed to be representative of much of the middle class in general: "He was afraid of our platform at the recent election because, on the whole, he did not understand it. He has the vague impression that humanitarianism is, in the last analysis, high-way robbery. He gazes at us from the windows of his stage-coach and imagines that we wear masks and carry revolvers."

In summary, Roosevelt's New Nationalism had called upon Americans to abandon regional, ethnic, traditional, and interest group alignments for the larger national interest. In a sense, he had asked Americans to repudiate much of their past, and even to disregard many existing social and economic realities. He had prophetically summoned his countrymen to look to the needs and problems of the future as they were being revealed in the present, and he had indicated a path that could be followed to realize the promise of the future. The majority of voters, however, had chosen instead one of the two familiar partisan roads. What remained to be seen was if after 1912 the New Nationalism and the new party could somehow be adapted and promoted so as to broaden the base of Progressive support.

3

Surveying the results of the state and congressional elections, the *Boston Herald* observed that the Progressive vote had an "inverted pyramid aspect" —it "tapers down very fast" from Roosevelt to the bottom of the tickets. Other commentators then and since have followed a similar analysis, stressing the point that in other election contests the new party in 1912 failed to match T.R.'s strength at the polls. It was true that no governor had been elected on a straight Progressive ticket, while 260 or so state legislators and 13 congressmen had been elected as Progressives, comparing unfavorably with the Populist score in 1892 of 3 governors, hundreds of state legislators, and 5 senators and 10 representatives. But such an analysis is misleading. In fact, a closer and more detailed analysis of returns reveals that the Progressive Party had made a strong showing in many states.

Roosevelt had outpolled the rest of the ticket in most states. But Beveridge in Indiana and Straus in New York, both running for governor, had won more votes than T.R., while in Colorado and North Carolina as well as Indiana the Bull Moose gubernatorial candidates came in ahead of their Republican opponents and placed second. And in Montana, Illinois, Michigan, Vermont, and other states, Progressive candidates for governor made a respectable showing. Moreover, though the national total of elected Progressive state legislators was relatively low, Progressives won the balance of power in the Illinois and New Hampshire legislatures, the majority in California, and strong minority positions in the legislatures of Washington, Montana, Michigan, Pennsylvania, and Vermont. Three California Republican congressmen, John I. Nolan, William D. Stephens, and C. W. Bell, joined with Republican congressmen A. Walter Lafferty of Oregon, Victor Murdock of Kansas, Charles A. Lindbergh of Minnesota, and Ira C. Copley of Illinois, all of whom had been endorsed in the election by the new party, and affiliated with the Progressive rather than the Republican organization in the House. Thus, when the dust settled the 13 Progressives in the House had become 20. In short, Progressive strength had been demonstrated in states from New England to the Pacific coast.

California, South Dakota, Nebraska, Kansas, West Virginia, and Maine, where the state G.O.P. had endorsed or indicated support for the Progressive Party nationally, were special cases. In these states there had been no third state tickets in 1912, and Roosevelt appeared on the Republican ballot in South Dakota and California. In California most of the state legislators elected on the G.O.P. ticket, a majority of the whole in both houses, declared allegiance to Governor Johnson and the new party, and only a handful registered for the Republican caucus. After the elections Roosevelt supporters in all six states moved to establish new state party organizations under the Progressive label so as to be consistent with national affiliation and separate from Republican leaders in these states who remained loyal to the national G.O.P. Thus, by 1914 every state in the nation had a separate and distinct Progressive party.

The political situation in 1912 was confusing in many states, with party lines being crossed back and forth, and with some state legislators being designated as "Republican-Progressive" or "Democrat-Progressive," but the election returns did reveal the areas of Progressive strength and weakness. In New England the new party emerged from the elections strongest in New Hampshire and Vermont. In New Hampshire Roosevelt and Winston Churchill ran third against the powerful Republican machine and an aggressive Democracy, but the gubernatorial election was thrown into the legislature since no candidate had a majority of the total vote. Progressives won the balance of power in the legislature, and joined with Democrats and some liberal Republicans to choose a Democrat for governor and a Progressive as speaker of the state house. In Vermont Fraser Metzger also polled enough votes to throw the election into the legislature. The G.O.P. had sufficient votes in the legislature to control the outcome, but it was the first time in Vermont history that a Republican candidate for governor had not been elected at the polls. Twenty-five Progressives were elected to the Green Mountain State legislature—three to the senate, where the Democrats won no seats. In the middle Atlantic area state Progressive parties did best in New York and Pennsylvania. In New York Oscar S. Straus came in ahead of T.R. but behind the Republican gubernatorial candidate and winning Democrat, though Straus and other new party candidates outpolled the G.O.P. in New York City, where Progressive Walter M. Chandler was elected to the U. S. House. The Washington Party of Pennsylvania not only carried the state with Roosevelt but also elected 25 members of the state legislature and 6 congressmen.

In the Midwest new party candidates made a strong showing in Michigan, Indiana, and Illinois. The Progressive candidate for governor in Michigan ran far behind Roosevelt's winning vote in the state, but Progressives elected 17 members of the state legislature and 2 congressmen, lawyer William J. MacDonald and Bay City Mayor Roy O. Woodruff. In Indiana Beveridge and the third party were opposed by two well-organized political machines, and the Democrats triumphed in most contests with the split in the normal Republican vote, but the defeated Beveridge polled 166,124 votes—T.R. received 162,007— to the Republican gubernatorial candidate's 142,850, and Progressives also ran second in most congressional races. Frank Funk in Illinois ran behind T.R. and third in the race for governor, but polled an impressive 303,401 votes to the Republicans' 318,469 and the Democrats' 443,120. The Progressives elected 28 members to the state legislature, giving them the balance of power, and Judge William H. Hinebaugh, the Chicago lawyer Charles M. Thomson, and incumbent congressman Ira C. Copley joined the Progressives in the U. S. House.

In the West the new party ran strongest in Colorado, Montana, and Washington. While the Democrats won in Colorado, Edward P. Costigan outpolled the Republican candidate for governor 66,132 to 63,061. In Montana in a preferential vote for senator (a feature in a few states in 1912), National Chairman Dixon lost his seat to the Democrat but defeated the Republican candidate 22,161 to 18,450, while 18 Progressives were elected to the legislature. In Washington the Bull Moose gubernatorial candidate Robert T. Hodge ran far behind Roosevelt's winning total, but James Wesley Bryan and Jacob A. Falconer were elected Progressive congressmen-at-large, and 37 Progressives were sent to the legislature. Hodge's low vote perhaps reflected the facts that he was an ex-boxer and divorced, in a state where women had the vote. The Democratic candidate was elected governor, but the Progressives elected more state legislators than the Democrats.

In the South and border states the Progressive vote was generally low from the top to the bottom of the tickets. Iredell Meares outpolled the Republican candidate for governor in North Carolina, but other candidates in the region trailed the Republicans, who themselves polled a small vote. Outside of North Carolina and pockets of strength in Louisiana and Missouri, it could be said that Dixie Progressives were present but not worth counting.

The Progressive Party had thus made a strong showing in about a dozen states across the country. What accounted for the strengths and weaknesses of the party in the various states? A well-organized state party with able leadership was obviously an important factor in Progressive gains in New Hampshire, Pennsylvania, Illinois, and other states, while relatively weak Progressive state organizations in Rhode Island, North Dakota, and elsewhere had been badly beaten. But in other states like New Jersey, Ohio, and New Mexico strong state Bull Moose organizations had made little headway at the polls. The candidates were important, of course, as witnessed by Hodge's low vote in Washington and the performances of Beveridge and Straus in outpolling T.R. In some states, however, able Progressive candidates had been buried by lackluster opponents. As with Roosevelt's voting strength, the new party did well only where the normal Republican vote was high. Yet new party candidates made a poor showing in some traditionally Republican states like Connecticut and Iowa. Regionalism played a role in Progressive voter support, helping the new party in the reform-minded Midwest and West and hindering Bull Moose advance in the more conservative East. But states where the new party ran strongly and poorly were remarkably evenly distributed across the country. In the final analysis, the most important factor in determining the Progressive Party's areas of strength and weakness was probably the political and social situation in the various states.

Progressives had prescribed a new party to answer reform needs for the separate states as well as for the nation as a whole. But once again the new party had come up against the fact of American pluralism in all its varied manifestations. Progressive voting strength in New Hampshire, Pennsylvania, and Illinois was in part perhaps a reaction against conservative and corrupt G.O.P. state machines, while in Iowa and Minnesota, though Roosevelt garnered a heavy vote, other candidates on the third ticket were badly defeated probably because the Republican Party in those states answered voters' demands for progressivism. In other states, like Connecticut and Rhode Island, the G.O.P. was standpat, but the voters seemed to have little interest in progressivism. In Vermont, Pennsylvania, and Michigan, the new party faced weak Democratic state parties, while in other states like New Jersey, Ohio, and New Mexico, the Democracy was well organized and able to capitalize on voter discontent with state Republican leaders. In short, the degree of success or failure of the New Nationalist party depended largely on local political and social conditions, conditions which the new party tried to meet, change, or channel with uneven results. In most states the Democrats won, usually doing better than Wilson in the vote count, because Progressives were able to win only Republican votes, because many who voted for T.R. refused to support Progressive state tickets, and because citizens in general seemed to find it more logical to punish Republicans by electing traditionally rival Democrats than by turning to the new party. If Progressives were to make gains in the next years, they had to perfect their state organizations, but they also had to convince all those who voted for Roosevelt to support the party on the state and local level, and prove to voters that the Democrats in the various states were no better than the rejected Republicans.

4

Although the Progressives had lost most of the contests, they were jubilant in the weeks after the elections. They acted like men vindicated, rejoicing in the G.O.P.'s crushing defeat and boasting of their successes. Most were certain that they had succeeded in establishing a permanent reform party. Victory would come in the next few years. First, Progressives would win in state, local, and congressional elections in 1913 and 1914, and then in 1916 Roosevelt would capture the White House. All realized, however, that victory would require a massive campaign of public education and an equally intensive effort to strengthen and extend the new party's organization on all levels. There was, therefore, no normal post-election, "off season" slump in the party's activities after election day. Enthusiasm continued to fuel their drive as Progressives held rallies and conferences around the country. Armageddon was to continue for the next four years; 1912 had only been the first skirmish of the great contest.

Chairman Dixon told the press on November 5 that the election results resembled those of 1856. "Some of our most enthusiastic leaders had hoped that possibly this might have been '1860'; it is evidently '1856,'" he said. He pointed out that the percentages of the vote polled by Buchanan, Fremont, and Fillmore in 1856 were close to those of, respectively, Wilson, Roosevelt, and Taft. Just as Fillmore represented the dying Whigs, so Taft's candidacy was the last gasp of the G.O.P. The Republicans of the 1850s, Dixon continued, had gone on to win the elections of 1858 and the presidency in 1860, and it would be the same with the Progressives in 1914 and 1916.

Roosevelt on November 11 issued a public statement on the elections: "What the Progressive Party has done since . . . last June is literally unparalleled in the history of free government. . . . The Progressive Party has come to stay. . . . So far from being over, the battle is just begun. We will not rest content until every feature of the Progressive program has been put into effect. . . ."

That was for public consumption, but what was Roosevelt thinking and saying in private? He had always been congenitally pessimistic in private about political situations, cautious in his assessments and forecasts. In the months after the election he was certain about only two things. First, he was positive that the principles and programs he had championed would triumph sooner or later. Second, he thought that whether or not the Progressive program would become reality under the new party was problematical, but he was determined to do all in his power to work for the survival and success of the party, since it was the Progressive Party alone which stood clearly and completely for those things necessary to the well-being of the nation.

He had expected defeat, T.R. wrote his English friend Arthur Hamilton Lee when the results were known, but he had hoped to do better. Still, he pointed out to diplomat Henry White, "it was a phenomenal thing to be able to bring the new party into second place and to beat out the Republicans." To James R. Garfield he wrote: "We have fought the good fight, we have kept the faith, and we have nothing to regret. Probably we have put the ideal a little higher than we can expect the people as a whole to take offhand." And there was much to be proud of in what the campaign had accomplished. ". . . I firmly believe," Roosevelt told Judge Lindsey, "that we have put forward the cause of justice and humanity by many years. The educational value of the campaign is worth very much." "It would have been better if we had succeeded," he wrote a California friend on November 14, "but much good came even though we failed.

We have really posed the vital questions that are now before the nation, and the parties will have to deal with them. . . ."

The ultimate fate of the Progressive Party could not be known yet, but it was certain its principles would not die. Roosevelt told Arthur Lee:

Whether the Progressive Party itself will disappear or not, I do not know; but the Progressive movement must and will go forward even though its progress is fitful. It is essential for this country that it should go forward. The alternative is oscillation between the greedy arrogance of a party directed by conscienceless millionaires and the greedy envy of a party directed by reckless and unscrupulous demagogues.

He wrote the philanthropist Alexander Smith Cochran at the end of December:

No one can tell the future of the Progressive Party as a party. I hope, and I am inclined to believe, that it will even as a *party* play a very important part in our social and industrial development. But I do not merely hope, I know, that the *principles* for which we stand will and must receive an extraordinary development and application within the next few years.

Much of the future of the party depended on the Democrats. If the Republican feats of 1858 and 1860 were to be duplicated, the Democrats would have to split as they had then. Progressives reminded each other that not only had the Democracy split in 1860, but it had also divided against itself in the days of Cleveland. Once again the tariff was a major issue before the Democratic administration, as it had been in Cleveland's era, and perhaps Democratic bungling would bring another depression like the one of the 1890s. On November 12 President Benjamin Ide Wheeler of Berkeley wrote Roosevelt about Wilson: "I should incline to expect that his party will be split before 1914." On the other hand, as T.R. wrote Arthur Lee, "If the Democratic Party as a whole acts wisely and sanely it may be that the Progressive Party will be eliminated." Yet there was only one way for this to happen, and that was for Wilson, like Jefferson before him, to abandon the views expressed before the election. Roosevelt predicted to the Episcopal Bishop Charles Henry Brent: "It is perfectly possible . . . that Wilson will succeed in making a good President, and will be hailed as a good President, just because he goes back on his own utterances and platform and adopts the principles of the Progressive Party, which he assailed during the campaign." Wilson was "a very adroit man," T.R. reminded President Wheeler. "I do not think he has any fixity of conviction; but this may be all the better for his chances of success under the present circumstances."

What course should the new party take? Roosevelt and the Progressive leaders were agreed on what the party should do. The duty was clear, the Colonel wrote Henry White: "Our business is to keep the Progressive Party in such shape that it will be ready to serve the Nation in any way that the Nation's needs demand." This required two things: further organization and public education on the social issues. Underscoring his words, T.R. reminded Gifford Pinchot in a letter on November 13 that the party needed *"a first-class organization."* The next day he wrote Governor Bass of New Hampshire: "The danger in sight is . . . that we may lose ground in the State elections during the next two or three years. We must do our best to strengthen our local organization." Along with organization a complementary campaign of public education on the issues was needed. Progressive leaders agreed with the assessment of Berkeley's Wheeler, who wrote Roosevelt:

The principles set forth [in the platform] were "quite fresh" . . . , and rather numerous. Many voters, for instance, who had just got as far as digesting Women's Suffrage wanted a little more time for masticating the various "recalls," —and *vice versa*. Many of the people who liked the new sociology might be just the ones to shudder about strong government and battleships. . . . Very many, as I know, who liked the rest of the "cause," did not like protection as a principle. I mean to say, to put it summarily, the time was too short wherein to reduce all these viands to an orderly menu. French *table d'hote* is an appeal to the majority based on long and successive experiences. You had no chance for that.

There was, however, an immediate problem facing the new party—the quarrel over the continued leadership of George W. Perkins. Now that the campaign was over, the opposition to Perkins within the party came boiling to the surface. Professor McCarthy and others told the press about the "missing plank," and the Pinchot brothers openly tried to have Perkins removed from chairmanship of the executive committee. Amos Pinchot wrote Roosevelt that Perkins's continued leadership "would be bad politics and bad ethics." Not only did his associations with Harvester and United States Steel make him suspect to many voters, but his opposition to the tenets of the "missing plank" would do great damage to the party. Medill McCormick informed Roosevelt that Progressives in the Midwest had found Perkins a "drag on the ticket." There were complaints that the *Progressive Bulletin* and party pamphlets contained far too many statements by or about Perkins. "Mr. Perkins replying to Mr. Bryan or Mr. Wilson and Mr. Brandeis," Charles E. Merriam wrote T.R., "places us in an extremely unfortunate light." *La Follette's Weekly* and other publications hostile to the Progressive Party happily fanned the flames of the dispute.

Roosevelt was alarmed and angered by the opposition to Perkins. He replied to the Pinchots' many letters that he would not "throw to the wolves one of the staunchest allies and supporters we have had. . . ." He reminded Gifford:

In this campaign we did not have half money enough. There never was a campaign managed with so little money. If Perkins had been excluded from all share in the management, if we had lost his very great organizing ability, his devoted zeal, and the money he so generously gave, and the money which men like [Frank A.] Munsey gave because of their associations with Perkins, and the newspaper support which men like Munsey and [Henry L.] Stoddard gave—why, I think our whole campaign would have gone to pieces.

The Pinchots rejoined that they did not wish to exclude Perkins from the party or even from the executive committee. Rather, they wanted him to cease being a spokesman and visible leader. Roosevelt, however, refused to consider any plan to remove Perkins from his office or muzzle him. Quickly he wrote letters to Progressive leaders declaring his support for Perkins. "Of course to fight in our own ranks, and to try to turn out Perkins now, would be worse than a calamity," he warned William Allen White. On the other hand, the Colonel agreed that the disputed Sherman Act clause should be used in all future editions of the platform, since there was question whether the lines had in fact been removed by the platform committee, and since the views expressed were indeed ones he agreed with and had used in the campaign. Soon other Progressives rallied to Perkins's support at the Colonel's urging: Judge Lindsey of Colorado, John Franklin Fort of New Jersey, National Committeeman Charles H. Thompson of Vermont, and others agreed that Perkins should stay. Most leaders were willing to follow Roosevelt's direction. The Pinchots reluctantly dropped the dispute by mid-December, and for the time being harmony was restored.

Both sides in the argument had been right. Perkins was, as McCormick said, a "drag" on the party's popular appeal, and as long as he remained in any party office the opposition would make the most of it, calling him an agent of Wall Street. The Pinchots' points were well taken. But it was also true that the party needed his business ability and—more particularly—his money. The party had many leaders who could make speeches and appeal to the public, but how many had Perkins's "zeal" with a checkbook? Roosevelt had not put it this bluntly, but his meaning was clear. His judgment on the matter would remain a subject of controversy among Progressives and later historians, for Perkins's contributions came at a high interest rate, not in special favors or the watering down of Progressive doctrine, but in the coin of factionalism and public distrust. Yet he was the only Progressive willing and able to contribute the massive sums necessary for the existence of the party.

5

Even though the Progressives quarreled about Perkins, they were united in their resolve to continue the work of building the new party. The striking fact was not that some wished to depose one of the party's leaders, for that was a commonplace occurrence in partisan politics after elections, but that the party acted as if the campaign were still in full swing. On November 9 the defeated Massachusetts Progressives held a rally at Boston's Tremont Temple, with an overflow meeting in Faneuil Hall. Over $8,000 was pledged for the state campaign of 1913. On November 19 the New York Progressives held a meeting at New York City's Holland House, attended by over 250 state committeemen, county chairmen, and party leaders, and addressed by Roosevelt. Soon it was announced that the national committee meeting scheduled for Chicago in December would be expanded into a three-day conference for Progressive leaders from all the states.

By December 9 over fifteen hundred delegates had arrived in Chicago. The affair was almost a reunion of the August convention. On December 10 Roosevelt addressed the conference in the ballroom of the La Salle Hotel. "We have accomplished more in ninety days than ever any other party in our history accomplished in such a length of time. We have forced all parties and candidates to give at least lip-service to Progressive principles," T.R. declared. He spoke contemptuously of the old parties, which were "but wings of the same party of reaction and privilege." There was no place for progressives except the new party. He urged as the first order of business the introduction of bills embodying the planks of the Progressive platform in Congress and as many state legislatures as possible. He spoke at length of the meaning of the platform, using the words of the "missing plank" to describe the Progressive position on the trusts. Defending the recall of judicial decisions, Roosevelt stubbornly insisted: "The doctrine of the divine right of judges to rule the people is every whit as ignoble as the doctrine of the divine right of kings. . . ." There was to be no lowering of the Progressive standard, no compromise on the "contract with the people."

After Roosevelt's call to arms Jane Addams presented "A Plan of Work" for the party, focusing on the two goals of political organization and social education, and proposing a novel structure for the national party organization. Between meetings of the national conventions and the whole national committee, the day-to-day work of the party would be directed by an administrative board. This board would be composed of the chairmen of the national committee, the executive committee, and those of four new departments: publicity, finance, political organization, and "Progressive Service." The Progressive Service department was to work for the education of the public and the promotion of Progressive legislation in Congress and the states. Each party department was to have a committee of workers and advisors, and the Service department would have various bureau subdivisions for legislative reference work and other concerns. This ambitious and unique blueprint was adopted at the national committee meeting the next day, and referred to the executive committee for implementation.

Following Jane Addams's address on party organization, the conference heard a speech by Walter Weyl proposing that the party adopt a plan of financial support based on a "dues-paying membership." Weyl's plan was referred to the executive committee along with Addams's plan, and became the basis of the "Progressive Volunteers" organization launched in 1913 to mobilize popular financial support for the new party. Weyl's speech was followed by a call by the evangelist Benjamin Fay Mills for a continuous campaign of propaganda and education during the next four years. His proposal was later translated into the "Progressive Lyceum" and a speakers' bureau, subdivisions of the Progressive Service.

The new party's approach to partisan program and organization reflected a union of traditional views of professional politics with concepts of social service and engineering, a union expressed in the two Progressive goals of political organization and social education, and representing the collective experience and thought of the professional politicians and social service and planning advocates in the ranks of the new party's leadership. Emphasis would be placed both on traditional partisan organization—local, county, and state committees, and the work of precinct captains, organizers, state chairmen, and the like— and on new, innovative partisan structures like the Progressive Service. The goal of perfecting and extending traditional forms of partisan organization and activity represented the *realpolitik* of professional politicians in the party like Beveridge and Dixon, and the recognition by previously nonpartisan reformers like Jane Addams and Walter Weyl that reform required partisan organization and methods in order to be effective. The goal of social education and service embodied the thinking, background, and skills of the party's social workers, academics, and other professional experts, and demonstrated that the party was dedicated to finding new ways to conduct partisan politics.

Since the Progressive Party differed from the old parties and the old politics, it was reasoned that these differences should be reflected in the party's day-to-day activities as well as in its platform. Party organization was to be elaborately bureaucratic, and run along principles of "modernism" and the "engineering mentality." Party structure in a sense would form a "shadow government" and a working model for the new politics. Social workers, trained experts, and other professionals were to be utilized on a regular basis, just as they would be in any local, state, or national administration run by the new party. Bills and governmental programs would be formulated "scientifically" by the appropriate specialists, and then presented to the public by the party. Popular participation would also be a hallmark of party work. Party members were to work at the grass roots level to solicit financial support and build local political organizations, while the party would try to involve all voters in a program of popular education. If the ward heeler and the boss were the backbone of the old parties, the volunteer worker and the expert were to be characteristic of the new politics. On the other hand, the new party's announced intention to continue at the same time with the traditional forms and techniques of professional politics was notice to all that the Progressive Party meant business—its business was partisan politics, and the old parties were to be given stiff competition on the traditional field of partisan battle. The Progressive Plan of Work was ambitious and unique in scope and conception, a plan whose efficacy could be tested only by the experience of the next years, but its adoption by the new party was witness to the realization that to win converts the Progressive faith had to make a difference in daily partisan life.

After the formal presentations by Addams, Weyl, and Mills, the conference was opened for general discussion by party leaders reporting on the political situations in the various states. That night a "family dinner" was held with a brace of Bull Moose orators. The next day the national committee met to approve proposals made the day before and garner pledges for the work of the national organization. There was a disagreement about the location of national headquarters. Midwestern and western members wanted it moved to Chicago, but it was voted 32 to 12 to keep the headquarters in New York City and establish the publicity bureau in Washington. A luncheon was held in honor of Jane Addams, bringing the conference to a close. Soon announcements were made of further Progressive conferences, rallies, and banquets to be held all over the nation in the near future. As William Allen White later recalled: "And so the year ended without an anticlimax."

CHAPTER SEVEN

1913: HANDS SET TO THE PLOW

*Our hands are set to the plow, and we will not quit
our task till the field is turned, the seed planted and
the harvest gathered.*

Albert J. Beveridge

For a new or third party every month and year of survival in the arena of
American politics is an accomplishment, and if such a party not only endures
but prospers and makes advances, then a victory has been won in the face of
tremendous forces and odds working against its very existence. This was in fact
the story of the Progressive Party in 1913. While Progressives in the states
worked to improve and extend local organizations, the national party built
an elaborate political structure that was innovative and impressive by any
standards. The dual campaign of organization and education proclaimed at the
December, 1912, party conference in Chicago was waged at all levels. The new
party's ability to compete with the old parties depended both on maintaining
and expanding partisan machinery and on educating the voters on the issues and
the party's positions. How might success be measured for 1913? The answer
seemed clear to Progressives by the end of the year. The enthusiastic response
of men and women who volunteered for party work on every level, the lack of
massive defections from the leadership of the party, the successes in improving
political organization, and the gains and victories scored in local and state
elections in 1913 seemed to prove that the party had a bright future. "If 1912
witnessed the birth of the Progressive Party," an Ohio Democratic newspaper
observed at the end of the year, "1913 has demonstrated its permanence. . . ."

It was, however, appropriate and natural that 1913 begin with a debate on
the continuation of the Progressive Party. The debate opened in January with
a call by Frank A. Munsey for the "amalgamation" of the Progressives and
Republicans. In articles printed in his newspapers and *Munsey's Magazine,* the
millionaire publisher proposed a national conference with an equal number of
delegates from both parties. The conference could reach agreement on principles, and then create another party—perhaps called the "Liberal Party,"

Munsey suggested—which would absorb the two existing parties. A merger was necessary to beat the Democrats, Munsey argued, and Republicans and Progressives could easily agree on the principles of nationalism and the protective tariff against the states rights and free trade of the Democrats, a division which formed "the true and only definite line of political cleavage" since progressivism was found in all three parties. Dan R. Hanna, a major financial backer of the Ohio Bull Moose, agreed that amalgamation was desirable and possible, as did former

Once upon a time there was an Elephant. He had won many races. Never-the-less, one day, just before a race it was decided that the Elephant had too much weight and not enough speed. Accordingly a new animal was chosen.

This animal was a Bull Moose. He was chosen on account of his speed, to enter the race which happened to be with a Donkey. But, sad as it may seem, he lost the race. The speed was there, but the weight was lacking.

It was quite evident that a combination of speed and weight was necessary to insure success. But how was that to be accomplished? Using the head of the Moose and the tail of the Elephant quite satisfied the followers of the Moose but

the Elephant's friends preferred the head of the Elephant and the tail of the Moose. To put the two heads together looking out in opposite directions would be folly. And what will become of the remaining halves? It's a difficult problem.

CARTOON COMMENT ON THE "AMALGAMATION"
DEBATE OF 1913

Governor Chase S. Osborn of Michigan. Munsey's proposal was followed in May by a Chicago meeting of more than thirty progressive Republicans, including former Governor Hadley and Senator Cummins, who issued a statement calling for a Republican convention in 1913 to reform party machinery and promote harmony. Former Speaker Cannon rejected the idea of any convention before 1916; Taft counseled Republicans to stand fast against the radicalism of the

Progressives as well as the Democrats; and the conservatism of the G.O.P. national committee foredoomed the possibility of an official gathering for purposes of reform. But Munsey reported that in general Republicans reacted favorably to the idea of amalgamation. It was the Progressives, he found, who were overwhelmingly opposed to any merger, for aside from Hanna and Osborn few members of the new party endorsed his pleas.

Charles J. Bonaparte reported to Roosevelt that he had met privately in Baltimore with Munsey, who had explained that he backed the Progressive Party in 1912 as a rebuke to the G.O.P. bosses for their actions at the Republican convention; Munsey also "spoke without sympathy of the wish to promote 'uplift' and, in his words, 'climb up moon beams' by the Progressives. . . ." The publisher was "pretty sore over the chilling reception his 'amalgamation' scheme has received," but "he admitted . . . that the test of sentiment afforded by his publication had satisfied him that, if the Progressive party broke up, not over 15 *per centum* would now join the Republicans. . . ." Roosevelt was sorry to see Munsey leave the party—it was like watching a million dollars walk out the door—but he and other leading Progressives quickly issued statements rejecting Munsey's proposal. The Colonel and other new party leaders were willing to see a union with Republicans or interested Democrats, but only on terms dictated by Progressives. "There is . . . much talk of 'amalgamation,'" T.R. said in a message to Maine Progressives. "There is just one way by which members of either of the old parties can amalgamate with the Progressives, and that is by taking the Progressive platform in its entirety and by retiring from leadership the old-type bosses, the Penroses and Murphys and the like." In short, only the converted need apply.

In an article in the *Saturday Evening Post,* "The Progressive-Republican Merger," Beveridge summed up the Bull Moose position and attacked both Munsey's and the progressive Republican efforts to join the two parties. Beveridge argued that the proposals for merger could not be considered because there were former Democrats in the Progressive Party, the G.O.P. as well as the Democracy was made up of men of "glaringly opposite beliefs," and the Progressives differed from conservative Republicans on the issues before the country. Munsey claimed that all Progressives and Republicans agreed on the tariff and nationalism. Beveridge replied that Progressives favored a tariff commission and opposed the methods that had led to the Republican Payne-Aldrich tariff of 1910, while the "broader, more logical and more helpful nationality" of the new party found expression in federal legislation for the abolition of child labor and other social measures opposed by both the old parties. Furthermore, the New Nationalism of the Progressives meant that unlike the Republicans and Democrats the new party stood for the same principles in every state. "What we fight for in Oregon we fight for in Florida. What we preach in Kansas we preach in Rhode Island. . . ." Progressives were not interested in a party made up of a patchwork of factions.

The question of merger was brought into sharp focus by contests for senator in the legislatures of Maine, New Hampshire, West Virginia, and Illinois. In Maine and West Virginia in 1912, Progressives had backed the Republican state tickets because of assurances that the state G.O.P. favored Roosevelt and the new party nationally, but after the elections Progressives found the victorious Republican organizations unwilling to cooperate with the new party. In Maine the Republican choice for the Senate, Edwin Burleigh, a Taft supporter and a member of the standpat machine of Senator Eugene Hale, was unacceptable to most Progressives, while in West Virginia the G.O.P. organization declined to endorse the candidacy of William Seymour Edwards, a former speaker of the state house who was the choice of Progressives. In the New Hampshire and Illinois legislatures third party men held the balance of power and could join with members of the old parties to determine the election of senators—two in Illinois because of the impeachment of Republican Senator William Lorimer for bribery in his election to the Senate. What should the policy of the new party be?

Directly after the 1912 elections Roosevelt had publicly advised Progressive state legislators to "stand aloof" and make no deals with the old parties over Senate seats. But soon Senator Bristow of Kansas suggested to Roosevelt that a deal might be made whereby a Democrat would be chosen in Maine and a Progressive in New Hampshire, while in Illinois William Jennings Bryan tried to work a compromise for one Democrat and one Progressive senator. Illinois Republicans also wanted to do business with the new party. Maine Progressives were not yet fully organized, and the choice resolved to voting for Burleigh or the Democratic candidate, but in New Hampshire Progressives nominated former Governor Bass against candidates of the old parties, while Edwards in West Virginia and Frank Funk in Illinois entered the field for the new party. Roosevelt replied to Bristow that he doubted a deal could be effected in Maine and New Hampshire without compromising the new party in the eyes of the public. "I do not want to seem impractical . . . ," he wrote Bristow. "But I do not want to hurt the Party by doing anything that would be misunderstood." He warned Illinois Progressives to stay clear of any alliance with machine Democrats or "Lorimer Republicans," both discredited by the Lorimer scandal in the legislature. "I would far rather see the Republicans and Democrats compelled to unite in electing the two United States Senators than that the Progressive Party should accept the Senatorship by any kind of compromise containing the least taint of discredit," he wrote State Senator Walter Clyde Jones of Illinois. It might be that the Progressives could "with self-respect" obtain one of the Illinois seats, Roosevelt told Merriam, but he doubted it. Roosevelt admitted to Progressives that Democrats in these states would be preferable to conservative Republicans, but he urged the party to stick with its own candidates as long as possible. On the surface it appeared that he was unrealistically throwing away the chance to gain senators for the party, but he believed that if Progressives made deals the party would compromise its independence and good name. The plans of the fusionists and compromisers did not seem good politics, since senators would be popularly elected in 1914 when the Seventeenth Amendment went into effect and the old legislative caucuses to choose senators were no more. Such a strategy, however, came at a price: the Progressives kept their independence and clean record, but the old parties won the Senate seats. In Maine Burleigh was elected, with seven Progressives voting for the Democratic candidate. The New Hampshire legislature cast forty-two ballots before choosing the Democrat Henry F. Hollis, whose election was finally made possible because eight Republican regulars and one Progressive broke ranks. In West Virginia the regular Republican Nathan Goff was elected over Edwards, though the defeated Progressive subsequently sent five legislators to jail for bribery. Republicans and Democrats in Illinois made a deal without the Progressives, electing the Democrat James Hamilton Lewis and the notorious Republican boss Lawrence Y. Sherman.

The clearest and most effective repudiation of the merger proposals, however, was not found in the statements of Roosevelt or the fights over the Senate seats but in the organizational work carried on by the Progressives during 1913. The series of meetings, banquets, and conferences which began immediately after the 1912 elections continued throughout the next year. On January 24 a conference of new party officials from the Dakotas, Minnesota, Wisconsin, and Michigan was held in St. Paul. On February 17 Nebraska Progressives met in Lincoln for a banquet addressed by former Governor Stubbs of Kansas. After the Republican custom, banquets were held in several cities on Lincoln's Birthday: 750 Kansas Progressives assembled in Topeka, while at the Hotel Astor in New York 2,500 attended a dinner sponsored by the National Progressive Club. Joseph Walker, former speaker of the Massachusetts house and G.O.P. candidate for governor in 1912, a leading New England insurgent, announced he was joining the Progressive Party, and appeared at a Washington's Birthday rally in Boston with his 1912 opponent Charles Sumner Bird. Every issue of the *Progressive Bulletin* catalogued many conferences and party functions like the February ones in Lincoln, Topeka, New York, and Boston. In March Progressive conferences were held in Santa Fe, Tulsa, Nashville, Baltimore, Augusta, Maine, and elsewhere; Illinois Progressives held a conference in Springfield April 28-29; in June the Washington Party gave a banquet in Scranton, and Arkansas Progressives met in Little Rock; in December the *Progressive Bulletin* reported recent state conferences in California, Colorado, Wyoming, and Kansas. "Our party duty now is organization, organization, and again, organization," Beveridge exhorted at the New York Lincoln Day banquet, and throughout 1913 Progressives worked systematically to strengthen party machinery at all levels. State Chairman Matthew Hale reported in February that 287 out of 354 towns in Massachusetts now had Progressive town committees and the rest would soon be organized, whereas in 1912 111 towns had been organized with committees. State Chairman U. S. Sartin of Kansas proudly noted that in leading progressive Republicans into the third party organization since the elections, the new Progressive committees in about half the counties had been formed by virtually all the members formerly on the G.O.P. county committees. In May it was announced that over five thousand Progressive clubs had been organized around the country. In the local and state elections in the spring and fall of 1913 there were Progressive campaigns for every office from school committee and town council on up nearly everywhere outside the South, testament to the extent of the party's organization. In short, if the Progressive Party failed to survive it would not be because of lack of organization.

Roosevelt himself worked hard for the party in 1913, conferring with leaders, writing letters and articles, making speeches and public appearances. Regularly he sent out streams of letters and telegrams encouraging Progressives in the ranks—to the Italo-American Progressive Club in Rhode Island, the Progressives of Bergen County, New Jersey, the North End National Progressive Club in Brooklyn, and others. In February he spoke at the New York Lincoln Day dinner and attended a reception for Nassau County Progressives on Long Island; in March he spoke for the party in Philadelphia, Albany, and Detroit; in June he was at party gatherings in Buffalo, Rochester, and Boston; in July he spoke in Newport, Rhode Island, for the Progressive Service. "If you could act as my secretary for a few days you would feel sympathy for that unfortunate individual," Roosevelt wrote a New Jersey Progressive in April. "I kept count for two weeks merely of the letters of declination I had to write to requests to attend banquets, rallies, and the like, and this is only a small part of my correspondence. In that two weeks I declined 171 invitations and there were hundreds of other letters to reply to." Yet, in spite of his work for the new party, Republicans continued to spread rumors that he would soon return to the G.O.P. After writing an article in the fall for the *Century* magazine, denouncing the old parties and amalgamation and affirming his loyalty to the cause of 1912, the Colonel wrote Matthew Hale:

My "Century" article on the Progressive Party will be out in a week or two, and if after that people think I am lukewarm about Progressivism, why there is nothing in the world I could do to make them feel otherwise. They are perfectly certain to take one of two tacks. If I speak often they will say it is a one-man party, dominated in the interests of personal ambition by me, and that I am officiously interfering everywhere. If I do not speak often they will say I have lost interest and am thinking of abandoning the Progressive Party. They are perfectly content to make one of these statements one week, and the other the next, and I do not see any way to stop them.

2

The "Plan of Work" presented by Jane Addams and adopted by the national committee at the December, 1912, Chicago conference was quickly implemented in 1913. Under the direction of the executive committee of the national committee and Chairman George W. Perkins of the executive committee, the work of the national organization was conducted by four divisions, Finance, Organization, Publicity, and Progressive Service, with the chairmen of the divisions plus Perkins and National Chairman Dixon constituting the party's administrative board. The executive committee, consisting of Perkins, Bill Flinn,

Walter F. Brown of Ohio, Jane Addams and veteran politician Chauncey Dewey of Illinois, Charles H. Thompson of Vermont, the Oklahoma oil man George C. Priestley, Ben Lindsey, and Meyer Lissner, met periodically between gatherings of the full national committee to review the work of the administrative board and the divisions.

The treasurer of the national committee, Elon H. Hooker, became chairman of the finance committee, whose members included Charles Sumner Bird, Arthur L. Garford, the Chicago businessman George F. Porter, Priestley, and Mrs. Kellogg Fairbank, later Democratic national committeewoman from Illinois. Hooker, a civil engineer with a Ph.D. from Cornell, had been deputy superintendent of public works when T.R. was governor, and was president of the Hooker Electrochemical Company of Niagara Falls. A skilled businessman, he made an excellent manager of party finances. The chairman of the organization committee was Walter F. Brown, a seasoned politician from Toledo, formerly Ohio G.O.P. chairman, subsequently postmaster general under Herbert Hoover. Brown was ably assisted by Charles H. Thompson, former mayor of Brattleboro and leader of the Vermont Progressives, young David S. Hinshaw of Kansas, later a noted public relations expert and writer, and periodically by others like Edwin M. Lee of Indiana, first G.O.P. and then Progressive state chairman of the Hoosier State. William Allen White was chairman of the publicity committee, but the work was done by Oscar King Davis, an experienced newspaper correspondent who had directed publicity during the 1912 campaign. Frances A. Kellor became director of the Progressive Service with its many bureaus and committees for research, drafting legislation, and social education. Kellor was a social worker who had received a law degree from Cornell. She had been secretary-treasurer of the New York State Immigration Commission and chief investigator of New York's Bureau of Industries and Immigration, and was the author of *Experimental Sociology* (1902) and *Out of Work* (1904). It was of course unprecedented for a woman to assume so prominent a role in a political organization. For her assistants, Donald R. Richberg, Paxton Hibben, and the suffrage worker Alice Carpenter were hired. Young attorney Richberg, active in Chicago politics, was subsequently a director of the N.R.A. and an assistant to Franklin D. Roosevelt. Hibben had entered the diplomatic service under T.R., serving in Russia, Mexico, and elsewhere, and later became a writer and historian. Perkins, Hooker, Kellor, and their staffs of assistants and secretaries set up offices in the Forty-second Street Building in New York City. Brown, Thompson, and Hinshaw reported in to New York headquarters between organizing road trips, while O. K. Davis directed a news service and published the *Progressive Bulletin* with a staff and offices in the Munsey Building, Washington, D. C.

Following Walter Weyl's proposal at the December Chicago conference, a concerted and publicized effort was made to provide the party with popular financing through small contributions. At the same time, however, Hooker and the national committee quietly organized large contributors to insure an adequate income. In the summer of 1913 the Progressive Volunteers organization was launched with "A Call to the Colors" signed by Beveridge, Straus, Poindexter, and John M. Parker, run as an ad in *Collier's* and other publications. "We want to hear from 1000 loyal Progressives . . . ," read the appeal. The plan was to enlist volunteer workers who would in turn enroll small contributors for monthly pledges of five cents or more to be paid over a three-year period. By May, 1914, some 2,000 volunteers had signed up nearly 20,000 contributors, with the average pledge two dollars per year. A goal of over 300,000 contributors was announced by the newsletter *Progressive Volunteer* in 1914, but the organization was unable to increase significantly the number of pledges. Voters apparently were not sufficiently aware of the necessity for continuous financial involvement in politics and a steady income to pay the bills of the new politics. By the end of 1915 the receipts for the entire three-year period totaled only $33,005.09—a sum smaller than W. Emlen Roosevelt's single contribution in 1912—while the running expenses of the Progressive Volunteers were about $4,000 per year. Countless hours of labor had been invested, but the return was too small to be of significant help to the party. The fate of the Progressive Volunteers was a pointed comment on the limitations of the new politics.

The efforts of Hooker and the national committee to obtain an income for the party from large contributors was much more successful. Over a dozen Progressives, including Treasurer Hooker, Charles Sumner Bird, W. Emlen Roosevelt, Gifford Pinchot, T.R., and Perkins, each pledged the national committee $1,000 per year. "We hope to educate the public within the next four years so that very large individual subscriptions will no longer be needed. In the meantime, . . . many friends of the movement are contributing $1,000 a year to carry forward its educational program," Hooker wrote a prospective donor. Smaller yearly pledges were also received, like $50 each from Winston Churchill and Learned Hand, $100 from the writer George Ade, and $200 from William Dudley Foulke. The total pledges assured the national committee an annual income of over $15,000. In addition, a war chest of about $130,000 was raised in 1913 from single contributions, like the philanthropists Willard and Dorothy Straight's $1,000, Bill Flinn's $1,133, and substantial sums raised by groups of Chicago businessmen and Indiana Progressives. These monies were supplemented in the years after 1913 by other individual contributions. Wealthy Progressives like Medill and Ruth Hanna McCormick, Everett Colby, and, of course, Perkins could be counted on for periodic and generous checks.

Though the national committee had succeeded in raising substantial sums for the party's work, the elaborate national organization's bureaus and divisions easily spent all available funds, and there were continual requests for and arguments about more money. In 1913 the national committee planned to spend about $30,000 on the work of the Progressive Service and over $44,000 for the expenses of the other divisions, including $20,000 for organizational work and $10,500 for the Washington publicity bureau. The Progressive Service, however, with its work and duties continually expanding, spent $41,416.97 in 1913, while O. K. Davis complained that his Washington office could not survive on the funds sent from New York. The state organizations initially had made pledges to the national committee, but few were ever paid since state leaders found it necessary to spend all funds locally. Often in fact the national organization was called upon to assist the state parties and aid local projects and campaigns. Hooker had hoped that Massachusetts Progressives would contribute at least $6,500 a year to the national committee, but in the summer of 1913 Bay State leaders demanded that the national organization raise a fund of $50,000 for their fall state campaign. The national organization of the Progressive Party was doubtless better funded than other third parties have been, but still there never was money enough to accomplish all the work the party found to do.

The Progressive Service was the most elaborately structured division of the national party organization. It was charged with the tasks of educating the public on the issues and assisting legislators and party leaders with information, research, and legislation. All the planks of the 1912 platform were to be translated into specific programs and bills, while the voters were to be converted to progressivism and the new party through pamphlets, lectures, and other educational techniques. The Service was divided into two bureaus and four departments: the Bureau of Education, the Legislative Reference Bureau, and the departments of Social and Industrial Justice, Conservation, Popular Government, and Cost of Living and Corporation Control. Each bureau and department in turn had its own committees and divisions. Professor Samuel McCune Lindsay of Columbia became chairman of the Bureau of Education and Paxton Hibben its full-time director. The bureau was in charge of literature, speakers, and public education, and its committee members included many distinguished academics. Functioning under the Bureau of Education were the Lyceum Service, the Association of Collegiate Progressive Clubs, the Division of Public Education Problems headed by John Dewey, the Division of Motion Pictures (a group headed by Booth Tarkington to prepare film scripts), and other groups and committees as well. William Draper Lewis was chairman of the Legislative Reference Bureau and Donald Richberg its director. The members of the committee assisting Lewis and Richberg in drafting legislation and preparing briefs included Gifford Pinchot, Jane Addams, Charles E. Merriam, Herbert Knox Smith, Ben Lindsey, and Walter Weyl. The four Progressive Service departments conducted research, devised programs, assisted the Legislative Reference Bureau, and waged propaganda campaigns. The roster of those who served and assisted in the departments was made up of the men and women most prominent in American social work. The Department of Social and Industrial Justice was directed by Jane Addams and included committees on men's and women's labor, social security insurance, child welfare, and other matters. Henry Moskowitz was in charge of men's labor and Mary E. McDowell of women's labor; Paul Kellogg of the *Survey* directed work on social security insurance; and the child welfare committee was chaired by Dean George W. Kirchwey of Columbia with Owen Lovejoy, Lillian Wald, and Ben Lindsey among its members. The Department of Conservation was directed by former Chief Forester Gifford Pinchot. The Department of Popular Government was headed by George L. Record, with Alice Carpenter a full-time secretary for women's suffrage. The Department of Cost of Living and Corporation Control had Robert G. Valentine, former commissioner of Indian affairs, as director, and Herbert Knox Smith chaired its committee on trusts and corporations. The heads of the two bureaus and four departments made up the Progressive Service Board under Frances Kellor.

It was planned that as many states as possible would organize state Services patterned on the national model, and by July, 1913, twelve states, and by June, 1914, twenty-one, had Progressive Services in operation. The Massachusetts Progressive Service formed fourteen committees to study the state's problems. In Illinois Merriam was chairman of the legislative reference bureau, and Mary E. McDowell and Jane Addams were active in the state Service, which Richberg had directed before being called to New York. New York State's legislative reference bureau had Henry Moskowitz as secretary and Lillian Wald among its members. Greenwich, Connecticut, and New York County had local service organizations in addition to the state Services. Everywhere the Service was greeted with enthusiastic support by social workers like McDowell and Wald and academics like Merriam and Kirchwey.

The Progressive Service was, as Frances Kellor said in an article in the *North American Review,* a "radical departure from all standard party organization," a novel experiment in American politics. In fact, there has never been before or since anything quite like the Progressive Service. Its antecedents were the legislative reference bureaus like Charles McCarthy's famous one in Wisconsin, and the many reform and social service organizations like the National Child Labor Committee and the College Settlements Association which had proliferated during the progressive era. Indeed, the Progressive Service recruited most of its members from these bureaus and groups. Most of the earlier organizations had been involved in politics in that they drafted plans and bills and lobbied and agitated for reforms. But the Progressive Service was partisan, expressing what Kellor called "a new spirit in party organization." The Service attempted to bring about a union between social scientists and politicians, to translate social service into the stuff of partisan activity. The Service also sought to coordinate and combine the interests and activities of many separate organizations into a single, nationalist structure. It was the ultimate expression of the desire of many social workers and reform-minded academics to move from fragmented and specialized social concerns and nonpartisan reform to partisan involvement and a comprehensive approach to the problems of society.

A few social workers dissented from the concept of partisan involvement. During the 1912 campaign when social workers had flocked to the Progressive banner, Edward T. Devine had insisted that it was "the first duty of social workers to be persistently and aggressively non-partisan to maintain such relations with men of social goodwill in all parties as will insure their cooperation in specific measures for the promotion of the common good...." But Kellor argued that for too long those interested in social work had been separated from power within the parties. How could reformers expect changes in government unless first the parties were changed? "The reforms of government begin in the party," she maintained. "There can be no reform in government administration without corresponding reform in parties." Furthermore, as Jane Addams and other social workers pointed out, it was the Progressive Party alone among the major parties which stood for measures long advocated by social workers, and which opened the door of the party organization to reformers like Merriam, Addams, and Kellor—and regardless of sex.

Paxton Hibben argued the case for the Service in an address before the Southern Sociological Congress in 1913, noting that for decades private groups had worked to end human misery and met with severely limited success. If it were true that social degradation could not be ended, Hibben declared, then democracy was a failure. He continued:

But the day of democracy is scarcely even begun. We have simply gone the wrong way about solving the problems of democracy. We have tried to do separately what must be undertaken in accurate and scientifically adjusted correlation of effort. It is not through charity, organized to special ends; not through individual or even locally collective social service that we may accomplish any permanent improvement of the conditions which we are met here to discuss. It is through harnessing these agencies of social betterment to an adequate machinery of practical legislation—in a word, it is only through an application of the spirit of social service to politics, that the ends of government for the people may be achieved.

The Progressive Service thus embodied many articles of the Progressive faith and the new politics. It combined beliefs in "modernism," the engineering mentality, government by experts, nationalism, and social science into an instrumentality of the new politics. The Service, wrote Kellor, was "a party laboratory, manned by experts." It was a modern approach to government and politics inspired by nationalism and social science. No longer were the problems of society to be approached in a haphazard manner, bills to be framed by uninformed officeholders, voters to be presented with vague generalities in place of concrete programs, or problems to remain unaddressed by parties.

The assumptions behind the formation of the Progressive Service, however, raised a number of questions about the party and the new politics. First, the functions and role of the service had implications for party authority and the conduct of politics. Second, the Service operated on the assumption that there could be universally agreed, "scientific" solutions for every social and economic problem. Third, the Service was the symbol and instrument of the commitment of many social workers and social scientists to the Progressive Party, but some critics thought such a commitment foolish and unjustified by the new party's political prospects.

The Service claimed to be the servant of the people through the vehicle of the new party. But was the Service the master or the servant of the party? The Service began its work with a program based on the 1912 platform adopted by the Progressive convention, but as the "party laboratory, manned by experts," the organization could logically be expected to write future party platforms.

This doubtless made at least as much sense as having platforms hastily drawn by convention committees of politicians and party satraps, and yet the end result would hardly be more democratic than the traditional process. Platform committees were appointed by party leaders; the officers of the service had been similarly chosen. Furthermore, the Service was established as a kind of self-perpetuating party elite. In a real sense, the elitist nature of the organization contradicted the direct democracy principles of the party. More importantly for the future of the party, however, it seemed almost inevitable that sooner or later the Service would clash with other party bureaus and groups over questions of authority, funds, priorities, and jurisdiction. The Progressive Party had established what was perhaps the most elaborate national organization in the history of American political parties, and for that very reason the party's potential for internal disputes was great.

The assumptions of the supporters of the Service that there were "scientific" solutions to every social and economic problem, and that the Progressive Party had a permanent place in American politics, were understandable in light of conditions in 1912 and 1913. The Democrats and the Republicans, and government at all levels, had failed to demonstrate any real understanding of the social and economic problems confronting an urban and industrial society. In short, the stage had not yet been reached when it could be seen for certain that there were many different possible solutions to problems like child welfare, many factors and values involved in considering any program worked out by the tools and research of social scientists. With children in the factories and nearly all laborers living on subsistence wages, 1912 and 1913 was not a time for considering the limitations of social science or national bureaucracies in a federal system, for considering the subtleties of reform. As for the faith of social workers and social scientists in the Progressive Party, not only did the future of the new party seem promising to many observers in 1912 and 1913, but social workers and social scientists could see that they had little to lose in throwing their weight behind it. If a campaign of social education were all that was accomplished by the party and the Service, would not this alone be worth the whole effort? And there was a chance of accomplishing much more. Further, it was not the Democrats or the Republicans who wanted their services. It was another Roosevelt—Anna Eleanor, T.R.'s niece—who was to prove through her career that it would take many years of hard work and stubborn persistence before one of the two old parties would listen to either social workers or women, and she learned that no victories won in this regard were necessarily permanent. The Progressive Service was indeed not only an ambitious undertaking but one of the most imaginative and interesting innovations in the history of American political parties. It was also eloquent testament of the new party's faith in its future and belief in economic justice, social science, the ability of women, and social engineering.

3

Throughout 1913 the Progressive Service operated to the fullest of its capacities. "Usually work ceased at midnight only because the elevators stopped running," Richberg recalled. A series of Progressive Service Documents was prepared and distributed, including speeches and articles by Roosevelt, Beveridge, and Kellor; pamphlets on sickness insurance, workmen's compensation, and unemployment; and three books: one on municipal government by Judge William L. Ransom, *The Progressive Movement* by the newspaperman S. J. Duncan-Clark, and a collection of T.R.'s 1912 campaign speeches. In all there were twenty titles, and by the end of March, 1913, thirty thousand pieces of literature had already been distributed. The Lyceum Bureau furnished speakers for local groups and meetings; and a set of six lectures on social issues, each illustrated by fifty stereopticon slides, prepared by the veteran lecturer Montaville Flowers and the Social Gospeler W. D. P. Bliss, could be rented from the Service for a nominal fee.

GOVERNOR JOHNSON
OF CALIFORNIA

The Service cooperated with Progressives in the states to introduce model bills in the legislatures. It sent out bills with supporting briefs and supplied experts to testify before legislative committees. Progressive state legislators, few in number, could not hope to pass bills on their own except in California, but in those states where the new party either held the balance of power in the legislature or had made a strong showing in the elections, Progressives could provide the impetus and pressure for the passage of reform measures, drawing support from members of the old parties. The new party made much noise in the legislatures, introducing bills and calling on the public to support progressive programs. The leaders of the old parties quickly realized that the Bull Moose challenge had to be met, and in state after state Democrats and Republicans moved to the left and passed reform legislation. In short, the Progressive strategy of initiative and challenge was productive in many states.

Progressive state legislators in Maine, holding the balance of power after 1914, helped Democrats pass bills for workmen's compensation and reduced working hours. Charles H. Thompson reported in February, 1913, that Progressives in Vermont were pressing for legislation on seventeen different issues, and had already seen at least some action taken on a dozen of them. In the next four years Vermont Progressives were instrumental in the adoption of the direct primary, particularly important in a state traditionally dominated by one party, and legislation for workmen's compensation, a state budget system, reduced working hours, and other reform measures. In Oregon the legislature passed three of the bills introduced by the Progressive Party, including a widows' pension bill and a measure requiring the direct popular election of party national committee members. The story was similar in other states, while in California Hiram Johnson and the Bull Moose legislature kept that state the leader in progressive government. In 1913 California Progressives passed laws creating a minimum wage, the Industrial Welfare Commission responsible for wages, hours, and working conditions, the Commission of Immigration and Housing, a cross-filing primary system, and the Industrial Accident Commission and insurance fund.

The activities of the Service were wide-ranging. In New York the Service went to the aid of the International Ladies Garment Workers' Union. The women and girls of the union were on strike in early 1913. The prosperous and large firms in the dress and waist trade came to terms on January 18, but the wrapper, kimono, and white goods manufacturers, described by one historian as "typical small-fry sweatshop bosses," held out against the strikers. At the urging of Madeline Doty, secretary of the child welfare committee of the Service's Department of Social and Industrial Justice, Roosevelt dramatically visited garment strikers at Henry Street and St. Mark's Place on January 21. On January 24 he lunched with strike leaders, and released a public letter to Progressive Assemblyman Michael A. Schaap reporting the conditions he had found on his tour: girls between the ages of 14 and 18, as well as other workers, who received well below the twelve dollars per week minimum experts said was necessary to keep body and soul together. "We cannot as a community sit in apathy . . . ," Roosevelt insisted. Schaap introduced a resolution calling for an investigation of conditions in the wrapper, kimono, and white goods trade. Roosevelt's well-publicized interest and Schaap's resolution in the legislature gave the cause of the strikers a boost. Gertrude Barnum of the I.L.G.W.U. reported that two firms had immediately settled with the union because of T.R.'s tour, and soon the whole strike was settled with a protocol favorable to the union. Shortly after the strike Madeline Doty was dispatched to Albany, armed with another public letter from Roosevelt, to testify on behalf of child labor legislation.

The Progressive Service also worked to aid the cause of women's suffrage. In the spring of 1913 Alice Carpenter was sent to Michigan to stump for a women's suffrage amendment in a state referendum on the issue, and on May 2 the Service joined other suffrage groups in sponsoring a rally at New York City's Metropolitan Opera House. Roosevelt was the speaker for the New York meeting. Beveridge, in his keynote convention speech in 1912, had offered women on behalf of the party the "chivalry of the state," but Roosevelt went further, proposing an "equal partnership of duty and right" between men and women. T.R. believed in a special vocation for women in the home, and many of his views on women were traditional, but he favored women having an equal place with men in government and politics. Dismissing arguments that women were inferior to men, he pointed out that "you cannot draw any line of intelligence or of conduct that wouldn't leave some of each sex on each side of it." He agreed that women had a duty to the home, but so did men, and if a man had more leisure to think of public affairs than his wife, "then it is a frightful reflection on him." "It is perfect nonsense to think that a woman who is not a doll or a drudge thereby loses respect," Roosevelt maintained. "On the contrary, I think that there is no surer sign of an advancing civilization than the advanced measure of respect paid to the woman who is neither a doll or a drudge."

Roosevelt's speech on women's suffrage and his public letters on behalf of the garment workers, child welfare, and other issues were part of his work in 1913 for the party and the Service as a social educator. As he helped with the tasks of organizing, so he labored to fulfill the party's other main objective— the education of the voters. The events of 1912 had shown that progressivism had a constituency, but the conservatism of many Republicans and the popularity of the laissez-faire platitudes of the New Freedom demonstrated that there was much more to be done before the majority of Americans understood or accepted the principles and programs of social welfare and industrial regulation. Roosevelt did what he could to bridge the gap between the voters and the social workers and academics who made up the Progressive Service.

In January T.R. published "Sarah Knisley's Arm" in *Collier's*, a brief for workmen's compensation based on a specific case of a woman injured in a factory. By dramatic use of a tragic accident, he sought to make the legal and social arguments come alive for the readers of the popular magazine. When he spoke at a conference of the Progressive Service held in Newport, Rhode Island, in July, 1913, the spring floods in the Mississippi basin, and the violent coal mine strikes which had plagued West Virginia since 1912, provided him with further vivid illustrations for the necessity of adopting the Progressive platform. The platform, he correctly predicted, would be recognized in the future "as one of the great documents in American political history." The tragedies of the Mississippi floods and the West Virginia strike both showed that the New Nationalist approach was needed. The Progressive platform had called for a federal, interstate development of the Mississippi for conservation, flood control, and commerce. And the platform had insisted that only federal laws and regulations could solve the problems of miners and workers. The problems of those who lived along the Mississippi River and of the coal miners transcended state lines. One of the problems that had led to the strike was that unionized mines in other states could not compete with the nonunion mines in West Virginia, and the United Mine Workers had sought to equalize working conditions and wages to benefit not only miners in West Virginia but in other states as well. Likewise, action in only one or two states could not meet the needs of all those who lived in the Mississippi River basin. What had the New

Freedom and the Wilson administration to offer in these situations, Roosevelt asked? Nothing. The competition in the coal industry was of the same kind that the New Freedom lauded, while the states rights philosophy of the New Freedom largely tied the hands of the federal government in relation to regional development for the Mississippi and laws and regulations to help labor. The consequences of the New Freedom for labor were particularly tragic:

The "New Freedom" means nothing whatever but the old license translated into terms of pleasant rhetoric. . . . The "New Freedom" when practically applied turns out to be that old kind of dreadful freedom which leaves the unscrupulous and powerful free to make slaves of the feeble. There is but one way to interfere with this freedom to inflict slavery on others, and that is by invoking the supervisory, the regulatory, the controlling, and directing power of the government precisely as the Progressives last year demanded in their platform....

During the first year of the Wilson administration, the president concerned himself almost exclusively with tariff and currency legislation, the traditional preoccupations of the Democratic Party. Wilson did not present Congress with a comprehensive reform program, and no proposals for trust regulation, Wilson's major issue in 1912, were forthcoming from the White House until mid-1914. And there were no indications in 1913 that the New Freedom would ever concern itself with such issues as women's suffrage, child labor, and the minimum wage, issues important to many progressives in all parties. As far as the Progressives and many progressive Republicans were concerned, the Wilson administration was only a slight improvement over the Taft regime.

In the front lines of the battle against the New Freedom were the Progressive congressmen, with whom Roosevelt, O. K. Davis and the Washington office, and the Progressive Service worked closely. In the Senate Miles Poindexter of Washington and Moses E. Clapp of Minnesota were the only members of the new party after Dixon's defeat in 1912. Joseph L. Bristow of Kansas tried to maintain relations with both the Progressives and the G.O.P., but by 1914 had decided to remain a Republican. At first it was uncertain how many representatives in the House would register with the third party organization, but ultimately twenty did, thirteen elected on Progressive tickets, the rest elected as Republicans with Bull Moose support. Victor Murdock of Kansas, a leading Republican insurgent, member of the House since 1903, became the third-party candidate for speaker and Progressive minority leader. The Progressives had hoped that more progressive Republicans, like George Norris in the Senate and William Kent in the House, would join the third party organization, and Roosevelt urged Bull Moose congressmen to cooperate with the progressive Republicans "with the idea that they may ultimately join with us." "We should be just as nice as possible with these near-Progressives," he wrote Representative William H. Hinebaugh and others, "but at the same time we should go good humoredly ahead with our own organization as a separate distinct National party."

But there were problems with this policy of cooperation. First, the national

Progressive organization outside of Congress was bitterly battling the progressive Republicans in the states over fusion and the issue of building third party organizations. Second, in Congress the progressive Republicans themselves were militantly independent, not only of all party caucuses but from each other as well. During the Wilson administration progressive Republicans could be found on nearly all sides of every foreign and domestic issue. O. K. Davis, Beveridge, the journalist John Callan O'Laughlin, and other Progressives close to Roosevelt feared that the Progressive congressmen might be as independent in their actions as their insurgent colleagues. "I am quite sure you will readily realize that the future of the Progressive Party will be largely influenced by the way its representatives in Congress act," O'Laughlin warned Congressman Walter M. Chandler of New York in February. "If they split up, some going with the Democrats and others with the Republicans, the effect will be bad." Murdock and a few of the others who joined the Progressive organization in the House had been in Congress before, but most were freshmen, and O'Laughlin reported to T.R. in March that they "are absolutely at sea as to what to do" when the session begins. O'Laughlin and O. K. Davis, both veteran observers of the Washington scene, therefore decided to take them in hand and show them what to do.

The first issue before Congress in 1913 was the Underwood tariff bill of the Democrats, reducing the levels of the Payne-Aldrich tariff. O. K. Davis later recounted that Beveridge and he had met with the Progressive representatives and told them to vote "present" on the tariff as a protest against the "log-rolling" and secret, "behind-the-doors" manner in which the tariff was framed. The Progressive platform, of course, favored drawing the tariff through a non-partisan commission of experts and the retention of the protective principle. The Bull Moose congressmen were indignant, saying they declined to be dictated to and would each vote as they saw fit. Davis then devised a second plan, whereby during the reading of the long bill Progressives would object to the "secret" and partisan way the tariff was constructed as each separate schedule was announced. Murdock agreed to do this, but only lodged a protest after one schedule, remaining silent for the rest of the reading. When the time came for voting on the Underwood bill, the 19 Progressives present on the floor split, 4 voting in favor of the bill, 14 against, and 1 voting "present." The pattern of splitting up was repeated on other bills proposed by the Democratic majority. Roosevelt did not think it mattered much as long as the Progressives first clearly presented alternative programs and pledged loyalty to the party by voting together for the speakership and other organizational issues. But Davis was disgusted with the independence of the Progressive congressmen. ". . . A flock of goats will run just about as many ways as there are goats," he wrote in his memoirs. He believed that lack of cohesion and the stubborn independence among the reformers who made up the Progressive Party both in Congress and outside was one of the main problems of the party.

Davis had a point. Many of the Progressive leaders were men to whom principle came before considerations of organizational necessity. "Ours is a party of great enthusiasm and great independence, and therefore with much less cohesion than the old parties," Roosevelt wrote Harold L. Ickes, who himself won the title "old curmudgeon" in later New Deal days. Hiram Johnson was stubborn and dour, a man driven, fired by righteousness and ambition. Beveridge was proud and sensitive, sometimes conceited, always easy to offend. The Pinchot brothers, Gifford and Amos, never seemed to learn the meaning of practical compromise. George L. Record was a fanatic about the single tax, bringing debilitating factionalism to the Progressive Party in New Jersey. "Reformers are a dreadful set, and it is awfully hard to try to do anything with them!" Roosevelt wrote his English friend Arthur Lee in September, 1913. "Yet it is an absolute necessity, for the alternative is to let the swinish forces of evil triumph," he added. "Of course I am having my usual difficulties with the Progressive Party, whose members sometimes drive me nearly mad," the Colonel wrote his son Quentin in the fall of 1913. "I have to remember, in order to keep myself fairly good-tempered, that even though the wild asses of the desert are mainly in our ranks, our opponents have a fairly exclusive monopoly of the swine."

Most minor, third, or new political parties attract adherents of unbending independence, and from what Roosevelt once called the "lunatic fringe" of reform movements. It is in the nature of such organizations. Furthermore, reformers were often the products of struggles with conservative machines, had spent their lives opposing organizations in business and politics, and hence had become congenitally independent. Yet, contrary to what Davis thought, the Progressive Party was less troubled by lack of cohesion than many such parties. Progressives in and outside Congress were able to agree on a definite program even if there were some differences. Moreover, most of the party's leaders were men experienced enough to keep the party together even when there were points of disagreement. Factionalism did not kill the Progressive Party. Moreover, Progressives accurately pointed out that factionalism in the Progressive Party hardly compared with the great divisions within the old parties. Finally, most of the leaders of the new party had compensating virtues to match their faults. Perhaps such men were the type attracted to Roosevelt, who was a mixture of obvious faults and evident virtues, righteousness and ambition, idealism and practicality. The public records left by men like Ickes, Johnson, Beveridge, and Gifford Pinchot proved that they were capable of accomplishments as well as attacks on their enemies. Once someone said to Roosevelt: "Oh, Beveridge is just a baby." "Ah, yes," replied T.R., "but a very brilliant baby." Roosevelt was inclined to let Progressive congressmen vote as they chose on bills not presented by Progressives; there was room for differences of opinion. He knew there were difficulties inherent in working with reformers, but he knew, too, what it was like to work with the "swine." He had, after all, been leader of another party for nearly eight years, and that experience had led him to establish the Progressive Party.

By the spring of 1913 the Progressives in Congress were in fact able to agree on a series of bills embodying the planks of the 1912 platform, the "Progressive Congressional Program." On April 8 the committee of the Service's Legislative Reference Bureau held a joint meeting in Washington with the Progressive congressmen and adopted eleven measures, and at a subsequent meeting five more measures were agreed upon. Each measure was assigned to a congressman and a member of the committee or another expert from the Service, who together drew up a bill with the help and supervision of Donald Richberg, the director of the bureau. The list of bills was impressive, and included a bill for a nonpartisan tariff commission with plenary powers of investigation, drafted by Murdock and Richberg; a bill drawn up by Congressman M. Clyde Kelley of Pennsylvania and Paul Kellogg calling for the creation of a commission to investigate social insurance plans; a bill prohibiting convict-made goods from interstate commerce, introduced by John I. Nolan of California, who had been a union leader before he was elected to the House; a measure for the prohibition from interstate commerce of goods produced by child labor, drafted by Representative Ira C. Copley of Illinois, William Draper Lewis, and Richberg; a bill for presidential preference primaries drafted by Congressman Hinebaugh and George L. Record; and a set of three bills, the "trust triplets," introduced by Murdock and drawn up by Richberg in consultation with Gifford Pinchot and Herbert Knox Smith, which called for the creation of a federal trade commission with powers to prevent unfair competition and suppress monopolies. Of course, none of the bills had a prayer of passing Congress, but Progressives hoped the pattern being followed on the state level might be repeated in Washington with the new party pointing the way for reform legislation resembling Progressive proposals. The Service made every effort to publicize the Progressive Congressional Program, as did Progressives on the floor of Congress. If the Wilson administration chose to ignore this challenge from the left, interested voters would know where to turn in 1914 and 1916.

Looking at the whole national organization of the Progressive Party, particularly the Service with its many bureaus and divisions, it almost seemed as if the new party had constructed a "shadow government," a demonstrator's model of the kind of government and types of bureaus, officials, and programs that could be expected from the new party in power. This was the final innovation of the new politics of Progressivism: an audacious attempt to translate the ideals and concepts of partisan responsibility and viable political alternatives into the life of everyday politics. If parties should represent clear choice, one from another, present alternative views and programs, then this had to be reflected in the organization and conduct of parties both in and out of office. And if a party was to be more than a coalition of state factions, its national identity had to be focused and created by a national organization that was more than just an office where the national chairman could hang his hat. The Progressive Party had taken all these facts into account, and its organization and program represented the incarnation of the new politics.

4

Throughout 1913 observers closely watched the results of the off-year elections. There were special elections in Maine, New Jersey, Massachusetts, and other states to fill vacant congressional and state legislative seats, and in the spring there were local elections in many states and a statewide contest in Michigan for judgeships and other offices. In the fall New Jersey and Massachusetts elected governors, elections were held in New York City and many other cities and towns, and legislatures were chosen in New York and Massachusetts. Observers looked to find the answers to the pressing questions posed by the nation's state of political flux. Would the Democrats continue their victorious momentum of 1912? Would the G.O.P. regain its former strength or continue to decline? Would the Progressive Party keep in the running, fall by the wayside, or continue to advance?

The national organization of the Progressive Party dispatched speakers to help local candidates. Roosevelt, Dixon, Alice Carpenter, and the organizers Edwin M. Lee and Charles H. Thompson went to Michigan to help the state party. In a special congressional election in July in New Jersey's sixth district, a squad of seven Progressive congressmen was sent to campaign, while James R. Garfield, Beveridge, and others spoke for the special election in Maine's third district in September. Roosevelt sent letters of endorsement everywhere. A special fund was raised outside the state to help the Massachusetts party. Beveridge helped out with local contests in Indiana. Progressives realized that the future of the new party depended in large measure upon the results. If there were victories, the party's ability to pull votes without T.R. at the head of the ticket would be proved. It would be shown that the party had penetrated to the grass roots. If, however, the party did not win some prizes or at least hold its 1912 strength, then it would be very difficult to launch a campaign in 1914; funds might dry up and office-seekers and local organizers return to the old parties; and the party might even dissolve altogether.

The political situation in New Jersey was complicated by a fight between the Progressive factions of Everett Colby and George L. Record. Proposing a platform of municipal ownership of utilities and the single tax, Record ran a candidate, Edmund B. Osborne, against Colby in the Progressive gubernatorial primary. Colby easily won the primary, but the new party faced the fall elections with divided ranks, while the G.O.P. ran former Governor Edward C. Stokes who appealed to Progressives by claiming to be a Roosevelt supporter. In New York State the political situation was extraordinary. The Democrat William Sulzer, promising reform, had been elected governor in 1912 with the support of the Tammany chief Charles F. Murphy. Once in office, Sulzer broke with Murphy over patronage and pushed for various reforms including a primary system. Roosevelt and the Progressives strongly backed Sulzer's program, but Murphy and Tammany checked the governor by having him impeached on charges that he had misused campaign funds. Tammany produced evidence Sulzer was unable to refute, and the governor was removed from office in

October. But many believed that Sulzer was guilty only of being a reformer. It was a case of recall, said Oscar Straus, but by Murphy not the people: "The reason Sulzer was recalled was because he would not play Murphy's crooked game straight." Sulzer returned to New York City and became a Progressive candidate for the state assembly, while the new party chose another independent Democrat, Samuel Seabury, to run with the able Learned Hand for the state court of appeals against nominees of the old parties. The situation in Massachusetts was also promising for the Progressives. The Republicans nominated for governor Henry Cabot Lodge's son-in-law Augustus P. Gardner, who was associated in the minds of the voters with the conservative organization of Senators Lodge and Crane, while the Progressives again chose Charles Sumner Bird, the candidate in 1912. Bird, endorsed by his 1912 Republican opponent Joseph Walker, made a vigorous campaign, touring the state by automobile and speaking in every town. Roosevelt issued an appeal to Massachusetts voters, recounting the actions of Murphy in New York, the alliance of Lorimer Republicans and Sullivan Democrats in electing senators in Illinois, and the domination of the Massachusetts G.O.P. by conservative leaders. All of this proved, the Colonel insisted, that throughout the union both old parties were in the grips of conservative machines, which frequently worked together in bipartisan alliance against the people.

In New York City the Progressive Party's fight against the machines took the form of a fusion movement. For months New York County Chairman Francis W. Bird, William L. Ransom, Roosevelt, and other Progressives carefully negotiated with independents in the old parties. Finally a fusion ticket was chosen with Democrat John Purroy Mitchel for mayor, Republican Charles S. Whitman for district attorney, and Progressives William A. Prendergast for comptroller and Ransom for justice of the city court, with nominations for other offices also divided among members of the three parties. In St. Louis, where Progressives nominated a Democrat against candidates of the old parties, and in Louisville, fusion movements of sorts assembled under the Bull Moose banner. The municipal fusion movements seemed to contradict the Progressive Party's repudiation of amalgamation with the old parties and the efforts to build a distinct new party, but a conference of Progressive city chairmen meeting in Cincinnati in April declared that the party favored nonpartisan commission government in the cities, and until such time as this became a reality Progressives should select and endorse municipal candidates "regardless of their party affiliations."

The results of the special elections in Maine, New Jersey, and other states were blows to the new party. Although a Bull Moose state senator was elected in Washington, all the Progressive candidates for Congress were badly defeated. The Michigan state elections in the spring indicated a Republican revival in a state Roosevelt had carried. While the total vote was smaller than in 1912, comparisons of the vote for governor in 1912 with that for supreme court justice in 1913 showed a G.O.P. gain of 11.37 percent from 1912, a Democratic loss of 4.22 percent, and a Progressive loss of 7.15 percent. The Democrats had won the governorship in 1912, but the Republicans won the elections of

1913. The results of the New Jersey gubernatorial election seemed a replay of the national contest in 1912 with the important difference that it was the Progressives who ran a poor third. The total Republican and Progressive vote combined was greater than the victorious Democrat's vote, but Colby polled only 41,132 votes to the Republican Stokes's 140,298. The results of all these elections seemed to indicate that the Democrats were still strong but might be beaten by a combined opposition, while the Republicans were making a comeback, with Progressive support on the wane. The outcomes of the other elections

THE LIGHT WILL SHINE ON

in 1913, however, showed the Progressives gaining in strength and a real threat to both old parties.

The local elections in the spring and fall brought good news for the Progressives. While the two old parties still retained control of most cities, towns, and counties in the nation, the new party impressively fought its way into this level of government, demonstrating some grass roots strength. In Michigan and New Jersey, where the party fared poorly in state contests, the Progressives did better on the local level, electing thirteen mayors in Michigan and six in the Garden State. The Progressives lost the elections in St. Louis and Louisville, but made an impressive showing against the Democrats in Louisville, where many political observers agreed that the elections had been won by fraud. In Illinois the Chicago returns were disappointing, but Progressives made notable gains in eleven counties, six of which had been carried by Wilson in 1912. In Indiana Progressive mayors were elected in Richmond, Seymour, Mount Vernon, and Marion. Ohio Progressives were elated at capturing the mayoralties in the cities of Canton and Akron, located in counties carried by Wilson in 1912, and Maine Progressives elected mayors in Auburn and Old Town. In the West the Progressive H. Russell Albee was elected mayor of Portland, Oregon, by a vote of 27,226 to the Republican candidate's 20,813 and the Democrat's 20,177. There were other victories as well, but the Progressives found their greatest cause for rejoicing in the election results in New York and Massachusetts.

In New York State the revulsion against Tammany was evident as the Republicans regained the Assembly and the Progressives scored impressive gains. Progressives were elected mayors in the cities of Syracuse, Amsterdam, and Johnstown, all located in counties where T.R. ran third in 1912. In New York City the fusion ticket of independents and Progressives swept into office, one of the winners being the Progressive Stanley M. Isaacs, beginning his half-century of distinguished service on the city council. Samuel Seabury was also victorious for the state court of appeals with independent Democratic as well as Bull Moose support. In 1912 the Progressives had elected only four members to the lower house of the legislature, but in 1913 twenty-three, including ex-Governor Sulzer and young Hamilton Fish, Jr., were elected to the Assembly. From the standpoint of the new party, the results in New York were, as the *Progressive Bulletin* said, "shining."

Running against the insurgent Republican Joseph Walker and Governor Eugene N. Foss in 1912, Charles Sumner Bird had come in third in Massachusetts. But in 1913 with Walker in the Bull Moose camp and the Republicans running a conservative, Bird polled 127,755 votes to the Republican candidate's 116,705, though the Democrat David I. Walsh was elected. Moreover, in 1912 only six Progressives had been elected to the state house and none to the senate, but in 1913 two were elected to the senate and sixteen to the house, tripling Progressive representation in the General Court and giving the new party the balance of power. The day after the fall elections Senator Poindexter of Washington issued a statement: "The results yesterday demonstrated the impossibility of the old Republican organization's winning out. This is particularly true of the results in Massachusetts. This was the first thing to be accomplished by the Progressive Party. The defeat of the Democrats will be cared for in the future." Hiram Johnson also issued a statement as a spokesman for the Progressives, noting that "from a national standpoint the theatre of action was Massachusetts. . . . In Massachusetts the issue of whether the people desired a third party was plainly put," he continued. "The results demonstrate that the new party is not for a day. It is here until its purposes are achieved, its principles triumphant. It is founded on a rock and will endure." In December the *Political Science Quarterly* concluded after surveying all the election returns: "The results of the election would seem to indicate the permanence of the Progressive party." In short, the new party had successfully weathered the challenges of 1913.

5

The Progressives had actually held what amounted to a victory celebration before all the returns were in, a show of confidence for party workers and defiance for their opponents. On October 3 the Progressive Service sponsored a farewell dinner at the New York City Roof Garden for Roosevelt, about to embark on a trip to South America. It was a gathering of the faithful and a display of leadership talent. Gifford Pinchot presided on behalf of the Service, and Beveridge, Raymond Robins, and T.R. spoke. Seated around the Colonel were workers from the Service like Kellor, Weyl, and Hibben; men from the New York Progressive Party like Frederick M. Davenport, Stanley M. Isaacs, Hamilton Fish, Jr.; Progressives from Congress; the seasoned organizers Bill Flinn and Timothy Woodruff; the "dough moose" Perkins; and representatives from the states: Bird and Walker from Massachusetts, former Governor Fort from New Jersey, Garfield from Ohio, former Governor Chester Aldrich from Nebraska. It was a representative group of Progressives, men and women of considerable talent and ability, leaders from the past and of the future. Roosevelt must have wondered, however, as he looked out over the tables at this dinner, the last of so many banquets, rallies, and meetings he had attended in 1913, whether this was all there was to be of the Progressive Party. Was this indeed the vanguard of the new politics, or did this group represent the high water mark of Progressivism? He had exchanged revealing letters on the subject with William Allen White the month before.

White wanted to write Roosevelt some observations about the party before the departure for South America. He reported that he had just returned from Colorado where he had attended a Progressive banquet in Denver. As far as he could judge, the new party was in good shape in Colorado, and in Arizona and California as well. "Coming home," the Kansas editor wrote, "I find that our state organization is intact, that not a man who had left the Republican party and joined our organization has gone back. Our county organizations, as nearly as I can tell, are perfect. . . . Yet I have a curious, indefinable feeling," he continued, ". . . this curious feeling that there has been an immense slump of what might be called the 'sheep vote.'" White explained:

As nearly as I can figure out, we have attracted to ourselves thousands of men of the college professor, country lawyer, country doctor and country merchant type, men of considerable education and much more than the average intelligence. . . . These men, in the aggregate, number a million votes. They are the leaders of thought in the community, and they have not been fazed. I think they are as strong, if not stronger, than they were last year in the faith, but their clerks and the small farmer and the unskilled laboring man have minds that are moved largely by two things—tradition and noise. Our noise has subsided and party tradition is pulling them. Whether or not our noise will attract them again, I cannot say. . . . There was, in addition to the sheep votes, in our four million total, I should think, a million, perhaps not quite so many, Teddy votes—votes of men who had confidence in you personally without having any particular intelligent reason to give why; except that you were a masculine sort of a person with extremely masculine virtues and palpably masculine faults, for which they loved you, but who voted with the Progressives, without caring a cent for the minimum wage or the initiative and referendum . . . , merely because they wanted to vote for you. We are going to lose the sheep votes and the Teddy votes, though we will probably get them from time to time, but it will be many years before we can hold the sheep votes. By all the chains of tradition, they are bound to the Republican Party and unless you are the candidate, we will not get the Teddy votes, and certainly will not get them in our Congressional and state elections. There are, it seems to me, a fairly good two million votes in the box that will not be shaken by defeat and that may be counted on to run along for four years, maybe six, possibly eight. . . .

What, White asked, should be done?

Personally, I would favor going ahead, holding our own, trusting to events to show the country the futility of having a so-called Progressive faction in either of the old parties, and hoping that either in three or five years we may accumulate enough from the Democrats and from the sheep votes of the Republicans to carry a national election and dominate Congress.

Roosevelt replied that White's analysis was "perfect." He agreed with White's listing of the types attracted to the new party, but added settlement workers, "upright" city lawyers, and the "best farmer and mechanic type" to the catalogue, "men whom I cannot help thinking will in the end be the leaders of thought in their several communities. . . . I feel just as you do, that we have got two million votes, but that it is purely problematical whether we get anything else." He concluded that White was correct: there was nothing to do but go ahead with the party, "hoping that gradually progressive Republicans or rational Democrats will come with us." He added in a message to Progressives at the farewell dinner on October 3: "All my life I have been engaged in work which culminated during the last eighteen months; and of all my political life it is these eighteen months to which I look back with most unalloyed satisfaction. . . . Win or lose, whatever the outcome, I am with you, and I am for this cause, to fight to the end."

As 1913 closed, Progressives were hopeful, but they knew that the elections of 1914 would bring the real day of judgment.

CHAPTER EIGHT

STRATEGIES FOR PROGRESSIVISM

> *. . . We have to give very much latitude to the local leaders in the several states and sections in the way they conduct the campaign.*
>
> T. R.

Progressives realized that the state, local, and congressional elections of 1914 would be the supreme test for the new party. After the 1912 elections Chairman Dixon had told reporters that like the Republicans after 1856 the Progressives would go on to win the state and congressional elections two years later and then capture the White House in the next presidential election. Thus, 1914 marked a crucial point on the Progressive timetable. At the very least, the party had to hold on to the vote polled for Roosevelt and the Progressive state tickets in 1912 in order to remain a credible and vital political force, and unless a significant number of Progressive candidates were elected it would be difficult to continue to claim that the party had a future. Since most Progressive support had been drawn from Republican ranks, and as yet there was no sign of collapse in the Democratic organization, it was particularly important that the new party come in ahead of the Republicans even if the Democrats again won most contests, because it was clear that unless the G.O.P. were eliminated there could be no Progressive victories in 1916 and beyond. The new party had survived the challenges of its first year and a half of existence, but without the hope of eventual triumph, which only election gains in 1914 could sustain, the party could not be expected to hold together for very long. Without such hope could the party expect men to continue to risk careers and make sacrifices by running for office or working for party organizations? Could voters be expected to continue to "waste" their ballots after 1914 for a party which on the basis of past performance had little chance of winning? The answers to these questions were obvious to Progressive leaders as they looked ahead to the elections of 1914. There were, however, disagreements among them about what strategies to follow.

First, a dispute arose over the policy of the party's national headquarters: should the emphasis of its work be on social education or conventional political organization? Second, Progressives continued to argue over the leadership of George W. Perkins. Third, they faced the option of "fusion" with the old parties. "Amalgamation" with the G.O.P. or any other party, as proposed by Frank A. Munsey in 1913, was out of the question, but "fusion" was another matter. Progressives might enter fusion movements in different states or districts in various ways. The same set of candidates could be run on the Progressive ticket and another party's column on the ballot; Progressives could simply endorse one or more candidates nominated by other parties; or, finally, a straight Progressive ticket might be composed of candidates from various parties. The same situation had faced the new party in 1912, but it was inevitable that it should arise again as politicians contemplated possible strategies in an election year. Some Progressives argued that the new party would lose its identity and compromise its principles if it trafficked with the old parties, while others maintained that as in the New York City elections of 1913, when the Progressives joined a fusion movement against Tammany Hall, it was possible for members of different parties to work together for common goals without destroying the integrity of the Progressive Party.

Then there was the question of issues. All Progressives were pledged to the 1912 platform, but some disagreed over which issues should be stressed in the campaign, while others wanted to add supplements to the 1912 "contract with the people." Proponents of Prohibition, government ownership of railroads and utilities, and other issues fought for the adoption of new planks in the state platforms. At the same time Progressives wondered which planks of 1912 should be emphasized in 1914. Should the keynote be antibossism, the trusts, social justice, direct democracy, the tariff? Should the Wilson administration be attacked? Should all the leaders of the old parties be attacked or only the conservatives? Finally, there were disputes over candidates and state leadership. Progressives in California and Washington fought over choices for the Senate, while in New York and Pennsylvania there were quarrels about gubernatorial nominations. Ironically, the primaries—which in a sense had given birth to the new party in 1912—became the field of combat in 1914 for party disputes as Progressives in several states took their causes to the voters in primary contests that weakened the party's strength and unity.

Progressives found no easy or quick answers for the problems confronting their party in 1914. And behind all the disagreements over strategy and issues lay the larger question of the New Nationalism. How far could Progressives in one state differ in program from their brethren in other states and still remain loyal to the concept of a nationalist approach to the issues? How much could the party adapt itself to American pluralism and yet preserve the integrity of the New Nationalism? It would be many months before the answers became apparent, and in the meantime Progressives locked horns over the more immediate questions of campaign strategy.

2

As Progressives considered possible courses of action to follow during 1914, a schism developed in the party between those who placed primary emphasis on political organization and the social educators connected with the Progressive Service. The split marked a division among Progressives over the two party objectives of education and organization proclaimed at the post-election Chicago conference in 1912. Throughout 1913, that year of hope and promise, these two goals had seemed not only complementary but integrally related. Voters had to be educated about the issues while at the same time organizational structures were perfected to house those gathered into the Progressive fold. Social education would preach the Progressive gospel, and partisan organization would translate faith into political good works. The Chicago conference had set forth what Jane Addams called "A Plan of Work," the program for building the new party which had met with considerable success in 1913, uniting the programs of reformers and social workers with the pragmatic realities of partisan political life. But as the campaign of 1914 approached, Progressive political organizers like Walter F. Brown, the former Ohio G.O.P. chairman who headed the national Progressive Organization Committee, and many of the more experienced politicians in the party, like Indiana's Beveridge, contended that the needs of the campaign placed a priority on traditional political activity and work.

The political organizers argued that the party had limited funds and therefore could not continue to support the elaborate bureaucracy and work of the Progressive Service. The monies of the national committee were needed to help Progressive candidates and state organizations, for the business of a party was to win offices, and without victory at the polls the programs of the Service could not be instituted into statute and government policy. Furthermore, the political organizers claimed that the Service had completed its work by drafting the Progressive Congressional Program and state bills in 1913, and by publishing the pamphlets and books explaining the 1912 platform. What was needed at this critical time in the party's development, the political organizers concluded, was a concentrated effort to elect Progressive candidates.

The social workers and academics like Frances Kellor, Jane Addams, Dean Lewis, Donald Richberg, and others who had worked for the Progressive Service believed, on the other hand, that social education, variously carried out through drafting model legislation, preparing and circulating programs and pamphlets, lectures, and other activities, was the most important work for the party to perform. They contended that voters could not be expected to give the new party power until they were properly educated about the need for the Progressive Party and its platform, until they were alive to the social and economic problems of the day. As Richberg later recalled: "Political education and a new political religion seemed to me necessary before a new political organization could accomplish anything." The process of educating the public, the social educators realized, could not be effected in a year or two, and indeed political victory might be delayed for some time, but victory would not come at all without preliminary social education. In 1913 the Progressive Service had made a beginning in the task of social education, but the service's supporters knew it was only a beginning. Moreover, as the social educators conceived it, the Progressive Party was not just another political party like the Republicans and Democrats. It was a party dedicated to social service, and the goals of social service transcended in moral value those of immediate political gain. The work of educating the public was a social service, and hence had top priority. Furthermore, immediate accomplishments in legislation and administration could often be at least partly won through lobbying in Congress and the state legislatures, with Progressives working with reformers in other parties to pass legislation resembling the Progressive model bills. In short, for the social educators the unique character of the new party demanded that social service and education have primacy over conventional politics. William Allen White expressed well the attitude of the social educators in a letter written to a friend in 1914:

We don't care what happens next autumn. We don't care what happens two years from now. We don't even care if we finally get into the St. John [perennial Prohibition candidate for president] class, for our work will be accomplished. Others shall reap where we have sown, which is all right. We don't care to reap, but we do care that there shall be a harvest. We are now chiefly interested in planting the seed.

The split between the political organizers and the social educators had not really been apparent or crucial before 1914 because of the broad areas of agreement existing between the two groups. First of all, the social educators were committed to partisan political action, differing in this from nonpartisan and single interest reformers. The Progressive Service had been founded on the belief that reform needed both partisan expression and a complete, all-inclusive program like that presented in the 1912 Progressive platform. For their part, the political organizers did not quarrel with the Progressive program, the model bills, or the objectives of the Service. They considered themselves as loyal to the party and its principles as anyone. The reform credentials of politicians like Beveridge were above question, and while opponents attributed base motives to some political organizers like Brown and Bill Flinn, most of the politicians active in the Progressive Party had paid their dues to progressivism in the coin of politically hazardous commitments to the new party and hard work for the cause of reform. Thus, the social educators and political organizers had been able to work together in harmony. But as the campaign approached it seemed to the politicians that the limited resources of the party had to be focused on the pressing demands of the campaign.

As early as April, 1913, Medill McCormick of Illinois suggested to Perkins that the Progressive Service would not be needed after the drafting of bills was completed and the legislatures adjourned for the year, explaining that while he believed in the Service he thought its work should "follow" the work of organization. Shortly thereafter the writer Hamlin Garland reported to Roosevelt that he had discussed the party's tasks with Ruth Hanna McCormick (Medill's wife) and others, and had come away agreeing with the politicians that organization had to precede the work of the Service, or else there would be little for the Service to work with in the future. "...It is my belief that the Progressive Party has become too academic," Richard Washburn Child of Massachusetts, later ambassador to Italy and chairman of the National Crime Commission, complained to Roosevelt. "It would please me to see the organization snuggle up to practical politics a little more, or perhaps, when it appears in public, to appear a little more as a political body, and a little less as a cult." Perkins sided with the political organizers in the pending dispute, thereby further convincing his enemies that he was no friend of reform. Roosevelt himself remained committed to both the Service and the organizers, believing the work of each essential to the other, but he was in South America and out of touch with the party early in 1914 when the politicians began to dismantle the Progressive Service.

The executive committee of the party met at New York headquarters on January 24, 1914. The majority of the executive committee represented the political organizers in the party. Perkins was chairman. Brown, his assistant Charles H. Thompson, and the veteran politicians Flinn, Lissner of California, Chauncey Dewey of Illinois, and George C. Priestley of Oklahoma were members along with Jane Addams and Ben Lindsey. For whatever reasons, Addams and Lindsey did not attend the January meeting. The first order of business was the future of the *Progressive Bulletin* and the Washington, D. C., Publicity Bureau. The *Bulletin,* a slick-paper magazine with a layout similar to *Collier's,* had been issued weekly during the 1912 campaign and monthly since January, 1913. During the campaign copies had been distributed free of charge, and thereafter for the nominal fee of one dollar per year. The newspaperman O. K. Davis, who had left a job with the *New York Times,* edited the *Bulletin,* ran a Progressive News Service, and directed a staff of nine or so at the party publicity bureau in Washington's Munsey Building. The national committee had budgeted a slim $10,500 for the work of the bureau in 1913, which Davis protested was insufficient to meet printing and office expenses, but by 1914 the executive committee had decided that even this appropriation was too much to spend on the Washington work. The *Bulletin* and the publicity bureau were under the authority of the party's publicity committee, but were part of the party's social education campaign along with the Progressive Service. The *Bulletin* reported party news and activities, but it also published articles popularizing the Progressive program. Davis worked closely with the Service, publicizing its activities and promoting its model bills. The trouble was that after the 1912 campaign the *Bulletin's* circulation was confined to its Progressive subscribers—it was preaching to the converted. At the January executive committee meeting Perkins therefore suggested that the *Bulletin* be discontinued, and the committee so voted. The funds for the Washington office were also cut back, and the office was finally closed altogether in June, 1914.

After disposing of the *Bulletin* and the Washington office, the committee turned to the Progressive Service. The minutes read: "The Chairman [Perkins] reported that in view of the fact that very few state legislatures met this year, and that the work of the Legislative Reference Bureau in drafting bills, *etc.*, had been largely completed in 1913 and was in comparatively slight demand now, it had been suggested that the Legislative Reference Bureau be discontinued for the present." The committee agreed with Perkins. Next Perkins recommended that "in view of the fact that this is a campaign year" the speakers' bureau be transferred from the service to Brown's organization committee, and this was also voted. The speakers' bureau had utility in the campaign and thus was retained although taken away from the social educators. The executive committee also cut back the appropriations for the service. In 1913 the service had spent over $41,000; in 1914 expenses were steadily reduced. The service spent $3,240.30 in January, 1914; $1,748.32 in February; $553.91 in May; expenses thereafter were always kept below $1,000 per month.

With the closing of the Legislative Reference Bureau, its director Donald Richberg returned to Chicago to practice law and assist Raymond Robins's campaign for the U. S. Senate. Paxton Hibben, director of the Service's bureau of education, returned to Indiana to run for Congress. Hibben had actually been fired by Frances Kellor before the cut in funds. The Service itself had not been free of internal squabbles, with the strong-willed chief of the Service often at odds with Richberg and Hibben. Thus, the young reformers found it not altogether unpleasant to take up new work. The suffrage worker Alice Carpenter continued at headquarters, but worked under Perkins's direction, while other service workers looked for new jobs. With a reduced staff and meager funds, Kellor struggled on with the service during 1914. After the elections Perkins informed her that the office space used by the Service at headquarters was to be given to the New York State Progressive Party. At Kellor's request the party then relinquished control of the Service. With the help of friends she tried to continue the Progressive Service as an independent organization for social research and education. But the attempt was short-lived and the Service soon withered away. No word of the gradual demise of the Service was leaked to the press, and for the sake of party unity no public protests were made by the social educators, thus keeping the news of the split between the organizers and social educators from the public. As Richberg later recalled, "the Service was chloroformed and buried privately. . . ."

Though the quarrel between the social educators and the political organizers had been a debate over priorities, and though there had been and continued to be substantial areas of agreement and common cause for the two groups of Progressives, in the last analysis the split was based on different conceptions of politics and political parties. The social workers and academics connected with the Progressive Service, experienced in the tactics of propaganda and lobbying, believed in the long-term strategy of social education. Addams, Kellor, and their cohorts had spent years in social work and reform, and had been frustrated many times, forced to accept the process of incremental change.

Time and again when faced with some defeat or frustrated by only partial success, they had pinned their hopes on the future and social education. Slowly the public would be made aware; gradually attitudes would change. For these reformers social education almost took on the attributes of a panacea. The social educators connected with the Progressive Service had broken with the past and their fellow nonpartisan reformers when they enlisted in the new party. Yet they had tried to convert the party into a social service agency as much as they had tried to employ the techniques and structures of social work for partisan ends. In short, they had confused the functions of a social service agency and a political party.

There were essential differences between a political party and an organization like the National Child Labor Committee or Wisconsin's Legislative Reference Bureau. A party depends on electoral successes for its lifeblood. Without victory or the hope of victory, a party can perform only the limited if important function of pressuring those who actually conduct government, of being merely a party of protest. By its very nature a protest party has an ephemeral existence. Without the chance of success at the polls, its voters, contributors, and party workers can be expected for the most part to turn after a time to more viable partisan vehicles. A political party can only afford long-term strategies when it is reasonably assured of a long lease on life, and such was not the case with the Progressive Party. The political organizers in the new party, schooled in the cyclical world of elections, knew that in the immediate future the Progressive Party could only increase or decrease in strength. It could not coast along in hopes of a better tomorrow. Either it would prove itself as a party in the near future by winning more offices, or it would cease to be a party. It might continue to exist as a reform organization like the National Municipal League, but it would not be a party. That is, it would no longer be directly involved in government through participation in the electoral process. The concept of a kind of partisan half-way house like the later Liberal and Conservative parties of New York State was still decades away. The Progressive Service had done valuable work for the party, but its functions had to be auxiliary to the business of electing candidates and organizing the political structure. Although a campaign of social education could accomplish much even in a short time, the fact of the matter was that if the American people were not ready to support the Progressive Party, now that it had clearly presented its program and personnel, then it was doubtful at best that the new party could survive long enough to wait for social and political attitudes to change.

3

The supporters of the Progressive Service did not air their dispute with the political organizers in public, but their resentment of Perkins for his leading role in the demise of the Service fed the flames of a new and publicized revolt against Perkins's continued leadership launched in the spring of 1914 by the executive committee chairman's old opponent Amos Pinchot. Pinchot and the social educators were joined in the revolt by many of the political organizers and state leaders who, like Medill McCormick of Illinois, found Perkins a "drag" on the party's popular appeal. On May 22 Amos Pinchot addressed a letter to Chairman Joseph M. Dixon attacking Perkins. Copies of the letter were sent to members of the national committee, and soon portions were published in the newspapers. "To talk against monopoly, to place the words 'Social and Industrial Justice' on our banner, and then to hand over this banner to a man who has been monopoly's ardent supporter and one of the most distinguished opponents of social and industrial justice . . . is, in my opinion, a handicap to the party, and a fraud on the public," Pinchot asserted. Once again Perkins's opponents said that his former partnership with J. P. Morgan, and his continued membership on the boards of United States Steel and International Harvester, trusts frequently attacked for their practices and hated by unions and farmers, made him unfit to be either the leader or spokesman of the party. These were the same old charges that had been heard in 1912, but they carried new weight because of Perkins's public statements in the months before the 1914 campaign.

In February and March, 1914, Perkins exchanged verbal blows with the progressive Republican Senator William E. Borah of Idaho. In a speech in Columbus, Ohio, in February, Borah attacked International Harvester and charged that the Progressive Party favored monopoly. Perkins angrily replied in an open letter on February 27 that the new party did not favor monopoly, and he vigorously defended the company of which he was a member: "I believe the Harvester Company is treating labor, consumers and competitors fairly and honorably...." Borah returned fire by claiming that Harvester paid its workers poorly. He also attacked United States Steel as antilabor. Perkins defended the labor policies of both corporations, although Harvester and United States Steel were under heavy attack from the unions. Perkins had earlier championed big business in 1913 by having articles published in the *Progressive Bulletin* praising Harvester and Standard Oil—this last in spite of the fact that Roosevelt had been a sharp critic of Standard Oil for over a decade. Perkins also publicly defended his former partner J. P. Morgan as a friend of labor. But the climax of his defense of big business came in June when President Wilson nominated Thomas D. Jones as a member of the newly created Federal Reserve Board. The controversy surrounding this appointment revealed much about the Wilson administration as well as the reasons for Perkins's unpopularity in the Progressive ranks.

After the passage of the Underwood tariff, Wilson had turned his attention to banking and currency reform, directing the Federal Reserve Act through Congress. The act was a milestone in the development of federal regulation of the economy, but then Wilson had chosen prominent bankers and businessmen rather than reformers as members of the Federal Reserve Board. Progressives in all parties loudly protested the appointments, maintaining that Wilson was giving control of a government agency to the very men it was supposed to regulate. One of the appointees, Thomas D. Jones, was an owner of the "Zinc Trust" and a director of International Harvester. An old friend of Wilson's, he had generously contributed to the president's campaign fund in 1912. Responding to progressive attacks on Jones, which noted that Harvester was currently under federal and state indictment as an illegal combination, Wilson wrote the Senate Banking Committee that Jones had joined Harvester in order to reform the company. At this point Perkins issued a public statement revealing that Jones had been elected to the board on the recommendation of Cyrus H. McCormick, also a Wilson supporter, and that at the time there was no dispute in the company over policy, nor had Harvester changed its policies since Jones joined the board. Perkins concluded that Jones was a good choice for the F.R.B., but pointed out that the appointment in effect represented a repudiation of the false charges Wilson had hurled against Harvester during the 1912 campaign. When Jones finally testified before the Senate Banking Committee, he admitted that he had not joined Harvester for purposes of reform, and said that in fact he approved of the indicted corporation's policies. The committee then refused to confirm Jones's appointment to the F.R.B., and Wilson was forced to withdraw the nomination, though his other big business appointments were eventually confirmed. In sum, with progressive Republicans and Bryan Democrats united in opposition to what they considered Wilson's attempted sabotage of the F.R.B., the executive committee chairman of the Progressive Party had rushed to the defense of Harvester and the president's most controversial nominee. Bull Moose leaders were in no position to enjoy the irony.

Many Progressive leaders thought it had been a mistake for Amos Pinchot to make his views on Perkins public, but agreed that Perkins should be replaced. Others urged compromise, doubtless realizing that Roosevelt would never consent to a purge. In July Medill McCormick wrote to Perkins urging him to resign his directorships with United States Steel and Harvester, maintaining that he must choose between the party chairmanship and his corporate connections. McCormick added that Dixon, Edward P. Costigan, William Allen White, Raymond Robins, and others agreed with him. In August Robins broached the subject of Perkins's directorships in a letter to Roosevelt. Admitting that Amos Pinchot was a "trouble maker," the Chicago Progressive said that nevertheless "his case against Mr. Perkins has certain strength for so long as Mr. Perkins remains a director in the U. S. Steel Corporation and the International Harvester Corporation, and these corporations continue their long maintained policy in relation to labor organizations."

Perkins, however, refused to resign his corporate positions because he believed that such action would prove, first, that a big businessman could not be sincerely dedicated to progressivism, and, second, that the charges leveled against United States Steel and Harvester were true. Ironically, J. P. Morgan, Jr., would have been pleased with Perkins's resignations, for he feared that the former Morgan partner's political activities would be misinterpreted—as they were—as proof of the involvement of the Morgan interests in politics. But Perkins was not without his defenders. His friend Beveridge wrote that Amos Pinchot's letter "amounts to treason in the ranks." Alexander H. Revell, a Chicago businessman who had contributed heavily to Roosevelt's campaign for the Republican nomination, and Robert Ruhl, editor of the *Medford* (Oregon) *Sun,* both wrote Roosevelt defending Perkins. "It seems to me," Ruhl contended, "that it is from men like Mr. Perkins, who understand the Big Business game and who sincerely want to secure justice not only for Big Business but for the people, that our greatest help can come." Yet of the most prominent members of the party only Beveridge, Flinn, and Roosevelt stepped forward to squelch Amos.

Troubled by many details of party management, Roosevelt was in no mood to cajole his fellow Progressives into supporting Perkins or to respond to Amos's detailed criticisms. With his business and management skills Perkins had become, as his biographer calls him, Roosevelt's "right-hand man" in the party. Roosevelt found Perkins useful, and he did not want to try to find a replacement at this late date when there was much to be done in organizing the fall campaign. Furthermore, Roosevelt felt that in order to preserve an air of competence and respectability the new party needed businessmen among its leaders as well as professional reformers like the Pinchot brothers. Then, of course, the problem of funds still remained. The party had to cut expenses in 1914 to meet its demands, and few new contributors had joined the ranks of those who had pledged monies in 1912 and 1913. In May, 1914, Perkins loaned the national committee $2,500, in July $8,500 more, and by February, 1915, he had loaned the national organization a total of $20,000. These loans were in addition to his regular pledges, a special donation of $5,000 in October, 1913, and the checks he sent to state and local Progressive organizations. State leaders complained that Perkins's business associations hurt the party, but regularly they asked the executive com-

GEORGE W. PERKINS

mittee chairman to send money for their work. Roosevelt had refused to dump Perkins in 1912, and he refused again in 1914. "When they read Perkins out they will have to read me out too," the Colonel angrily told reporters. He was adamant on the subject, and once more Perkins's opponents in the party gave up the fight rather than face a confrontation with Roosevelt.

Roosevelt had ended the incipient revolt, though only for a time, but he had not squarely faced the issues involved. "No man has served with greater zeal or disinterestedness," he said to reporters of Perkins's work for the party. Perkins had indeed worked long and hard, late and soon, for the party, and he had not, as his opponents charged, consciously tried to twist or dilute Progressive doctrine. Richberg had found to his surprise that Perkins did not try to change or amend the programs and bills drawn up by the Progressive Service, and in fact had praised the "trust triplets," the three bills introduced in Congress by the Progressives, which included stiff antimonopoly and unfair trade practice provisions. Yet in the Borah and Jones controversies and his frequent defenses of United States Steel and Harvester, Perkins had not served the party with "disinterestedness." He had permitted his private connections and views to control his statements as public spokesman for the party. Perkins did not seek to corrupt or use the party for his own purposes, but he had done the party grave damage by allowing his private concerns to influence his public role.

4

The possible strategy of fusion caused further quarrels among Progressives in 1914, and offered evidence of the limitations of nationalist ideology in the pluralistic American context, as did debates over which issues to emphasize in the campaign. The question of fusion was raised by Roosevelt himself after his return from South America in May, 1914. In October, 1913, the leader of the Progressives had gone to South America on a lecture tour, and then in February, 1914, had led an exploring expedition down Brazil's River of Doubt (now Roosevelt River), an uncharted tributary of the Amazon. The expedition took a heavy physical toll of Roosevelt, but as he explained to a friend, "It was my last chance to be a boy." During the trip he had suffered from dysentery and a severe leg wound, incurred while attempting to save boats in the rapids, and had contracted a serious case of malaria. T.R. was now in his mid-fifties, and the malaria proved to be the beginning of a series of illnesses that led to his death in 1919. " . . . I am now an old man," he wrote his fellow Rough Rider Leonard Wood in June, 1914. But there was little time for rest when Roosevelt, temporarily supported by a cane, returned home in May. With new state primaries set for September, the New York State campaign was already under way.

New York politics resembled a kaleidoscope that year. Governor William Sulzer, elected as a reform Democrat in 1912, had been impeached the next year through the efforts of Tammany Hall and its chief Charles F. Murphy, after Sulzer refused to cooperate with the party machine. Elected to the assembly as a Progressive in the fall of 1913, Sulzer declared his candidacy for governor and sought the Bull Moose nomination. At the same time the reform Democrats John A. Hennessy and Assistant Secretary of the Navy Franklin D. Roosevelt, the Colonel's distant cousin, announced candidacies respectively for the Democracy's gubernatorial and senatorial nominations. Murphy and Tammany supported incumbent Governor Martin H. Glynn, the stalwart lieutenant governor promoted by Sulzer's impeachment, and James W. Gerard, a Tammany member and Wilson's ambassador to Germany, for the U. S. Senate. The aspirants for the G.O.P. gubernatorial nomination included the conservative Job E. Hedges, defeated candidate in 1912, as well as District Attorney

Charles S. Whitman of New York City and the upstate Republican Harvey D. Hinman, both liberals, while James W. Wadsworth, Jr., of the Old Guard was favored to win the Republican senatorial nomination.

What should the Progressive Party do? The party looked to Roosevelt for the answer. Assemblyman Hamilton Fish, Jr., and a few others urged the nomination of "Plain Bill" Sulzer, but most Progressive leaders considered him a demagogue, discredited by Tammany's well-documented charges that he had mishandled campaign funds. Sulzer pressed Roosevelt either to endorse him or remain neutral. Roosevelt found it impossible to favor Sulzer because, as he wrote privately, although impeachment proceedings had been begun as a result of what the former governor had done that was "right," they had succeeded because of what he had done that was "wrong." ". . . My dear Hamilton, he has a record that would make it a very ugly thing for us to back him," T.R. wrote Fish. Sulzer, however, told Progressives that he would continue in the race with or without Roosevelt's blessing.

Many New York Progressives urged Roosevelt to run himself, believing that only he could head off Sulzer in the primaries and go on to win in November. ". . . I have at present not the slightest doubt of your election, though I would hardly expect any other man on the ticket . . . to win," the former state chairman William H. Hotchkiss wrote Roosevelt in July. Beveridge also thought T.R. should run, and lectured the Colonel at Sagamore Hill that it was his duty to the party. But most Progressives outside New York thought Roosevelt should not be a candidate. Leaders from all over the country wrote urging him not to run. Poindexter of Washington, Johnson of California, Congressman Hinebaugh of Illinois, chairman of the Progressive congressional campaign committee, Garfield of Ohio, and others declared that Roosevelt owed it as his duty to campaign for Progressive candidates throughout the nation, and pointed out that a defeat in New York in 1914 could destroy his chances for the Presidency in 1916. ". . . I do not think," National Committeeman Pearl Wight of Louisiana said, "that the Progressives of New York, can afford, for the sake of making a showing, to endanger the chances of the Colonel for President in the next election." Roosevelt for that matter did not want to run for governor. He had been governor as a young man; now he was primarily interested in national affairs. Moreover, he felt that his duty lay with the party nationally, and if he were a candidate he could not answer the calls of Progressives in other states for campaign appearances.

If Roosevelt would not run—and he was adamant in his refusal from the first— and Sulzer was unacceptable, who then should the Progressives choose as a candidate? There was much talk of fusion. Some favored a union with the Hennessy reform Democrats, but Roosevelt pointed out that Tammany would continue to support Governor Glynn, which would mean two Democrats and Roman Catholics in the gubernatorial race. What was needed, cautioned T.R., was a Protestant who could appeal to upstate Republicans. ". . . Names and prejudices count a great deal with the average voters and it is simply folly and not virtue to fail to recognize this fact," he explained to Hiram Johnson. Other

Progressives favored the candidacy of the Republican Charles S. Whitman, famous for his battles with the New York City underworld, and lawyer Royal W. France and other members of the new party helped form a Whitman Non-Partisan League.

Whitman in fact tried to enlist Roosevelt's support, but the Colonel and many Progressives distrusted and were bitter towards the dapper district attorney because as a fusion candidate in 1913 he had accepted Tammany backing at the same time the hall was fighting the rest of the municipal fusion ticket. Moreover, Progressives reported that the Republican boss William Barnes favored Whitman's candidacy for governor. But in private the reformer C. S. Duell, Jr., became an intermediary between Whitman and Sagamore Hill. Duell brought word to Roosevelt that not only was Whitman opposed to the bosses in both old parties but that he had voted for Roosevelt in 1912. Duell asked if Roosevelt would back Whitman if the district attorney issued a letter condemning both Barnes and Murphy. Roosevelt cagily replied that if Whitman opposed Barnes and Murphy he should publicly say so, and then the matter of his candidacy could be discussed further. Whitman issued no public statement against the bosses, and when word of his negotiations with Sagamore Hill was leaked to the press, he quickly affirmed his loyalty to the G.O.P., saying that in the past he had always supported Republican candidates. Royal France and Duell then repudiated Whitman. Duell angrily told the whole story of Whitman's overtures to the Progressives, and declared that the district attorney's protestations of Republican loyalty and regularity in the light of his messages to Roosevelt were "so conclusive of the lack of any real character in the man that I don't see how any man this fall who respects his vote can vote for Mr. Whitman either at the primaries or at the polls."

There remained the candidacy of former state Senator Harvey D. Hinman, an upstate Republican who had been a supporter of the primary system, and who was an anti-Barnes candidate for the G.O.P. nomination. In Hinman, Roosevelt thought that he had at last found a solution to the problems of the Empire State Bull Moose. After conferring with Hinman and state Progressive leaders, the Colonel proposed that Hinman become a candidate simultaneously in the Republican and Progressive primaries, and on July 22 he issued a lengthy statement explaining the New York political situation.

"In this campaign I have a duty to the Progressives of the nation and a duty also to the State of New York," Roosevelt explained. "In national politics . . . I shall endeavor to strive for the success of the principles embodied in the Progressive National Platform. . . . But in this state the prime duty is a good citizens' movement—a fusion movement to save the state from the bi-partisan control of Messrs. Barnes and Murphy. . . ." This would be a fusion movement like the one in New York City in 1913. "It is impossible to secure the economic, social and industrial reform to which we are pledged until this invisible government of the party bosses . . . is routed out of our governmental system." No good could come from choosing between the candidates of Barnes and Murphy, Roosevelt continued, because the two bosses were of "exactly the same moral and political type." Furthermore, Barnes and Murphy worked together. "The interests of Mr. Barnes and Mr. Murphy are fundamentally identical, and when the issue between popular right and the corrupt and machine-ruled government is clearly drawn the two bosses will always be found fighting on the same side— openly or covertly—giving one another such support as can with safety be rendered." The situation in other states was different, Roosevelt explained, but in New York conditions demanded an alliance between Progressives and the "honest rank and file of the old parties" to overthrow the Barnes and Tammany machines.

Roosevelt's statement landed like a bombshell on the New York political scene. Barnes's response was prompt. The Republican state chairman denounced Hinman as a traitor, and announced that he was suing Roosevelt for libel for saying that he had entered into deals with Tammany. The habitual practice of bipartisan deals in the Empire State was common knowledge, and both the Republican *New York Tribune* and Democratic *New York Times* defended and praised T.R. and Hinman. The reaction among most Progressives, however, was almost as hostile to the Hinman fusion as Barnes had been.

Some New York Progressives, like Frederick M. Davenport and Perkins, did fall in line dutifully behind Hinman and the Colonel, and Perkins issued a letter explaining fusion to Progressive leaders in New York and throughout the country. "The question of governor in this state is a local and not a national question," wrote the chairman of the executive committee. "A great many of our people in this state at first blush will doubtless feel that we have amalgamated, that we have surrendered to the Republicans, and all that sort of thing. Exactly the opposite is the fact." Since Roosevelt would not run, Perkins continued, Hinman offered the only chance to beat Barnes as well as Tammany. "We, independent Republicans, were beaten in Chicago by Mr. Barnes and his machine," and hence "nothing is more natural" than that the Progressives should join with Hinman Republicans to destroy the same machine.

Most New York Progressives disagreed with Perkins's analysis. "While it is true that the formation of the Progressive Party was hastened by the theft of the Republican nomination in 1912," the Hudson County leader John J. O'Connell wrote, "still, after the adoption of the Chicago platform in August, 1912, it became a party with new and radical principles and not merely a rebellious offshoot of Republicanism. . . . Mere opposition to the corrupting influence of bossism . . . is a very unsubstantial and flimsy basis for a new party." Chauncey J. Hamlin of Buffalo, Erie County leader, did not agree that fusion was, as Perkins said, "a local and not a national question."

The difficulty about the situation . . . is that more is at stake, than the governorship of New York State [he wrote Roosevelt]. The Progressives throughout the U. S. have manfully stood up and are making a fight for the principles of our party and clean leadership, and pretty generally are going it severely alone. That has been the expressed policy of our party and in that policy lies, I believe, certain elements of strength I cannot bring myself to believe it would be well to abandon.

Hamlin added that he would resign from the party unless a straight ticket were run in New York.

"Progressives throughout the U. S." were soon heard from. The consensus was that fusion in New York would hurt the party in all states. "There is a determined effort on the part of the standpatters to create the impression of amalgamation everywhere," Senator Moses E. Clapp reported to Perkins from Washington. Although there was a distinction between "fusion" and "amalgamation," the Republican newspapers were using the Hinman candidacy to "befog the minds of the uninformed," warned the Ohio congressional candidate George M. Leopold. Similar reports came into Progressive headquarters from Colorado, North Dakota, Minnesota, Indiana, and other states. "It is hard to estimate the enormous damage which you have done the Progressive cause by your endorsement of Hinman," Charles Sumner Bird wrote T.R. "It will be called a surrender to the Republicans. . . ." Beveridge was outraged. The Hinman statement would stop Republicans "from coming over to us, who are ready to come . . . , provided they think that the Progressive Party is here to stay . . . ," he told Perkins. "So it is not very nice, is it, after all the work we have done out here in Indiana . . . and the sacrifices we have made, to have this bombshell thrown into us?"

Less emotionally Congressman Victor Murdock of Kansas, Progressive leader in the House, replied to Perkins's letter:

I have just read your letter about Hinman, so have most of the other Progressives here. . . . No one here is over-enthusiastic over the proposition. The only explanation, to my mind, is the one in which you put emphasis upon the New York situation being a purely local one. That will stand for elaboration. But the proposition of cleaning up the Republican Party from within is killing on us and I hope you will soft-pedal there. Take Kansas for instance—when the Progressive Party was formed we had been working at that job in Kansas for about eight years, with fair progress [,] but the Chicago events demonstrated that it is a national, not a state proposition. That is as true of New York as it is of Kansas. I long ago put behind me any thought of future alliance with the Roots and Barnes. . . . The trouble with the New York situation is to keep it local.

Roosevelt quickly replied to the critics of the Hinman candidacy. Progressives should not be guilty of "idolatry of names," he told Hiram Johnson. To Charles Sumner Bird he explained that there was no difference between fusion in New York City in 1913 and fusion in New York State in 1914. He added in letters to Johnson and Dwight B. Heard of Arizona that he hoped Progressives, "while running straight tickets in any state where the conditions demand it," would fuse with Democrats or Republicans if one of the old parties endorsed the Progressive platform of 1912. On July 31 he issued a public statement clarifying his position: "We appeal to the honest rank and file of the two parties, Republican and Democratic alike, and we will be delighted to fuse with them against the bosses, the machines, the Bourbons, and the reactionaries of both business and politics."

Yet although Roosevelt claimed fusion was possible and desirable in any state if the old parties agreed to Progressive principles, at the same time he explained that conditions in New York were peculiar. He wrote Raymond Robins on August 12:

New York is not a progressive community. Most of the so-called reformers have in the past been purely swallowtails and silk-stockings who objected to corruption really on aesthetic grounds and who sided with the corruptionists as soon as economic privilege was attacked. There are anarchists and ultrasocialists in some numbers and there are plenty of decent citizens whose minds move in old and worn grooves; but there are not any great numbers of the men who believe as you and I believe. . . . It is entirely impossible at the present moment to get any attention in this state for the consideration of questions of abstract social and industrial justice. It is possible—I do not say . . . [probable], but at any rate possible—to wake up the people on the issue of the overthrow of both the old bosses and the old machines and the establishment of clean and decent rule at Albany. . . .

Roosevelt's position, however, was contradictory. On the one hand, he insisted on a nationalist policy which would allow fusion only where Republicans or Democrats endorsed the 1912 platform with its emphasis on social and industrial justice as well as popular rule, and on the other hand he declared that a "good government" movement based solely on antibossism was the solution for New York. As he had stated on July 22: "In this campaign I have a duty to the Progressives of the nation and a duty also to the State of New York. In national politics . . . I shall endeavor to strive for the success of the principles embodied in the Progressive National Platform. . . . But in this state the prime duty is a good citizens' movement. . . ." But when Flinn and the publisher Alexander P. Moore asked him to confine his speeches in Pennsylvania that year to attacks on Barnes and Penrose "and to make this purely an anti-boss campaign," he refused, saying that the whole of the Progressive platform should be emphasized including the "economic and social side." In an analysis resembling that of New York's John J. O'Connell in his attack on Perkins's defense of fusion, Roosevelt wrote Dean Lewis in Pennsylvania: ". . . I believe we cannot build a permanent party merely by attacking the bosses. We have got to attack them always . . . ; but we have to have something else on which to lay great emphasis or we are not really a party." He had, of course, also argued that in New York neither a campaign for social justice nor a straight Bull Moose ticket would have any chance for success, but considerations of immediate victory had had no part in the decision to run state tickets in 1912, nor did Roosevelt claim that success was probable in other states in 1914.

The fact of the matter was that in the summer of 1914 there were forces pulling in opposite directions in Roosevelt's mind—a tension between the demands of practical politics and those of nationalist and reform ideology. As an experienced politician he knew that considerations like the ethnic background of candidates and the needs of particular state situations had to be taken into account, that, as he wrote Robins, "we have to give very much latitude to the local leaders in the several states and sections in the way they conduct the campaign." But as the apostle of the New Nationalism and the champion of social reform, he insisted that the party in all states outside New York stand four-square for the binding "contract with the people" covenanted in 1912. The paradox and inner tension were built into Roosevelt's dual role as leader of the national party and chief of the New York Progressives within the context of the pluralistic American federal system. As a New Nationalist he fought for a vision as large and broad as the whole country, for a national reform ethos; as a New York politician he jealously contended for the practical needs of his own state. The New York political situation, however, soon took on a completely different shape from what Roosevelt had first envisioned.

5

At first Hinman seemed to be making headway in his campaign for the Republican gubernatorial nomination, and though most New York Progressives opposed fusion, many of them, as Perkins euphemistically put it, in the end "yielded to Colonel Roosevelt's broad experience and judgment." But the Barnes machine was powerful, and Whitman, favored by the G.O.P. organization, was an attractive candidate, seen by many voters as a crusading district attorney. Soon Judge Ransom was worriedly reporting to Sagamore Hill that the G.O.P. nomination was "fast slipping away from Senator Hinman," who was playing a "'gum-shoe' game," muting his calls for reform and trying to mollify the Republican regulars. Then in late August Hinman issued a statement affirming his Republican loyalty. "I am and shall continue to be a Republican even if not nominated in the Republican primaries," he said. "I shall not . . . leave my party either before or after the September primaries nor seek support for any nominee of any other party." This meant that Hinman would not continue in the race if he won the Progressive but lost the Republican primary. The Progressives had been double-crossed by Hinman, and they moved quickly to find another candidate. ". . . The Hinman movement offered infinitely the most effective—and I am sorry to say perhaps the only effective—method of smashing the Barnes controlled Republican organization," Roosevelt sadly wrote a Michigan critic of fusion, but "Hinman failed in the supreme test and we promptly threw him to one side and will now nominate a Progressive as the only alternative."

The New York Progressives met in convention at Utica on August 27. Mayor Samuel A. Carlson of Jamestown had suggested the adoption of a comprehensive platform like that of 1912, but Perkins and T.R. favored, and the convention issued, a brief statement which declared that "the time is not opportune to write new platforms in this state." Until the people again controlled the government, "all discussion of social and industrial and political justice . . . is idle and futile. . . ." The Progressives "bid Godspeed" to reformers in both old parties, and then proceeded to form their own ticket. Frederick M. Davenport, professor of law and politics at Hamilton and a former state senator, was endorsed for governor, with the opponent of fusion Chauncey J. Hamlin and New York attorney Bainbridge Colby selected for lieutenant governor and U. S. senator respectively. The ticket also included the Democrat Samuel Seabury for chief judge of the court of appeals and a distinguished slate of delegates, headed by Oscar S. Straus, as candidates for the 1915 state constitutional convention.

The results of the September primaries were a blow to progressives in all parties. Tammany's candidates Governor Glynn and Ambassador Gerard were nominated for governor and senator over John A. Hennessy and Franklin D. Roosevelt by a vote of more than two to one in the Democratic primary. In the G.O.P. primary Hinman polled only 61,952 to Whitman's 120,073, while standpatter James W. Wadsworth, Jr., was nominated for the Senate. As Bull Moose leaders had feared, "Plain Bill" Sulzer ran strongly in the Progressive primary, and Davenport won by only a small margin. Sulzer continued in the race as the candidate of the Prohibition Party and his own newly created American Party. Progressives worried that he would outpoll Davenport in November.

Although the fusion movement was dead in New York, the option remained open in other states. As in 1912 many Republican officeholders and candidates badgered Roosevelt for endorsements, but the Progressive leader laid down the rule that fusion was possible only if candidates endorsed the 1912 platform and otherwise demonstrated unity with the purposes of the Progressive Party. In Vermont the Republican Charles A. Prouty, former member of the Interstate Commerce Commission, received the endorsement of the Progressive, Democratic, and Prohibition parties against the conservative G.O.P. incumbent Senator William P. Dillingham, but the three parties ran separate candidates against the Republicans for other offices. As in 1912, the Republican candidates in South Dakota and Wisconsin were backed by Roosevelt supporters. In Utah, the bastion of Senator Reed Smoot and conservative Republicanism, Progressives and Democrats united on a common platform following the 1912 Progressive platform, and agreed on a fusion ticket of Democrats and Progressives. In the end, with these exceptions and a few others, Progressives ran straight third tickets for all offices. Few local and state Republican or Democratic organizations were willing or able to meet the strict standards laid down by the Progressives for fusion.

The situation in Pennsylvania was complicated. Gifford Pinchot was the unanimous choice of the Washington Party to run against the Republican boss Senator Boies Penrose, but support for the gubernatorial nomination was divided between Dean Lewis of the University of Pennsylvania, H. D. W. English, president of the Pittsburgh chamber of commerce and enemy of the party leader Bill Flinn, Judge Charles N. Brumm, and others. Eventually Lewis, Pinchot's own choice, was endorsed by the Washington Party organization, but Judge Brumm also entered the primaries. In 1912 when the Penrose machine had preempted the names "Progressive," "National Progressive," "Roosevelt," and others by having them legally registered as party labels belonging to Penrose henchmen, Flinn and the organizers of the new party had adopted the name

"Washington Party," but they had also established a "Bull Moose Party" and a "Roosevelt-Progressive Party" to provide T.R.'s supporters with several columns to choose from on the confused Pennsylvania ballot. The Bull Moose Party had an organization in Lancaster County, but the Roosevelt-Progressive Party largely existed only on paper. Being legally constituted, these two parties had to participate in the May primaries along with the Washington and other parties—there were at least nine parties in the Keystone State in 1914. Pinchot was unopposed in the three Progressive primaries, but Lewis lost the Bull Moose nomination to Brumm while winning the Washington and Roosevelt-Progressive endorsements. This was, of course, an embarrassing development for the Washington leaders, though it was hoped Brumm could be induced to withdraw. But before negotiations with Brumm were completed, Lewis himself announced that he was withdrawing from the gubernatorial race in favor of the Democratic candidate Vance McCormick, saying that "the forces making for evil are united, those making for good should not be divided."

Gifford Pinchot at first opposed any fusion, but then came to believe it would help him win Democratic votes. Flinn supported fusion, but H. D. W. English and those in the Washington Party opposed to Flinn's leadership were against it. English declared that Lewis had no right to accept primary endorsement and then turn the nomination over to someone else. A Philadelphia party conference in September reluctantly approved Lewis's withdrawal, and then the Washington Party state committee voted to substitute Vance McCormick's name on the party ballot in place of Lewis. Lewis argued that McCormick and he stood for the same progressive principles, and fusion would unite the anti-Penrose forces, but he made it clear that he had entered into no deal with the Democrats and no fusion had been arranged for other offices. Progressives hoped, however, that Congressman A. Mitchell Palmer, the Democratic candidate for the Senate, would reciprocate by withdrawing in favor of Pinchot. But Palmer, a staunch supporter of the Wilson administration, refused to yield to the Progressives. Pinchot campaigned for McCormick, but McCormick declined to back Pinchot over Palmer. Democrats in fact urged Pinchot to resign in favor of Palmer, claiming the congressman was the stronger candidate—an assertion which the election figures in November later disproved. Many Progressives were furious. ". . . When there is so-called fusion, I want to *see a fuse,*" English wrote T.R. When the Democrats refused to drop Palmer, Brumm remained in the gubernatorial race as the Bull Moose nominee and a protest candidate, although he was opposed by Pinchot and the Washington Party. Pinchot, on the other hand, would not withdraw for Palmer, pointing out that the Progressives had carried the state in 1912, and that Pennsylvania was a protectionist state and would not elect a senator pledged to Democratic tariff policies. In short, with neither the Progressives nor the Democrats agreed on what fusion should mean, the Pennsylvania political scene was confused, and observers believed that the Penrose machine had a good chance of victory in November.

The divisions among Progressives in New York and Pennsylvania were exacerbated by the primary system, with many Empire State voters supporting Sulzer's independent candidacy in the Progressive primary, and Keystone voters being presented with a choice between Washington and Bull Moose party candidates as a result of the primaries. Yet this was not the end of the new party's problems with the primaries. In North Dakota the Progressives failed to poll enough votes in the primary to win a place on the ballot and had to resort to petition, while in Washington, Oregon, and California the new party's unity was threatened by primary contests between different Progressive factions.

In Washington the Progressive Congressman Jacob Alexander Falconer announced his candidacy for the Senate, only to be opposed in the Bull Moose primary. And Congressman James Wesley Bryan, the other new party member of the U. S. House from the state, was contested for renomination. Both Falconer and Bryan were defeated in the Progressive primaries, and thus the new party lost two incumbent congressmen even before the November elections. In Oregon A. Walter Lafferty, elected to the U. S. House from the third district in 1912 on the Republican ticket with Progressive support, and joining the Bull Moose caucus in Congress, found himself opposed after a bitter primary contest by Republican and "Progressive-Republican" as well as Democratic candidates. Designating his political gender as "Republican-Progressive," Lafferty was defeated for reelection in November by the straight Republican candidate. There was also a contest in the Oregon Progressive primaries for the gubernatorial nomination. In California the Progressive national committeeman Chester H. Rowell, Fresno newspaper publisher, and Francis J. Heney, the fiery graft prosecutor, opposed each other for the new party's senatorial nomination. Rowell was favored by most leaders close to Governor Johnson, but Heney appealed to the rank and file of the party for support. Roosevelt carefully remained neutral. Heney won the primary, but the ill will between Heney and the Johnson camp threatened the success of the Progressive ticket in November.

It was ironic that the primaries should have hurt the Progressive Party, which so vociferously championed the system. Intraparty quarrels were probably inevitable, but a party with many problems to face could ill afford the luxury of divisions aired in public through primary contests. Primaries offered voters an opportunity to choose their candidates, and leaders a method of deciding party control, but a new party depends on unity even more than established organizations because the image of a party is blurred in the minds of voters when its leaders fight in public. In short, the direct democracy reforms of the New Nationalism had resulted in a reinforcement of the pluralistic nature of the American polity by bringing local factionalism to the surface. Fusion had been attempted in various states to bring the Progressive Party added strength in the 1914 elections, and factionalism over candidates was in part a function of the party's search for the strongest champions to lead the fall campaign, but the disputes over fusion and in the primaries had in fact weakened the party's standing in many states.

Progressives, however, faced other problems as well. Still another question remained to be resolved before the fall campaign: what issues should the party raise and emphasize?

6

Roosevelt wanted the Progressives in 1914 to wage a campaign equally against the G.O.P. and the Democrats, attacking both Republican bossism and the failures of the Wilson administration, but many Progressives urged him to concentrate his fire on the G.O.P. "I am firm in my conviction that our fight must be directed principally against the Taft-Penrose-Barnes-Cannon-Lorimer brand of Republicanism and only incidentally against the Democrats," declared Congressman William H. Hinebaugh of Illinois, chairman of the Progressive Congressional Campaign Committee. The New York publisher Henry L. Stoddard agreed. "Progressive candidates are not going to get the anti-Wilson votes cast next November," Stoddard advised Roosevelt in July. "Even you cannot deliver them. Republican candidates will get them. Your anti-Wilson speeches will make more Republican votes than Progressive votes. The American people are very practical, and they will take the simplest, surest way to accomplish their purpose. That way is the Republican ticket." Many Progressive leaders seemed to agree with the assessment of the *Baltimore Sun:* "Colonel Roosevelt must ruin the old Republican Party beyond repair before either the Progressives can triumph or the G.O.P. be given into his hands. Therefore his main struggle, however much he may rage against the President and Congress, is with the Old Guard."

Roosevelt, however, did not think his advisors correct in their judgment that he should confine his campaign assaults to the G.O.P. When Washington Party leaders urged such a policy, he replied to the publisher Alexander P. Moore:

I do not agree with you as regards your views that I should only attack the bosses, and particularly Barnes and Penrose. In my judgment to confine ourselves to that attitude is practically to eliminate us as a national party. There is a very strong feeling against the bosses and we must make that fight a prominent feature of our program—indeed . . . I could not conscientiously do otherwise. But just as prominent must be the fight against the national Administration. Permanently there is only room for two national parties in this country and one of these must be the opposition. I feel as conscientiously in my opposition to Wilson as in my opposition to Barnes and Penrose. I cannot compromise with either. My judgment is that the discontented Democrats and the men who voted with us but have a tendency to join the Republicans would refuse entirely to go with us if we failed to make an active fight against Wilson.

What was the record of the Wilson administration? Wilson had directed the Underwood tariff and the Federal Reserve Act through Congress, but as of Labor Day, 1914, when T.R. began touring the country for the Progressive Party, the administration had not produced the promised new antitrust law, nor had Wilson acted on most of the issues emphasized by the Progressives in 1912: a federal trade commission, a nonpartisan tariff commission with powers to direct tariff making, workmen's compensation, social security insurance, abolition of child labor, federal regulation of working conditions and hours, and women's suffrage. The president was still arguing that most of these measures were unconstitutional, while at the same time the so-called Susan B. Anthony amendment to the Constitution had been defeated in Congress largely because of Democratic opposition. Moreover, the vaunted Underwood tariff had been passed during the cyclical recession of 1913-14, which lasted about twenty months, the worst economic reverse since the depression of 1893 under the Cleveland administration. The Underwood tariff was not really responsible for the recession, though Republican and Bull Moose orators claimed otherwise. But the reduction in sugar rates had adversely affected the cane and sugar beet industries in Louisiana, Colorado, and other states. And the reduction in steel rates came at a time when production and sales were declining, with mills in Chicago, Pittsburgh, and other cities operating well below capacity. It was unfair to blame the recession on Wilson, though he did little to relieve the situation, but since he had virtually said in 1912 that a reduced tariff would solve most of the nation's economic ills, there was justice in pointing out that such had hardly proved to be the case. Finally, Roosevelt wanted to condemn Wilson's foreign as well as domestic policies. The Colonel opposed the payment of an indemnity to Colombia for his actions in securing the Panama Canal, a measure proposed by the administration in 1914, and he condemned Wilson's risky and ever-changing Mexican policy. In short, as the fall campaign approached Roosevelt was convinced that there was a long bill of indictment to be lodged against the Wilson administration.

Roosevelt wanted the Progressives, except in New York, to emphasize the issues raised by the party's 1912 platform, but Progressives in various states believed the time had come to raise new issues as well. The introduction in Congress of the so-called Sheppard-Hobson amendment to the Constitution, providing for national Prohibition, had elevated this old issue to a new political prominence. The Sheppard-Hobson amendment, which had failed to win the necessary two-thirds vote in the House, had been supported by nearly all the Bull Moose congressmen, and many Progressives insisted that in 1914 their party should declare for Prohibition. Progressives like William Allen White had long favored Prohibition, and Roosevelt had had a hard time keeping a dry plank out of the party platform in 1912. Now the argument was advanced in many states that with the G.O.P. and the Democracy largely silent on the issue, the new party would gain moral and political strength by speaking out for an end to the liquor traffic. For many progressives in all parties, particularly reformers in the Midwest and West, Prohibition was as desirable as direct democracy and industrial justice, because it was a social reform which would attack the problems accompanying drunkenness like disease, broken homes, pauperism, and accidents.

In 1914 at least fourteen Progressive state conventions declared for Prohibition in one form or another. Joseph Walker in Massachusetts, Republican candidate for governor in 1912 and Progressive nominee in 1914, strongly advocated Prohibition. At the October state convention there was a sharp debate on the issue, but a dry plank was passed 232 to 130 over the objections of Charles Sumner Bird. The Michigan Progressives also declared for Prohibition, and nominated a well-known temperance worker, Samuel Pattengill, for governor. In Ohio both James R. Garfield, Progressive candidate for governor, and Arthur L. Garford, running for the Senate, endorsed statewide prohibition for the Buckeye State. "I am going out in this campaign and bust the liquor interests in the eye every chance I get," Garford proclaimed. In view of this stand the Ohio Prohibition Party opted for fusion and endorsed the Progressive state ticket. "The temperance men of both old parties are coming to us.... With the tide running our way ... victory may be gained. The temperance problem has completely changed the campaign," Garfield enthusiastically reported to Roosevelt in October. "... As part of the new nationalism for which we contend," declared the Nebraska Progressive platform, "we take our stand for national, constitutional prohibition of the liquor traffic throughout the U. S...." The Progressive platforms of Maine, Vermont, Pennsylvania, Georgia, Indiana, Iowa, Kansas, Arizona, Colorado, and Utah also declared for some form of Prohibition, though several adopted compromise planks like that in the Vermont platform which favored congressional passage of the Hobson amendment "in order that the people of the United States as a whole may decide" through the votes of the state legislatures.

Roosevelt, a moderate social drinker himself, had some sympathy for the cause but believed that Prohibition could not be enforced, and knew the issue would alienate workers and immigrants. When Joseph Walker asked for his endorsement of Prohibition, "the right and righteous side," Roosevelt replied: "I cannot back up National Prohibition. I have carefully refrained from committing myself on the subject because as yet it seems to me that it would not be the right thing to do." To William Allen White he explained:

As for prohibition nationally, it would merely mean free rum and utter lawlessness in our big cities.... I will favor prohibition whenever the sentiment is strong enough actively and locally to support it, but I do not believe that the American people can be dragooned into being good by any outside influence, whether it is a king or the majority in some other locality.

It was too late to stop Progressives from joining the crusade for national Prohibition, but that was one issue they would have to fight for without T.R.'s help.

The espousal of Prohibition revealed much about the Progressive Party. "Of course I am entirely out of sympathy with prohibition, and felt bound to make a fight against it," attorney Arthur Dehon Hill told Roosevelt after the Massachusetts convention, "but it is in no way surprising that in a gathering of this character a movement of that kind ... should have great weight." The widespread support for Prohibition in the Progressive Party showed the Protestant and Anglo-Saxon background of many of its members, and also indicated that for many social reform was integrally related to moralism. There was also an element of social control and a certain implicit nativism present in the arguments for Prohibition. In most states those opposed to Prohibition were laborers and immigrants for whom the neighborhood saloon, the beer garden, wine with meals and for religious occasions, and liquor at social gatherings were a way of life, a part of ethnic and cultural heritages. But liquor and spirits were often alien and suspect to Protestants of British descent in New England, west of the Appalachians, and south of the Mason-Dixon Line. Unfortunately for the Progressive Party, the cultural and ethnic myopia displayed by the advocacy of Prohibition offended the very groups the party had not attracted in 1912 and needed to win in 1914–the immigrants and the working class.

Prohibition was not the only new issue taken up by Progressives in 1914. George L. Record of New Jersey agitated for the single tax and government ownership of utilities, and while the single tax attracted little attention in 1914, Amos Pinchot and Francis J. Heney joined Record to promote the concept of government ownership. Amos was unable to convince his brother Gifford to run for the Senate in Pennsylvania on such a program, and soon Hiram Johnson was agreeing with Roosevelt that Amos had become, in the governor's words, "a terrible and bloodthirsty parlor Anarchist." But Johnson's running mate Heney was also proposing a new "radical" platform for Progressives. As the Bull Moose candidate for the Senate in California, Heney issued a personal platform which advocated, among other measures, government ownership of remaining timber, coal, oil, natural gas, water power, and fertilizer resources; a government-owned steamship line connecting the east and west coasts through the Panama Canal; and public ownership of railroads, telephones, and telegraph. The concept of government ownership, however, was taken up by few Progressives.

Heney's platform also contained a "peace plank," calling for world peace and the elimination of war profits through government manufacture of all arms, ammunition, and battleships. Walker in Massachusetts also ran on a "peace plank." The gubernatorial candidate declared that the "two great moral and social reforms" needed were Prohibition and the "substitution of law for war in the settlement of international disputes" through an "international Court of Justice" and a "real international parliament." These planks were in obvious conflict with Roosevelt's lifelong advocacy of military preparedness and nationalism, but as with Prohibition and government ownership the Colonel kept his peace and let the candidates say what they wished.

7

The discussion among Progressives of the issues of 1914 and the debates over fusion revealed weaknesses in Roosevelt's New Nationalism. Roosevelt claimed that fusion had to be considered from the perspective of each locality, and yet he soon learned fusion in any one state had implications national in scope. The storm over fusion in New York and elsewhere was an illustration of the difficulties involved in following a nationalist ideology in the context of the American federal system. Furthermore, while the primary system had been included in the New Nationalism to provide plebiscitory mandates for powerful leadership, in practice the system had meant diffusion of power and a breakdown in central partisan authority. The Progressive Party could ill afford factionalism, but the primaries had enforced factionalism and made it public.

In 1912 the Progressives had said that unlike the old parties they stood for the same principles in every state, and except on the race question this had indeed been true. In 1914 the Progressive state platforms affirmed allegiance to the 1912 "contract with the people," and again there were many large areas of agreement on issues like women's suffrage and industrial reform, but definite differences had emerged as to what Progressivism meant in different states. In Massachusetts, Ohio, Michigan, and other states, the party stood for Prohibition, but in New York, California, and still other states the party did not. In New York the Progressives emphasized antibossism, and while all Progressives opposed the tribe of Barnes and Penrose, in other states the emphasis was on labor legislation or other issues. In short, it looked as if the Progressive Party was coming to stand for different things in the various states. The seamless garment of the New Nationalism was beginning to unravel; pluralism was infiltrating the ranks at Armageddon. As Roosevelt girded himself for the fall campaign, it remained to be seen if he could salvage enough from the New Nationalism, if he could reformulate the faith of 1912, to meet the new conditions and present voters with a coherent nationalist gospel.

CHAPTER NINE

"THEY WILL NOT ENDURE
SOUND DOCTRINE"
The Campaign and Elections of 1914

*For the time will come when they will not endure
sound doctrine; but after their own lusts shall they
heap to themselves teachers, having itching ears;
And they shall turn away their ears from the
truth, and shall be turned unto fables.*

II Timothy 4:3-4

As the campaign of 1914 approached, Roosevelt faced the problem of how
to shape and frame the Progressive appeal to the voters. His unsuccessful negotiations for fusion in New York had been widely interpreted as an attempt to return to the G.O.P. The national image of the Progressive Party was further
blurred and confused by pluralism: the Prohibition stands of state Bull Moose
parties in Massachusetts, Ohio, and other states; the individual platforms of
various candidates like California's Heney, who urged government ownership;
and the fusion in some states and districts with Democrats or Republicans.
Yet it soon became clear that however much he might disagree with the
strategies of individual candidates and state parties, Roosevelt felt that it was
both possible and logical for there to be Progressive pluralism and particularism
within the folds of the New Nationalism. He believed, in short, that the sum
of the parts of the Progressive Party in 1914 still added up to a meaningful
whole. It was his responsibility as national leader and spokesman to demonstrate how the parts fitted into and related to the Progressive whole. In this
attempt to reconcile pluralism with nationalist ideology, Roosevelt presented
what amounted to a third version of the New Nationalism, expanding the
earlier versions of 1910 and 1912.

Roosevelt's restatement of the Progressive faith in 1914 in part consisted of
a contention that there was a juncture between the New Nationalism and the
particular and pluralistic needs of the states. Again and again he argued that
differing state situations required different political tactics and emphases on the
issues. He had said as much in 1912, but during the hectic days of the presidential campaign there had been little opportunity for him to stress the peculiar

needs of different states, or to relate these particularisms to the New Nationalist ideology. In the campaign of 1914, however, there were both the chance and the necessity for elaboration on the thesis that the New Nationalism could serve the individual parts of the federal system. For Roosevelt the paradox of the American polity, the paradox of a national union of separate states, was resolved and the ideological integrity of the New Nationalism preserved by the fact that every state party remained pledged to the Chicago platform of 1912, and individual state issues were addressed within the context of the national platform.

Even the brief New York antiboss platform of 1914 stated: "We, the Progressives of the State of New York . . . , hereby ratify and confirm our national and state platforms adopted in 1912," though in New York "all discussion of social and industrial and political justice through law . . . or improved constitutional provision" was "idle and futile" as long as Barnes and Murphy held power. All the Progressive state platforms contained clauses like Connecticut's affirming that "we hereby indorse the national platform of the Progressive Party adopted at Chicago, August 7, 1912." And except in New York the state platforms presented detailed enumeration of the 1912 pledges for women's suffrage, minimum wage, abolition of child labor, primaries, and other reforms. Conditions in various states necessitated an emphasis in state platforms on special problems, like the depression of the sugar industry in Louisiana or the need for a new state constitution in Rhode Island. But Roosevelt argued that such local concerns showed the relevancy and prescience of the state parties, while at the same time all remained pledged to the same goals of political democracy and social and industrial justice in state and nation. In those states or electoral districts where the new party had entered into fusion with Democrats or Republicans based on a common agreement on platform, as in Utah, Progressives had merely thereby proved that they were indeed a party of principles, a party that stood for something and was not guilty of narrow partisanship or what T.R. called the "idolatry of names."

The Progressive attempt to adapt the New Nationalism to the particular needs of the various states was illustrated by the party's campaign in Colorado. The political situation in Colorado in 1914 was dominated by issues arising from the coal strike called by the United Mine Workers in September, 1913. The causes of the strike had been building for decades with an accumulation of labor grievances. In 1903-04 the U.M.W. had led a strike for an eight-hour day and other measures against the Colorado Fuel and Iron Company owned by the Rockefeller family, but the miners had been crushed by the operators with the help of the state militia. When all efforts to obtain negotiations and union recognition failed in 1913, the vast majority of miners left the pits and the company towns and moved into tent colonies. The operators imported strikebreakers and "plug-uglies," and convinced the Democratic governor to call out the Colorado National Guard. On April 20, 1914, the state troops attacked and burned the tent colony at Ludlow, killing strikers, women, and children. Further bloodshed and virtual civil war followed the Ludlow Massacre. John D.

Rockefeller, Jr., and Colorado Fuel and Iron rebuffed President Wilson's efforts to mediate, and the president was forced to send federal troops to restore order. The U. S. House sent a subcommittee to Colorado to investigate, and Edward P. Costigan, the Denver lawyer who led the state's Progressive Party, served as U.M.W. counsel for the lengthy hearings. Costigan also became defense attorney for miners accused of conspiracy to murder in indictments resulting from a fight near Walsenburg, Colorado, and was chosen to present the strikers' case before the federal Commission on Industrial Relations. Costigan's masterful defense of the U.M.W. won widespread sympathy for the union's cause throughout the country, and eventually the indicted miners were acquitted, but the mine owners still refused to accept arbitration. Worn down by the long struggle, the U.M.W. was forced to end the strike in December, 1914, and shortly thereafter the Rockefeller interests dictated their own settlement.

In 1914 the Colorado Progressives nominated a distinguished state ticket headed by Costigan for governor and Benjamin Griffith for the senate, with Merle D. Vincent for attorney general and Agnes L. Riddle for secretary of state. Costigan had been the Progressive gubernatorial candidate in 1912, coming in second behind the winning Democrat. Griffith was a former attorney general of the state; Vincent a veteran of the legislature who had long been a foe of the G.O.P. state machine; and Mrs. Riddle a two-term member of the legislature, whose presence on the ticket was witness to the Progressive commitment to women's rights. The party adopted a comprehensive platform, which attacked Democratic misrule and the 1914 Colorado G.O.P. slogan of "law and order." "The Progressive Party and its candidates stand for law, order, and justice," the platform declared. ". . . We yield to no party in our devotion to . . . orderly government and the settlement of all disputes without destruction of life and property. . . . We also hold that there can be no permanent orderly government, under law without justice; that is, justice to all, to labor, to capital and to the public alike." The platform went on to call for recognition of unions, government investigation of labor disputes, enforcement of the right to counsel and habeas corpus for prisoners held in connection with labor disturbances, direct democracy reforms, and the federal labor measures included in the 1912 national platform like workmen's compensation and the abolition of child labor. The Colorado platform also advocated state control of prices and working conditions in coal mining on leased public lands. "Coal is a public necessity," the platform stated, "and we believe that the state constitution should be amended, making coal a public utility. This accomplished, then . . . legislation could be enacted, not only governing sanitary working conditions in mines, but regulating the price of coal to the consumer, if need be, in public crises. . . . And we believe that the state should be permitted, in case of necessity, to purchase, develop and condemn coal lands, now privately owned. . . ."

The Colorado Democrats generally favored the same state labor and coal mining reforms as the Progressives, but the Democratic platform was silent on primaries, trusts, federal welfare and labor legislation, and other issues covered by the Bull Moose state platform. Although the Democrats claimed to be champions of labor, Progressives pointed out that the Democratic state administration had called out the troops who attacked the Ludlow tents, and that the Democrats had failed to adopt a platform as comprehensive as the Progressive reform program. The G.O.P. state platform, which took few positions on proposed reforms, declared that law enforcement was the paramount issue, and "We will not be diverted from this issue by those who have openly violated the laws, or by their sympathizers, attorneys, or bondsmen"—a pointed reference to Costigan.

Costigan asked Progressives outside Colorado to help in the campaign. New York headquarters dispatched O. K. Davis to help the Colorado party, and the Pinchot brothers sent funds. Davis reported to Roosevelt that while the Democrats and Republicans were guilty of ignoring labor's just demands for the past thirty years, the Progressives were being hurt because it was widely believed they had not taken a firm enough stand in favor of "law and order." In the summer when Costigan and other Colorado Progressives made a well-publicized pilgrimage to Sagamore Hill to receive Roosevelt's blessing, the Colonel remarked to Costigan about the Republican "law and order" crusade:

Fifteen years ago, no, not fifteen years ago, because I was governor then, such a movement might have caught me, but not now. Of course, we all believe in law and order, . . . but we must never forget that law and order are means to justice, and where there is no justice, there is and can be no permanent peace. They had law and order in Warsaw under Russia.

On August 15 Roosevelt issued a lengthy public letter to Costigan, which was widely circulated in pamphlet form in Colorado.

Roosevelt had condemned the Colorado Fuel and Iron Company for its antilabor practices when he toured the state in 1912, further noting that the mining concern was not a monopoly, not one of those corporations attacked by the New Freedom. He had argued that it was clear that the company and similar firms should be regulated by the federal government, and yet Wilson's program provided for no such supervision. In 1914 Roosevelt feared, as he told Walter Weyl, that Costigan would suffer from a backlash against the miners' battles with the authorities. Hence, in his public letter he sought to expose the forces behind the Republican "law and order" crusade.

"It seems to me that not since the creation of the Progressive Party have there been in any state conditions so peculiarly and strongly calling for the exact application of the Progressive program of social and industrial justice as now in Colorado," Roosevelt began. The "first necessity," he continued, was to realize that the "war" in Colorado was a result of the "governmental bankruptcy" of both Democratic and Republican administrations in the state "for many years past."

The second necessity is to recognize the folly, the worse than folly of asserting that the present conditions can be met by mere shouting for "law and order," when what is thereby meant is exerting the power of the government to see that the lawbreakers on one side are forced to obey the law and refusing to exert the power of the government to make the lawbreakers on the other side obey the law. . . . They [the law and order advocates] demand that we shall police the lawlessness of the workingmen. In the same breath they demand that we shall not police those who by their misconduct have created the conditions which provoked this lawlessness. . . . We, on the contrary, hold that it is the duty of the government both to "police" the rioting and the violence and also to "police" the causes that have led to the industrial unrest, and not stand supine until these causes produce this inevitable result by provoking the sense of injury and resentment which creates disorder.

Roosevelt further pointed out that nationally as well as in Colorado the old parties had not produced a thoroughgoing program for industrial justice and business regulation. Only with the Progressive Party's plan of regulating and supervising all aspects of industrial life, from wages through trade, "will it be possible to undo the evils that have arisen not only in connection with the unscrupulous insolence of uncontrolled combinations but in connection with the merciless cut-throat competition which has resulted in unrestricted and un-controlled private war, either under business forms or in the shape of frankly lawless violence."

The social and political situation in Colorado thus provided Roosevelt with a case in point for his contention that the New Nationalism and the Progressive Party were addressing the needs of both the nation as a whole and the individual states. The New Nationalism, in the version presented by Roosevelt in 1914, sought to complement the powers and programs of the states with national policies designed to serve the entire federal union. The solution of the problems of Colorado required in part the adoption of the kind of legislation and programs set forth in Costigan's 1914 state platform, and in part the institu-tion of federal policies outlined in the national Progressive platform of 1912. The individual states had to work out their own salvation in regard to peculiar problems like the terms and conditions for coal mining leases on Colorado state lands, but the national government alone could deal with issues affecting several states. If Colorado were to adopt strict labor regulations for its mines and mills while other states did not, then Colorado commerce would be placed in an unfavorable competitive position. As Roosevelt had pointed out in his Newport, Rhode Island, speech in 1913, such a situation had arisen between the nonunion mines of West Virginia and the unionized mines in neighboring states. The result had been a bloody strike in West Virginia as the U.M.W. moved to equalize labor conditions, a strike which Roosevelt argued could have been prevented by federal regulations for all mining concerns involved in interstate commerce, regardless of whether or not they were trusts. In short, there was no necessary contradiction between the New Nationalism and the state govern-ments, and the new party had proved itself cognizant of the needs of state and nation through its national platform and state platforms like Costigan's in Colorado.

While helping the state campaigns, Roosevelt sought to sound the Progressive keynote on the national issues in a speech in Pittsburgh on June 30. Wilson had based his campaign in 1912 on the issues of the tariff and the trusts, Roosevelt noted, but the Wilson administration had failed to solve either problem. The Underwood tariff had reduced duties, but had done so in the old "log-rolling" manner, and a recession had followed. The Democrats had promised to reduce the cost of living and solve the trust question by reducing the tariff, but what had happened? "The cost of living has not been reduced. But the ability of the average man to earn a living has been greatly reduced. Not the slightest progress has been made toward solving the trust question." The Progressive Party favored the protective principle in tariff making: "We wish to pass prosperity around and for that very reason we desire that there may be . . . prosperity sufficient to pass around." The new party also advocated the tariff be made by a "scientific" nonpartisan commission of economic experts. Nothing could be gained, T.R. maintained, by returning to the unfair and economically archaic high tariff policy of the Republicans, by a "violent oscillation" between an Underwood and a Payne-Aldrich tariff.

In 1912 Roosevelt had called the tariff a "red herring," used by the old parties to divert voters from more important and substantive issues. But in 1914 the tariff issue was clearly still alive and crucial. Roosevelt feared that the G.O.P. would benefit in a reaction against the Underwood tariff and hard times, and he sought to steal the Republicans' "full dinner pail" appeal while at the same time advancing the Progressive commission stand to meet criticisms of the old Republican high tariff policies of the past. Progressives, therefore, were to go before the voters as protectionists, but as protectionists who favored the third option of a tariff commission of experts rather than the two old paths of high tariff and free trade. During the campaign Progressive candidates around the country followed Roosevelt's keynote and emphasized protection and the tariff commission as among the most important issues of the new party.

The trust question had been the other major issue of the Democrats in 1912, when Wilson called for trust busting and the enforcement of competition in business, and Roosevelt had proposed a federal trade commission for the regulation of all business. In his Pittsburgh address Roosevelt pointed out that the Democrats had yet to produce antitrust legislation and no trust-busting crusade had been launched. He went on to give the clearest and most detailed exposition of the Progressive stand since the formation of the party. Antitrust and regulatory legislation, according to T.R., should be based on seven principles. First, it should be recognized that Americans needed "large units to do our work." Second, "We cannot make every man compete with every other man"; there were limits to the possibility and desirability of competition. Third, "We cannot destroy monopoly by attacking all forms of concentration whether monopolistic or not." Fourth, not only the "legal form" but also the "real economic basis of monopoly" should be taken into account. Fifth, it was futile to expect "effective results" from the courts since lawsuits were time-consuming and courts lacked competence to deal with complex economic problems. Sixth, business should be encouraged by allowing the degree of corporate concentration necessary for service to the public and reasonable profit. Seventh, government should promote cooperation among business, labor, and farmers. Each interest group should receive its just rewards, and at the same time the commonweal should be guarded by the government. These should be the principles guiding a federal trade commission, Roosevelt argued. Arthur L. Garford, Progressive candidate for the Senate in Ohio, best summed up this clearer and more balanced trust stand of 1914: "What the Progressive Party plan seeks to establish is a proper balance between unlimited monopoly and unlimited competition, both of which are destructive to sound business if unrestrained."

ON THE TRACK OF PROGRESS

In his Pittsburgh address Roosevelt also condemned the administration for continuing to ignore federal welfare and labor reforms like the minimum wage, abolition of child labor, improved working conditions, and other issues. And he renewed his party's commitment to direct democracy and women's suffrage. That same day—June 30—an irate delegation of suffragettes at the White House berated the president for refusing to come to their aid.

During the rest of the summer Roosevelt sounded further blasts on the Progressive bugle. The *New York Times* claimed that since the Pittsburgh speech was primarily directed against the Democrats, it was an appeal for the G.O.P. as well as the Progressives. "Without saying a word about reunion he has made an effective argument for it." Some observers linked the indictment of the administration with his attempts to promote fusion in New York, and concluded that the Colonel was preparing to return to the Republican camp. Indeed, some of Roosevelt's friends like Cal O'Laughlin were urging him not to offend the Republicans in 1914 because the G.O.P. would surely nominate him in 1916. But Roosevelt responded to suggestions that he was about to return to the G.O.P. by saying that he favored fusion or reunion only on Progressive terms, and that he had only considered fusion in New York as a tactic to defeat the Republican Barnes machine before taking on Tammany in the fall. On July 31 he issued an appeal for the Progressive congressional candidates, lauding the work of Murdock and the Progressives in the House: "I hold that, on the one hand, the Democratic National Administration in Washington with its control of the Presidency and both houses of Congress, has shown its complete incapacity. . . . I hold no less that the Republican national organization, dominated as it is by men of the stamp of Messrs. Barnes, Penrose, and company, is utterly incapable of affording the slightest permanent relief." On August 27 he wrote O'Laughlin: "Now, my dear Cal, you say you think the Republicans wish me to run for President in 1916. I do not for one moment believe anything of the kind." He pointed out that the Republican organizations in the major states of Massachusetts, Pennsylvania, Ohio, Illinois, and elsewhere remained as reactionary as in 1912. The failure of fusion in New York was proof of the impossibility of working with the G.O.P.:

You say you want us to back the proper Republican candidates who are willing and desirous of supporting our principles. Yes! But there are really no such candidates this year. . . . It is perfectly obvious that there is but one course for me to follow this fall . . . ; and that is to fight straight-out for the Progressive Party in Illinois, in New York, in Kansas and in Louisiana, all alike.

In Boston in August Roosevelt reviewed the record of the party he asked voters to support. "The Progressive Party focused the Progressive movement," he recounted. "Instantly, it gave cohesion and powerful effect to the theretofore heterogeneous and unorganized forces, which, during years of effort, had been able to give concrete expression to its aims and principles only here and there. . . ." Formerly, he explained, the old parties had existed for only "one real purpose"—winning and holding office. He was preaching the gospel of the social educators and the Progressive Service: "Power and place were always first with them [the old parties], principle and service always subordinate. But with the Progressive Party, principle and service are always first, power and place always subordinate. . . ." What had been the results now that reform had its own party? The old parties, fearing the Progressives, had moved to pass reform measures in the state legislatures. The California legislature, directly controlled by Progressives, had made the best record in the nation, while in other states reforms had been enacted under pressure from Progressives and against the backdrop of the threat posed by the new party.

State legislation that had been urgently demanded for years, but which the forces of reaction had successfully resisted, was at last put on the statute books. More direct advance, more practical improvement in conditions of living . . . [has] been achieved in the last two years than in the previous quarter of a century; and this advance has been the practical result, the immediate effect of the organization of the Progressive Party. . . . So in compelling the other parties, sometimes one, sometimes the other, reluctantly to move forward for the service of human-kind, and the betterment of conditions of life, and of government, the Progressive Party, without office and without power, has yet fulfilled the highest mission a political organization can have.

Thus, by the end of the summer Roosevelt had formulated the Progressive campaign appeal "to the conscience and common sense of the people" on behalf of "the party of sane radicalism." In summary, this appeal, which amounted to an expanded or third version of the New Nationalism, was based on the propositions that there was no necessary contradiction between nationalism and the needs of the states, and that on the national issues of the tariff, trusts, business regulation, democracy, and social welfare the Progressives offered the only comprehensive program and real solutions. Progressives in New York emphasized clean government and antibossism in a state where corruption was rampant and reforms were blocked by the two old party machines, while in Colorado the emphasis was put on labor problems in a state suffering from virtual civil war. But Progressives in both states, and all other states as well, were pledged to the same ultimate goals of state reform and national legislation. In contrast to the old parties, Progressives were pictured as consistent, straightforward, and courageous in their championship of reform.

Roosevelt's attempt to reconcile the New Nationalism with the pluralism found in the states was not completely successful. How could he logically argue that Prohibition was justified in one state and not another, or that there was no substantive difference between the regulation of utilities and railroads advocated by most Progressives and the public ownership favored by Heney, Record, and Amos Pinchot? Moreover, though Roosevelt had tried to reconcile American social and economic pluralism with the New Nationalism, he continued to cling to a traditional general interest theory of society. By 1914 the Progressive nationalist theorists Croly, Lippmann, and Weyl, who launched the *New Republic* magazine at the end of the year, were evolving to an interest group theory of liberalism. But Roosevelt continued to preach the commonwealth gospel, seeking to paper over the reality of class and interest group divisions. He had brought the New Nationalism to the threshold of an ideological breakthrough, but he refused to take the final step to interest group theory. From an intellectual and theoretical standpoint there was much to be said in favor of the idea of commonwealth, but Roosevelt failed to realize that the "general interest of society" as usually conceived and understood amounted to little more than the interest group needs of the middle class.

There were also problems with the Progressive positions on the tariff and the trusts. The Progressive arguments for a tariff commission made good sense, but the equation of protectionism with prosperity and the reduced Underwood rates with the recession was inaccurate and bordered on the demagogic. In January, 1915, in a New York City speech on the unemployment problem, Roosevelt advocated a massive national public works program to provide work and accomplish needed tasks like highway building and flood control. But during the 1914 campaign he instead proposed protectionism to solve the recession and unemployment. Roosevelt's new statements on business regulation and the trusts were improvements in terms of detail on all his earlier pronouncements since 1901, but he still had not completely defined what he meant by such concepts used in the Pittsburgh address as "necessary concentration," "social and economic efficiency," and "good service to the public." Perkins thought that International Harvester, United States Steel, and even Standard Oil met the measurements of necessary concentration, efficiency, and public service, but labor leaders, many economists, and most Progressives disagreed. The fact of the matter was that Roosevelt probably did not know exactly how "necessary concentration" and other such concepts should be defined in everyday economic life. These questions of business regulation have also plagued economists and other social theorists down to the present day, and it seems accurate to say that there are no simple and clear solutions in this field. But Roosevelt's ambiguity had distinct political disadvantages, because while he refused to give easy answers others were willing to do so.

Roosevelt's position on the tariff and trust questions in a sense justified the existence of the new party by showing that Progressives represented a third and differing alternative to the Democrats and Republicans. He was seeking to present an image of the Progressive Party as the party in responsible opposition to the Democratic administration, while at the same time maintaining that the Republican Party was incapable of giving the country the reforms needed to solve the tariff, trust, and other problems. But the *Nation*, reviewing the Pittsburgh address, decided that Roosevelt had fallen between two stools, and that his antitrust arguments would benefit the Democrats, who had often used the issue in the past, while his tariff arguments would help the traditionally protectionist G.O.P. "If any party is to profit by ringing the changes on the ruinous effects of a low tariff, it is the Republican, not the Progressive," the *Nation* predicted. Roosevelt was attempting a necessary but by its nature delicate balancing act. The question was: would the voters perceive the crucial distinctions Roosevelt so carefully made between the three parties? Or would those opposed to the G.O.P. rally to the Democrats, while those opposed to the Wilson administration turned to the Republicans?

2

Thirty-two states elected governors in 1914, and thirty-two Senate seats in thirty states were at stake in this first election in which senators were popularly elected. In most southern and border states as well as a few others, the new party decided not to enter gubernatorial contests. In Pennsylvania the Washington Party backed the Democratic nominee for governor, while in South Dakota Roosevelt supporters backed the Republican state ticket and in Wisconsin an independent Republican candidate for governor. In the end Progressives ran candidates for governor in some twenty-one states. The new party did not run senatorial candidates in several heavily Democratic states, mainly in the South, but there were Progressive candidates for the Senate in the southern states of Alabama and Georgia, and the border states of Missouri, Kentucky, and Maryland. In Vermont and Utah the Progressives fused with Democrats in Senate races, while in South Dakota and Wisconsin Roosevelt partisans fell in behind G.O.P. candidates for the Senate. In all, there were twenty-three Progressive senatorial candidates in twenty-one states running against Democratic and Republican opponents in 1914.

In 1914 the Progressive Party was faced with the challenge of finding more state candidates than in 1912 because of the popular election of senators and more gubernatorial contests. At least twenty-five of the forty-four Progressive gubernatorial and senatorial candidates were qualified for office by the normal standards of background and experience. In some states, like Idaho, Iowa, Rhode Island, and others, Progressives were forced to turn to men whose only prominence depended on their work within the party or to political unknowns, because of weak state organizations or other local factors. But in most of the more populous states, and many smaller ones as well, in 1914 as in 1912 the party was able to field distinguished candidates for governor and senator, men well qualified for office in terms of background, ability, and experience, thus presenting a partisan image of credibility and responsibility.

The gubernatorial candidates Halbert P. Gardner in Maine, Henry D. Allison in New Hampshire, Joseph Walker in Massachusetts, Frederick M. Davenport in New York, and F. M. Gill in Oregon had all served in the legislatures of their states. Gardner had led the fight for railroad regulation in Maine; Walker had been speaker of the state house in Massachusetts; and Davenport was identified as a champion of the primary system in New York. Professor Willard Fisher of Wesleyan, Bull Moose candidate for governor in Connecticut, was a former mayor. Henry J. Allen, nominee in Kansas, was a well-known newspaper publisher and political leader. Johnson was running for reelection in California. Colorado's Costigan and Ohio's Garfield, both running for governor, were nationally known figures. Progressive candidates for the Senate such as Herbert Knox Smith in Connecticut, Gifford Pinchot in Pennsylvania, Beveridge in Indiana, Robins in Illinois, Congressman Murdock in Kansas, and Heney in California were also nationally known public figures. Bainbridge Colby, Bull Moose senatorial candidate in New York, was a distinguished attorney, subsequently United States secretary of state, and candidates for the Senate Arthur L. Garford in Ohio, Benjamin Griffith in Colorado, and William Hanley in Oregon were all prominent public leaders in their states. The Progressive lineup was impressive, and indeed Progressive candidates received more support and praise from the press and periodicals in 1914 than in 1912, testimony to the quality of the Bull Moose candidates when compared with many of the standard bearers of the old parties.

Collier's endorsed Beveridge for the Senate, declared Davenport the best of the four major candidates for governor of New York, and argued that Robins in Illinois "ought to be supported by everyone who favors the new order." *La Follette's Weekly* had been consistently hostile to the Progressive Party since 1912, but in 1914 Senator La Follette endorsed Robins, the fusion candidate Charles Prouty in Vermont, and Heney for the Senate in signed editorials. "Go to the support of Francis J. Heney with all your might and strength," the Wisconsin senator urged his readers. By 1914 the venerable *Harper's Weekly* had become a nonpartisan reform journal under the new editorship of Norman Hapgood, the former *Collier's* editor who had supported Wilson in 1912. In articles and editorials in 1914 *Harper's* and Hapgood supported the candidacies of Heney, Costigan, Davenport, Smith, and other Progressives. "The best ticket in New York is the Progressive ticket," *Harper's* informed readers, and Herbert Knox Smith was the "best candidate of the three" for the Senate in Connecticut, while Gifford Pinchot was an example of "the highest type of American citizen."

Raymond Robins and Gifford Pinchot in particular received support from outside the new party. The nonpartisan National Popular Government League issued an appeal for Robins in Illinois signed by Democratic Senators Robert L. Owen of Oklahoma and Thomas J. Walsh of Montana. Robins's opponents, the Republican Lawrence Y. Sherman and the Democrat Roger L. Sullivan, were both conservative, machine politicians. Bryan had condemned Sullivan in the primaries. In an open letter to Robins Senator Owen examined the conservative and unsavory pasts of the nominees of the old parties and concluded: "The real issue is the Rule of the People (Democracy) vs. the Rule of the Machine (Commercialized Autocracy). I believe that you deserve to be trusted on this issue and that Sullivan and Sherman do not." Owen campaigned for Robins, and Illinois Democrats organized a "Raymond Robins Democratic League." In Pennsylvania Pinchot's candidacy won the support of Republican Senator George W. Norris, Harvey Wiley, the pure food and drug crusader who had championed Wilson in 1912, and the independent Republican William Kent, congressman from California and ally of La Follette. Norris, Wiley, and other noted reformers were joined on the stump for Pinchot in the Keystone State by Progressives from all over the country like Jane Addams, Senator Poindexter, and Judge Lindsey.

The Progressive Party, of course, also faced the challenges of local, state legislative, and U. S. House contests. In August O. K. Davis, working as field organizer, reported that "especial emphasis has been laid upon the importance of nominating township and county tickets, because, particularly in the agricultural districts, it is these tickets which furnish the great body of strength and support to the Congressional, district, and state organization." Davis found that in most northern states township and county tickets had been nominated. "It is the strongest evidence of the permanency and enthusiasm of the Progressive organization," the veteran newspaper man concluded. Further reports received by Roosevelt and the New York headquarters indicated the high quality of local, county, and state legislative tickets in many places. For one example, in Delta County, Michigan, a county carried by T.R. in 1912, the Progressive candidate for state representative was the president of a local businessman's association; a police chief was the nominee for county sheriff; the candidate for county surveyor was a city surveyor; and the nominee for registrar of deeds was a local alderman. In Montgomery County, Kansas, the energetic local campaign of the county chairman Alfred M. Landon was winning notice from state political leaders, and in many localities around the nation men later prominent in public affairs were active in Bull Moose campaigns.

Most of the Progressive members of the House of Representatives were standing for reelection. Congressman Hinebaugh, as chairman of the Progressive Congressional Campaign Committee, predicted that the party would more than double its twenty members in the House: "A political revolution is on, and revolutions never go backward." Although most political observers found Hinebaugh's forecast overly optimistic at best, as in 1912 the Progressive Party assembled an impressive array of House candidates. In Minnesota's tenth district the blind attorney Thomas D. Schall, subsequently a representative (1915-25) and a senator (1925-35), ran a campaign that was a textbook model of organization. In California attorney John A. Elston of Berkeley began a stint of six years in the House as the Progressive candidate in the sixth district. In Indiana's seventh district the former diplomat Paxton Hibben, returned from the Progressive Service in New York, was the Bull Moose nominee. In Connecticut's third district Professor Henderson of Yale was again candidate, and in T.R.'s home district, New York's first, the former governor of Puerto Rico Regis Post was the nominee.

The Progressive campaign in the South was given new hope in 1914 by factional revolts among Democrats in Georgia and Louisiana, and in both states the new party was optimistic of making gains. In Georgia the noted Democratic leader G. Rufe Hutchens bolted his party and ran for one of the two Senate seats at stake with dime-store chain owner C. W. McClure. Progressives hoped to win support from cotton farmers angry with the Wilson administration for poor cotton prices in the wake of the Underwood tariff. In Louisiana a major revolt shook the Democratic Party when sugar was placed on the free list by the

Underwood tariff. Democratic officeholders and district committee members deserted and joined the energetic state Progressive organization run by John M. Parker and Pearl Wight. In the third district, the "sugar bowl," Judge Whitmell Pugh Martin, a Democratic leader who had once been a chemist in a sugar refinery, became the Progressive candidate for Congress. Political observers predicted that Martin's chances were excellent, while there was also the possibility of victory in other districts. Roosevelt, ever anxious to break the solid South and eager to exploit opposition to the Underwood tariff, announced that he would begin his fall campaign for the Progressive Party with a Labor Day address in New Orleans.

3

In the New Orleans Opera House on September 7, Roosevelt delivered the first of his many campaign speeches that fall. In spite of troubles with his health resulting from the South American trip, in the campaign of 1914 Roosevelt delivered over 110 speeches in fifteen states. The schedules for his tours in Louisiana, New York, and elsewhere resembled a railroad timetable. To William Allen White he wrote on September 14: "Oh Lord, I wish you could be in my place for a little while! I am speaking literally, not figuratively, when I say that there are certainly a dozen states, each of which has demanded that I spend so much time with it this fall that I could not devote very much time to all the other states combined." As usual everywhere Roosevelt was greeted by enthusiastic crowds, but as in 1912 it was uncertain how many voters intended to support the Progressive Party and how many simply turned out to see "Teddy" in person. On October 6 the Music Hall was packed when T.R. arrived in Troy, New York, and crowds surrounded the auditorium hoping for a glimpse of the Colonel. But the *Troy Times* reported that as soon as Roosevelt finished his speech and left the hall, the audience departed too, few remaining to hear Bainbridge Colby and other New York candidates. It was an ominous sign.

Many of the Progressives were confident of victory or at least predicted close races. Heney and Murdock were sure they would be elected to the Senate; Beveridge thought victory within his grasp in Indiana; supporters of Robins and Pinchot were confident; and Garfield reported the Republicans were beaten in Ohio and the Progressives were pressing the Democrats. But as the campaign continued everything seemed to go wrong for the new party.

Wilson signed the Federal Trade Commission Act on September 26 and the Clayton Antitrust Act on October 15. The president had originally supported a weak trade commission bill for a federal agency with no real power, and Roosevelt had attacked the administration measure in his Pittsburgh address on June 30. But then the president had swung his support behind a strong commission bill written by Louis D. Brandeis and George L. Rublee. After further study of the problem, Brandeis, an architect of the New Freedom of 1912, seemed to be converted to the New Nationalist approach to the trade commission. He turned to

New York attorney Rublee, a Progressive and friend of Roosevelt's who had worked on the 1912 Bull Moose platform, to collaborate in drawing up a bill. Wilson's change of heart promptly followed Brandeis's conversion. The Clayton bill as originally conceived was to be a traditional trust-busting measure, but when it emerged from Congress it had been modified so that it closely resembled New Nationalist formulas. In addition, the Clayton Act as finally adopted contained

WORSE THAN JUNGLE FEVER

provisions supposedly protecting unions from the courts, leading Samuel Gompers to celebrate the law as labor's "Magna Carta." The Wilson administration's record by the end of October, 1914, was thus not only progressive but progressive in the image of the New Nationalism. The Progressives had not preached in vain—Wilson was moving to the left. But Roosevelt's arguments against the New Freedom, delivered in the summer and early fall, had been undermined and made at least partially obsolete, although it was still true that the administration had not yet adopted many of the reforms advocated by the new party like women's suffrage and minimum wage.

With Gompers and the A.F.L. praising Wilson for the Clayton Act, the Progressives as in 1912 were unable to enlist the support of labor, except in California where the unions were pleased with Johnson's record. In New York Alice Carpenter, employed by national headquarters, helped organize and run a Working Man's Progressive Party League, but her efforts came to nothing after the New York County Progressive organization refused to nominate any of the league's leaders for offices in 1914. Costigan's appeal to labor in Colorado was undercut by the Democrats' support for the unions and the new party's support for Prohibition. Indeed, the Prohibition planks in many Progressive state platforms hurt the party's appeal to labor everywhere, perhaps particularly in Pennsylvania where Penrose had long been identified with the wets. Furthermore, the Progressives were in general caught in a "whip-saw" between the old parties, as Judge Lindsey put it. In Colorado labor was alienated by Prohibition, and at the same time many of Costigan's supporters from 1912 deserted him over the Republican issue of law and order. Nationally, the Democrats pointed to the Clayton Act and Gompers's support, while the Republicans promised a return to good times with the protective tariff. In Pennsylvania posters entitled "Full Dinner Pail" were distributed, showing Senator Penrose shielding a family at a dinner table in the folds of a capacious cloak. On the cloak appeared the legend: "Protection and Prosperity to the Wage-Earner." The Senate G.O.P. leader's campaign for reelection, which sounded the keynote for many Republican candidates that year, was aptly summed up by the publisher Alexander P. Moore, who reported to Roosevelt:

Penrose's only plea is practically this:—You must save me to save the Republican party; and you must save the Republican party to save the tariff; and you must save the tariff to insure plenty of work for the workingman—and plenty of business for the business man—and parenthetically (though not expressed) to provide ample graft for machine politicians.

Alarmed at the downward turn of Progressive prospects, Roosevelt flailed out at Penrose and the bosses in both old parties when he appeared in Pennsylvania to support Pinchot:

The people who, whether from timidity or sloth, or desire for selfish ease, or desire for selfish gain, surrender themselves to the leadership of a boss are not really free men. There is a serfage of the soul that is fully as degrading as any serfage of the body. The men who have surrendered their will and their judgment into the keeping of Mr. Barnes, or Mr. Penrose, or Mr. Murphy, or Mr. Sullivan, are not fit to be free citizens in a free republic.

"Be sovereigns of your own souls"—this was Roosevelt's message to the voters during the last weeks of the campaign as he toured the country. He exhorted voters not to be bound by party labels or past allegiances, not to surrender their freedoms to the bosses of the old parties, not to be fooled by insincere professions of progressivism or reform measures adopted only because of public pressure, but rather to vote for what they knew was right—the principles of popular government and humanitarianism championed by the Progressive Party. ". . . Be true to yourselves," he urged citizens in Monticello, New York. "I wish, fundamentally, to make my appeal to you not in the interest of . . . the candidates, but in your own interest." The new party had proved itself in public service by presenting carefully framed programs and candidates of the caliber and stature of Johnson, Costigan, Murdock, Robins, Beveridge, Garfield, and Pinchot. The rest, Roosevelt stressed, was up to the voters. In Roosevelt's campaign rhetoric the elections were thus transformed from the crucial test for the Progressive Party that they in fact were into a time of testing for the American people.

In public he predicted Progressive victory—"if we can only get the rubbish off the souls of the weary plain citizens. . . ." But in private he admitted that Bull Moose chances were slim, and he feared, as he wrote George Record, that the "Progressive Party will make such a pitiful showing at the fall elections that by common consent its existence as a separate political party will at once be ended." The Colonel kept up a brave front, but as he stepped into the Oyster Bay voting booth on November 3 he knew full well that all the months of campaigning had been futile.

4

"The Progressive Party has come a cropper," Roosevelt wrote Charles J. Bonaparte on November 7. Indeed, in every state but California the party had been defeated, and in most states had come in a poor third, while in Arizona, Montana, Oklahoma, Rhode Island, and elsewhere, Progressives had placed fourth behind the Socialists. In Minnesota, a state carried by T.R. in 1912, the Progressive candidate for governor was outpolled by Socialist, Prohibitionist, and Labor candidates as well as by the Republicans and Democrats. California and Louisiana were "the two bright spots in the election," Roosevelt wrote Hiram Johnson. But in Louisiana only the "sugar bowl" third district had been won, and in California Heney was defeated for the Senate though Johnson and three Bull Moose congressmen were elected. Johnson's reelection as governor, Meyer Lissner observed, was not really a triumph for the Progressive Party, but rather a "victory for Hiram Johnson, the man and public official, and for progressivism with a small 'p.'" Thomas Schall was elected to the House from Minnesota, and Copley of Illinois and Chandler of New York were reelected, but incumbents Hinebaugh and Thomson in Illinois, MacDonald in Michigan, and the entire Pennsylvania Progressive congressional delegation went down to defeat.

In New York the Republican Whitman was elected governor, and Davenport came in fourth behind Glynn and Sulzer, while in Massachusetts Walker received less than 10 percent of the vote, although Charles Sumner Bird had placed second in the 1913 gubernatorial race. In Connecticut Herbert Knox Smith polled only 3.8 percent of the vote for senator. In Pennsylvania Pinchot out-polled the Democrat Mitchell Palmer, but Penrose was comfortably reelected. In Ohio Garfield and Garford won less than 10 percent of the vote. "East of Indiana there is no state in which the Progressive Party remains in condition even to affect the balance of power between the two old parties," T.R. reported to Johnson. But to the west the party had been badly defeated as well. Beveridge, Robins, and Murdock could do no better than place third in their senatorial races, and in Colorado Costigan polled less than half the vote he had won in 1912. In all, the Progressives in 1914 polled about 2 million votes, as compared with Roosevelt's over 4 million in 1912, while the Democrats and Republicans each won about 6 million votes.

Although the Democrats won several important state races and retained control of both houses of Congress, the elections were viewed by political observers as a victory for the Republicans because the party had made a spectacular comeback, capturing governorships from incumbent Democrats in New York and Ohio, and reducing the Democratic margin in the House from 147 to 29. The Old Guard seemed to be in the saddle as Joseph G. Cannon and William B. McKinley, the old enemies of the insurgents, regained House seats lost in 1912, and as Penrose, Lawrence Y. Sherman, Reed Smoot, and others were reelected to the Senate, while Warren G. Harding became the new senator from Ohio. "As for the Republican Party, at the moment the dog has returned to its vomit," Roosevelt wrote William Allen White.

What were the causes for the overwhelming Progressive defeat? In part it seemed to fit the pattern of general reaction against progressives of all parties. ". . . The people were sick of reformers," T.R. explained to Lissner. "Johnson is the only exception so far as I know. Aside from him, the people have had enough of all reformers and especially me." He hoped the "revulsion" was temporary, he added in letters to friends. Moreover, he was certain that sooner or later the substance of the entire Progressive platform would be adopted, "even although it is done in formulas superficially so different as to enable people to say that it is not the same thing." But he doubted that it would be possible to run another Progressive Party campaign in most states.

Why were the voters "sick of reformers," as the returns seemed to indicate they were? The victory of high tariff Republican conservatives seemed to point to hard times as the major factor. Workers "felt the pinch of poverty; they were suffering from hard times; they wanted prosperity and compared with this they did not care a rap for social justice or industrial justice or clean politics or decency in public life," Roosevelt said. The progressive movement had come in with a wave of prosperity at the turn of the century, and it seemed to be ebbing as the stock market declined. As Roosevelt explained in the *Outlook:*

We cannot pay for what the highest type of democracy demands unless there is a great abundance of prosperity. . . . In practice this means that when a nation suffers from hard times wage-workers will concern themselves . . . primarily with a return to good times, and not with any plan for securing social and industrial justice. If women cannot get any work, and nevertheless have to live, they will be far more concerned with seeing a factory opened in which they can work at night or work twelve hours every day than they are concerned with the abolition of night-work or the limitation of hours of labor. Exactly the same is true of men. In the recent election in Pennsylvania the majority of the miners and wage-workers generally voted for the Republican machine, although this Republican machine had just defeated a workmen's compensation act, a child-labor law, a minimum wage for women law, and various other bits of desirable labor legislation. The attitude of the wage-workers was perfectly simple. They wished employment. . . . They believed that they had more chance if the candidates of the Republican machine were elected than they would otherwise have. Personally I very strongly believe that they were in error; but it was their belief that counted. The average voter usually sees what he is voting about in very simple form. He does not regard the political picture as an etching and follow out the delicate tracery. He treats it as a circus poster, in which the colors are in very vivid contrast and are laid on with a broad brush.

In the wake of the Progressive debacle, Roosevelt was voicing doubts about the assumptions behind the direct democracy reforms he had championed. "The people" did not seem as wise as he had once hoped. Economically, he was expressing a concept held in common with many of his generation: that reform depended on what Walter Weyl called the "social surplus," the wealth produced by the nation over and above what was necessary to meet essential needs like food. The "social surplus" could be used for social improvements and, as Beveridge put it, to "pass prosperity around." But without such a "surplus" men and women were forced to turn their attentions and energies to a struggle for the bare necessities, were prevented from pursuing humanitarian goals, blinded to the needs of others and to the commonweal. The concepts behind later Keynesian economics and the potentials of massive tax revenues for social improvements were largely absent from progressive thinking. The belief that prosperity and reform had to go hand in hand gave a certain ambivalence to progressive attitudes toward business, an ambivalence reflected in the policies of the Roosevelt and Wilson administrations alike, for capitalism was at once the threat to and the promise of the good life. For most reformers, particularly those who had joined the Progressive Party, reform was equated with morality and humanitarianism. Close observers of society that they were, as the years passed many such reformers sadly concluded that both morality and humanitarianism were luxuries in the modern world. The sadness and disillusionment experienced by many Progressives after the elections of 1914 were the experience, sooner or later, of much of a whole generation of reformers nurtured on belief in democracy and Protestant morality.

Though Progressives knew there were many reasons for their defeat, some were convinced—at least at first—that the main cause lay in the fact that "the people" had been weighed in the balance and found wanting. All realized there were many local factors in their defeat, ranging from the Prohibition planks to state factionalism, and all counted such reasons for defeat as Wilson's legislative record and the G.O.P. identification with protectionism and the "full dinner pail," but some Progressives maintained that it was "the people" who really had gone down to defeat in 1914. "The fact is the people have not yet 'caught up,'" Congressman Jacob Alexander Falconer of Washington wrote. The Progressives "are way ahead of the country as a whole in morality, and the country will need a long time to catch up with them," T.R. wrote his daughter Ethel. "The fault is not yours; the fault is in the people themselves," he consoled Heney. "Probably we have erred in thinking that even in this country men were a little better and more intelligent than they actually are." Replying to defeated Congressman Willis J. Hulings of Pennsylvania, T.R. agreed that "the trouble with our party is just what you said: that the American public had a mind about four inches long." When the press asked the Colonel for a statement, he refused and told reporters to read II Timothy 4:3-4. On November 5 the newspapers printed the verses:

For the time will come when they will not endure sound doctrine; but after their own lusts shall they heap to themselves teachers, having itching ears;
And they shall turn away their ears from the truth, and shall be turned unto fables.

It was perhaps natural for Roosevelt and some of the Progressives who had placed so much trust in the electorate to turn to a measure of cynicism in the cold dawn of defeat. But upon further reflection most Progressives realized that it was simplistic to blame the people for their defeat. Charles Sumner Bird wrote Roosevelt on November 19: "Well! we surely were hit hard. The people were sick of the Democratic party and concluded that a vote for the Republican party was the best way out. Perhaps they were right." Frederick M. Davenport told the press: "The country still favors a two-party system and prefers to try to better conditions by alternating between the two parties, first disciplining one and then the other, according as one or the other goes wrong." Many of the Progressives came to believe that about half of those who voted for Roosevelt in 1912 had done so for the most part merely to protest and rebuke the policies of Taft and the "theft" of the G.O.P. nomination, rather than to establish a permanent new party. William Allen White's analysis in 1913 seemed accurate: in 1914 the Progressives had been unable to hold the "sheep votes" and the "Teddy votes" from 1912, ending up with about two million votes. "This was not the Republican party born over; it was the Free Soil party of our day... ," Roosevelt concluded.

The Progressive Party had been defeated in 1912 largely because of the forces of American pluralism and conservatism—a conservatism expressed in part through allegiance not only to the two-party system but to the traditional two parties as well. In 1912 Taft had polled nearly 3.5 million votes virtually on the strength of the Republican name. In 1914 pluralism and conservatism again played a major role in the Progressive defeat. To some extent, however, the new party had met the challenge of pluralism with state campaigns addressed to the particular needs of various states. But the Progressive Party was usually caught in a political whip-saw between Republicans and Democrats. Whenever the Progressives made a case against one of the old parties, it seemed to benefit the other established party. The chief effect of the Progressive campaign seemed to be to provide each of the old parties with ammunition to use against its traditional rival.

In Maine, Michigan, and some other states, vigorous Progressive state campaigns had helped Democrats by discrediting the traditionally dominant G.O.P., and by drawing votes to the Bull Moose or the Democracy itself. In Maine in 1912 Republican William T. Haines had been elected governor by a margin of 3,295 with Progressive support. In 1914 the Democrats won and Haines was defeated for reelection by 3,177 while the Progressive Gardner polled 18,225 votes. In Michigan the Democrat W. N. Ferris was elected governor in 1912 because of the vote polled by the Progressive Whitney Watkins; in 1914 the Progressive vote was greatly decreased, but Ferris was reelected by a margin almost equal to the number of votes won by the Bull Moose gubernatorial candidate. In most states in 1914, however, the Progressive campaigns seemed to strengthen the hands of the Republicans.

"Your anti-Wilson speeches will make more Republican votes than Progressive votes," publisher Henry L. Stoddard had warned Roosevelt in July, 1914. "The American people are very practical, and they will take the simplest, surest way to accomplish their purpose. That way is the Republican ticket." After Roosevelt's Pittsburgh address in June, the *Nation* had predicted that "if any party is to profit by ringing changes on the ruinous effects of a low tariff, it is the Republican, not the Progressive." And after the elections the Colonel had sadly concluded that indeed it had been the "full dinner pail" which reelected Penrose. Furthermore, Robins's attacks on Roger Sullivan in Illinois had apparently helped elect the Republican Sherman. The steady campaign against Tammany in New York State—first in the 1913 New York City fusion race, and then in 1914 against Governor Glynn—had, it seemed, resulted in the defection of Progressive voters to Sulzer and Whitman. In 1912 Straus had polled 393,183 votes for governor on the Progressive ticket; in 1914 Davenport garnered only 45,586, while Sulzer won 126,270 and the Republican Whitman's plurality was 145,507. The Progressives had, of course, also denounced the Illinois G.O.P. and Barnes and Whitman in New York, but perhaps voters had decided to choose the lesser of two evils, turning to the G.O.P. as "the simplest, surest way to accomplish their purpose." As Lindsey had observed in Colorado, the old parties had spread the "paralyzing psychology" that the Progressive Party had *"no chance."* Some of the magazines which had endorsed Progressives like Davenport and Herbert Knox Smith had gone on to explain that while the Progressive candidate was the best choice, there was little chance of the new party winning in New York, Connecticut, and other states. Thus, the Progressive Party in 1914 had been the victim of a vicious cycle: the more the new party delivered telling blows to the old parties, the more likely it was that "practical" Americans would turn to the less objectionable of the old party candidates. "Perhaps they were right," concluded Charles Sumner Bird. Many Progressives found that judgment impossible to accept as they surveyed the wreckage of their hopes, but it was clear that the Progressive attempt to change the traditional party system had been a failure.

CHAPTER TEN

THE ARMAGEDDON OF WORLD WAR

The Last Days of the Progressive Party

It is impossible for us Progressives to abandon our convictions. But we are faced with that fact that as things actually are the Progressive national organization no longer offers the means whereby we can make these convictions effective in our national life. Under such circumstances, our duty is to do the best we can, and not to sulk because our leadership is rejected.

T. R.

"What next?" was the question Progressives asked each other in the months following the 1914 election defeats. Some like William Allen White remained optimistic that the party would yet win sometime in the future. Others were more pessimistic, but agreed that the party should continue, and wait for further developments which might suggest a course of action. The consensus was that unless conditions changed dramatically, it would be almost impossible to launch local, state, and congressional campaigns in 1916. But Progressive leaders were convinced that, whatever happened, the party could play an important role in the presidential election. The Republicans might nominate Roosevelt as the only candidate who could reunite the G.O.P. and beat Wilson. Many Progressives viewed the party's continued existence as a means of forcing the Republicans to choose between Roosevelt and defeat, with the possibility of a third ticket being used as a sword of Damocles over the heads of the G.O.P. leaders. Others favored running T.R. or perhaps Hiram Johnson as a further protest against the old parties, regardless of the course of the Republicans and Democrats in the campaign, though few believed a lone Progressive ticket could win. A significant minority of Bull Moose leaders, however, decided to return to the G.O.P. without further delay, and work within that party for Roosevelt and progressive principles. In New York Davenport and State Chairman Theodore Douglas Robinson, T.R.'s nephew, announced they were returning to the Republican fold; and Medill McCormick of Illinios, State Chairman Edward C. Toner of Indiana, and others also joined the exodus to the G.O.P. But Johnson, Beveridge, Murdock, Costigan, Garfield, and most of the prominent Bull Moose leaders remained loyal to the Progressive Party.

In the days immediately after the elections, Roosevelt was "very gravely in doubt about what we ought to do about the Progressive Party." But soon he decided that "as a party we should simply sit tight." It was impossible, he explained, for Progressives to go to the Democrats under Wilson or the Republican Party led by Penrose, Cannon, and the conservatives, and thus the Progressive Party had to continue as an independent organization for the foreseeable future. ". . . We should hold on to our party integrity and organization without courting defeat by unnecessarily nominating candidates in local elections . . . ," he told National Committeeman N. Winslow Williams of Maryland. "I will keep you posted as to anything that is done," he wrote John M. Parker on November 12, "but my own view is that we have got to go on with the fight on the one hand, and that on the other hand there should be very little activity on our part for a year to come." He expressed regrets but no bitterness or condemnation when McCormick and others left the party, because, as he explained to his son Archie, "I know that I would have great hesitancy in appealing to young men to come forward and identify themselves with it [the party] and vote for it now when to do so may prevent their doing more effective work in some other way."

On November 6, 1914, three days after the elections, the party's executive committee held a summit meeting of leaders at the New York City headquarters. In addition to the regular members of the committee, representative leaders were summoned to give their opinions—Beveridge, Robins, Straus, Harold L. Ickes, Mark Sullivan, and others. It was decided that the party needed a national conference to restore morale and announce that the party would continue. The conference was set for Chicago on December 2.

At the same time that the decision was made to hold a conference in Chicago on the future of the party, Amos Pinchot and George Record came forward with suggested new programs for the Progressive Party. Writing in the socialist magazine the *Masses* shortly after the elections, Amos argued that the Progressive Party had been defeated because it was not "radical" enough. He therefore proposed that the party adopt a program of government ownership. And George Record sent Roosevelt an elaborate and lengthy paper which called for T.R. to announce a "radical" platform based on government ownership and the single tax, and then lead the Progressives back into the Republican fold. Roosevelt was furious. The party had lost, he fumed, because people associated foolish reformers like Amos Pinchot and George Record with the Progressives. He suggested that if Amos and Record went to Chicago, they should be thrown out because neither man could be considered a Progressive any longer since Amos was consorting with the Socialists and Record with the Republicans. He added, however, that of course the Progressives at Chicago should not be misled by their opposition to the pair "into taking a position in any way reactionary." Finally, when Amos publicly charged that Roosevelt and Perkins had corrupted the Progressive Party with their conservative views, the Colonel wrote Amos: "Sir: When I spoke of the Progressive Party as having a lunatic fringe, I specifically had you in mind. On the supposition that you are of entire sound mind, I should be obliged to say that you are absolutely dishonorable and untruthful. I prefer to accept the former alternative."

Perkins and others favored issuing a restatement of the party program at the Chicago conference, and Roosevelt was asked to prepare such a proclamation. He declined and advised that "all that should be done should be an announcement that we stand unflinchingly by our principles and will never abandon them...." He explained to E. A. Van Valkenburg:

As a matter of fact, what we now say is of very small consequence. Immediately after election is a poor time for the beaten party to expect to be listened to or to start a propaganda. People at such times are sick of politics and above all sick of the politics of the defeated crowd. They wish to wait and see what the victors and near-victors do. They are interested at present in what the Republicans and Democrats *do* and not at all in what *we say* of the Republicans and Democrats....

When the "defeated crowd" assembled in Chicago on December 2, however, it was voted to have William Allen White and Chester H. Rowell draw up a public statement. At first Roosevelt planned to attend the conference but then decided against it, maintaining that the public was not interested in anything he might have to say so soon after his leadership had been repudiated at the polls. Over ninety Progressive leaders did attend: members of the executive committee including Perkins, Meyer Lissner, and Jane Addams; Frank Funk, Ickes, Robins, and others from Illinois; Albert D. Nortoni and a delegation from Missouri; Senator Clapp and Congressman-elect Schall from Minnesota; Parker from Louisiana; Garfield and Garford from Ohio; Gifford Pinchot from Pennsylvania; and many others. Victor Murdock of Kansas was chosen as the new chairman of the national committee to succeed Joseph M. Dixon, and the conference heard reports and speeches from Clapp, Robins, and others. The statement drafted by White and Rowell emphasized the Progressive tariff plank:

The industrial depression and the consequent reaction against the Democratic tariff was undoubtedly the issue which primarily determined the reactionary results of the recent election.... The way to provide stable industrial conditions and business peace is to accept the principle of protection as a fixed national policy and to take the tariff out of politics. The Progressive Party specifically declared this doctrine in its platform of 1912, and pointed out the only way to take the tariff out of politics by the creation of a permanent expert nonpartisan tariff commission....

It was also announced that the party definitely would hold a national convention in 1916 and had no intention of retiring from the political field. Perkins's opponents hoped that with the dynamic Murdock as the new national committee chairman, the manager of the New York headquarters would be heard from less in public, and at long last T.R. privately informed Progressives that he, too, hoped this would be the case. But Perkins paid no attention, and continued to make speeches and issue statements.

The Chicago conference inevitably invited comparisons with the post-election convocation held in the same city in December, 1912, two years before. Most of the same leaders attended both meetings, but instead of discussing direct democracy and social justice as in 1912, the Progressives at the second Chicago conference merely declared that their theory of tariff protectionism was superior to the Republicans'. White reported his observations of the conference to Roosevelt on December 15:

. . . I was struck by the fact that everyone was spiritually weary. We were sapped dry. We could reach down in the well and bring up courage, more or less of it. We could bring up enthusiasm, or a good counterfeit of enthusiasm. We could even laugh, and that was genuine. But we were all dead tired. For two or three, and in some cases for four years—since 1910—we have been living upon our emotions. We have been putting spirit into others. We have been spurring literally thousands at first hand, and holding ten thousands almost at first hand, in fighting trim. And the thing I saw was that we went through the motions—all the wonted motions of real crusading soldiers—but the whole thing was automatic. The spiritual well from which we dipped was *physically* low. We need emotional rest. We need complete change. . . .

The Kansas editor added: "Give that crowd a year or eighteen months to restore itself, and it can whip the world." That remained to be seen.

2

Roosevelt did not lose interest in the cause of progressivism and reform after 1914, though he devoted most of his time and energies to preparedness and the issues of the World War, which had begun in August, 1914. On January 26, 1915, after touring New York City agencies to inspect conditions among the unemployed, he spoke at the Metropolitan Opera House under the auspices of the Inter-Church Unemployment Committee. What was needed, he declared, was a federal employment bureau, with the government providing work for the unemployed through reclamation and river and harbor projects. Expanding upon his earlier proposals, T.R. urged the government to begin flood control and development projects on the Ohio and Missouri Rivers, Mobile Bay, Boston harbor, and the mouth of the Columbia River as well as in the Mississippi Valley. A few days earlier he had addressed an open letter to the New York Short Ballot Organization commending proposals for the new state constitution. In February he wrote to Assemblyman Michael Schaap urging Progressives to oppose a bill providing for compulsory Bible reading in New York public schools. On October 15, in a letter to Ethel Eyre Valentine Dreier of the League of Women Voters, he appealed for the adoption of women's suffrage amendments in referendums in New York, New Jersey, and Massachusetts. Women deserved the "equality of right," Roosevelt maintained, "this they are entitled to and this they ought to have." It was a message he was to repeat often in the next years. But Roosevelt's major battle for reform in 1915 was with his old enemy the Republican leader William Barnes.

The trial resulting from the libel suit Barnes had launched in the summer of 1914, after Roosevelt had charged the Republican boss with allying with Tammany in the conduct of state government, began in Syracuse on April 19, 1915. Barnes's attorney William M. Ivins constructed a case designed to prove that during his long career T.R. himself had employed the same kind of political methods he accused Barnes of using—that, in short, Roosevelt and Barnes were the same type of politician. Ivins assembled letters from T.R. to various political leaders, and put particular emphasis on Roosevelt's dealings with machine politicians while governor of New York. "I am going to Syracuse tomorrow to nail Roosevelt's hide to the fence," Ivins told Elihu Root the day before the trial began. "Ivins, let me give you a piece of advice," Root replied. "I know Roosevelt and you want to be very sure that it is Roosevelt's hide that you get on the fence."

Although his kinsman Franklin D. Roosevelt, long an opponent of Tammany, supported the Colonel's charges against Barnes, T.R. was unable to persuade Charles Evans Hughes and others to testify to the details of the G.O.P. boss's career. T.R. was thus himself forced to give the evidence of bipartisan collusion and corruption which he had gleaned from Hughes, Mark Sullivan, and others. At the close of Roosevelt's testimony Ivins cross-examined the former president for six days, asking him about many incidents and letters from his past. Ivins's strategy backfired, however, as T.R. quickly became the master of the court-room, explaining to the fascinated jury and spectators the details of New York politics during the preceding twenty years. It was a skillful public performance, and Ivins protested: "You need not treat me as a mass meeting. . . . Now, if your honor please, I ask that this witness be requested to testify without gesticulation. . . . I do not want to be eaten up here and now." But Ivins and Barnes were "eaten up," and the jury brought in a verdict for Roosevelt. After his defeat in the courtroom Barnes's influence in New York politics soon declined, and his days as G.O.P. boss of the Empire State were over. Roosevelt had not only been vindicated, but he had also defeated Barnes as he had failed to do in 1912 and 1914. Observers decided that the Colonel was on his way to a political comeback, even though his party had been over-whelmingly defeated only months before.

There were those who said Roosevelt's campaign for military preparedness was opportunistic, a politically inspired attempt to use the charger of militarism to ride back to the White House in 1916, and his renewed association with conservative Republicans like Senator Henry Cabot Lodge, Elihu Root, and others in the preparedness movement was sometimes taken as proof that he was abandoning progressivism. Actually, when Roosevelt began agitating for preparedness in the fall of 1914 the cause was not a popular one, and only gradually did the country begin to respond. His friend and biographer Hermann Hagedorn later referred to Roosevelt in the war years as "the bugle that woke

America," but it was not at all clear in 1914 or 1915 that his call would be heeded.

In October, 1914, Wilson spoke slightingly of preparedness talk as merely "good mental exercise," and in his annual message in December he pledged adherence to the American tradition of a small navy and army: "We shall not alter our attitude . . . because some amongst us are nervous and excited." Secretary of State William Jennings Bryan, speaking not only for his followers in the Democracy but for many other liberals as well, defended the administration. "The President knows that if this country needed a million men, and needed them in a day, the call would go out at sunrise and the sun would go down on a million men in arms," declared the Great Commoner. At the same time Secretary of the Navy Josephus Daniels claimed that the navy was in "fine shape." But what were the facts? According to the report of the navy's General Board, the navy was unfit for combat duties. Because of neglect of target practice and maneuvers, a large proportion of the men serving with the Atlantic fleet had never even heard a ship's guns fired. The crews of the nation's two largest battleships had never fired a gun. And former Secretary of War Henry L. Stimson charged that the army had only enough ammunition for a single day's battle. The army was small as well, and even with later increases in manpower, supplies, and training, it was over a year after the United States entered the war before a significant number of troops could be assembled in France. It was, therefore, with accuracy and justice that Roosevelt commented on Bryan's famous remark:

. . . Mr. Bryan had a good precedent. . . . Pompey, when threatened by Caesar, and told that his side was unprepared, responded that he had only to "stamp his foot" and legions would spring up from the ground. In the actual event, the "stamping" proved as effectual against Caesar as Mr. Bryan's "call" would under like circumstances. I once heard a Bryanite senator put Mr. Bryan's position a little more strongly than it occurred to Mr. Bryan himself to put it. The senator in question announced that we needed no Regular Army, because in the event of war "ten million freemen would spring to arms, the equals of any regular soldiers in the world." I do not question the emotional or oratorical sincerity either of Mr. Bryan or of the senator. Mr. Bryan is accustomed to performing in vacuo. . . . This was equally true of the senator in question. If the senator's ten million men sprang to arms at this moment [1914], they would have at the outside some four hundred thousand modern rifles to which to spring. Perhaps six hundred thousand more could spring to squirrel pieces and fairly good shotguns. The remaining nine million men would have to "spring" to axes, scythes, hand-saws, gimlets, and similar arms. As for Mr. Bryan's million men who would at sunset respond under arms to a call made at sunrise, the suggestion is such a mere rhetorical flourish that it is not worthy even of humorous treatment. . . .

To an extent, the preparedness issue cut across geographical and ideological divisions. It has sometimes been assumed that only easterners and conservatives, particularly representatives of the business interests, favored preparedness, while progressives of all parties, especially in the South, Midwest, and West, opposed it. There is some basis for this assumption. The preparedness movement was in fact strongest in the East, and was financed and supported to a large degree by conservative Republicans and businessmen, while prominent progressives from other sections of the country like Bryan and La Follette opposed the movement, asserting that armaments invited wars from which eastern financiers would profit. There were Bull Moose leaders like Jane Addams of Illinois who opposed preparedness and any involvement in the European conflict. But there were also Progressives from the Midwest and West, like Robins, Richberg, and Ickes of Illinois, Murdock of Kansas, and Robert D. Carey of Wyoming, who strongly supported T.R.'s campaign for preparedness. Moreover, though such eastern conservatives as Lodge and Root favored preparedness, so did Henry L. Stimson, considered one of New York's leading liberal Republicans, and such eastern Bull Moose leaders as Bainbridge Colby, Frances A. Kellor, Charles J. Bonaparte, and Gifford Pinchot. Pinchot informed an Ohio civic group in late 1915: "The only subject upon which I am willing to speak, because it seems to me the paramount question now, is the interest of the United States in the war. The talk . . . will not be relished by any pro-Germans in my audience." Kellor, the former chief of the Progressive Service, published a book, *Straight America* (1916), which called for universal military training as a means for developing the spirit of nationalism necessary for reform. In New Jersey both the "moderate" Everett Colby and the "radical" Edmund B. Osborne, a leader of the Record faction, favored preparedness. In short, while many reformers like La Follette opposed preparedness, many other reformers from all sections of the country favored the movement.

Roosevelt was willing to work for national defense with his old opponents the conservative Republicans, but he never pretended, nor did they suppose, that this alliance and agreement extended to domestic issues. Roosevelt never abandoned the platform of 1912. He was well aware, however, that many in the reform camp like Jane Addams opposed preparedness. As early as 1912, he had written:

Very early I learned through my reading of history, and I found through my association with reformers, that one of the prime difficulties was to get the man who wished reform within a nation also to pay heed to the needs of the nation from the international standpoint. . . . Here at home I too often found that men who were ardent for social and industrial reform would be ignorant of the needs of this nation as a nation, would be ignorant of what the navy meant to the nation, . . . of what it meant to the nation to get from the other nations of mankind the respect which comes only to the just, and which is denied to the weaker nation far more quickly than it is denied to the stronger.

In 1912 Roosevelt had taken care to include demands for preparedness in his "Confession of Faith" and a plank in the Progressive platform calling for the construction of two battleships per year. During the campaign he had asserted:

I feel that the Progressive party owes no small part of its strength to the fact that it not only stands for the most far-reaching measures of social and industrial reform, but in sane and temperate fashion stands also for the right and duty of this nation to take a position of self-respecting strength among the nations of the world. . . .

While that was a dubious claim, with the coming of the war Roosevelt tried to make his party live up to the preparedness positions he had taken as president and in 1912. He argued that it was in the interests of reform to have the nation armed. Indeed, he claimed that preparedness was an integral part of the New Nationalism, just as Herbert Croly had earlier insisted in *The Promise of American Life* in 1909. Universal military training could be a great school for democracy, with rich and poor, southerner and northerner, native and immigrant learning the meaning of equality and patriotism as they served side by side. "Universal service . . . would be educational in the highest and best sense of the word," the Colonel claimed.

Roosevelt's view of war was romantic. Some of his contemporaries saw through the clichés of Tennyson and Kipling, the mystique of "The Charge of the Light Brigade," but Roosevelt was not among them. He once remarked that the popular pacifist song "I Didn't Raise My Boy To Be a Soldier" should be "sung with a companion piece entitled 'I Didn't Raise My Girl To Be a Mother' . . . The two would stand on precisely the same moral level." Roosevelt of course was no fascist. As president he had worked hard at the Portsmouth and Algeciras conferences for peace in Asia and Europe. And he was the first American to win the Nobel Peace Prize. But in his heart he always remained the perennial Rough Rider, charging up San Juan Hill to the glory that comes to the brave and reckless. "Actually Roosevelt was confused about the whole question of war and peace," the historian Howard K. Beale has written. "Though he valued the blessings of peace, he craved the excitements of war."

Yet while Roosevelt was a confused romantic on the subject of war, he considered himself the supreme realist on the question of defense. To him Bryan and Wilson were naive dreamers at best, and he had no patience with reformers who believed that progressivism and pacifism went hand in hand. In December, 1915, he was asked to contribute a paper to the American Sociological Congress on the subject of "the effect of war and militarism on social values." The opportunity was perfectly tailored to addressing reformers on the subject of defense:

. . . Infinitely the most important fact to remember in connection with the subject in question is that if an unscrupulous, warlike, and militaristic nation is not held in check by the warlike ability of a neighboring non-militaristic and well-behaved nation, then the latter will be spared the necessity of dealing with its own "moral and social values" because it won't be allowed to deal with anything.

Belgium had had a keen sense of proper social values, he continued, but that creased to matter after the German invasion of July, 1914. History provided further illustrations for the point that national defense was necessary for internal national progress:

If Lincoln had not been willing to go to war, to appeal to the sword, to introduce militarism on a tremendous scale throughout the United States, the sociologists who listened to this . . . , if they existed at all, would not be considering the "social values" . . . [we have today], but the "social values" of slavery and of such governmental and industrial problems as can now be studied in the Central American republics.

To Roosevelt the "moral" of history was obvious:

Nothing is gained by debate on non-debatable subjects. No intelligent man desires war. But neither can any intelligent man who is willing to think fail to realize that we live in a great and free country only because our forefathers were willing to wage war rather than accept the peace that spells destruction. No nation can permanently retain any "social values" worth having unless it develops the warlike strength necessary for its own defense.

Throughout the years before the United States entered the war, Roosevelt continued to argue for preparedness as simply a policy of common sense. He also maintained that it was in American national interest for the Allies to defeat the Central Powers, basing his arguments for intervention mainly on the tradition of *realpolitik*. He did confuse the separate issues of preparedness and intervention in the public mind, though he advocated both; but he himself maintained the logical distinction in his writings and speeches. After the sinking of the *Lusitania* in May, 1915, however, he introduced the arguments of neutral rights and national "honor" into his arsenal, and thus, as William Henry Harbaugh has noted, Roosevelt clouded questions of national interest and *realpolitik* with rhetorical smoke screens of specious issues based on simplistic conceptions of modern war. Roosevelt was in Syracuse at the libel trial when the British liner was torpedoed by a German submarine, with the resulting death of many American passengers, including the New York County Progressive Chairman Lindon Bates—passengers who had been warned by the German embassy that they traveled on a British ship at their own risk. The Colonel was called from bed by a phone call from a New York City editor giving him the details of the tragedy. "That's murder!" he told the editor. "Will I make a statement? Yes, yes, I'll make it now. Just take this," and he dictated over the phone:

This represents not merely piracy, but piracy on a vaster scale of murder than old-time pirates ever practiced. . . . It is warfare against innocent men, women, and children, traveling on the ocean. . . . It seems inconceivable that we can refrain from taking action in this matter, for we owe it not only to humanity but to our own national self-respect.

It was fitting that Roosevelt chose the image of pirates. He was using the imagery and sentiments of the eighteenth and nineteenth centuries, and this accurately reflected the feelings of a man to whom the concept of "national honor" had a meaning apart from considerations of practicality and national interest. By the summer of 1915 he agreed with his old friend Rudyard Kipling, who had written him in September, 1914, that America had to arm, "otherwise, if Europe fails, there will be no place left for freedom and the decency of things in any part of the earth."

TUT, TUT, THEODORE

3

Roosevelt was successful in winning the Progressive Party to the cause of preparedness. Some Progressives like William Allen White disagreed with T.R.'s criticisms of Wilson's foreign and defense policies, and some like Jane Addams were seen no more in party councils, but the majority of party leaders by late 1915 not only supported preparedness but did so with enthusiasm. As the war dragged on, and it became clear the Allies were not going to win a quick victory, and indeed might lose, the widespread support for neutrality manifested in 1914 began to give way to a feeling that American national interests were involved in the outcome of the battles in Europe. Progressives in company with many Americans came to favor preparedness as the minimal step for national protection, while interventionist sentiment grew in many quarters.

"HE'S GOOD ENOUGH FOR ALL!"

Roosevelt applied a steady pressure on his party's leaders, but their willing response and the near-unanimity of their pronouncements indicated that preparedness and even war itself were not policies they found alien to progressivism. There was to be no surrender of the principles of 1912, but Progressive Party leaders made it plain that defense and the war were to be their chief issues in 1916.

Throughout 1915 and during the first half of 1916, Roosevelt devoted most of his energies to preparedness. In July, 1915, he was in California to preach the need for national defense, and during the next twelve months he spoke in Missouri, Illinois, Michigan, Pennsylvania, and other states. He also regularly contributed articles on defense and the issues of the war to the *Metropolitan* magazine, publishing them early in 1916 in a collection entitled *Fear God and Take Your Own Part*. Working closely with the Progressive National Chairman Victor Murdock and George Perkins, Roosevelt began to expand the meaning of national defense to encompass a program described by Murdock as "military and economic preparedness" or the "broader Nationalism," a program which the *New Republic* termed the "Newer Nationalism." As outlined by Murdock, Perkins, and T.R., the Newer Nationalism combined domestic reform and the issues of the war. Military defense included the need for a "strong" home front, where businessmen, farmers, and workers pulled together to work for the nation, each group receiving social justice and a fair share of the national wealth in return. At the same time social justice now required the defense of American "rights" abroad as well as industrial reforms at home. In a sense, the whole country was to be "drafted" into a kind of "universal service" which included military training and duty, the cooperation of all sectors of the economy, and a rebirth of patriotism and national purpose. In short, military requirements and domestic and humanitarian needs were viewed as symbiotically related under the Newer Nationalism.

This Newer Nationalism may be seen as the fourth version of the New Nationalism that Roosevelt had presented since 1910. The original Osawatomie speech of 1910 had given only a broad outline of a nationalist policy which was to replace states rights and laissez-faire government. With the formation of the Progressive Party in 1912, it had become clear what the New Nationalism meant in detail: a strong federal government which would implement a specific program of social and industrial reform, and a direct democracy realized through primaries and other plebiscitory measures as well as through a new popular party. Defeated in 1912 by the forces of American pluralism, in 1914 the New Nationalism was expanded to include a recognition of the particular needs of the various states, needs which were addressed by state Progressive parties adapting the 1912 platform to specific local problems like those connected with Colorado mining. In 1914, however, the New Nationalism and the new party had been defeated once again. Then the war had provided the inspiration and occasion for the fourth and Newer Nationalism. Taking the preparedness proposal for universal military service, the so-called Swiss system, Roosevelt and his fellow partisans had expanded the concept to include "economic preparedness," a kind of universal social service wherein all Americans would serve the commonweal like soldiers. In a sense this Newer Nationalism was an ironic commentary on the fate of the nationalist reform ideology of 1910 and 1912. In 1912 the Progressives had appealed to the people in the name of Christian humanitarianism, but by 1916 the Bull Moose leaders were hoping that commonweal could be created perforce by the threat of the Germans. "Service"—

that favorite Progressive term and concept—now became "mandatory service" like the military draft. This ideological twist was as ominous as it was, perhaps, pathetic. It was as if the traditional quest of reformers for "an analogue to war," a quest illustrated by images of "Armageddon" and "Christian soldiers marching as to war," had come to a dead end in a real Armageddon. But as the Progressive Party sounded the keynote for the election of 1916, at a meeting of the Progressive National Committee in Chicago in January of that year, the Newer Nationalism seemed to be a way out of political and ideological difficulties for the party instead of a cul de sac.

Forty-six states were represented at the Chicago meeting on January 11-12, 1916, and many of the familiar Bull Moose leaders were there: Dixon from Montana, Funk and Ickes from Illinois, Mark Sullivan of *Collier's,* Van Valkenburg and Flinn from the Washington Party, Smith from Connecticut, and many others. Telegrams of support were read from T.R., Johnson, Straus, Beveridge, and various state leaders. Perkins and Bainbridge Colby delivered speeches stressing the war issues. Referring to one of Wilson's most quoted remarks, Perkins declared: "Of late we Americans have been hearing a new and strange doctrine; it is that men can be too proud to fight. Thank God, no one has been able to say that of the Progressive Party." Under Wilson, he continued, "our honorable name and our flag are dishonored and dragged in the dust." Bainbridge Colby's speech, entitled "Our Country," also referred to a famous Wilson statement:

It has been said recently in this country and on high authority that it is the duty of Americans to be neutral in word and deed, aye, even in thought; to fight down any generous response which the significance of the immeasurable struggle, now being waged, may evoke within us. The principle of democracy may be battling for its life. We must sit still. The cause of liberty may be gravely imperilled. We must not cry out, much less lift up our hands.

A public statement unanimously adopted by the national committee affirmed allegiance to the 1912 platform, and declared that Progressives favored "a broader Nationalism, to make possible an effective program of social and industrial justice at home and the protection of American citizens and rights abroad." This "broader Nationalism" required "complete preparedness":

It is . . . our supreme duty to protect American institutions and American standards of justice. This momentous hour therefore demands a complete preparedness, not merely in military armament, but preparedness that will mobilize our economic resources, agricultural, industrial and financial, a preparedness that will unify American citizenship and create a loyalty to our institutions such as peoples of other nations have so patriotically shown since the terrible test of war; the preparedness of self-defense, that preparedness which creates a spirit, unalterably opposed to militarism, and the ultimate object of which is universal peace, but a national spirit and soul which views the doctrine of peace-at-any-price as futile, cowardly and unrighteous and which will unhesitatingly make any needed sacrifice to uphold American standards of humanity and justice.

The Wilson administration, the statement continued, had failed to protect "national honor and industrial welfare." "It first among American administrations has shown the supine spirit, whose sure consequence is the contempt of the world." The need of the hour was "leadership of the highest order and most courageous character," and thus it was vital that the Wilson administration be defeated in 1916. "Keenly alive to this," the national committee announced that the Progressive convention would meet in Chicago at the same time the Republicans met. "We take this action, believing that the surest way to secure for our country the required leadership will be by having, if possible, both the Progressive and Republican Parties choose the same standard-bearer and the same principles." Such a result would be possible if the two parties rose above petty partisanship. "In this turning-point in world history, we will not stick on details; we will lay aside partisanship and prejudice. But we will never surrender these principles for which we stand and have stood. We will follow only a leader who, we know, stands for them and is able to put them through."

Nobody doubted that the Progressives had Roosevelt in mind as the man to unite the two parties. It had earlier been announced by the Progressive executive committee that he would not permit his name to be entered in the Republican primaries, and that "so far as possible delegates to our convention should go uninstructed. . . ." The Progressives found no use for the primaries in 1916, the system they had promoted in 1912. Roosevelt would not enter divisive factional fights with Republicans in primary states—primaries he might well lose—but would be presented to the conventions as a statesman above the political battles involved in a traditional campaign for a presidential nomination. All knew, of course, that uninstructed or not, the Bull Moose delegates would favor their party's acknowledged chief.

After the 1912 election Roosevelt had realized that the Progressives would want him to run again in 1916. "I have had too much experience in the past to make any definite promises even to myself; so all I can say is that it would be a real misfortune if we did not develop someone else to lead the fight in 1916," he wrote to George E. Miller of the *Detroit News* on November 8, 1912. In 1914 he thought that either Johnson or Beveridge would make a good candidate in 1916. But Beveridge's defeat in Indiana that year eliminated him as a possibility. Furthermore, in 1916 Beveridge refused to allow his name to be used in the Hoosier Progressive primaries even as a favorite son candidate. Roosevelt hoped Hiram Johnson could develop some support, but he doubted the Republicans would ever accept the California Progressive as their nominee. In 1916 Johnson entered the California G.O.P. presidential primary, hoping to win a nucleus of delegates to the Republican convention, but he was defeated, and all hopes for his candidacy then faded.

By 1915 Roosevelt had definitely decided he wanted to be president again. In May, when the German embassy warned Americans not to travel on Allied vessels, he wrote Cal O'Laughlin: "It makes my blood boil to see how we are regarded. . . . All the European nations look down upon us; but the Germans are the worst. . . . Lord, how I would like to be President. . . ." Roosevelt was certain, however, that the Republicans would not nominate him so soon after the battles of 1912 and 1914. He told Lodge that from the standpoint of foreign affairs, Murphy, Barnes, or Penrose would make a better president than Wilson. But when word reached Sagamore Hill that these sentiments had been quoted in Washington, he hastily asked Lodge not to repeat his remarks. As he explained to Republican and Progressive friends, the G.O.P. could not expect and would not deserve Bull Moose support if a conservative candidate were nominated. Roosevelt agreed with the preparedness and foreign policy pronouncements of such G.O.P. presidential hopefuls as Elihu Root, Senator John W. Weeks of Massachusetts, and Taft's Secretary of State Philander C. Knox, but he was at odds with them on domestic policy, and knew they would never be chosen by the Progressives. No Republican seemed to be making much headway in the race for the G.O.P. nomination except Supreme Court Justice Charles Evans Hughes.

Although the justice declined to enter the race formally, Hughes attracted much support and attention as a potential nominee. He had been a reformer as governor of New York from 1907 to 1911, and had won T.R.'s praise for his work. Appointed to the Supreme Court by Taft, he had been able to avoid the fights of 1912 and 1914. Moreover, his position on the Court had kept him from stating his views on the 1912 Progressive platform, preparedness, and other issues. As a man with a progressive but not a Bull Moose past, and a candidate whose views were unknown, Hughes seemed the perfect choice to many Republicans. Yet Roosevelt opposed him precisely because his views on the issues had not been made public. "We do not want to find that we have merely swapped Wilson for another Wilson with whiskers," T.R. explained to a friend. The movement for Hughes was a "politician's movement," Roosevelt wrote, "made for the very reason that no one knows where he stands, and therefore [he] represents the ideal, dear to the soul of the politician, of the candidate against whom no one can say anything. . . ."

At the beginning of 1916 Roosevelt still thought the odds were against his being nominated by the Republicans, but he sensed that public opinion was changing in favor of preparedness, and by May he thought popular sentiment was building for his nomination. "My own judgment is that among the rank and file of the Republican voters . . . there is very much more sentiment for me than for any other candidate," he wrote a friend on May 6. "But—I think—the convention at Chicago will be in the hands of a very sordid set of machine masters. . . ." He explained to his English friend Arthur Lee on June 7: "I do not believe the Republicans have any intention of nominating me. I now have a considerable following, whereas a year and three-quarters ago I had none. But I do not think I have the majority of the people with me as yet, nor do I feel that a sufficiently deep and widespread impression has been made on them to reflect itself among the politicians."

Yet, if Roosevelt's candidacy did not seem destined for success in June, it was not because of a lack of effort on the part of his supporters. In 1915

Meyer Lissner of California and others surveyed Progressive state chairmen to find out how much support there was for Roosevelt among Republicans in the various states. In state after state the answer was the same: many Republicans favored T.R., but commitments to numerous favorite son candidates, or to political organizations favoring a conservative candidate, or to the "safe" front-runner Hughes, prevented these sentiments from being translated into delegate votes for the Colonel. Roosevelt's supporters nevertheless proceeded

with their campaign. George von L. Meyer, postmaster general in the Roosevelt administration and then secretary of the navy under Taft, had remained with the G.O.P. in 1912, but as a leader of the Navy League and other preparedness groups he was once again in the Roosevelt camp. Meyer became president of the Roosevelt Republican Committee, and enlisted such Republicans as Ogden Reid of the *New York Tribune*, George B. Cortelyou, Senator Albert B. Fall of New Mexico, and J. Ogden Armour. Meyer's group was complemented by the Theodore Roosevelt Non-Partisan League, headed by the banker-philanthropist Guy Emerson and the building contractor Thomas Charles Desmond, and by Alice Carpenter's Women's Roosevelt League. T.R.'s Harvard classmate Charles G. Washburn prepared a campaign biography, and the magazine writer Julian Street published *The Most Interesting American,* another campaign document. Pamphlets were distributed and advertisements placed in newspapers and magazines. Meyer claimed that his organization had "no relations whatsoever with the Progressive Party," but in fact he was in close contact with the Bull Moose leaders, and it was Perkins who arranged for the committee's headquarters in the Congress Hotel. Typical of Meyer's efforts was his advice to the Arkansas banker F. E. Patrick in a telegram sent May 25:

SUGGEST YOU INTEREST MANY PEOPLE IN YOUR LOCALITY AS POSSIBLE IN CREATING ROOSEVELT TALK AND SENTIMENT EMPHASIZING THE FACT THAT HE IS THE WINNING CANDIDATE AND REPRESENTS THE ISSUE OF THE DAY WHICH IS AMERICANISM. IF YOU CAN GET LETTERS FOR ISSUE IN LOCAL PUB-LICATIONS FROM REGULAR LINE REPUBLICANS ENDORSING ROOSEVELT AND THUS CREATING SUPPORT AND PUBLICITY IT WILL BE OF VALUE....

A publicity campaign, however, was simply not enough. Meyer and his cohorts assembled an elaborate card file on all the Republican delegates, noting business and political associations and the appeals which might move each to vote for Roosevelt. It was soon discovered, however, that the mass of the delegates could not be convinced to turn to the Colonel. For the most part the G.O.P. Old Guard remained opposed to Roosevelt. Furthermore, there seemed to be no political necessity to nominate him. Roosevelt and the Progressive leaders had stated they would unite with the Republicans if a candidate could be found acceptable to both parties. Hughes seemed to fill the bill with his progressive record. Moreover, it became apparent that the Progressive National Committee's decision to hold the Bull Moose convention at the same time as the Republican convention was a tactical blunder. As Donald Richberg recalled: "... The Progressive Party advertised that it would be on a certain corner at a certain time, wearing a red carnation, and that its intentions were matrimonial!" The better course would have been to hold the Progressive convention first, nominate Roosevelt, and then wait for the Republicans to act. But Roosevelt had feared that such a plan might backfire, and result in another three-cornered race and the reelection of Wilson. Finally, Meyer's efforts were also doomed because until the last minute Roosevelt had refused to work on his own behalf. On March 9 he had issued a statement declining to allow his name to be used in the Republican primaries, adding "that it would be a mistake to nominate me unless the country has in its mood something of the heroic...." He spent the final months before the conventions, not in trying to round up delegates, but in preaching preparedness in cities like Detroit, the home of pacifist presidential hopeful Henry Ford, where he thought the sentiment for national defense was weakest.

4

The two conventions opened in Chicago on June 7. Raymond Robins presided, and delivered the keynote speech, at the Progressive conclave, while Warren G. Harding chaired the Republican convention. Though the contrast between the two chairmen seemed marked, this difference was not reflected in the platforms adopted by the two parties. Dean William Draper Lewis and Senator Henry Cabot Lodge, heads of the respective platform committees, had been in close consultation, and both platforms emphasized the preparedness issue while giving brief if definite endorsements for reform. Each convention appointed a committee to confer on a joint nominee, and Roosevelt talked by private line from Sagamore Hill with Hiram Johnson, Nicholas Murray Butler, and other members of the committees. But no agreement was reached. "We'll take any one you offer but Roosevelt," Reed Smoot said on behalf of the Republican committee. But the Progressives refused to offer any candidate but Roosevelt. Roosevelt suggested several names which were rejected, and finally proposed Lodge as the joint nominee, probably in disgust at the intransigence of both sides. Lodge, a man with no national following, who was unpopular even with some of his fellow conservative Republicans, had no chance of being nominated. Roosevelt "was evading, not seeking, responsibility for the nominee," the Progressive Henry L. Stoddard later explained.

The outcome of the Republican convention, however, was obvious as soon as the first ballot was cast on June 9. Hughes with 253½ votes was far ahead of Root, Weeks, and all the other candidates; Roosevelt received only 65 votes. On the second ballot Hughes passed the 300 mark, while Roosevelt only climbed to 81 votes, and it was clear that the Justice would be nominated the next day. At the same time a split was developing in the Progressive ranks. Most of the delegates apparently were willing to consider fusion if Roosevelt were the nominee of the Republicans, but wanted union on no other terms. Furthermore, while Progressive leaders like Harold Ickes were interested in taking over the Republican Party, they feared the reverse would be the case if the new party accepted a Republican candidate. Some state leaders also wanted to preserve a distinct Progressive Party because they still had political ambitions. John M. Parker had made a strong showing for governor in the Louisiana election that spring, and the demise of the party would leave him without a political home, while Albert Nortoni and Joseph P. Fontron of Missouri had already made plans to run for office on the Progressive ticket in the fall. Some of the Indiana Progressives had also been organizing a state campaign for 1916. Yet it was evident to all observers that the majority of Progressive delegates had come to Chicago for one purpose—to nominate Roosevelt. They had hoped that lightning would strike and the G.O.P. turn to their leader and hero, but whatever course the Republicans took they were determined that Roosevelt be a candidate.

On June 10 the Progressive convention, disregarding the pleas of Perkins, nominated Roosevelt at 12:37 P.M., minutes before the Republican convention chose Hughes. John M. Parker was then nominated for vice president, and the Progressives began to raise pledges in the hall for a campaign fund. Soon a telegram arrived from Sagamore Hill:

I AM VERY GRATEFUL FOR THE HONOR YOU CONFER ON ME BY NOMINATING ME AS PRESIDENT. I CANNOT ACCEPT IT AT THIS TIME. I DO NOT KNOW THE ATTITUDE OF THE CANDIDATE OF THE REPUBLICAN PARTY TOWARD THE VITAL QUESTIONS OF THE DAY. THEREFORE, IF YOU DESIRE AN IMMEDIATE DECISION, I MUST DECLINE THE NOMINATION. BUT IF YOU PREFER IT, I SUGGEST

T.R.—"THIS HURTS ME WORSE THAN IT DOES YOU!"

THAT MY CONDITIONAL REFUSAL TO RUN BE PLACED IN THE HANDS OF THE PROGRESSIVE NATIONAL COMMITTEE.... THEY CAN CONFER WITH ME AND THEN DETERMINE ON WHATEVER ACTION WE MAY ... DEEM APPROPRIATE TO MEET THE NEEDS OF THE COUNTRY.

William Allen White recalled the scene:

For a moment there was silence. Then there was a roar of rage. It was the cry of a broken heart such as no convention ever had uttered in this land before.

Standing there in the box I had tears in my eyes, I am told. I saw hundreds of men tear the Roosevelt picture or the Roosevelt badge from their coats, and throw it on the floor. . . .

A resolution empowering the national committee "to fill any vacancies that may occur on the ticket" was rushed through by Perkins's cohorts, and then the second and final Progressive national convention adjourned.

"The rest of the story is anticlimactic," writes the historian John A. Garraty. Hughes issued statements pledging himself to preparedness and progressivism,

"COME, MOOSIE! GOOD MOOSIE! NICE MOOSIE!"

and Roosevelt then endorsed the Republican nominee. The Progressive National Committee met in Chicago on June 26. A letter from T.R. was read asking the committee to back Hughes. The Progressives argued for six hours. Perkins, Garfield, Ickes, and Flinn, representing a cross section of the Bull Moose leadership, supported Hughes. Parker, Bainbridge Colby, Nortoni, and Matthew Hale, all of whom were prominent almost solely as leaders in the Progressive organization, opposed Hughes. A motion to substitute Victor Murdock as the candidate was defeated 31 to 15, another to postpone any decision was rejected

34 to 13. Garfield then moved that Hughes be endorsed, and the vote was 32 in favor, 6 opposed, 9 declining to vote.

Later John M. Parker and Victor Murdock issued a call for a new Progressive convention. A group of antifusionists assembled on August 2 in Indianapolis, but Murdock had announced he would not be their candidate, and no substitute was found. Parker, Bainbridge Colby, Edwin M. Lee, Matthew Hale, Murdock, and C. W. McClure were the only well-known Progressives who attended, and less than twenty states were represented. A committee of fifteen was chosen to direct the "party," and it was decided to put up electoral tickets for the vice presidential candidate Parker with the hope that a balance of power could be won in the electoral college. Parker, however, soon announced for Wilson and returned to the Democratic Party.

Most of the Progressive leaders followed Roosevelt into the Republican camp, but a significant minority supported Wilson. When the lineup was completed, those endorsing Hughes included Gifford Pinchot, Garfield, Perkins, Beveridge, Ickes, Hiram Johnson, Charles J. Bonaparte, and Raymond Robins, while those backing Wilson included Ben Lindsey, Francis J. Heney, John M. Parker, all of whom had previously been Democrats, and Edward P. Costigan, Bainbridge Colby, and Albert Nortoni. Vance McCormick, the fusion nominee of the Washington Party in 1914, headed Wilson's campaign, and every effort was made to attract former Progressives. Wilson had continued to adopt Progressive planks after 1914, and by 1916 he was an advocate of preparedness too. Thus, such proponents of the Newer Nationalism as Bainbridge Colby could find reason to support the president along with Progressives like Jane Addams who favored peace. Wilson's Democratic-Progressive coalition was victorious at the polls, and an analysis of the returns shows that the Bull Moose vote provided the president with the margin of victory in New Hampshire, Kansas, California, and other states. The election was one of the closest in American history, and hence in a real sense the Bull Moose vote reelected Wilson. The Progressive Party had defeated the Republicans at its birth, and in death it did so again.

EPILOGUE: THE DIASPORA

Those who stood at "Armageddon and battled for the Lord" with Theodore Roosevelt were never united again after June, 1916. In the following years former Progressives could be found in every political camp. After the election, on December 5, 1916, William Allen White, Chester H. Rowell, Gifford Pinchot, Raymond Robins, James R. Garfield, and Harold L. Ickes issued a statement declaring that they were "firm in the conviction that in the existing two-party system constructive progressivism may best be achieved through the Republican Party." This group probably represented the sentiments of the majority of Bull Moose leaders. But by then Bainbridge Colby, John M. Parker, Ben Lindsey, Victor Murdock, Edward P. Costigan, and Francis J. Heney had joined the Democrats in the belief that the party of Wilson was the best vehicle for reform. A few antifusionists, however, continued to work for a new progressive party. In December, 1918, the Committee of 48 was organized by Amos Pinchot, George L. Record, and other former Progressives to replace the committee organized at the 1916 antifusionist conference in Indianapolis.

By 1918 Roosevelt was again the most prominent leader of the Republican Party and the odds-on favorite for the nomination in 1920. The Colonel made plans for 1920, chose a campaign manager, and began drawing up a new progressive program. The dream of a reconstructed, progressive G.O.P., however, was not to be. Roosevelt died on January 6, 1919, and the progressive Republicans then divided their support among Hiram Johnson, the old Rough Rider Leonard Wood, Miles Poindexter, and other candidates. In the resulting convention deadlock the Old Guard was able to nominate the dark horse Warren G. Harding. At the same time the antifusionist Committee of 48 split, with some members supporting the Farmer Labor Party, and others holding out for a new party controlled by the committee. The antifusionist remnant merged with La Follette's Progressive Party in 1924.

The Progressives who joined the Democrats in 1916 weathered the party's defeats in the 1920s, but when the day of victory came in 1932 with the second Roosevelt, some like Bainbridge Colby, along with some Wilsonian Democrats like Vance McCormick, joined with the former Bull Moose leaders James R. Garfield, Hamilton Fish, Jr., Amos Pinchot, and others in opposing the New Deal. The New Deal, however, won the support of such former Progressives as Francis E. McGovern, William Draper Lewis, Ben Lindsey, and most of the old social educators connected with the Progressive Service. Donald Richberg, former director of the Service's Legislative Reference Bureau, worked with the N.R.A. Harold L. Ickes left the Republican Party to become F.D.R.'s secretary of the interior, while in the Senate Republican Bronson Cutting of New Mexico joined with Democrat Edward P. Costigan to defend the New Deal. In 1936 the Republican presidential and vice presidential candidates Alfred M. Landon and Frank Knox were former Progressives, but so were Ickes, Costigan, Heney, Paul U. Kellogg, and others who supported F.D.R. for reelection.

In short, after 1916 there was no Progressive consensus on parties, leaders, or issues. The explanation seems to be that various Progressives came to emphasize different tenets of the old faith. At a unique point in history the Progressives had been united by the political and ideological circumstances of their environment and by the direction of a charismatic leader. History did not repeat itself; the Bull Moosers never gathered in a common herd again. Thus, the Progressives went their different ways after 1916, each trying to preserve as best he could a faith which no longer had a single directive.

For the antifusionists of the Committee of 48, the most important goal was the creation of an ideologically pure party dedicated solely to reform. If in their quest they lost the quality of practicality and the sense of what T.R. called "realizable ideals," this was perhaps understandable since their task became increasingly difficult after 1914. Other Progressives like Hiram W. Johnson returned to the G.O.P. and the old strategy of factional politics, while still others like Costigan decided to become Democrats. In the 1920s both old parties were unfriendly to reform, both partisan paths seemed equally difficult, and it was natural that many of the old Progressives decided to hold on to whatever partisan power they were able to win and never deserted partisan homes again. There were, of course, those free spirits of reform like Ickes and Richberg who asked only for a fight and a cause, not partisan security. There were also some Progressives like Winston Churchill who retreated from public concerns, disillusioned by the turn of events after 1912. As followers of the apostle of the "strenuous life," however, most Progressive leaders continued in public life. Some like James R. Garfield and Everett Colby turned to charity and civic good works. Following the Progressive beliefs in management and government planning, others served as bureaucrats and government experts. John Franklin Fort and Victor Murdock were appointed to the Federal Trade Commission by Wilson. Frederick M. Davenport founded the National Institute of Public

Affairs to train bureaucrats. When the institute was incorporated into the Civil Service Commission, Davenport continued as chairman under F.D.R. and Truman.

Many more Progressives continued to be active in politics. Henry J. Allen became governor of Kansas, and John M. Parker governor of Louisiana, the offices they had been defeated for as Progressives, while Joseph M. Dixon was elected governor of Montana and Gifford Pinchot governor of Pennsylvania. Costigan, Cutting, Medill McCormick, and Hiram Johnson as well as other former Progressives were elected to the Senate—T.R.'s old running mate serving from 1917 until his death in 1945. Many of the old Bull Moose members of the U. S. House returned to Congress after the defeats of 1914. Roy O. Woodruff of Michigan retired from the House after thirty-four years of service, in 1953. The list of former Progressives who won office after 1916 is long. In sum, a Bull Moose past did not prove to be a political liability.

Some old Progressives like Hamilton Fish, Jr., and Minnesota's Thomas D. Schall became identified as conservatives after 1916; others like Cutting and Costigan were leaders of the liberal wing in their parties. Emphasizing Progressive efficiency through economy, Fish and others opposed the Keynesian spending and bureaucratic "wastes" of the New Deal, while Republican Cutting and Democrat Costigan found the New Deal the embodiment of the social and industrial justice of the 1912 platform.

Most of the Bull Moose platform eventually became law. But the dream of a progressive party pledged to common principles and programs, free from a conservative faction, nationalist and reformist in ethos, was never realized by either liberal Republicans or progressive Democrats, and the old Progressives made their way as best they could in a new world which often looked back at the Progressive Party as a futile and naive venture. In the early 1940s William Allen White tried to write an obituary for his old party and the men who led it. The result was a characteristic affirmation of the Progressive faith:

Looking back now more than thirty years, I can shut my eyes and see that Bull Moose convention of 1912, see their eager faces—more than a thousand of them—upturned, smiling hopefully with joy beaming out that came from hearts which believed in what they were doing; its importance, its righteousness.

It seemed to matter so very much, that convention of zealots, cleansed of self-interest and purged of cynicism. I never have seen before or since exactly that kind of crowd. I impressed it on my memory because I felt as they felt. . . .

And now they are dust, and all the visions they saw that day have dissolved. Their hopes, like shifting clouds, have blown away before the winds of circumstance. And I wonder if it did matter much. Or is there somewhere, in the stuff that holds humanity together, some force, some conservation of spiritual energy, that saves the core of every noble hope, and gathers all men's visions some day, some way, into the reality of progress?

I do not know. But I have seen the world move, under some, maybe mystic, influence, far enough to have the right to ask that question.

NOTES AND BIBLIOGRAPHICAL REFERENCES

An extensive bibliography on the Progressive Party, including all primary and secondary sources used for this book, has been placed on deposit for the use of students at the Theodore Roosevelt Collection at Harvard.

The following abbreviations are used throughout.

BDAC–Biographical Directory of the American Congress, 1774–1961 (Washington, 1961).
DAB–Dictionary of American Biography (20 vols.: New York, 1928–1937, and supplements).
*Letters–*Elting E. Morison and associates, editors, *The Letters of Theodore Roosevelt* (8 vols.: Cambridge, 1951–1954).
NCAB–The National Cyclopedia of American Biography (continuing series of volumes: New York, 1892–).
*NWTR–*Hermann Hagedorn, editor, *The National Edition of the Works of Theodore Roosevelt* (20 vols.: New York, 1926).
T.R.–Theodore Roosevelt
TRCH–The Theodore Roosevelt Collection at the Harvard University Library, Cambridge, Massachusetts.
TRLC–The Theodore Roosevelt Papers at the Library of Congress, Washington, D.C.
WWW–Who Was Who (continuing series of volumes: New York, 1963–).

For the *BDAC, DAB, NCAB,* and *WWW* volume numbers and page references are omitted since they may be found in the indexes of these series under the names of subjects.

PREFACE

". . . In the prophet business," T.R. to E.A. Van Valkenburg, April 23, 1918, *Letters,* VII, pp. 1312–1313; "bully pulpit," quoted by George Haven Putnam in "Roosevelt: Historian and Statesman," *NWTR,* IX, pp. ix–xix, quotation, p. x. On historians' views of T.R., see I. E. Cadenhead, Jr., *Theodore Roosevelt and the Paradox of Progressivism* (Woodbury, N.Y., 1974), pp. 242–268; Richard H. Collin, "Henry Pringle's Theodore Roosevelt: A Study in Historical Revisionism," *New York History,* 52 (1971), pp. 3–35; Dewey W. Grantham, Jr., "Theodore Roosevelt in American Historical Writing, 1945–1960," *Mid-America,* XLIII (1961), pp. 3–35; Dewey W. Grantham, Jr., editor, *Theodore Roosevelt* (Englewood Cliffs, N.J., 1971); Morton Keller, editor, *Theodore Roosevelt: A Profile* (New York, 1968). The best full-length scholarly biography is William Henry Harbaugh, *Power and Responsibility: The Life and Times of Theodore Roosevelt* (New York, 1961). This classic work has been printed in a revised edition by the Oxford University Press as *The Life and Times of Theodore Roosevelt* (New York, 1975), which has the most comprehensive and recent annotated bibliography of scholarly writings on T.R. (Page references to Harbaugh in these Notes are taken from the first edition of this biography.) For a negative view of T.R. as a compromising politician, see Henry F. Pringle, *Theodore Roosevelt: A Biography* (New York, 1931). For an appreciation of T.R. as a *realpolitiker*, see John M. Blum, *The Republican Roosevelt* (Cambridge, 1954). Blum's view of T.R.'s last years is essentially also that of Joseph L. Gardner, *Departing Glory: Theodore Roosevelt As Ex-President* (New York, 1973). The view of the Progressive Party as wasted effort and damaging to liberalism and personal careers is expressed in George E. Mowry, *Theodore Roosevelt and the Progressive Movement* (Madison. 1946). Important studies of the theory and workings of political parties as viewed by T.R. , generation are Charles E. Merriam, *The American Party System: An Introduction to the Study of Political Parties in the United States* (New York, 1922); and Austin Ranney, *The Doctrine of Responsible Party Government, Its Origins and Present State* (Urbana, Ill., 1954). On the general history of parties, see Arthur M. Schlesinger, Jr., editor, *History of U.S. Political Parties* (4 vols.: New York, 1973), which includes George E. Mowry, "The Progressive Party, 1912 and 1924," III, pp. 2541–2570; and on third parties, Howard P. Nash, *Third Parties in American Politics* (Washington, 1959). On Hamiltonian means for Jeffersonian ends, see T.R., *Autobiography* (1913), *NWTR*, XX, p. 414.

1. THE ROAD TO ARMAGEDDON

Page 3: "You know, Charley...," T.R. to Charles Grenfill Washburn, June 23, 1915, *Letters*, VIII, pp. 941–942; "the swift culmination...," Herbert Knox Smith, "The Progressive Party," *Yale Review*, October 1912, pp. 18–32, quotation, p. 18; T.R.'s statement, "To the Republican Convention," June 22, 1912, *Letters*, VIII, pp. 562–563.

Pages 3–5 and 14–17: For accounts of the 1912 Republican convention and the Orchestra Hall meeting, see William Jennings Bryan, *A Tale of Two Conventions* (New York, 1912); *Chicago Trubune*, June 18–24, 1912; *Great Leaders and National Issues of 1912* (Philadelphia, 1912); Alice Roosevelt Longworth, *Crowded Hours* (New York, 1933), pp. 196–205; Mowry, pp. 237–255; *New York Times*, June 18–22, 1912; *Official Report of the Proceedings of the Fifteenth Republican National Convention* (New York, 1912); Amos R. E. Pinchot, *History of the Progressive Party, 1912–1916* (New York, 1958), edited by Helene Maxwell Hooker, pp. 165–172; Nicholas Roosevelt, *Theodore Roosevelt: The Man As I Knew Him* (New York, 1967), pp. 75–101; Victor Rosewater, *Backstage in 1912* (Philadelphia, 1932); Mark Sullivan, *Our Times: The United States 1900–1925* (6 vols.: New York, 1926–35), IV, pp. 512–532; James E. Watson, *As I Knew Them: Memoirs of James E. Watson* (Indianapolis, 1936), pp. 148–162; William Allen White, *The Autobiography of William Allen White* (New York, 1946), pp. 462–475.

Page 5: T. R. quoted in Joseph Bucklin Bishop, *The Life and Times of Theodore Roosevelt* (2 vols.: New York, 1920), II, pp. 334–335; George Ade, "90–Count 'Em–90," *Collier's*, July 6, 1912, pp. 11–12, 29, quotation, p. 11.

Pages 4–8: For a survey and bibliography of the extensive literature on the progressive movement, see David M. Kennedy, editor, *Progressivism: The Critical Issues* (Boston, 1971). The earliest scholarly work on the movement is still useful and informative: Benjamin Parke DeWitt, *The Progressive Movement* (1915: University of Washington Press edition, Seattle, 1968). The most influential interpretations of the movement are Richard Hofstadter, *The Age of Reform, From Bryan to F.D.R.* (New York, 1955); and Robert H. Wiebe, *The Search for Order, 1877–1920* (New York, 1967). Other important studies include John Chamberlain, *Farewell to Reform: The Rise, Life and Decay of the Progressive Mind in America* (New York, 1932); Harold U. Faulkner, *The Quest for Social Justice, 1898–1914*

(New York, 1931); Samuel P. Hayes, *The Response to Industrialism, 1885-1914* (Chicago, 1957); Gabriel Kolko, *The Triumph of Conservatism: A Reinterpretation of American History, 1900-1916* (Glencoe, Ill., 1963); Arthur S. Link, *Woodrow Wilson and the Progressive Era, 1910-1917* (New York, 1954); Arthur S. Link and William M. Leary, Jr., *The Progressive Era and the Great War, 1896-1920* (New York, 1969); George E. Mowry, *Theodore Roosevelt and the Birth of Modern America, 1900-1912* (New York, 1958); David P. Thelan, *The New Citizenship: Origins of Progressivism in Wisconsin* (Columbia, Mo., 1972).

Page 6: Paul U. Kellogg, "The Industrial Platform of the New Party," *Survey,* August 24, 1912, pp. 668-670, quotation, p. 70. On the readiness of social workers for a new party, also see Jane Addams, *The Second Twenty Years at Hull House* (New York, 1930), pp. 23-24.

Page 7: Gifford Pinchot quoted in "Pinchot's 'Fighting Speech,'" *Literary Digest,* June 25, 1910, pp. 1245-1246, quotation, p. 1245.

Pages 7-8: The best accounts of the Roosevelt administration are Blum; G. Wallace Chessman, *Theodore Roosevelt and the Politics of Power* (Boston, 1969); Harbaugh; Mowry, *Birth of Modern America;* T.R., *Autobiography, NWTR,* XX. For accounts of the Taft administration, see Paolo E. Coletta, *The Presidency of William Howard Taft* (Lawrence, Kansas, 1973); Mowry, *Birth of Modern America;* Henry F. Pringle, *The Life and Times of William Howard Taft* (2 vols.: New York, 1939). Taft's philosophy of the Presidency is outlined in Taft, *Our Chief Magistrate and His Powers* (New York, 1916). On the increasing militancy of conservative Republicans after 1906, see Chessman, pp. 129-130, 141-156; Harbaugh, pp. 337-349, 363-372; Mowry, *Birth of Modern America,* pp. 208-225. On the split between Taft and the conservatives on the one hand, and T.R. and the progressives on the other, see Archibald B. Butt, *Taft and Roosevelt: The Intimate Letters of Archie Butt, Military Aide* (2 vols.: New York, 1930); Kenneth W. Hechler, *Insurgency: Personalities and Politics of the Taft Era* (New York, 1940); William Manners, *TR and Will: The Friendship That Split the Republican Party* (New York, 1969); Mowry, *Progressive Movement,* chs. II-VIII (unless otherwise noted, all further citations from Mowry refer to *Theodore Roosevelt and the Progressive Movement,* and will be cited as "Mowry"); Alpheus T. Mason, *Bureaucracy Convicts Itself: The Ballinger-Pinchot Controversy* (New York, 1941); James Penick, Jr., *Progressive Politics and Conservation: the Ballinger-Pinchot Affair* (Chicago, 1968); Gifford Pinchot, *Breaking New Ground* (New York, 1947), pp. 376, 391-504. On the split between conservative and progressive Democrats in the 1900-1912 period, see De Witt, pp. 35-43, 71-76. On the attempted purge of progressive Republicans by the conservatives and the Taft administration, see Mowry, pp. 98-156.

Page 8: "On a shutter," Senator Jonathan Dolliver of Iowa quoted in White, p. 426; for the "back from Elba" movement, see *Literary Digest,* January 22, 1919, p. 126; and "The 'Return From Elba,'" *Literary Digest,* March 5, 1910, pp. 427-428. "By 1910 the split . . . ," Smith, p. 22. On the 1910 and 1911 sentiment for Roosevelt's candidacy, see Mowry, pp. 118, 147.

Pages 8-9: On the St. Paul Roosevelt Club banquet, see *Literary Digest,* June 25, 1910, pp. 1245-1246, from which the *Atlanta Journal, Kansas City Star,* and *Boston Transcript* quotations are taken.

Page 9: For Roosevelt's attitudes on the factional struggles in 1910-1911, see particularly T.R. to Nicholas Longworth, July 22, 1910, *Letters,* VII, pp. 105-106; T.R. to Theodore Roosevelt, Jr., August 10, 1910, *Letters,* VII, pp. 108-110; T.R. to William Allen White, December 12, 1910, *Letters,* VII, pp. 181-185; T.R. to Robert Bacon and family, January 2,

1911, *Letters*, VII, pp. 198-200; T.R. to Theodore Roosevelt, Jr., May 5, 1911, *Letters*, VII, pp. 26-261. On the New York State fight, see Butt, II, pp. 479-482; Mowry, pp. 134-142, 148-152; Watson, pp. 144-147.

Pages 9-11: Roosevelt quotations from T.R., "The New Nationalism," speech at Osawatomie, Kansas, August 31, 1910, *NWTR*, XVII, pp. 5-22. On T.R.'s 1910 speaking tour, see Mowry, pp. 142-148; Pringle, *Theodore Roosevelt*, pp. 540-544 (all further citations from Pringle refer to *Theodore Roosevelt: A Biography*, and will be cited as "Pringle"); and a colorful contemporary account, Charles Morris, *Battling For the Right: The Life Story of Theodore Roosevelt* (New York, 1910). The speeches of the tour were published in T.R., *The New Nationalism* (New York, 1910). See Herbert Croly, *The Promise of American Life* (New York, 1909); and for discussions of T.R., Croly, and the New Nationalism, see Charles Forcey, *The Crossroads of Liberalism: Croly, Weyl, Lippmann and the Progressive Era, 1900-1925* (New York, 1961), particularly pp. 3-51, 121-217; Eric F. Goldman, *Rendezvous With Destiny: A History of Modern American Reform* (New York, 1952), pp. 188-212; Harbaugh, pp. 390-393. Goldman's analysis of Croly and the New Nationalism is perceptive, but he fails to see, as Forcey and Harbaugh note, that New Nationalist concepts were at the core of Roosevelt's political philosophy long before 1910. Indeed, Croly had used T.R. as a model and inspiration for his book. For a discussion of Roosevelt's early nationalist views, see John Allen Gable, "Theodore Roosevelt As Historian and Man of Letters," introduction to Theodore Roosevelt Association American Revolution Bicentennial Edition of T.R., *Gouverneur Morris* (1888; Oyster Bay, N.Y., 1975), pp. vii-xxiv.

Page 11: *Boston Traveler, New York Commercial,* and *New York Herald* quoted in *Literary Digest,* September 10, 1910, pp. 367-369; the Nebraska conference is reported in Mowry, p. 147; on the failure of the purge and the election of 1910, see Mowry, pp. 126-156. On polarization in the Republican Party, see De Witt, pp. 71-150; for the Lincoln-Roosevelt Clubs of California, see George E. Mowry, *The California Progressives* (Berkeley, 1951), Chapter III, and Spencer C. Olin, Jr., *California's Prodigal Sons: Hiram Johnson and the Progressives, 1911-1917* (Berkeley, 1968), pp. 11-68; for the Progressive-Republican League of Illinois, see Thomas E. Vadney, *The Wayward Liberal: A Political Biography of Donald Richberg* (Lexington, Kentucky, 1970), pp. 18-19; for Wyoming, see biographical information on Joseph M. Carey in *BDAC* and *NCAB;* for the Republican Progressive League of New Mexico, see Patricia Cadigan Armstrong, *A Portrait of Bronson Cutting Through His Papers, 1910-1917* (Albuquerque, 1959), pp. 4-6, 11, and Robert W. Larson, "The Profile of a New Mexico Progressive," *New Mexico Historical Review,* XLV (1970), pp. 233-244; for the Citizens' Party of Denver, see biographical information on Edward P. Costigan in *NCAB,* and Colin B. Goodykoontz, editor, *Papers of Edward P. Costigan Relating to the Progressive Movement in Colorado, 1902-1917* (Boulder, Colo., 1941), p. 155.

Page 12: "My hat is in the ring," quoted by Pringle, p. 556; "merely means to ends," T.R. to Jonathan Bourne, Jr., January 2, 1911, *Letters,* VII, pp. 196-198. On the launching of the Roosevelt National Committee, and on the seven governors' letter, see Harold Howland, *Theodore Roosevelt and His Times: A Chronicle of the Progressive Movement* (New Haven, 1921), pp. 210-211; Mowry, pp. 183-225; T.R. to Chase S. Osborn, *Letters,* VII, pp. 484-485. The text of the letter of the seven governors, February 10, 1912, and T.R.'s response, February 24, 1912, are printed in "The Nomination for President," *NWTR,* XVII, pp. 149-150. On LaFollette's candidacy, see Robert M. LaFollette, *LaFollette's Autobiography: A Personal Narrative of Political Experiences* (1913; University of Wisconsin Press edition, 1960), Chapters XI-XIII and Appendix; Mowry, pp. 173-174, 177-178, 185-187, 200-201, 205-208, 221, 233, 235, 236, 253; Amos Pinchot, pp. 121-157. T.R.'s most important speeches in the campaign for the Republican nomination are published in *NWTR,* XVII, and in T.R., *Progressive Principles* (New York, 1913). For a detailed discussion of T.R.'s decision to run in 1912, see John Allen Gable, "The Bull Moose Years: Theodore Roosevelt and the Progressive Party, 1912-1916," Ph.D. dissertation, Brown University, 1972, pp. 26-34, 63-71. This earlier study, upon which this book is largely based, will be cited hereinafter as "Gable, dissertation."

Pages 12-13: T.R., "A Charter of Democracy," address, Ohio Constitutional Convention, Columbus, Ohio, February 21, 1912, *NWTR,* XVII, pp. 119-148. For reactions to the speech, see Harbaugh, pp. 419-426; Mowry, pp. 212-219; Watson, pp. 147-148.

Pages 13-14: For accounts of the pre-convention campaign, see Harbaugh, pp. 412-436; Mowry, pp. 220-236.

Page 14: T.R., "The Right of the People to Rule," address, Carnegie Hall, New York City, March 20, 1912, pp. 151-171, quotation, p. 151. Primary election figures and results are taken from Mowry, pp. 228-236; and *The World Almanac and Encyclopedia for 1913* (New York, 1913), p. 719.

Pages 14-15: On the delegate disputes, see Bishop, II, pp. 320-333; Lewis L. Gould, "Theodore Roosevelt, William Howard Taft, and the Disputed Delegates of 1912: Texas as a Test Case," *Southwestern Historical Quarterly,* LXXX (1976), pp. 33-56; Harbaugh, pp. 431-436; Mowry, pp. 237-241; Pringle, pp. 562-565; Gilbert E. Roe, "The Truth about the Contests," *LaFollette's Weekly,* July 20, 1912, pp. 7-8, July 27, 1912, pp. 8-9, 14, August 3, 1912, pp. 7-9, 15; T.R., "Thou Shalt Not Steal," *Outlook,* July 13, 1912, *NWTR,* XVII, pp. 232-242; Rosewater; and Watson, pp. 149-152.

Page 15: T.R.'s estimate is in "Thou Shalt Not Steal," p. 233; headline from *Chicago Tribune,* June 18, 1912. For Senator Boies Penrose's remark and an account of the activities of conservative Republicans at the convention, see Watson, pp. 149-152. James E. Watson was Taft's floor leader at the convention.

Page 16: "I quite agree . . . ," William Howard Taft to William Barnes, Jr., January 29, 1912, quoted in James Holt, *Congressional Insurgents and the Party System, 1912-1916* (Cambridge, 1967), p. 61; "I THINK . . . ," Hiram W. Johnson to Meyer Lissner, telegram, June 9, 1912, quoted in Olin, p. 62.

Pages 16-17: Roosevelt quotations from T.R., "The Case Against the Reactionaries," speech at the Chicago Auditorium, June 17, 1912, *NWTR,* XVII, pp. 204-231. The Johnson, Munsey, and Perkins quotations are from Amos Pinchot, pp. 164-165. On the decision in advance to bolt in case of "theft," see Longworth, p. 196; Mowry, p. 248; Nicholas Roosevelt, p. 87; White, pp. 452-454; T.R. to Chase S. Osborn, April 16, 1912, *Letters,* VII, p. 196. On the conference where the decision was made to form a new party, see Mowry, pp. 248-249; Amos Pinchot, pp. 164-165; Henry L. Stoddard, *As I Knew Them: Presidents and Politics from Grant to Coolidge* (New York, 1927), pp. 305-306.

Page 18: Smith, p. 23; Albert J. Beveridge, "Pass Prosperity Around," keynote address at the Progressive National Convention, August 5, 1912, in *First National Convention of the Progressive Party,* ms. typed minutes, copies in TRCH and TRLC, pp. 12-41, quotation, p. 13; T.R. quotation from "Confession of Faith," address to Progressive National Convention, August 6, 1912, *NWTR,* XVII, pp. 254-299, quotation, p 254.

2. FORMING THE RANKS AT ARMAGEDDON

Page 19: "Will the new party . . . ," *Literary Digest,* July 6, 1912, p. 2; formation of the organizational committee, *New York Times,* June 25, 1912; on the term "bull moose," see Manners, pp. 237-238; the "call" for the Progressive Party, *New York Times,* July 8, 1912.

Pages 20-21: For accounts of the campaign for the Democratic nomination, see Arthur S. Link, *Wilson: The Road to the White House* (Princeton, 1947); Link, *Woodrow Wilson and the Progressive Era,* pp. 7-12. The vote for conservative Democrat Alton B. Parker in 1904 was 5,084,223 to Roosevelt's 7,628,461. In 1900 progressive Democrat William Jennings Bryan received 6,356,734 votes and in 1908 6,412,294. These figures suggest, though of course they do not prove, that had the Democrats nominated a conservative in 1912 they might have lost over one million votes to a progressive candidate.

Page 21: "I'm praying . . . ," B. F. Harris to Medill McCormick, June 28, 1912, copy in TRLC; Dixon quoted on "bob-tailed" ticket by *New York Times,* July 21, 1912.

Pages 21-22: The problems of electors and state tickets are discussed at length in Gable, dissertation, pp. 78-80, 92-106, 148-153.

Page 22: *Washington Star* quoted in *Literary Digest,* July 27, 1912, p. 138; T.R. to William Dudley Foulke, July 1, 1912, *Letters,* VII, p. 568; Walter Lippmann, *Drift and Mastery* (1914; Prentice-Hall edition: Englewood Cliffs, N.J., 1961), p. 135. On the question of Roosevelt continuing in the race, see *New York Times,* June 25, 1912; T.R. to Chase S. Osborn, July 5, 1912, *Letters,* VII, pp. 569-570; T.R. to Alford Warriner Cooley, July 10, 1912, *Letters,* VII, p. 575.

Page 23: Bryan quoted in Link, *Woodrow Wilson and the Progressive Era,* p. 12; Franklin D. Roosevelt quoting Kermit Roosevelt, *New York Times,* July 4, 1912; Heney's meeting with Bryan reported in *New York Times,* June 26, 1912; also see report to T.R. from Baltimore, John Callan O'Laughlin to T.R., June 26 [?], 1912, telegram, TRLC; Marshall quoted in *Literary Digest,* July 13, 1912, p. 1245. Proposals for alliance with Bryan or Wilson in case of a conservative Democratic nominee: John E. Sykes to T.R., June 26, 1912, Henry White to T.R., June 26, 1912, S. L. Noe, William McNellis, George J. Sloan to T.R. (one letter), June 27, 1912, Edwin T. Earl to T.R., July 15, 1912, TRLC. For accounts of the Democratic convention, see *New York Times,* June 26-July 2, 1912; Link, *Woodrow Wilson and the Progressive Era,* pp. 12-13.

Pages 23-24: Roosevelt's statement to the press on Wilson's nomination, *New York Times,* July 3, 1912.

Page 24: Everett Colby to T.R., July 3, 1912, TRLC; on the Wilson Progressive Republican League, see *Letters,* VII, p. 574; for La Follette's position see Holt, p. 67.

Pages 24-25: Osborn's statement to the press is quoted in Robert M. Warner, "Chase S. Osborn and the Presidential Campaign of 1912," *Mississippi Valley Historical Review,* XLVI (1959), pp. 19-45, quotation, p. 39; "Woodrow Wilson represents . . . ," Chase S. Osborn to T.R., July 6, 1912, TRLC; "excellent man . . . ," T.R. to Chase S. Osborn, July 5, 1912, *Letters,* VII, pp. 569-570. Eugene Thwing, editor of *Success Magazine* and the *Circle,* wrote and wired Osborn and sent copies to T.R.: "perhaps Woodrow Wilson...," Eugene Thwing to Chase S. Osborn, July 10, 1912, copy, "WHY EXCHANGE...," Eugene Thwing to Chase S. Osborn, telegram, July 4, 1912, TRLC. Osborn's public letter of June 25 is quoted in *Letters,* VII, p. 566. Further Osborn-T.R. exchanges: Chase S. Osborn to T.R., July 1, 1912, Osborn to T.R., July 10, 1912, TRLC; T.R. to Osborn, June 27, 1912, telegram, *Letters,* VII, pp. 565-566; T.R. to Osborn, June 28, 1912, *Letters,* VII, pp. 566-567; T.R. to Osborn, July 5, 1912, *Letters,* VII, pp. 569-570. Warner's article details Osborn's positions throughout 1912. On Progressive attitudes after Wilson's nomination, also see Elon H. Hooker to T.R., July 3, 1912, and Herbert Knox Smith to T.R., July 6, 1912, TRLC.

Pages 25-26: Roosevelt quotations from T.R., "Platform Insincerity," *Outlook,* July 27, 1912, in *NWTR,* XVII, pp. 245-253. Platform quotations from the "National Platform of the Democratic Party Adopted at Baltimore, Md., July 2, 1912," *World Almanac: 1913,* pp. 687-690. "The Democratic platform shows . . . ," T.R. to Herbert Knox Smith, July 13, 1912, TRLC. For Roosevelt's views on the Democratic Party and Baltimore platform, also see T.R. to Miles Poindexter, July 2, 1912, T.R. to Albert Bushnell Hart, July 10, 1912, TRLC; T.R. to Madison Clinton Peters, July 9, 1912, *Letters,* VII, p. 574.

Page 26: Friend in London: T.R. to William Watson, July 10, 1912, TRLC.

Page 27: *Yale Review* quotations from Smith, pp. 30-31; Smith's prediction that Progressives will be in power within eight years, p. 31; Beveridge's letter to the *Indianapolis Star* quoted in *Letters,* VII, p. 581. On Beveridge's decision to join the Progressive Party, see James R. Parker, "Beveridge and the Election of 1912," *Indiana Magazine of History,*

LXIII (1967), pp. 103–114. Beveridge's career has been studied in two excellent biographies: Claude G. Bowers, *Beveridge and the Progressive Era* (Cambridge, 1932); John Braeman, *Albert J. Beveridge: American Nationalist* (Chicago, 1971).

Pages 28–29: "I have been careful . . . ," T.R. to Paul A. Ewert, July 5, 1912, *Letters,* VII, pp. 570–572; "if I could . . . ," T.R. to W. F. Cochran, July 16, 1912, TRLC; Johnson quoted from his acceptance speech as Vice Presidential nominee, *Convention of Progressive Party,* p. 295; "I suppose that . . . ," T.R. to Henry Rider Haggard, June 28, 1912, *Letters,* VII, pp. 567–568.

Page 29: The seven governors were (see page 12) Chester H. Aldrich of Nebraska, Robert Perkins Bass of New Hampshire, Joseph M. Carey of Wyoming, William E. Glasscock of West Virginia, Herbert S. Hadley of Missouri, Chase S. Osborn of Michigan, and Walter R. Stubbs of Kansas. The letter of February 10, 1912, was later endorsed by Governors Hiram W. Johnson of California and Robert S. Vessey of South Dakota. Carey, Johnson, and Vessey signed the "call" for the Progressive Party, July 8, 1912. Carey, Johnson, and Vessey also attended the Progressive convention in August. Johnson was nominated for vice-president on the Progressive ticket in 1912, and reelected governor of California as a Progressive in 1914. Aldrich was endorsed for reelection as governor of Nebraska by the Progressives in 1912, and he was among the party leaders who attended the Progressive Service dinner in New York City in October, 1913. Bass served as chairman of the New Hampshire state Progressive convention in 1912, and was the Progressive candidate for the U.S. Senate in New Hampshire in 1913. Stubbs supported Roosevelt in 1912, and served as a leader of the Kansas Progressive Party in the following years. Osborn's position was the same as that of Senator Albert B. Cummins of Iowa. Both endorsed T.R. but not the new party. Glasscock tried to remain neutral during the campaign. Hadley finally came out for Taft, the only one of these nine governors to do so. In summary, of the seven who signed the February 10 appeal asking T.R. to run, Aldrich, Bass, Carey, and Stubbs continued to support Roosevelt after the Republican convention, and also endorsed the Progressive Party. Glasscock was neutral; Osborn backed T.R. but not the Progressive Party; and Hadley endorsed Taft. Johnson and Vessey, who had endorsed the February appeal after it was issued, backed Roosevelt and the new party in the fall. There has been much confusion among historians on the positions of these Republican governors, probably because of confusing and sometimes erroneous reports published in newspapers and magazines in the summer and fall of 1912. Mowry, p. 257, states: "Of the original seven only Hiram Johnson of California and Osborn of Michigan stood by." (Johnson, of course, was not one of the "original seven.") Mowry's assertion has often been repeated by historians, and has contributed to the belief that few prominent politicians joined the Progressive Party.

Pages 29–30: On the Kansas plan, see Robert Sherman La Forte, *Leaders of Reform: Progressive Republicans in Kansas, 1910–1916* (Lawrence, Kansas, 1974), pp. 189–197.

Pages 30–31: The Hadley-Roosevelt exchange: T.R. to Herbert S. Hadley, June 28, July 15, and July 23, 1912, three letters, TRLC; Hadley to T.R. July 5, July 9, July 18, and July 29, 1912, four letters, TRLC; "while there is a strong . . . ," Hadley's letter of July 5; ". . . I take the view . . . ," T.R.'s letter of July 15; "I hold that . . . ," T.R.'s letter of July 23; Hadley comes out for Taft, see William T. Miller, "The Progressive Movement in Missouri," *Missouri Historical Review,* XXII (1928), pp. 456–501.

Page 31: "I cannot consent . . . ," T.R. to E. A. Van Valkenburg, July 16, 1912, *Letters,* VII, pp. 576–577; "I hold that . . . ," T.R. to Joseph R. Baldwin, July 12, 1912, *Letters,* VII, p. 576; "I never knew . . . ," T.R. to Charles J. Bonaparte, July 9, 1912, copy in TRCH. On the Pennsylvania situation, see William Flinn to T.R., July 17, 1912, Flinn to W. Frank Gorrecht, August 10, 1912, copy, E. A. Van Valkenburg to T.R., July 17, 1912, TRLC; Martin L. Fausold, *Gifford Pinchot: Bull Moose Progressive* (Syracuse, 1961), pp. 128–133; Mowry, pp. 258–261; *New York Times,* July 16, 1912; meetings with Pennsylvania leaders and T.R. are recorded in "Chronology [of T.R.], March 5, 1909–January 8, 1919," Appendix IV, *Letters,* VIII, pp. 1466–1496, see pp. 1477–1478. On the general situation in regard to electors, see *Literary Digest,* July 20, 1912, pp. 87–88;

Mowry, pp. 258-261; T.R. to W.R. Orchard, July 18, 1912, T.R. to Robert Perkins Bass, July 17, 1912, TRLC.

Page 32: On South Dakota, see Stitzel X. Way to Medill McCormick, July 3, 1912, copy, TRLC; Holt, p. 68. Governor Johnson reported the California situation to Roosevelt in Hiram W. Johnson to T.R., July 8, 1912, and Johnson to T.R., January 21, 1913, TRLC. On California, see Mowry, *California Progressives,* pp. 188-189. On the Pennsylvania party label situation, see William Flinn to T.R., July 17, 1912, TRLC; Fausold, pp. 131-132. On the Idaho situation, see T.R. to James Herrick Gipson, October 12, 1912, telegram, *Letters,* VII, p. 628; T.R. to James Herrick Gipson, January 3, 1913, telegram, January 3, 1913, *Letters,* VII, pp. 687-688. The main offense for which the Idaho editors were jailed was publishing T.R.'s blunt telegram of October 12 condemning the Republican judges.

Pages 33-34: "Now wherever . . . ," T.R. to F. A. Johnson, July 25, 1912, TRCH. On the question of state tickets, see Holt, pp. 67-70; and the detailed discussion in Gable, dissertation, pp. 98-106, 112-131, 149-160, 273-284. On West Virginia, also see Paul Douglas Casdorph, "Governor William E. Glasscock and Theodore Roosevelt's 1912 Bull Moose Candidacy," *West Virginia History,* 28 (1966), pp. 8-15; Carolyn Karr, "A Political Biography of Henry Hatfield," *West Virginia History,* 28 (1966), pp. 33-63. Lists of gubernatorial and Congressional candidates and contests in *World Almanac: 1913,* pp. 721-769.

Page 35: On former Populists in the Progressive Party, see Thomas E. Watson to T.R., January 4, 1913, Mary E. Lease to T.R., undated [March, 1913], John O. Zabel to T.R., undated [1912], TRLC; Butler met with T.R. on July 11, "Chronology," p. 1477; John D. Hicks, *The Populist Revolt* (Minneapolis, 1931), p. 421; C. Vann Woodward, *Tom Watson: Agrarian Rebel* (1938: Oxford University Press edition: New York, 1963), p. 430. On the "Gold Democrats," see biographical information on Bird, Straus, and Dickinson in *DAB, NCAB,* and *WWW;* Richard B. Sherman, "Charles Sumner Bird and the Progressive Party in Massachusetts," *New England Quarterly,* 33 (1960), pp. 325-340; Naomi W. Cohen, *A Dual Heritage: The Public Career of Oscar S. Straus* (Philadelphia, 1969); Oscar S. Straus, *Under Four Administrations* (Boston, 1922).

Pages 35-37: For biographical information on Pettigrew, Cockran, Garvin, Parker, Lindsey, and Robins, see *BDAC, DAB, NCAB,* and *WWW.* Also see R. F. Pettigrew to T.R., July 19, 1912, and October 25, 1912, two letters, TRLC; James McGurrin, *Bourke Cockran: A Free Lance in American Politics* (New York, 1948); chapter on Lindsey in Lincoln Steffens, *Upbuilders* (1909; University of Washington Press edition: Seattle, 1968), pp. 94-243; Allen F. Davis, "Raymond Robins: The Settlement Worker as Municipal Reformer," *Social Service Review,* XXXIII (1959), pp. 131-141.

Pages 37-38: Amos Pinchot, p. 171; on Lippmann, see Forcey, pp. 88-118; on Hourwich, see Benjamin Stolberg, *Tailor's Progress: The Story of a Famous Union and the Men Who Made It* (Garden City, N.Y., 1944). For biographical information on Roosevelt's associates, see *BDAC, DAB, NCAB,* and *WWW.* Some of Roosevelt's old friends and associates of course remained with the Republican Party, including Elihu Root and Henry Cabot Lodge. But more typical was the attitude of Isaac L. Hunt, who had served with T.R. in the New York Assembly in the 1880s. He telegraphed T.R.: "I AM WITH YOU HEART AND SOUL. ENLISTED THIRTY YEARS AGO. SHALL REMAIN TO THE FINISH," Hunt to T.R., July 29, 1912, telegram, TRLC.

Pages 38-39: "What a miserable showing . . . ," T.R. to John Callan O'Laughlin, July 9, 1912. On Republican insurgents and the Progressive Party, see Holt, pp. 63-80; Mowry, pp. 256-263; T.R. to John MacVicar, July 10, 1912, Hugh T. Halbert to T.R., July 20, 1912, Gilson Gardner to T.R., July 26, 1912, Moses E. Clapp to T.R., August 8, 1912, TRLC.

Page 39: On Republican "bosses" who joined the Progressive Party, see Mowry, p. 263; Hoyt Landon Warner, *Progressivism in Ohio, 1897-1917* (Columbus, 1964), pp. 373-374; on Flinn, Fausold, pp. 128-134; *NCAB* and *WWW* for Brown and Woodruff.

Pages 39–40: "The churches, as such . . . ," S. J. Duncan-Clark, *The Progressive Movement* (Boston, 1913), p. 291; "recrudescence of the religious spirit . . . ," Duncan-Clark, p. 288. Duncan-Clark's important and suggestive book on the Progressive Party was sponsored by the party, and published with an introduction by T.R.; copy in TRCH. On the Social Gospel and the new party, also see Duncan-Clark, pp. 287-291. T.R. was Contributing Editor of Lyman Abbott's *Outlook* magazine; for Gladden, see Jacob H. Dorn, *Washington Gladden: Prophet of the Social Gospel* (Columbus, Ohio, 1967); for Newton, see T.R. to R. Heber Newton, November 28, 1912, *Letters*, VII, pp. 659–660; on Metzger, see Alon Jeffrey," Vermont's Pastor-Politician: Fraser Metzger and the Bull Moose Campaign of 1912," *Vermont History*, XXXVIII (1970), pp. 58–69; on writer Churchill, see chapter in Robert W. Schneider, *Five Novelists of the Progressive Era* (New York, 1965), pp. 205-251.

Pages 40–41: ". . . The launching of the new third party . . . ," Kellogg, p. 669; "the libraries and laboratories . . . ," Duncan-Clark, p. 296; "found a political . . . ," Duncan-Clark, p. 294; "social reform has the services . . . ," Henry Moskowitz to Lillian Wald, quoted in Walter I. Trattner, "Theodore Roosevelt, Social Workers, and the Election of 1912: A Note," *Mid-America*, 50 (1968), pp. 64-69, quotation, p. 65; "my last fourteen years . . . ," Mary Kingsbury Simkhovitch to T.R., August 15, 1912, TRLC. On the Progressive Party and social workers, see Jane Addams, "My Experiences As a Progressive Delegate," *McClure's*, November, 1912, in Christopher Lasch, editor, *The Social Thought of Jane Addams* (Indianapolis, 1965), pp. 162-169; Jane Addams, *The Second Twenty Years at Hull House*, pp. 10-48; Allen F. Davis, *American Heroine: The Life and Legend of Jane Addams* (New York, 1973), pp. 184-197; Allen F. Davis, "Raymond Robins;" Allen F. Davis, "The Social Workers and the Progressive Party, 1912-1916," *American Historical Review*, 69 (1964), pp. 671-688; Allen F. Davis, *Spearheads for Reform: The Social Settlements and the Progressive Movement, 1890-1914* (New York, 1967), pp. 194-217; Allen F. Davis, "Theodore Roosevelt, Social Worker," *Mid-America, 48 (1966),* pp. 58-62; Duncan-Clark, pp. 293-295; Kellogg, "The Industrial Platform of the New Party;" Daniel Levine, *Jane Addams and the Liberal Tradition* (Madison, Wisconsin, 1971), pp. 188-198; Trattner article; Homer Folks to T.R., July 19, 1912, Jane Addams to T.R., November 20, 1912, TRLC. On social workers drawing up the platform, see Davis, *Spearheads for Reform*, pp. 195-201.

Pages 41–42: ". . . I do not believe . . . ," Edwin R. Seligman to T.R., July 19, 1912, TRLC; "as a teacher. . . ." William Henry Crawshaw to T.R., December 16, 1912, TRLC; "I was loath . . . ," Albert Bushnell Hart to T.R., August 26, 1912, TRLC. On academics and the Progressive Party, see Duncan-Clark, pp. 295-296; biographical data on academics mentioned in *BDAC, DAB, NCAB, WWW;* also on DeWitt, see Arthur Mann, "Introduction" in University of Washington Press edition, DeWitt, *Progressive Movement,* pp. xiii-xx; for Merriam, see Barry D. Karl, *Charles E. Merriam and the Study of Politics* (Chicago, 1974); for Fisher, Henderson, and Luther, see Herbert Janick, "The Mind of the Connecticut Progressive," *Mid-America,* 52 (1970), pp. 83-101. Letters of support and counsel to Roosevelt from academics include Joseph Schafer to T.R., November 2, 1912, James A. Woodburn to T.R., November 9, 1912, Benjamin Ide Wheeler to T.R., November 12, 1912, Tyrell Williams to T.R., April 4, 1913, TRLC. Also see Albert Bushnell Hart, "A New Party: Do the People Want It?" *American Review of Reviews,* August, 1912, pp. 197-200; Yandell Henderson, "The Progressive Movement and Constitutional Reform," *Yale Review,* October, 1913, pp. 78-90.

Page 42: On women and the Progressive Party, see Duncan-Clark, pp. 90-108, 291-293; *From the Women Delegates to the National Convention of the Progressive Party to the Women of the United States* (Chicago, 1912), and *To the Women Voters of the United States from the Women in Political Bondage: Vote the Progressive Ticket and Make Us Free* (Chicago, 1912), pamphlets in TRCH. Mrs. Helen J. Scott of Tacoma, Washington, is featured in the *American Review of Reviews,* December, 1912, p. 657.

Pages 42–43: *Boston Journal* quoted in *Literary Digest,* July 6, 1912; "my generation was . . . ," Donald R. Richberg, *Tents of the Mighty* (New York, 1930), p. 32; "Rublee told me . . . ," Learned Hand to T.R., August 11, 1912, TRLC. On Borglum and

Henderson, see Janick, "Mind of the Connecticut Progressive." For a survey of occupational groups in Progressive Party leadership, see Alfred D. Chandler, Jr., "The Origins of Progressive Leadership," Appendix III, *Letters*, VIII, pp. 1462-1465. For biographical information see *BDAC, DAB, NCAB,* and *WWW;* and for Richberg, Donald R. Richberg, *My Hero: The Indiscreet Memoirs of an Eventful but Unheroic Life* (New York, 1954), *Tents of the Mighty,* and Vadney; for Weyl, see Forcey, pp. 52-87; for Ickes, see Harold L. Ickes, *The Autobiography of a Curmudgeon* (New York, 1943); for Pell, see Leonard Baker, *Brahmin in Revolt: A Biography of Herbert C. Pell* (Garden City, N.Y., 1972); for Isaacs, see *Stanley M. Isaacs: An Interview on Theodore Roosevelt* (New York, 1962), pamphlet in TRCH; for Costigan, see Goodykoontz; for Everett Colby, see chapter in Steffens, pp. 47-93; for Cutting, see Armstrong.

Pages 42-44: Ages, occupations, religious and ethnic backgrounds, education, and other data on Progressive leaders compiled from *BDAC, DAB, NCAB,* and *WWW.* Conclusions here and elsewhere on the Progressive leaders as a group are based on a sample of 80 leaders, including state chairmen, Congressmen, national committeemen, candidates for governor, and others, as well as on secondary sources. For studies of age, occupations, and the general sociological background of Progressive Party leaders, see Chandler; Janick; Jeffrey; Larson; E. Daniel Potts, "The Progressive Profile in Iowa," *Mid-America,* XLVII (1965), pp. 257-268; Sherman; Norman M. Wilensky, *Conservatives in the Progressive Era: The Taft Republicans of 1912* (Gainesville, Florida, 1965). For a discussion of the findings and the limitations of Chandler's classic study, see Gable, dissertation, pp. 154, 157-159. Chandler's sample did not, it appears, include many of the most important state leaders of the new party.

Page 45: Biographical information from *BDAC, DAB, NCAB, WWW;* and on Watson, Vann Woodward; on Hodges, *Bench and Bar of Florida* (Tallahassee, Florida, 1935); on Poston, *Who's Who in Tennessee, 1911* (Memphis, 1911); on Meares, *History of North Carolina* (Chicago, 1919). See Chapter Three for information on the "lily white" policy and on the Progressive Party in the South.

Pages 45-46: On the Progressive Party in the New England states, see Richard M. Abrams, *Conservatism in a Progressive Era: Massachusetts Politics, 1900-1912* (Cambridge, 1964), pp. 217-294; Robert P. Bass, *Address of Governor Robert P. Bass as Chairman of the First New Hampshire Convention of the Progressive Party Held at Concord, N.H., September 22, 1912* (Manchester, N.H., 1912), pamphlet, TRCH; Winston Churchill, *To the Men and Women of New Hampshire: An Open Letter* (Manchester, N.H., 1912), pamphlet, TRCH; Winston Allen Flint, *The Progressive Movement in Vermont* (Washington, D.C., 1941), particularly pp. 52-107; Halbert Paine Gardner, *Political Experiences, 1898-1938* (privately printed, 1938), copy in TRCH; Joseph A. Interrante, "The Politics of Robert Perkins Bass," unpublished seminar paper, Brown University, 1973, copy in TRCH; Janick; Jeffrey; Erwin L. Levine, *Theodore Francis Green: The Rhode Island Years, 1906-1936* (Providence, 1963), particularly pp. 1-90; John Meck, "New Hampshire: The Effect of Progressivism on State and National Politics from 1912-1916," unpublished senior thesis at Dartmouth College, 1967, copy in Dartmouth College Library; Elizabeth Ring, *The Progressive Movement of 1912 and Third Party Movement of 1924 in Maine* (Orono, Me., 1933); and Sherman. For biographical information see sources cited above, and *DAB, NCAB, WWW;* on Churchill, also see Schneider, pp. 208-210; on Humes, see Robert Grieve, *An Illustrated History of Pawtucket, Central Falls and Vicinity* (Pawtucket, R.I., 1897), p. 350.

Page 47: On the New York State ticket, see *New York Times,* September 5-7, 1912, and press clippings in the Mabel A. Styles scrapbooks, TRCH. On the Progressive Party in New York State, also see Cohen, pp. 205-212; *Collier's,* October 19, 1912, p. 7; *New York Times,* July 12, 1912; *State Platform: National Progressive Party of the State of New York* (New York, 1912), pamphlet, TRCH; Straus, pp. 313-326. On the background of the party in New Jersey, see Ransom E. Noble, Jr., *New Jersey Progressivism Before Wilson* (Princeton, 1946), pp. 12-99, 130-145; on Colby, see Steffens, pp. 47-93; on Fort and Record, see *NCAB, WWW.* On the Washington Party, see Fausold. On the Progressive Party in Ohio, see Warren Miles Hoffnagle, "Arthur L. Garford: A Biography of an Ohio Industrialist and Politician, 1858-1933," unpublished Ph.D. dissertation, Ohio State University, 1963; Jack M. Thompson, "James R. Garfield: The Career of a Rooseveltian Progressive, 1895-1916," unpublished Ph.D. dissertation, University of South Carolina, 1958; Warner, pp. 354-384.

Page 48: On the organization of the Progressive Party in Michigan, see *New York Times,* July 21, 1912; for biographical information on Watkins, see *Michigan Biographies* (Lansing, 1924). On the Progressive Party in Indiana, see Bowers, pp. 423-454; Braeman, pp. 220-253; Will H. Hays, *The Memoirs of Will H. Hays* (Garden City, N.Y., 1955), pp. 81-82, 89-90, 93, 96, 98-99, 139-149; Carl Painter, "The Progressive Party in Indiana," *Indiana Magazine of History,* XVI (1920), pp. 173-283. On the Illinois Progressive Party, see *New York Times,* August 3, 1912; biographical information on Illinois leaders from *BDAC, DAB, NCAB, WWW;* and on Robins, see Davis, "Robins;" on Merriam, see Karl; Richberg, see Vadney; Ickes, *Autobiography.* On Illinois politics, also see Joel Arthur Tarr, *A Study in Boss Politics: William Lorimer of Chicago* (Urbana, Ill., 1971).

Pages 48-49: On Maryland, see T.R. to Charles J. Bonaparte, June 25, 1912, Letters, VII, p. 564; biographical information on Bonaparte in *DAB.* On the Progressive Party in Kentucky, see Leslie Combs to T.R., October 31, 1914, TRLC. Delaware was one of the states that did not sign the Progressive Party "call," *New York Times,* July 8, 1912; biographical information on Hynson is in *Delaware: A Guide to the First State* (New York, 1935), p. 214. On the new party in Missouri, see Miller, pp. 492-501; for biographical information on Nortoni, see *NCAB* and *WWW.*

Pages 49-50: On Progressive Party activities in 1912 in Kansas, Iowa, Nebraska, North Dakota, Minnesota, and South Dakota, see Holt, pp. 67-71. On Kansas Progressives in 1912, also see David Hinshaw, *A Man from Kansas: The Story of William Allen White* (New York, 1945), pp. 109-139; LaForte, pp. 185-207. On Progressive leaders in California, see Mowry, *California Progressives,* pp. 23-198; Olin, pp. 11-99. Halbert is identified, *Letters,* VII, p. 95; for biographical information on Collins and Stevens, see *WWW;* for Sweet, see obituary in *Fargo Forum,* February 10, 1923. On the Progressive Party in North Dakota, also see Elwyn B. Robinson, *History of North Dakota* (Lincoln, Nebraska, 1966), pp. 267-269. On the party in Iowa, see Potts. On the party in Oregon, see Warren Marion Blankenship, "Progressives and the Progressive Party in Oregon, 1906-1916," unpublished Ph.D. dissertation, University of Oregon, 1966; Henry Waldo Coe to T.R., November 22, 1912, TRLC.

Page 50: The only two states where T.R. was not on the ballot in 1912 were Idaho and Oklahoma, and in Nevada a new party never really got off the ground. Utah was one of the two states carried by Taft in 1912. See on Idaho, Holt, p. 66, and biographical information on Martin in *History of Idaho: Gem of the Mountains* (Chicago, 1920), IV, pp. 339-340; on Oklahoma, Edwin C. Reynolds, *Oklahoma: A History of the Sooner State* (Norman, Oklahoma, 1954), p. 323; on Nevada, Russell R. Elliott, *History of Nevada* (Lincoln, Nebraska, 1973), p. 250; on Morris of Utah, *NCAB.*

Pages 50-51: On the Progressive Party in Arizona, see George S. Hunter, "The Bull Moose Movement in Arizona," *Arizona and the West,* X (1968), pp. 343-362; John C. Greenway to T.R., July 29, 1912, TRLC. On the new party in New Mexico, see Armstrong; George Curry, *George Curry, 1861-1947: An Autobiography,* edited by H. B. Hening (Albuquerque, 1958), pp. 268-276, 280-284; and Larson. On the party in Wyoming, see T. A. Larsen, *History of Wyoming* (Lincoln, Nebraska, 1965), p. 326; biographical information on Joseph and Robert Carey in *BDAC.*

Page 51: On the Progressive Party in Colorado, see Goodykoontz; Ben Lindsey to T.R., July 17, 1912, TRLC. The Progressive Party in Washington, Griffiths, Poindexter, and Hodge are discussed in Howard W. Allen, "Miles Poindexter: A Political Biography," unpublished Ph.D. dissertation, University of Washington, 1959; Howard W. Allen, "Miles Poindexter and the Progressive Movement," *Pacific Northwest Quarterly,* LII (1962), pp. 114-122; biographical information on Hodge in *Notable Men of Washington* (Tacoma, 1912). Dixon's career, Montana politics, and the Progressive Party in Montana are studied in detail in Jules A. Karlin, *Joseph M. Dixon of Montana* (2 vols.: Missoula, Montana, 1974); biographical information on Edwards, see obituary in *Helena Independent Record*, July 21, 1945.

Page 52: On Brown and Ohio, see Francis Russell, *The Shadow of Blooming Grove: Warren G. Harding and His Times* (New York, 1968), pp. 232-233.

Pages 53-54: "Progressive candidates for Congress . . . ," *American Review of Reviews*, December, 1912, p. 653. For a complete listing by state and district of all elections for the House of Representatives in 1912, see *World Almanac: 1913*, pp. 721-769. Biographical information on Congressional candidates in *BDAC, NCAB, WWW.* There were third ticket Progressive candidates for the U.S. House in 1912 in districts in at least thirty-two states. In the states of California, Kansas, Nebraska, South Dakota, West Virginia, and Maine, where the state Republican parties were recognized in 1912 as part of the National Progressive Party, Republican Congressional nominees were backed by the new party. In North Dakota, Minnesota, and Wisconsin the Republican Congressional candidates were considered friendly to the Progressive cause, and only one district was contested in these states. Some Republican nominees in other states who endorsed Roosevelt were in turn backed by the Progressives, and in a few instances Democratic candidates were backed against Republicans. In the Southern states of Arkansas, Georgia, Louisiana, Mississippi, and South Carolina, where the G.O.P. frequently did not contest Congressional seats, the third party ran no candidates for the House, nor did Progressives in Nevada, Oklahoma, and Vermont run candidates for the House.

Page 54: Press reactions to Straus's nomination quoted from *New York Times*, September 7, 1912; Wilson quoted by *New York Times*, September 8, 1912.

Pages 54-57: For biographical information on Progressive candidates for governor, see sources previously cited for each; most are included in *NCAB* and *WWW.* In Kansas, Maine, Nebraska, South Dakota, and West Virginia, where state Republicans had endorsed or indicated support for the Progressive Party nationally, the Republican gubernatorial candidates were backed by the Bull Moose, as was Governor Francis E. McGovern in Wisconsin, who supported T.R. in spite of the hostility of the LaFollette organization to Roosevelt. Progressives ran no candidates for governor in Arkansas and South Carolina. In the other thirty-two states which elected governors in the fall of 1912, there were third ticket Progressive candidates for governor.

Page 57: *Philadelphia Record* quoted by *Literary Digest*, July 6, 1912, p. 7; Taft quoted from "President Taft's Speech of Acceptance," *National Issues of 1912*, pp. 213-217, quotation p. 217; George B. Morewood, "Thou Shalt Not Steal," *New York Times*, July 17, 1912; La Follette's views are given in *La Follette's Weekly*, June–November, 1912; *New York Tribune* cited in *Literary Digest*, July 20, 1912, pp. 87–88.

Page 58: *Chicago Record-American* quoted from *Literary Digest*, August 3, 1912, p. 178; "tomorrow at noon . . . ," *New York Times*, August 5, 1912; also see *New York Times*, July 28, 1912.

Page 59: Dixon quoted from *Official Report of the Proceedings of the Provisional National Progressive Committee*, typed ms., pp. 2-3, copies in TRCH and TRLC; Smith, p. 18; Richberg, *Tents of the Mighty*, p. 32.

3. LILY-WHITE PROGRESSIVISM

Pages 60-61: "One of the really puzzling questions . . . ," T.R. to the Rev. Bradley Gilman, July 24, 1912, TRLC; "negro incubus," George N. Wise to T.R., [*ca*. June 30], 1912, TRLC; "nearly every letter . . . ," John M. Parker to T.R., July 15, 1912, TRLC; "cannot and will not . . . ," and "recognizing the superior . . . ," John M. Parker to T.R., July 24, 1912, TRLC. The lower case "n" for "Negro" has been retained wherever it so appears in original sources. T.R. considers Parker for Vice President in 1912, see *New York Times*,

August 1, 1912. Letters to T.R. urging a lily-white policy in the South include W. Fred Long of Mississippi to T.R., June 27, 1912, J. M. Fuller of Georgia to T.R., July 1, 1912, Cecil A. Lyon of Texas to T.R., July 13, 1912, TRLC. On the delegate disputes and the Progressive lily-white policy in the South, see George N. Green, "Republicans, Bull Moose, and Negroes in Florida, 1912," *Florida Historical Quarterly*, XLIII *(1964), pp. 153–164;* Arthur S. Link, editor, "Correspondence Relating to the Progressive Party's 'Lily White' Policy in 1912," *Journal of Southern History*, X (1944), pp. 480–490; Arthur S. Link, "The Negro as a Factor in the Campaign of 1912," *Journal of Negro History* XXII (1947), pp. 81–99; Arthur S. Link, "Theodore Roosevelt and the South in 1912," *North Carolina Historical Review*, XXIII (1946), pp. 313–324; George E. Mowry, "The South and the Progressive Lily White Party of 1912," *Journal of Southern History*, VI (1940), pp. 237–247; Mowry, pp. 267–269. For general information on the Progressive Party in the South, see the above, and also Paul Douglas Casdorph, "The 1912 Republican Presidential Campaign in Mississippi," *Journal of Mississippi History*, XXXIII (1971), pp. 1–19; Paul Douglas Casdorph, *A History of the Republican Party of Texas, 1865-1965* (Austin, Texas, 1965), pp. 98–117; Chandler; Richard H. Collin, "Theodore Roosevelt's Visit to New Orleans and the Progressive Campaign of 1914," *Louisiana History*, XII (1971), pp. 5–19; Gould; William F. Mugleston, "The 1912 Progressive Campaign in Georgia," *Georgia Historical Quarterly*, LXI (1977), pp. 233–245; Howard W. Smith, "The Progressive Party and the Election of 1912 in Alabama," *Alabama Review*, IX (1956), pp. 5–21; Joseph F. Steelman, "Richmond Pearson, Roosevelt Republicans, and the Campaign of 1912 in North Carolina," *North Carolina Historical Review*, XLIII (1966), pp. 122–139; Joseph F. Steelman, "The Trials of a Republican State Chairman: John Motley Morehead and North Carolina Politics, 1910-1912," *North Carolina Historical Review*, XLIII (1966), pp. 31–42.

Page 61: Roosevelt quotations from *NWTR*, XIV: "by inheritance . . . ," *Boston Herald* interview, July 20, 1884, pp. 39–40, quotation p. 40; "the party that tried . . . ," address, Winchester, Mass., October 30, 1884[?], pp. 52–57, quotation p. 57; "as long as . . . ," speech, Young Republican Club, Brooklyn, N.Y., October 18, 1885, pp. 58–67, quotation p. 66. On T.R.'s family and background, see Carleton Putnam, *Theodore Roosevelt: The Formative Years, 1858-1886* (New York, 1958); on his general racial and ethnic views, James E. Amos, *Theodore Roosevelt: Hero to His Valet* (New York, 1927), Howard K. Beale, *Theodore Roosevelt and the Rise of America to World Power* (1956; Collier's edition: New York, 1962), pp. 41–45, Edward Wagenknecht, *The Seven Worlds of Theodore Roosevelt* (New York, 1958), pp. 230–236; for his views on the Negro, T.R., "The Education of the Negro," address, Tuskegee Institute, October 24, 1905, *NWTR*, XVI, pp. 351–355, T.R., "The Negro in America," *Outlook*, June 4, 1910, *NWTR*, XII, pp. 214–222, T.R., "The Negro Problem," address, Lincoln dinner, Republican Club of New York City, February 13, 1905, *NWTR*, XVI, pp. 342–350.

Pages 61–62: "Three-fourths of them . . . ," T.R. quoted by Blum, p. 45; on T.R.'s political activities in the South as President, see Blum, pp. 43–47. For Roosevelt's policies as President toward the Negro, see Bishop, I, pp. 166, 168–170, 192, 193, 247, 248, 441, 442; Harbaugh, pp. 303–308; Mowry, *Birth of Modern America*, pp. 165–166, 212–214; Willard B. Gatewood, Jr., *Theodore Roosevelt and the Art of Controversy* (Baton Rouge, La., 1970); Seth Scheiner, "President Roosevelt and the Negro, 1901-1908," *Journal of Negro History*, XLVII (1962), pp. 169–182. On race relations and the blacks during the progressive era, see particularly Stephen R. Fox, *The Guardian of Boston: William Monroe Trotter* (Boston, 1970); Dewey W. Grantham, Jr., "The Progressive Movement and the Negro," *South Atlantic Quarterly*, LIV (1955), pp. 461–477; Gilbert Osofsky, "Progressivism and the Negro," *American Quarterly*, XVI (1964), pp. 153–168; August Meier, *Negro Thought in America, 1880-1915: Radical Ideologies in the Age of Booker T. Washington* (Ann Arbor, Michigan, 1963).

Pages 62–63: "The colored delegates . . . ," Ralph W. Tyler to T.R., March 25, 1913, TRLC; "they loved Massa . . . ," Amos Pinchot, p. 162; "equality . . . ," and "the colored people . . . ," William H. Maxwell, July 28, 1912, TRLC. The role of the black delegates in the contest for the Republican nomination, and the use of bribery are discussed in Mowry, pp. 227–228, 245; "The Negro Delegates," *Nation*, June 20, 1912, p. 606; Amos Pinchot, pp. 162–163. On blacks' interest in and support for the new party, see Fox, pp.

164–168; W. E. B. DuBois, *The Autobiography of W. E. B. DuBois* (New York, 1968), pp. 263–264. On the Negro delegates to the Progressive convention, see T.R., "The Progressives and the Colored Man," *Outlook,* August 24, 1912, *NWTR,* XVII, pp. 300–305; *Know the Truth! Statement from Entire Colored Delegation of the National Progressive Convention, August 7, 1912* (New York, 1912), pamphlet in TRCH. The statement was signed by 24 black delegates from 13 states, and noted that two blacks had been on each of three convention committees.

Pages 63–64: "Most certainly . . . ," T.R. to William H. Maxwell, July 30, 1912, TRLC.

Page 64: Letter to Gilman, T.R. to the Rev. Bradley Gilman, July 24, 1912, TRLC; Roosevelt's reaction to Southern disputes, *New York Times,* July 28, 1912; also see T.R. to Ryerson W. Jennings, July 30, 1912, TRLC.

Page 65: The T.R.–Harris exchange: T.R. to Julian LaRose Harris, August 1, 1912, *Letters.* VII, pp. 584–590; Harris to T.R., August 3, 1912, TRLC; Roosevelt's letter was published in pamphlet form under several titles including *Attitude of the Progressive Party toward the Colored Race* (New York, 1912), copy in TRCH; the T.R.–Harris exchange has also been published in Link, editor, "Correspondence Relating to the Progressive Party's 'Lily White' Policy of 1912." On black reaction to the Harris letter, see the Rev. J. Gordon McPherson, editor of the Los Angeles *Voice of the West,* to T.R., August 6, 1912, telegram, and August 17, 1912, TRLC. For the views of Addams, Spingarn. and Moskowitz, see *New York Times,* August 6, 1912; see Flavel L. Luther to T.R., August 8, 1912, Albert Shaw to T.R., August 2, 1912, Shaw to T.R., August 7, 1912, telegram, TRLC; the views of Dixon, McCormick, and other Progressive leaders were expressed in *Proceedings of the Provisional National Progressive Committee,* typed ms. minutes, copies in TRCH and TRLC.

Pages 66–67: "In this country . . . ," T.R. to Julian LaRose Harris, August 1, 1912, *Letters,* VII, pp. 584–590; "ugh!" T.R. to Brander Matthews, January 7, 1913, TRLC; "really if I could carry . . . ," T.R. to John M. Parker, July 15, 1912, TRLC. The Minor cartoon is reproduced in *Current Literature,* October, 1912, p. 461.

Pages 67–71: All quotations from *Proceedings of the Provisional National Progressive Committee,* typed ms., TRCH, which are the minutes of the hearings at the Congress Hotel. Most of the previously cited sources on the Progressive Party in the South include information on the delegate disputes. The committee hearings are examined in detail in Gable, dissertation, pp. 162–215.

Page 72: For "dangerous person" quotation and text of the plank prepared by DuBois, see W. E. B. DuBois, *The Autobiography of W. E. B. DuBois* (New York, 1968), pp. 263–264; the meeting of Spingarn, Hayes, Moskowitz, and T.R., and the text of the plank brought to Chicago by Spingarn are reported in *New York Times,* August 6, 1912; T.R.'s response to the question from the gallery, which does not appear in printed versions of the speech, is in *New York Times,* August 7, 1912; reports of the New York caucus and the platform committee deliberations are in *New York Times,* August 6, August 7, 1912, including the text of the plank presented by Halbert; McCarthy's objection to a plank on Negro rights was noted in T.R. to Amos Pinchot, December 5, 1912, *Letters,* VII, pp. 661–670. The DuBois, Spingarn, and Halbert versions of the civil rights planks differ one from another in crucial respects. See Gable, dissertation, pp. 211–212.

Page 73: Addams quotations from Jane Addams, "The Progressive Party and the Negro," *The Crisis,* November, 1912, pp. 30–31; William Monroe Trotter to Jane Addams, August 6/7, 1912, telegram, quoted by Fox, p. 166; statement by Negro delegates, *Know the Truth! Statement from Entire Colored Delegation of the National Progressive Party;* meeting of "National Progressive Party of Colored Men" in Chicago, *New York Times,* August 7, 1912; on activities of blacks in the Progressive Party, see *Progressive Bulletin,* October, 1912, publication in TRCH; for information on James H. Hayes, see Fox, pp. 82, 112, and Meier, pp. 174, 175, 176, 237; on the Ohio black Progressives, see Henry Taylor to T.R., December 10, 1912, TRLC; for list of letters of support to T.R. from blacks, see Gable, dissertation, p. 213. On Negroes and the Progressive Party, also see

Attitude of the Progressive Party toward the Colored Race; Meier, p. 188; T.R., "The Progressives and the Colored Man;" Hanes Walton, Jr., *The Negro in Third Party Politics* (Philadelphia, 1969), pp. 46–52; *What Southern Colored Men Say About Roosevelt and the Progressive Party* (New York, 1912), pamphlet, TRCH. On black support for Wilson and Democratic efforts to win the black vote, W. E. B. DuBois, "Quo Vadis," *The Crisis,* November, 1912, pp. 44–45; Fox, pp. 161–168; Link, "The Negro as a Factor in the Campaign of 1912," from which the vote and funds estimates are taken; Link, *Wilson: The Road to the White House,* pp. 501–505. For Wilson's policies towards the blacks as President, see Fox, pp. 168–187; Arthur S. Link, *Wilson: The New Freedom* (Princeton, 1956), pp. 244–248; Kathleen Wogelmuth, "Woodrow Wilson and Federal Segregation," *Journal of Negro History,* XLIV (1959), pp. 158–173.

Page 74: Daniels quoted in Link, "Theodore Roosevelt and the South in 1912," p. 319; "Democrats will surely . . . ," William E. Gonzales, editor, *Columbia State,* quoted *New York Times,* August 19, 1912. The views of the *News* of Birmingham and other Southern newspapers are given in "Few in South for Roosevelt," *New York Times,* August 19, 1912. Southern reaction to Roosevelt's campaign and racial views are examined in Link, "Theodore Roosevelt and the South in 1912."

4. CONSECRATION IN THE COLISEUM

Page 75: "Never doubt . . . ," Albert J. Beveridge, "Pass Prosperity Around," keynote address, August 5, 1912, *First National Convention of the Progressive Party,* typed minutes, copies of ms. in TRCH and TRLC, pp. 12–41, quotation p. 40; quotations from *New York Times,* August 6, 1912; Davis quoted from Richard Harding Davis, "The Men at Armageddon," *Collier's,* August 24, 1912, pp. 10–11; hymn quoted from Arthur Ruhl, "The Bull Moose Call: A New Sound in American Politics and Those Who Answered It," *Collier's,* August 24, 1912, p. 21. For contemporary accounts of the Progressive convention, also see Ernest Hamlin Abbott, "The Progressive Convention," *Outlook,* August 17, 1912, pp. 857–864; Jane Addams, "My Experiences As A Progressive Delegate," *McClure's,* November, 1912, in *Social Thought of Jane Adams,* pp. 162–169; Edward S. Lowry, "With the Bull Moose in Convention," *Harper's Weekly,* August 17, 1912, p. 9; William Menkel, "The Progressives at Chicago," *American Review of Reviews,* September, 1912, pp. 310–317; Mark Sullivan, "Armageddon at Chicago," *Collier's,* August 24, 1912, p. 13. And see *National Progressive Program* (Chicago, 1912), copy, TRCH.

Page 76: Quotations: Menkel, pp. 310–317; Davis, p. 11; Amos Pinchot, pp. 17–171; White, both quotations, p. 483; *New York Times,* August 6, 1912. It is impossible to determine the number of women delegates at the convention because the roll of delegates sometimes denotes gender by "Miss" or "Mrs.," and sometimes does not. For certain there were six women delegates from New York, six from Massachusetts, two from Illinois, one from Colorado, and two from Utah. See *Roll of Delegates and Alternates to the First National Progressive Convention* (Chicago, 1912), copy, TRCH. Two Progressive Party pamphlets in TRCH, *From the Women Delegates* and *To the Women Voters,* were signed by 19 and 18 women delegates respectively.

Pages 77–81: All Beveridge quotations from "Pass Prosperity Around," keynote address, August 5, 1912, *Convention of the Progressive Party,* pp. 12–41. "It reminded me . . . ," Davis, p. 11. See accounts of Beveridge's address in Bowers, pp. 423–431; Braeman, pp. 221–222; *New York Times,* August 6, 1912.

Pages 81–85: Roosevelt quotations from "A Confession of Faith," address to Progressive convention, August 6, 1912, *NWTR,* XVII, pp. 254–299; and *Convention of the Progressive Party,* pp. 52–138. On T.R.'s speech, see Abbott; Davis; *New York Times,* August 7, 1912. On Roosevelt's position as president on corporations, see particularly Harbaugh; and Robert H. Wiebe, "The House of Morgan and the Chief Executive," *American Historical Review,* LXV (1959), pp. 49–60. On the general problems of corporation control, see Harold U. Faulkner, *The Decline of Laissez-Faire, 1897–1917* (New York,

1951); Charles R. Van Hise, *Concentration and Control* (New York, 1912); Simon N. Whitney, *Antitrust Policies: American Experience in Twenty Industries* (2 vols.: New York, 1958); Robert H. Wiebe, *Businessmen and Reform: A Study of the Progressive Movement* (Cambridge, 1962).

Pages 85-86: "He stood . . . ," and "it is unmistakable . . . ," *New York Times,* August 7, 1912, which quotes the *New York Press* and *New York Sun;* Albert Bushnell Hart quoted from *Progressive Bulletin,* October 7, 1912, copy in TRCH; "I am well aware . . . ," *NWTR,* XVII, p. 265; "I am opposed . . . ," T.R., "Speech at Hartford, Connecticut, September 2, 1912," typed ms., TRCH. Further press reaction to the "Confession of Faith" cited in *Literary Digest,* August 17, 1912, pp. 244-246, which quotes the Wisconsin Socialist Victor Berger; *New York Times,* August 14, 1912, reported that the Socialist Presidential candidate Eugene Debs said that the red bandannas of the Progressives, the so-called "battle flag" of the new party, were replacing the red flag of socialism; General King made his statement in a speech seconding Roosevelt's nomination, *Convention of the Progressive Party,* pp. 197-205; the Progressive platform of 1912 was usually titled the "contract with the people," see *A Contract With the People: Platform of the Progressive Party Adopted at Its First National Convention, Chicago, August 7, 1912* (New York, 1912), pamphlet, TRCH. For the view that the Progressives of the new party and the whole progressive movement were counterrevolutionary, see Kolko.

Page 87: "None of us . . . ," *NWTR,* XVII, p. 230; "more and more . . . ," Miles Poindexter, "Why I Am for Roosevelt," *North American Review,* October, 1912, pp. 468-483, quotation p. 483. For the evolution of Roosevelt's New Nationalism, see the speeches and articles from 1910-1912 published in *NWTR,* XVII, and T.R., *Progressive Principles* (New York, 1913). On Wilson as a classical "liberal," see Richard Hofstadter, "Woodrow Wilson: The Conservative as Liberal," in *The American Political Tradition* (New York, 1948), pp. 234-278; for a comparison between the nationalist views of Roosevelt and Lodge and Root, see Harbaugh, pp. 71-72, 127-128, 228-230, 351.

Page 88: ". . . The Progressive Movement . . . ," T.R., "Introduction," Duncan-Clark, *The Progressive Movement,* pp. xiii-xxi, quotation p. xx; "an American commonwealth . . . ," *NWTR,* XVII, p. 265; "malefactors of great wealth," *NWTR,* XVI, p. 84; "invisible government," Beveridge, "Pass Prosperity Around," *Convention of the Progressive Party,* p. 17; "sinister forces . . . ," Paxton Hibben, *Politics and Social Service: An Address Delivered Before the Southern Sociological Congress by Paxton Hibben, April 29, 1913* (New York, 1913), copy in TRCH, p. 7. And see Croly, particularly Chapters I, V, VII, XI, XII.

Page 89: On the "engineering mentality," see particularly Wiebe, *Search for Order.*

Page 90: Walter Lippmann, *A Preface to Politics* (1914; University of Michigan Press edition: Ann Arbor, Mich., 1962), first Lippmann quotation, p. 55, second, p. 200; third Lippmann quotation from Lippmann, *Drift and Mastery,* p. 115; "human wreckage," *NWTR,* XVII, p. 265; "you see . . . ," Will Irwin, "Why Edison is a Progressive," *Progressive Bulletin,* September 30, 1912, copy, TRCH. Arthur L. Garford manufactured, among many other products, an automobile named the "Garford," which first appeared in 1911. Garford was the Progressive candidate for governor of Ohio in 1912 and for the U. S. Senate in 1914. See Hoffnagle.

Page 91: On "rural Toryism," see T.R. to Horace Plunkett, August 3, 1912, *Letters,* VII, pp. 591-594; see John Braeman, "Seven Progressives: A Review Article," *Business History Review,* XXXV (1961), pp. 581-595. For a survey of progressive and conservative views on competition, see Edwin C. Rozwenc, editor, *Roosevelt, Wilson and the Trusts* (Boston, 1950). For Lippmann's views on culture and morals, see *Preface to Politics,* Chapters II, IX; *Drift and Mastery,* Chapters 10, 13. On Viereck, see Niel M. Johnson, *George Sylvester Viereck: German-American Propagandist* (Urbana, Ill., 1972). On the progressive movement and culture, see Henry F. May, *The End of Innocence: A Study of the First Years of Our Time, 1912-1917* (New York, 1959).

Page 92: On Weyl's concept of the "social surplus," see Forcey, pp. 80–87, 162, 296, and Walter Weyl, *New Democracy: An Essay Concerning Certain Political and Economic Conditions in the United States* (New York, 1912); Lippmann quotations, *Drift and Mastery,* pp. 68–69.

Page 93: Beveridge quotation, *Convention of the Progressive Party,* p. 19; T.R. quotation, *NWTR,* XVII, p. 299. On the problems and promise of "direct democracy" measures, see T.R., "Nationalism and Popular Rule," *Outlook,* January 21, 1911, *NWTR,* XVII, pp. 53–65; on the Progressives compared to the early Republicans, see T.R., "The Heirs of Abraham Lincoln," speech at Lincoln Day banquet of Progressive Party, New York City, February 12, 1913, *NWTR,* XVII, pp. 359–378.

Pages 96–97: Edison quoted in Irwin, "Why Edison is a Progressive"; Beveridge quoted, *Convention of the Progressive Party,* "savage individualism," p. 13, "special interests," p. 17; for information on Father Curran, see T.R.'s *Autobiography;* on Straus, see Cohen. On the middle class during the progressive era, see Hofstadter, *Age of Reform;* Thelan, *New Citizenship;* Wiebe, *Search for Order.* For examples of the Social Gospel appeal of the Progressive Party, see Winston Churchill, *To the Men and Women of New Hampshire: An Open Letter;* and Duncan-Clark, pp. 287–291.

Pages 86–98: The Progressive "faith" is expressed in party publications like *Progressive Bulletin,* Vol. I, nos. 1–16 (1912–1913), Vol. II, nos. 1–11 (1913), copies in TRCH, and Duncan-Clark; in works on political and social theory written by Progressives, such as Herbert Croly, *Progressive Democracy* (New York, 1914), Croly, *The Promise of American Life,* De Witt, *The Progressive Movement,* Lippmann, *Drift and Mastery,* Lippmann, *Preface to Politics,* and Weyl, *New Democracy;* as well as in the speeches, letters, and writings of Beveridge, Roosevelt, and other party leaders. Biographies of Progressive leaders, like those cited previously on Beveridge, Dixon, Richberg, and Roosevelt; and memoirs, such as those noted by Ickes, Richberg, and White, have much material on the Progressive "faith." Articles and monographs on the party, like Chandler, "Origins of Progressive Leadership," Davis, "Social Workers and the Progressive Party," Janick, "The Mind of the Connecticut Progressive," Jeffrey, "Fraser Metzger and the Bull Moose Campaign of 1912," Mowry, *Theodore Roosevelt and the Progressive Movement,* and others cited, contain important information on Progressive thought. Likewise, monographs on the Progressive movement on the state level and particular aspects of the progressive movement, including Davis, *Spearheads for Reform,* Flint, *The Progressive Movement in Vermont,* Mowry, *The California Progressives,* and others cited, are valuable in studying the ideas of the Progressives. Finally, more general works on progressivism and the progressive movement often include relevant and useful material on the ideology of those who joined the Progressive Party. See particularly Braeman, "Seven Progressives;" Forcey, *Crossroads of Liberalism;* Goldman, *Rendezvous With Destiny;* Otis L. Graham, Jr., *An Encore for Reform: The Old Progressives and the New Deal* (New York, 1967); Hofstadter, *Age of Reform;* May, *End of Innocence;* David W. Noble, *The Paradox of Progressive Thought* (Minneapolis, Minn., 1958); Robert H Wiebe, *Businessmen and Reform;* and Wiebe, *Search for Order.*

Page 98: On the conferences at Sagamore Hill in July on the platform, see daily listings of visitors and meetings in "Chronology," *Letters,* VIII, pp. 1477–1478. Letters to T.R. about the platform include Joseph L. Bristow to T.R., July 15, 1912, James R. Garfield to T.R., July 15, 1912, Francis E. McGovern to T.R., July 15, 1912, Hamilton Fish, Jr. to T.R., July 19, 1912, R. F. Pettigrew to T.R., July 19, 1912, William Dudley Foulke to T.R., July 29, 1912, William L. Sims to T.R., July 29, 1912, TRLC. William Allen White later recalled that Kirchwey, Lewis, the Pinchot brothers, and he had each worked up separate preliminary drafts of a platform. See White, p. 485. McCarthy and the Roosevelt supporters in Wisconsin had another draft platform. See Edward A. Fitzpatrick, *McCarthy of Wisconsin* (New York, 1944), pp. 157–174. Foulke's letter of July 29 reports that Rowell had also prepared a platform draft for the party.

Pages 98-102: A list of the members of the platform or "resolutions" committee is given in *Convention of the Progressive Party,* p. 47e. The committee had one member from each state and the District of Columbia. Members of the committee included Chester H. Rowell of California, Herbert Knox Smith of Connecticut, Charles E. Merriam of Illinois, William Dudley Foulke of Indiana, William Allen White of Kansas, Joseph M. Dixon of Montana, George L. Record of New Jersey, George W. Kirchwey of New York, Chairman William Draper Lewis of Pennsylvania, Lucius F. C. Garvin of Rhode Island, and Joseph M. Carey of Wyoming. The manuscript minutes of the platform committee, together with surviving manuscript drafts for the full platform and drafts for individual planks are in TRCH, as are other remaining records of the Progressive Party. The platform and plank drafts are mostly typed pages with a few in handwriting. There appear to be six full platform drafts in all, as well as a set of drafts for the "business plank" and miscellaneous other planks. Four of the six full platform drafts appear to be the same platform at different stages of revision. A fifth draft is identified as that prepared by Chester H. Rowell; and a sixth is marked "Dean Lewis" (William Draper Lewis). Many of the sheets are annotated personally by T.R. in handwriting, and are so identified. Other sheets are marked with the initials or names of Progressive leaders Herbert Croly, Learned Hand, Dwight B. Heard, W. D. Lewis, Gifford Pinchot, and George Rublee, and have various annotations. Most of the plank drafts included in the final platform have "adopted" written on them. No minutes for the deliberations of the platform subcommittee have been located. The members of the subcommittee appear to be those indicated on a "ballot tally sheet" with the committee and platform manuscripts: Chester H. Rowell of California, Charles E. Merriam of Illinois, William Allen White of Kansas, Pearl Wight of Louisiana, Joseph M. Dixon of Montana, George L. Record of New Jersey, George W. Kirchwey of New York, William Draper Lewis of Pennsylvania, and Wheeler P. Bloodgood of Wisconsin. The standard accounts of the platform deliberations are Bowers, pp. 431–432; O. K. Davis, *Released for Publication* (Boston, 1925), pp. 326–336; Fitzpatrick, pp. 157–174; John A. Garraty, *Right-Hand Man: The Life of George W. Perkins* (New York, 1960), pp. 264–273; Harbaugh, pp. 443–444, 545; William Draper Lewis, *The Life of Theodore Roosevelt* (Chicago, 1919), pp. 369–376; Mowry, pp. 269–273; Amos Pinchot, pp. 170–177; White, pp. 482–488. The final platform has been printed in many places, including Kirk H. Porter and Donald Bruce Johnson, editors, *National Party Platforms, 1840-1964* (Urbana, Ill., 1964), pp. 175–182.

Page 99: On the post-election dispute over the Sherman Act paragraph, and the disagreements in August over various other planks, see the works cited above on the platform deliberations; and on Jane Addams's reactions to the battleship construction plank and other party matters, see Addams, *Second Twenty Years at Hull House,* pp. 10–48.

Pages 100-102: Quotations from platform and plank drafts in platform committee mss., TRCH; "I was sitting . . . ," White, p. 487; "the substituted business plank . . . ," William Draper Lewis to T.R., August 11, 1912, TRLC. Roosevelt discussed the dispute over the Sherman Act paragraph, and his own role in the making of the platform in letters written after the election when McCarthy and the Pinchot brothers made the quarrel public. See T.R. to Amos Pinchot, December 5, 1912, *Letters,* VII, pp. 661–670; T.R. to Francis J. Heney, December 13, 1912, *Letters,* VII, pp. 672–676; T.R. to Henry F. Cochems, November 19, 1912, T.R. to George L. Record, December 13, 1912, T.R. to Walter W. Strong, January 30, 1912, TRLC. The incident involving Perkins and the printed text of the platform is documented in Davis, pp. 326–336; Amos Pinchot, p. 177; White, p. 486; also see Garraty, pp. 268–270. Since there was a question about whether the Sherman Act lines had been adopted or not, and since most Progressives including T.R. had no quarrel with these lines, the Sherman Act paragraph was put back into printed versions of the platform by action of a party conference in December, 1912.

Page 103: On Amos Pinchot's cost of living plank draft T.R. wrote: "utter folly; but harmless." The last two words, however, were crossed out. See platform committee mss., TRCH. For Amos Pinchot's views on the cost of living, trusts, Perkins, and other related matters, see Amos Pinchot, pp. 170–212; for Roosevelt's views on the cost of living question, see T.R. to Amos Pinchot, December 31, 1912, *Letters,* VII, pp. 682–683. On the views of

Munsey and Perkins, see George Britt, *Forty Years—Forty Millions: The Career of Frank A. Munsey* (1935; Kennikat Press edition: Port Washington, N.Y., 1972); Garraty, *George W. Perkins;* Goldman, pp. 205-207.

Pages 103-104: Joseph L. Bristow to T.R., July 15, 1912, TRLC. On the general problems inherent in business regulation, see Goldman, pp. 202-207, 214-219.

Pages 104-105: William Dudley Foulke to T.R., July 29, 1912, TRLC. On the agreement of California Progressives with T.R.'s stand on the trusts, see Olin, pp. 67-68.

Pages 105-106: On White's views in 1912, and his later assessment of those views in his memoirs, see White, pp. 487-491; on Dixon, see Davis, pp. 267-268, and Stoddard, pp. 406-407; the finances of the Progressive convention are discussed in *Progressive Bulletin,* September, 1912, TRCH; the photograph incident is related by O. K. Davis, pp. 340-341; the political preferences of trust executives are discussed in T.R., "The Control of Corporations and the 'New Freedom,'" Appendix B to the 1913 Macmillan Co. edition of *Autobiography,* pp. 621-630; on J. P. Morgan, Jr.'s efforts to remove Perkins from United States Steel, see Garraty, pp. 282-283; for Perkins's election as executive committee chairman, see "Minutes of the Progressive National Committee, August 8, 1912," typed ms., TRCH, and White, pp. 490-491; for biographical on Perkins, see Garraty.

Page 106: J. F. Cleveland quoted in O. K. Davis, pp. 339-340; "from the shorter catechism . . . ," Amos Pinchot, p. 201; "it is the most . . . ," Winston Churchill, "The Progressives' Creed," *Progressive Bulletin,* September 16, 1912, TRCH; "it was fortunate . . . ," *New York Times,* August 8, 1912.

Page 107: Quotations from *Convention of the Progressive Party,* Prendergast, p. 176; Lindsey, pp. 191-193. Eliot quoted from *New York Times,* August 21, 1912. See *Convention of the Progressive Party,* for committee reports, pp. 144-173; nominating speeches for T.R., pp. 174-242. On Demonstration for Addams and suffrage, see *National Issues of 1912,* p. 278.

Pages 108-109: Robins quoted from *Convention of the Progressive Party,* pp. 282-283; "Roosevelt and Johnson" banner described in *National Issues of 1912,* p. 282; the hymn "Roosevelt" by C. H. Congdon in Congdon, *Progressive Battle Hymns* (n.p., 1912), copy in TRCH, and see *National Issues of 1912,* p. 282; T.R. quoted from acceptance speech, *Convention of the Progressive Party,* pp. 292-295; Johnson quoted from acceptance speech, *Convention of the Progressive Party,* pp. 295-297; description of Johnson quoted from "Johnson of California: A Progressive in a Hurry," *Current Literature,* August, 1912, pp. 306-309. See *Convention of the Progressive Party,* for reading and adoption of platform, pp. 243-268; T.R. nominated, pp. 268-269; nominating speeches for Johnson and his nomination, pp. 269-291; acceptance speeches, pp. 292-297.

Page 110: Spingarn's verse quoted by Mark Sullivan, "Armageddon at Chicago," p. 13.

5. THE CRUSADE

Pages 111-112: Campaign song quoted in Mowry, p. 263; "he will draw . . . ," *Providence Daily Journal,* August 16, 1912. For accounts of the Progressive campaign, see Gardner, pp. 260-280; Harbaugh, pp. 445-450; Frank K. Kelly, *The Fight for the White House: The Story of 1912* (New York, 1961); Manners, pp. 265-291; George E. Mowry, "Election of 1912," in Arthur M. Schlesinger, Jr. and Fred L. Israel, *History of American Presidential Elections* (4 vols.: New York, 1971), pp. 2135-2242; Mowry, pp. 274-283. T.R.'s campaign schedule is given in "Chronology," *Letters,* VIII, pp. 1478-1479. Some of T.R.'s campaign speeches are published in *Progressive Principles* and *NWTR,* XVII; manuscripts of other speeches are in TRCH and TRLC. On Hiram W. Johnson's campaign, see Mowry, *California Progressives,* pp. 188-198.

Page 112: T.R. quoted on Taft, *Boston Sunday Globe,* August 18, 1912, and *New York Times,* August 19, 1912; Taft quoted from *Chicago Tribune,* September 29, 1912.

Pages 113-115: "Regulated competition," characterization of Wilson program by Link, *Wilson and the Progressive Era,* p. 20; "the men who are on the make," quoted by Richard Hofstadter, *American Political Tradition* (New York, 1948), p. 252; "legalized monopoly," "God forbid . . . ," and "self-appointed divinity," *New York Times,* September 3, 1912; "this is a second struggle . . . ," Link, *Wilson and the Progressive Era,* p. 21; "ready to admit . . . ," John Wells Davidson, editor, *A Crossroads of Freedom: The 1912 Campaign Speeches of Woodrow Wilson* (New Haven, 1956), p. 265; "no government has . . . ," *New York Times,* September 5, 1912; ". . . the history of liberty . . . ," Davidson, p. 130; "a giant republic . . . ," T.R., "Speech of Honorable Theodore Roosevelt Delivered at Point of Pines, Mass., August 17, 1912," typed ms., TRCH. On Wilson's campaign, see Ray Stannard Baker, *Woodrow Wilson: Life and Letters* (8 vols.: Garden City, N.Y., 1927-1939), III, pp. 364-412; Link, *Wilson and the Progressive Era,* pp. 1-24; Link, *Wilson: The Road to the White House,* pp. 467-520. Wilson's campaign speeches have been collected in Davidson, *Crossroads of Freedom.* On Wilson and Brandeis, also see Alpheus T. Mason, *Brandeis: A Free Man's Life* (New York, 1946); Melvin I. Urofsky, "Wilson, Brandeis, and the Trust Issue, 1912-1914," *Mid-America,* XLIX (1967), pp. 3-28.

Pages 115-116: "Like a cuttle fish . . . ," *New York Times,* August 23, 1912; "embodies a far worse . . . ," T.R. to Moses E. Clapp, August 28, 1912, *Letters,* VII, pp. 602-625, which was T.R.'s public response to the charges of *Hearst's,* Archbold, and Penrose. On the trip to Wilkes-Barre, see *New York Times,* August 22, 23, 1912. On the 1912 Standard Oil controversy, see *American Review of Reviews,* October, 1912, pp. 387-394; *Hearst's Magazine,* August, 1912, pp. 2-16; and the Clapp subcommittee testimony in *Campaign Contributions: Testimony Before a Subcommittee of the Committee on Privileges and Elections, United States Senate* (2 vols.: Washington, 1913). For Penrose, see Walter Davenport, *Power and Glory: The Life and Times of Boies Penrose* (New York, 1931).

Pages 117-120: "Wanted, 100,000 earnest citizens . . . ," quotation and *World* cartoon in Link, *Wilson: The Road to the White House,* p. 483; Roosevelt quoted from T.R. to Moses E. Clapp, August 28, 1912, *Letters,* VII, pp. 602-625; also see T.R. to Hermann Hagedorn, August 21, 1912, *Letters,* VII, p. 602. For the exchanges between T.R. and Wilson over trust support, see *Chicago Tribune,* August 8-13, 1912. Schiff's support for Wilson announced *New York Times,* September 2, 1912; the support of Cyrus H. McCormick, the Jones brothers, and Baruch noted in Link, *Wilson: The Road to the White House,* p. 485. The finances of the Democratic campaign are discussed in detail in Link, *Wilson: The Road to the White House,* pp. 483-487; Taft's campaign fund and contributors listed *New York Times,* December 3, 1912; the figures and contributors of the Progressive Party are taken from *Progressive National Committee–Financial Records,* two account books in TRCH. It should be noted that campaign figures from national committees do not include monies spent by state communities, various special campaign organizations, and state and local candidates. T.R. told a reporter in 1916 that he would have appointed Perkins Secretary of Treasury or Commerce. See John J. Leary, Jr., *Talks With T.R.* (Boston, 1920), pp. 79-80. On Munsey, T.R., and the Progressive Party, see Britt, particularly, pp. 158-184.

Page 120: *New York Sun* quoted by Mowry, p. 279; "Roosevelt was the first . . . ," George Harvey, "Roosevelt or the Republic!" *North American Review,* October, 1912, pp. 433-448, quotations p. 442; Watterson's views quoted from *Louisville Courier-Journal,* August 24, 1912; "Roosevelt lies . . . ," Ishpeming, Michigan *Iron Ore,* October 12, 1912, clipping in TRCH. There are other clippings and letters in TRCH and TRLC recording charges that Roosevelt was a drunkard. Since the slander that he was a drunkard had plagued Roosevelt for years, he decided to sue the editor of the *Iron Ore* to set the record straight, as it was in the trial in 1913. T.R. was a moderate social drinker on occasion, but he seldom had more than one or two drinks during a single day. See Wagenknecht, pp. 92-97.

Pages 120-121: Brandeis quoted in *Progressive Bulletin,* September 30, 1912, TRCH; "... we were not ...," *Collier's,* November 9, 1912, p. 8; see Link, *Wilson: The Road to the White House,* on Wilson's Fall River speech, p. 509, and on Gompers and Wilson's relations with organized labor, pp. 470-471, 500. Brandeis's signed articles in *Collier's* were: "Trusts, Efficiency, and the New Party," *Collier's,* September 14, 1912, pp. 14-15; "Trusts, the Export Trade, and the New Party," *Collier's,* September 21, 1912, pp. 10-11. Brandeis's unsigned editorials in *Collier's* were: "Monopoly," September 7, 1912, p. 8; "Labor and the Trusts," September 14, 1912, p. 8; "The Wastes of Monopoly," September 21, 1912, p. 8; "Concentration," October 5, 1912, p. 8; "The Method," October 19, 1912, p. 8. On the Brandeis articles and the dispute between Hapgood and Collier and Sullivan, see Norman Hapgood, *The Changing Years: Reminiscences of Norman Hapgood* (New York, 1930), pp. 219-222; Link, *Wilson: The Road to the White House,* p. 492; Mark Sullivan, *The Education of an American* (New York, 1938), pp. 229-308.

Pages 121-122: "I need hardly ...," George Sylvester Viereck to National German-American Roosevelt League, July 23, 1912, TRLC. Gillette's speeches are mentioned in *Chicago Tribune,* October 26, 1912; Lillian Russell's publicity photograph is in TRCH; see "Why Edison Is a Progressive"; on the Progressive writers' syndicate, see "A Group of Bull Moose Writers," *Progressive Bulletin,* September 30, 1912, TRCH; copies of foreign language Progressive literature are in TRCH. The following letters from TRLC mention various ethnic organizations: Danish National Progressive League, V. A. M. Mortensen to T.R., November 15, 1912; Austrian and Hungarian Club of New York, Bernard Hirsh to T.R., December 19, 1912; Italo-American Progressive Club of Rhode Island, Antonio Massaniso to T.R., December 28, 1912; National German-American Roosevelt League, George Sylvester Viereck to T.R., June 26, 1912.

Pages 122-124: "Red herring," T.R., "Speech at Hartford, Connecticut, September 2, 1912," typed ms., TRCH; Hiram Johnson quoted from speech in Columbus, Ohio by *Chicago Tribune,* September 6, 1912; "our proposal ...," T.R. quoted from speech in Helena, Montana, *New York American,* September 8, 1912; "I am not for monopoly ...," T.R. quoted in *Collier's,* November 2, 1912, p. 9; T.R. response to Wilson on commissions, *Chicago Tribune,* September 7, 1912; T.R. on minimum wage, *Chicago Tribune,* September 3, 1912; T.R. on Colorado Fuel and Iron Company, *Chicago Tribune,* September 20, 1912. For Roosevelt's statements on the trust issue late in the campaign, see statement in *New York Tribune,* October 20, 1912; and T.R., "Governor Wilson and the Trusts," speech, Oyster Bay, N.Y., November 2, 1912, *NWTR,* XVII, pp. 341-348.

Pages 124-125: Quotations from T.R., "Limitation of Governmental Power," address, San Francisco, California, September 14, 1912, *NWTR,* XVII, pp. 306-314. Roosevelt was quoting from Wilson's speech to the New York Press Club, September 9, 1912, which is printed in Davidson, pp. 122-135. On the Press Club speech, see Gable, dissertation, pp. 322-323.

Pages 125-126: For a lengthy and day-by-day account and analysis of T.R.'s 1912 campaign, see Gable, dissertation, pp. 270-333.

Pages 126-128: "... This is my big chance ...," quoted in Manners, p. 281. Quotations from T.R., "The Leader and the Cause," address, Milwaukee, Wisconsin, October 14, 1912, text from stenographic report, *NWTR,* XVII, pp. 320-330. The most complete account of the Milwaukee shooting is Oliver E. Remey, Henry F. Cochems, Wheeler P. Bloodgood, *The Attempted Assassination of Ex-President Roosevelt* (Milwaukee, 1912); Roosevelt described the event in T.R. to Edward Grey, November 15, 1912, *Letters,* VII, pp. 647-650; also see Manners, pp. 279-288. TRLC contains court transcripts, sanity hearing records, and other documents relating to Schrank and his attack.

Pages 128-129: Quotations from T.R., "The Purpose of the Progressive Party," address at Madison Square Garden, New York City, October 30, 1912, *NWTR,* XVII, pp. 334-340. The conclusion of T.R.'s October 30 speech was a quotation from his speech "The Right of the People to Rule," March 20, 1912, the passage found *NWTR*, XVII, p. 270. For accounts of the October 30 rally, see Hermann Hagedorn, *The Roosevelt Family of Sagamore Hill* (New York, 1954), pp. 322-325; Corinne Roosevelt Robinson, *My Brother Theodore Roosevelt* (New York, 1921), pp. 274-275. While still in the hospital, Roosevelt issued a statement, "The Stricken Standard-Bearer," *NWTR*, XVII, p. 331, read in Louisville, Ky., October 16, 1912, by Albert J. Beveridge. T.R. issued further statements to the press before the close of the campaign, including "The Fight Goes On," October 17, 1912, *NWTR*, XVII, pp. 332-333. His speech for the New York State Progressive ticket on November is reported *New York Times*, November 2, 1912; his final campaign speech, in Oyster Bay on November 2, was "Governor Wilson and the Trusts," *NWTR*, XVII, pp. 341-348.

6. COUNTING THE BALLOTS AND CHARTING THE FUTURE

Page 131: "We have fought . . . ," T.R. to James R. Garfield, November 8, 1912, *Letters*, VII, p. 637; "we are full of spirit . . . ," Richard Washburn Child to T.R., November 6, 1912, TRLC. Child, a lawyer and writer, was one of the leaders of the Progressive Party in Massachusetts, and in later years Ambassador to Italy.

Pages 131-133: Election figures differ slightly in various sources, because there was no official national compilation of election results. Figures for the national totals are from Svend Peterson, *A Statistical History of the American Presidential Elections* (New York, 1963); figures for the vote in states and counties are from *World Almanac: 1913*, pp. 721-769.

Pages 133-142: "Not agrarian but urban," Mowry, p. 280; on the vote in Vermont and education of Vermont state legislators, see Jeffrey. Figures for vote in states and counties from *World Almanac: 1913*, pp. 721-769. Information and figures on cities, urban growth, population, farm lands, ethnic composition of the states, illiteracy, and other demographic characteristics are from *Thirteenth Census of the United States Taken in the Year 1910* (11 vols.: Washington, 1913).

Pages 142-144: "The crime of 1911," Collins quoted from speech seconding T.R.'s nomination, *Convention of the Progressive Party*, pp. 222-240; "Teddy votes," William Allen White to T.R., September 24, 1913, in Walter Johnson, editor, *Selected Letters of William Allen White* (New York, 1947), pp. 144-146. For discussion of the political situation in the various states see Chapter II. On the factor of the Canadian Reciprocity Treaty of 1911, see Mowry, pp. 160-164, 166-167; Ring, pp. 24, 26-44, 53-54. On the Payne-Aldrich Tariff of 1909, see Mowry, pp. 46-64. The Payne-Aldrich Tariff had been one of the first issues dividing Taft from the progressives, as the progressives fought for downward revision of the tariff, and Republican conservatives, with Taft's support, successfully sought to maintain a high tariff. On the "full dinner pail" and protection issue, see Levine, p. 61; Frank A. Munsey to T.R., August 16, 1912, TRLC. On the trust issue, see Mowry, pp. 269-272, 280. On the issues of "honesty" and "bossism," see White, p. 503.

Page 145: ". . . While Mrs. Medill McCormick . . . ," Maude Howe Elliott to T.R., January 28, 1913, TRLC; the Tuxedo Park situation is discussed in Baker, pp. 71-73.

Page 146: "Tired business man," Edward S. Van Zile to T.R., December 16, 1912, TRLC; *Boston Herald* quoted by *Literary Digest*, November 30, 1912, p. 997.

Pages 146-149: See election results in *World Almanac: 1913*, pp. 721-769, which gives returns for gubernatorial elections and Congressional elections in each district as well as the partisan alignments in state legislatures. The populist victories of 1892 are discussed in Harold U. Faulkner, *Politics, Reform and Expansion, 1890-1900* (New York, 1959), pp. 134-136. The 20 members of the Progressive Party in the U.S. House, Sixty-Third Congress, 1913-1915, are listed in *Progressive Congressional Program* (New York, 1914), copy in TRCH. Two senators in the Sixty-Third Congress, Moses Clapp of Minnesota and

Miles Poindexter of Washington, both elected as Republicans before 1912, affiliated with the Progressive Party. On the exodus of California Republicans into the organization of the new party after the November elections, see Mowry, *California Progressives*, pp. 188–198; Olin, pp. 67–68. In 1912 the Progressives had endorsed five Republican gubernatorial candidates: William T. Haines of Maine, H. D. Hatfield of West Virginia, Arthur Capper of Kansas, incumbent Chester H. Aldrich of Nebraska, and Frank M. Byrne of South Dakota. Haines, Hatfield, and Byrne were elected; Capper and Aldrich were defeated.

Page 150: Dixon quoted, *New York Times,* November 6, 1912; T.R.'s statement to the press on the election, *New York Times,* November 12, 1912; "it was a phenomenal thing . . . ," T.R. to Henry White, November 12, 1912, *Letters,* VII, p. 639; "we have fought the good fight . . . ," T.R. to James R. Garfield, November 8, 1912, *Letters,* VII, p. 637; ". . . I firmly believe," T.R. to Ben Lindsey, November 16, 1912, *Letters,* VII, p. 650; T.R. to Arthur Hamilton Lee, November 5, 1912, *Letters,* VII, pp. 633–634.

Pages 150-151: "It would have been . . . ," T.R. to Charles Dwight Willard, November 14, 1912, *Letters,* VII, pp. 645–647; "whether the Progressive Party . . . ," T.R. to Arthur Hamilton Lee, November 5, 1912, *Letters,* VII, pp. 633–634; "no one can tell . . . ," T.R. to Alexander Smith Cochran, December 31, 1912, TRLC; "I should incline . . . ," T.R. to Benjamin Ide Wheeler, November 12, 1912, TRLC; "if the Democratic Party . . . ," T.R. to Arthur Hamilton Lee, December 31, 1912, *Letters,* VII, pp. 683–684; "it is perfectly possible . . . ," T.R. to Charles Henry Brent, January 14, 1913, TRLC; "a very adroit man," T.R. to Benjamin Ide Wheeler, November 20, 1912, *Letters,* VII, pp. 652–653; "our business . . . ," T.R. to Henry White, November 12, 1912, *Letters,* VII, p. 639.

Page 152: *"A first-class organization,"* T.R. to Gifford Pinchot, November 13, 1912, *Letters,* VII, pp. 640–645; "the danger . . . ," T.R. to Robert Perkins Bass, November 14, 1912, *Letters,* VII, p. 647; "the principles . . . ," Benjamin Ide Wheeler to T.R., November 12, 1912, TRLC. On the need for education of the voters, also see Charles E. Merriam to T.R., November 20, 1912, TRLC.

Pages 152-153: "Would be bad politics . . . ," Amos Pinchot to T.R., December 3, 1912, TRLC; "drag on the ticket," Medill McCormick to T.R., November 18, 1912, TRLC; "Mr. Perkins . . . ," Charles E. Merriam to T.R., November 20, 1912, TRLC; "throw to the wolves . . . ," and "in this campaign . . . ," T.R. to Gifford Pinchot, November 13, 1912, *Letters,* VII, pp. 640–645; "of course to fight . . . ," T.R. to William Allen White, November 19, 1912, copy in TRCH. For the position of the Pinchot brothers, also see Amos Pinchot to T.R., December 23, 1912, and Gifford Pinchot to T.R., four letters, November 23, 1912, December 17, 1912, January 1, 1913, January 20, 1913, TRLC. For Roosevelt's responses, also see T.R. to Amos Pinchot, two letters, December 5, 1912, *Letters,* VII, pp. 661–670, December 31, 1912, *Letters,* VII, pp. 682–683; and T.R. to Gifford Pinchot, two letters, November 11, 1912, *Letters,* VII, pp. 637–638, December 21, 1912, *Letters,* VII, pp. 677–679. Letters from Roosevelt to Progressive leaders on the Perkins controversy also include T.R. to Ben Lindsey, November 16, 1912, *Letters,* VII, p. 650; T.R. to Charles E. Merriam, November 23, 1912, *Letters,* VII, pp. 657–659; T.R. to Francis J. Heney, December 13, 1912, *Letters,* VII, pp. 672–676. The issue of the "missing plank" is discussed in most of Roosevelt's letters concerning Perkins, and also in T.R. to Henry F. Cochems, November 19, 1912, T.R. to George L. Record, December 13, 1912, T.R. to Walter W. Strong, January 30, 1913, TRLC. Support for Perkins is found in Charles H. Thompson to T.R., November 20, 1912, John Franklin Fort to T.R., November 21, 1912, James Bronson Reynolds to T.R., December 14, 1912, Ben Lindsey to T.R., December 18, 1912, telegram, Ben Lindsey to T.R., December 20, 1912, TRLC. William Allen White also agreed at this time that Perkins should stay: White to T.R., November 25, 1912. On the Perkins controversy of December, 1912, also see Mowry, pp. 294–296.

Pages 153-166: "We have accomplished . . . ," "but wings . . . ," and "the doctrine . . . ," from T.R., "The Future of the Progressive Party," speech at Progressive conference, Chicago, Ill., December 10, 1912, *NWTR,* XVII, pp. 349–356; "Progressive Service" proposal, Jane Addams, "A Plan of Work," typed ms., TRCH; "dues-paying membership," from "Voluntary Popular Subscriptions, To the National Committee of the Progressive Party, Assembled at Chicago, December 10, 1912," typed ms., TRCH, which appears to be Walter Weyl's address on finances, noted in all articles on the conference; "and so the year ended . . . ," White, p. 496. The November 9 Boston rally, addressed by novelist Winston Churchill and Charles Sumner Bird, is described in *Progressive Bulletin*, November 20, 1912, TRCH; the New York City meeting, addressed by Bourke Cockran and Oscar S. Straus as well as by T.R., is reported in *New York Evening Mail*, November 19, 1912. On the Chicago Progressive conference in December, see Elbert E. Martin, "The National Progressive Conference," *Progress*, January, 1913, TRCH; *Progressive Bulletin*, December 14, 1912; and *New York Times*, December 9-12, 1912.

7. 1913: HANDS SET TO THE PLOW

Page 157: "Our hands are set . . . ," Albert J. Beveridge in a speech in New York City, October 3, 1913, quoted from *Progressive*, October 18, 1913, a New York Progressive journal, copy TRCH; "if 1912 witnessed . . . ," *Cincinnati Enquirer* quoted by *Progressive Bulletin*, December, 1913, TRCH.

Pages 157-159: Munsey quoted from Frank A. Munsey, "A Possible Scheme for Amalgamating the Republican and Progressive Parties That Should Be Acceptable to Each," *Munsey's Magazine*, February, 1913, pp. 729-733; Munsey, "Amalgamation No. 2," *Munsey's Magazine*, March, 1913, pp. 888-892; Munsey, "Amalgamation No. 3," *Munsey's Magazine*, April, 1913, pp. 14-21. On Dan R. Hanna, see Warner pp. 468-471; Dan R. Hanna to T.R., two letters, April 28, 1913, May 24, 1913, TRLC. For the views of Osborn, Taft, and the press, see "Rejecting Republican Reunion," *Literary Digest*, January 25, 1913, pp. 166-168. On the Chicago meeting of progressive Republicans, see *LaFollette's Weekly*, May 24, 1913, pp. 10-11; "Setting the Republican Fracture," *Literary Digest*, May 31, 1913, pp. 1210-1212.

Page 159: "Spoke without sympathy . . . ," Charles J. Bonaparte to T.R., February 15, 1913; "there is . . . much talk . . . ," T.R. to Frank L. Dingley, August 28, 1913, *Letters*, VII, p. 744; Beveridge quoted from Albert J. Beveridge, "The Progressive-Republican Merger," *Saturday Evening Post*, June 28, 1913, pp. 3-5, 49-52. Also see Albert J. Beveridge, "A Party Afraid of Itself," *Collier's*, January 31, 1914, pp. 7-8, 24-26, in which Beveridge attacks the Republican National Committee for refusing to call a special convention; and Medill McCormick, "Republican-Progressive Fusion Impossible," *North American Review*, May, 1914, pp. 700-708. Roosevelt wrote many letters rejecting "amalgamation," and calling on Progressives to stand firm. See, for instance, T.R. to Robert S. Vessey and the state chairmen and national committeemen of Michigan, Minnesota, Wisconsin, North Dakota, and South Dakota, January 22, 1913, *Letters*, VII, pp. 691-693; T.R. to Frank A. Munsey, February 15, 1913, T.R. to Charles J. Bonaparte, February 17, 1913, T.R. to George von L. Meyer, June 9, 1913, T.R. to William H. Hinebaugh, September 2, 1913, T.R. to Herbert S. Hadley, September 10, 1913, T.R. to Charles Sumner Bird, September 18, 1913, TRLC.

Pages 159-161: "Stand aloof," T.R. quoted in *Progressive Bulletin*, November 30, 1912, TRCH; "I do not want to seem . . . ," T.R. to Joseph L. Bristow, January 9, 1913, TRLC; "I would far rather . . . ," T.R. to Walter Clyde Jones, February 25, 1913, TRLC; "with self-respect," T.R. to Charles E. Merriam, March 18, 1913, TRLC. On the situation in Maine, see Ring, pp. 32-34; Frank L. Dingley to T.R., November 16, 1912, Halbert P. Gardner to T.R., November 30, 1912, Frank L. Dingley to T.R., January 8, 1913, Irving E. Vernon to T.R., January 9, 1913, Charles S. Hichborn to T.R., February 4, 1931, TRLC; T.R. to A. C. Wheeler, December 31, 1912, *Letters*, VII, pp. 684-685; T.R. to Frank L. Dingley, November 22, 1912, T.R. to Halbert P. Gardner, December 3, 1912, TRLC. For the New Hampshire situation, see Robert Perkins Bass to T.R., January 23, 1913, George

Ray Wicker to T.R., February 7, 1913, TRLC; T.R. to Robert Perkins Bass, January 28, 1913, *Letters*, VII, pp. 701–702; T.R. to George Ray Wicker, February 13, 1913, TRLC. On the West Virginia political picture, see William Seymour Edwards to T.R., January 16, 1913, O. K. Davis to T.R., January 28, 1913, TRLC; T.R. to O. K. Davis, January 21, 1913, *Letters*, VII, pp. 690–691; T.R. to Joseph L. Bristow, January 21, 1913, TRLC. On the Illinois senatorial contests, see Medill McCormick to T.R., February 8 and February 21, 1913, two letters, Walter Clyde Jones to T.R. February 22, 1913, Charles E. Merriam to T.R., April 7, 1913, B. F. Harris to T.R., May 1, 1913, TRLC; T.R. to Ruth Hanna McCormick, December 4, 1912, *Letters*, VII, p. 661; T.R. to B. F. Harris, March 4, 1913, T.R. to Charles E. Merriam, April 11, 1913, TRLC. On Maine, New Hampshire, West Virginia, and Illinois, also see letters listed in Gable, dissertation, pp. 450–454.

Pages 161–162: "Our party duty...," Albert J. Beveridge, *Senator Beveridge's Lincoln Day Speech, Hotel Astor, New York City* (New York, 1913), pamphlet, TRCH; "if you could...," T.R. to J. M. Wall, April 8, 1913, TRLC; "my 'Century' article...," T.R. to Matthew Hale, September 16, 1913, TRLC. See T.R., "The Progressive Party," *Century Magazine*, October, 1913, NWTR, XVII, pp. 388–409; on St. Paul conference, *Progressive Bulletin*, February, 1913, TRCH; Nebraska banquet, F. P. Corrick to T.R., February 19, 1913, TRLC; Kansas banquet, La Forte, pp. 213–214, and *Progressive Bulletin*, March, 1913, TRCH. On the New York City Lincoln Day dinner, see *Lincoln Day Banquet, National Progressive Club, Wednesday evening, February 12, 1913, New York* (program), *List of Diners* (pamphlet), *Progress*, March, 1913 (magazine), *Senator Beveridge's Lincoln Day Speech*, TRCH; T.R., "The Heirs of Abraham Lincoln," speech at Lincoln Day Banquet, New York City, February 12, 1913, NWTR, XVII, pp. 359–378. On Joseph Walker and the Massachusetts Progressives, see Abrams, pp. 240–243; *Progressive Bulletin*, February and March, 1913, two issues, TRCH. On other Progressive meetings and conferences in 1913, see *Progressive Bulletin*, issues of February-December, 1913, TRCH; Hale's report is in *Progressive Bulletin*, March, 1913; on organization in Kansas, see U.S. Sartin to T.R., February 15, 1913, TRLC, and *Progressive Bulletin*, December 28, 1912, and March, 1913 issues, TRCH; for the Progressive clubs, see *Progressive Bulletin*, June, 1913, TRCH. The Roosevelt letters mentioned, examples of many written on behalf of the party, are T.R. to Antonio Mattaniso, Italo-American Progressive Club, Providence R. I., January 15, 1913, T.R. to Herbert M. Bailey, Bergen County, N. J., January 27, 1913, T.R. to Edward J. Montagne, North End National Progressive Club, Brooklyn, N.Y., May 22, 1913, TRLC. There were other letters in 1913 to Progressive state conventions in Michigan and Maryland, the Progressives in Ward 19 of Roxbury, Mass., Progressive leaders in Vermont, Missouri, Kansas, etc. For a list of such messages, see Gable, dissertation, p. 457. Roosevelt's speaking schedule in 1913 is given in "Chronology," *Letters*, VIII, pp. 1480–1483. As T.R. told Hale, there were persistent rumors, circulated by the Republicans, that T.R. intended to abandon the Progressive Party. Historians have sometimes accepted these assertions as fact. But T.R.'s private letters and public statements and actions show that in 1913 and 1914 Roosevelt made every effort to establish the Progressive Party on a permanent basis. On this point, see Gable, dissertation, pp. 396–398, 411–412, 448–458. In addition to his work for the party, in 1913 and 1914 T.R., the apostle of the "strenuous life," found time for other activities. He regularly contributed reviews and essays to the *Outlook* magazine; wrote his autobiography; served as president of the American Historical Association; and with Edmund Heller published a two-volume natural history of African big game. In May, 1913 he went to Marquette, Michigan for the libel trial of the editor who during the 1912 campaign had called him a drunkard. The editor, George A. Newett, could produce no evidence, and after a battery of witnesses testified as to T.R.'s personal habits Newett recanted his charges. Roosevelt then asked the court to award nominal damages of six cents. In the summer of 1913, T.R. went camping in the deserts of the Southwest, and in October he left for South America to give a lecture tour and lead an exploring expedition into the jungles of Brazil. See Harbaugh, pp. 453–465; T.R., *Autobiography;* T.R., *History As Literature* (New York, 1913); Edmund Heller and T.R., *Life-Histories of African Game Animals* (2 vols.: New York, 1914); *Roosevelt vs. Newett: A Transcript of the Testimony Taken at Depositions Read at Marquette, Michigan* (privately printed, 1914), copy in TRCH.

Pages 162-163: See Addams, "A Plan of Work;" *Organization of the Service* (New York, 1913), pamphlet, TRCH; for biographical information, *DAB, NCAB, WWW;* and on Richberg, see Vadney.

Pages 163-165: For "A Call to the Colors" and the launching of the Progressive Volunteers, see *Progressive Bulletin,* August, 1913, and "Voluntary Popular Subscriptions," TRCH; "we hope . . . ," Elon H. Hooker to Charles Henry Davis, January 4, 1913, Progressive National Committee Files in TRCH. Also see *Progressive Volunteer* (newspaper), May and October, 1914, two issues, and material on the Progressive Volunteers in the "Volunteers" folder, Progressive National Committee Files, TRCH. The financial records of the Progressive Party consist of two ledgers, and letters, notes, and bills in the Progressive National Committee Files, TRCH. The planned budget for 1913 is given in Elon H. Hooker to O. K. Davis, May 3, 1913; the expenditures for the Progressive Service in 1913 are given in Frances A. Kellor to Elon H. Hooker, January 27, 1914; both in Progressive National Committee Files, TRCH. The ledger books give lists of contributors and pledges. The correspondence, in the Progressive National Committee Files, between Elon H. Hooker and Charles Henry Davis of Massachusetts reveals much about the finances of the party on the national and state levels.

Pages 165-168: Kellor quoted from Frances A. Kellor, "A New Spirit in Party Organization," *North American Review,* June, 1914, pp. 872–892; Devine quoted by Davis, *Spearheads for Reform,* pp. 204-205; "but the day of democracy . . . ," Paxton Hibben, *Politics and Social Service: An Address Delivered Before the Southern Sociological Congress.* The organizational meetings of the Progressive Service and the Legislative Reference Bureau were held in New York City, January 9, 1913: "Minutes of the Progressive Service Committee held January 9, 1913," "Minutes of the First Meeting of the Legislative Reference Committee," typed ms., TRCH. The work of the Progressive Service and its bureaus, departments, committees, and state organizations, as well as the members of these bodies, are reported in *First Quarterly Report of the Progressive National Service* (New York, 1913), *Organization of the Service,* and issues of *Progressive Bulletin,* TRCH. There are also letters, notes, pamphlets, and other materials in the Progressive National Committee Files, TRCH, relating to the Progressive Service. There are brief accounts of the Progressive Service in Davis, *Spearheads for Reform,* pp. 194-217; Richberg, *My Hero,* pp. 42-77; Richberg, *Tents of the Mighty,* pp. 36-57; Vadney, pp. 22-27. Lists of the members of the various organizations of the Progressive Service are given in Gable, dissertation, pp. 418-420, 462-464.

Pages 169-170: "Usually work ceased . . . ," Richberg, *Tents of the Mighty,* p. 42. Titles in the Progressive Service Documents series included Duncan-Clark, *The Progressive Movement;* William L. Ransom, *The Making of a Municipal Platform* (New York, 1913); T.R., *Progressive Principles; Sickness Insurance* (New York, 1914); *Standards of Workmen's Compensation* (New York, 1914); Frances A. Kellor, *Unemployment: A Program of Relief* (New York, 1914). All Progressive Service publications are in TRCH. The work of the Progressive Lyceum Bureau is outlined in two Lyceum pamphlets in TRCH; the distribution of Progressive Service literature is discussed in *First Quarterly Report.* On the Progressive Party and the state legislatures, see *First Quarterly Report;* and for Maine, Ring, pp. 39-44; for Vermont, Flint, pp. 61-103; for Oregon, Blakenship, pp. 217-222, 226; for California, Mowry, *California Progressives,* pp. 135-224; for Massachusetts, Arthur Dehon Hill to T.R., February 14, 1913, TRLC.

Pages 170-171: "We cannot as a community . . . ," T.R. to Michael A. Schaap, January 23, 1913, *Letters,* VII, pp. 696-701; "chivalry of the state," Albert J. Beveridge's keynote address, *Convention of the Progressive Party,* p. 36; T.R. quoted on women's rights from T.R., "Woman Suffrage Demanded In the Interests of Good Government," speech, Metropolitan Opera House, May 2, 1912, typed ms., TRCH. On the ILGWU and the 1913 strike, see Paul M. Angle, *Crossroads: 1913* (New York, 1963), pp. 80-84; Stolberg, pp. 76-87. On the Progressive Party and the strike, see Gertrude Barnum to T.R., January 22, 1913, Julius Henry Cohen to Frank Harper, January 23, 1913, Madeline Doty to T.R., January 23, 1913, J. E. Bailey to T.R., telegram, January 24, 1913, Michael A. Schaap to

T.R., January 27, 1913, Mary E. Dreier to T.R., January 29, 1913, TRLC. On the party and women's suffrage, see *First Quarterly Report.*

Pages 171-172: T.R., "The 'New Freedom' and the Courts," speech at the National Conference of the Progressive Service, Newport, R.I., July 2, 1913, *NWTR,* XVII, pp. 379-387, quotations pp. 379, 380. See T.R., "Sarah Knisley's Arm," *Collier's,* January 25, 1913, pp. 8-9, 22-23, and February 1, 1913, pp. 8-9, also printed as a Progressive Service pamphlet. On the Newport conference, see Richberg, *My Hero,* pp. 56-58, and Richberg, *Tents of the Mighty,* pp. 44-47; on the West Virginia coal strike, see Angle, pp. 123-126; on the first year of the Wilson administration, see Link, *Wilson: The New Freedom* (Princeton, 1956).

Page 172: "With the idea ... ," and "we should be ... ," T.R. to William H. Hinebaugh, March 19, 1913.

Page 173: "I am quite sure ... ," John Callan O'Laughlin to Walter M. Chandler, February, 1913, TRCH; "are absolutely at sea ... ," John Callan O'Laughlin to T.R., March 23, 1913, TRLC; "a flock of goats ... ," Davis, p. 416, and account of plan on tariff bill, pp. 409-416.

Pages 173-174: "Ours is a party ... ," T.R. to Harold L. Ickes, April 11, 1913, *Letters,* VII, p. 719; "reformers are ... ," T.R. to Arthur Hamilton Lee, September 24, 1913, TRLC; "of course I am having ... ," T.R. to Quentin Roosevelt, September 29, 1913, TRCH; "lunatic fringe," see Albert Bushnell Hart and Herbert Ronald Ferleger, *Theodore Roosevelt Cyclopedia* (New York, 1941), p. 319; "oh, Beveridge ... ," quoted in Richberg, *My Hero,* pp, 57-58.

Pages 172-175: The Progressive members of the U.S. House, 1913-1915, were: C. W. Bell, William D. Stephens, and John I. Nolan of California, elected on the Republican ticket, which in California in 1912 was headed by T.R.; A. Walter Lafferty of Oregon, Charles A. Lindbergh of Minnesota, Ira C. Copley of Illinois, and Victor Murdock of Kansas, all elected on the Republican ticket with Progressive backing; M. Clyde Kelley, Fred E. Lewis, Arthur R. Rupley, Anderson H. Walters, Henry Willson Temple, and Willis J. Hulings of Pennsylvania, members of the Washington (Progressive) Party, some elected with Republican endorsement; and Walter M. Chandler of New York, Roy O. Woodruff and William J. MacDonald of Michigan, William H. Hinebaugh and Charles M. Thomson of Illinois, and James Wesley Bryan and J. A. Falconer of Washington, all elected on the Progressive ticket. These twenty Representatives joined the Progressive caucus in the U.S. House. Listings in various directories, including *Official Congressional Directory, 63rd Congress, 1st Session, 1913* (Washington, 1913), are confusing, with partisan affiliations such as "Progressive Republican" given, and the above list is taken from Progressive Party sources. See *Progressive Congressional Program* (New York, 1914), TRCH, for a list of Progressive Congressmen. On Bristow, see A. Bower Sageser, *Joseph L. Bristow: Kansas Progressive* (Lawrence, Kansas, 1968); on progressive Republicans in Congress, see Holt, pp. 63-164; on Progressives in Congress, see Davis, pp. 409-416. Accounts of the Underwood tariff bill in the *Progressive Bulletin,* May and June, 1913 issues, TRCH, include useful information on Progressives in Congress. On the Progressive Congressional Program, see Progressive Bulletin, July and September, 1913 issues, TRCH; *Progressive Congressional Program,* which was published by the Progressive Service; Richberg, *My Hero,* pp. 51-57, 68-69; Richberg, *Tents of the Mighty,* pp. 41-48; T.R. to Donald L. Richberg, June 27, 1913, *Letters,* VII, p. 735; William H. Hinebaugh to T.R., November 16, 1912 and December 18, 1912, two letters, William Draper Lewis to T.R., April 4, 1913, Victor Murdock to T.R., telegram, April 7, 1913, Ira C. Copley to T.R., April 5, 1913, Victor Murdock to T.R., telegram, April 7, 1913, Frances A. Kellor to T.R., April 9, 1913, Herbert Knox Smith to T.R., April 9, 1913, William Draper Lewis to T.R., May 13, 1913, Victor Murdock to T.R., June 28, 1914, TRLC. On the Progressives in Congress, also see Joseph M. Dixon to T.R., February 7, 1913, James Wesley Bryan to T.R., March 11, 1913, Albert J. Beveridge to T.R., March 16, 1913, T.R. to William Draper Lewis, April 1, 1913, John Callan O'Laughlin to T.R., August 24, 1914, TRLC; T.R. to William H. Hinebaugh,

November 19, 1912, *Letters*, VII, p. 651; T.R. to the Progressives in Congress, April 2, 1913, *Letters*, VII, pp. 718–719; and see other letters listed in Gable, dissertation, pp. 467–470.

Pages 176–178: "The reason Sulzer was recalled . . . ," Straus quoted from *The Progressive Cause and Its Meaning and Its Purpose: Speech by Oscar S. Straus to Home Progressive Club of New York City, December 10, 1913* (New York, 1913), pamphlet, TRCH; "regardless of . . . ," resolution on Progressive municipal policy adopted at Cincinnati conference of city chairmen quoted from *Progressive Bulletin*, May, 1913, TRCH. On the Michigan election, see T.R. to Henry M. Wallace, February 14, 1913 and February 21, 1913, two letters, Charles H. Thompson to T.R., March 10, 1913, Joseph M. Dixon to T.R., telegram, March 24, 1913, and other letters in TRLC. On the special Congressional election in New Jersey, see *Progressive Bulletin*, August, 1913, TRCH; on Maine's, see Ring, pp. 34–36. On the fund for Massachusetts, see Elon H. Hooker to Hugh T. Halbert, November 12, 1913, Progressive National Committee Files, TRCH. Beveridge's many services for the party in 1913 are noted in Braeman, *Beveridge*, pp. 231–233. On the New Jersey situation in 1913, see O. K. Davis to T.R., April 3, 1913, George L. Record to T.R., April 30, 1913 and May 8, 1913, two letters, TRLC; T.R. to George L. Record, September 2, 1913, *Letters*, VII, p. 746; *Progressive Bulletin*, October, 1913, TRCH. On the New York State political scene in 1913, see Jacob A. Friedman, *The Impeachment of Governor William Sulzer* (New York, 1939); J. Joseph Huthmacher, *Senator Robert F. Wagner and the Rise of Urban Liberalism* (New York, 1968), pp. 26–37; *Speech of Acceptance Delivered by Samuel Seabury* (New York, 1913), pamphlet, TRCH; *Speech by Oscar S. Straus;* T.R. to William Sulzer, September 2, 1913, *Letters*, VII, pp. 744–745. On Massachusetts Progressive politics in 1913, see Abrams, pp. 284–286; Sherman; and *Progressive Party Platform, Adopted in Convention, October 6, 1913* (n.d., n.p.), pamphlet, TRCH; T.R. to Charles Sumner Bird, September 18, 1913, TRLC. On the 1913 New York City election, see Ransom, *Making of a Municipal Platform;* Francis W. Bird to T.R., February 21, 1913, William L. Ransom to T.R., March 22, 1913, June 1, 1913, and June 17, 1913, three letters, Lillian Wald to T.R., May 17, 1913, TRLC; and see other letters listed in Gable, dissertation, pp. 472–473. Roosevelt early favored fusion in New York City. See T.R. to William H. Hotchkiss, June 24, 1913, *Letters*, VII, pp. 734–735. In St. Louis Progressives nominated Democrat Frank H. Gerhart for mayor. See Joseph A. Wright to T.R., with enclosure of St. Louis platform, February 8, 1913, TRLC. For Louisville, see *A Contract With the People: Platform of the Progressive Party of Louisville and Jefferson County* (Louisville, Ky., 1913), pamphlet, TRCH. On the Cincinnati conference, see Yandell Henderson to T.R., April 26, 1913, TRLC; *Cincinnati Commercial Tribune*, April 22, 1913. The spring Michigan state election results are given in Henry M. Wallace to T.R., with enclosure, May 20, 1913, TRLC; on the election of state Senator Jens Jensen in Washington, see *Progressive Bulletin*, February, 1913, TRCH; for the results in the special elections in Maine and New Jersey see sources cited above for these elections; for the New Jersey gubernatorial election results see *Manual of the Legislature of New Jersey, 1914* (Trenton, N.J., 1914).

Pages 178–180: Poindexter and Johnson quotations and quotation on New York results are from *Progressive Bulletin*, November, 1913, TRCH; "the results of the election . . . ," Carlton Hayes and E. M. Sait, "Record of Political Events," *Political Science Quarterly*, December, 1913, p. 723. Results of all 1913 elections are reported in *Progressive Bulletin*, March-December, 1913, TRCH; and on Massachusetts see *Manual of the General Court* (Boston, 1914); and on New York State see *The New York Red Book for 1914* (Albany, N.Y., 1914).

Pages 180–181: White quotations from William Allen White to T.R., September 24, 1913, Walter Johnson, editor, *Selected Letters of William Allen White* (New York, 1947), pp. 144–146; T.R.'s response is T.R. to William Allen White, September 29, 1913, TRLC; "all my life . . . ," T.R. quoted in *Progressive Bulletin*, October, 1913, TRCH. On the farewell dinner, see *Farewell Dinner Given to Theodore Roosevelt By the Progressive National Service and the Progressive Service of New York*, program, TRCH.

8. STRATEGIES FOR PROGRESSIVISM

Page 182: "... We have to give ... ," T.R. to Raymond Robins, August 12, 1914, *Letters,* VII, pp. 796–802.

Pages 184–188: "Political education ... ," Richberg, *Tents of the Mighty,* p. 49; "we don't care ... ," William Allen White to J. A. Burnette, *Letters of William Allen White,* pp. 151–154; "follow" the work of organization, Medill McCormick to George W. Perkins, April 7, 1913, TRLC; "... it is my belief ... ," Richard Washburn Child to T.R., May 3, 1913, TRLC; "the Chairman [Perkins] reported ... ," "Minutes of Meeting of the Executive Committee of the National Committee of the Progressive Party, held January 24, 1914," typed ms., copies in TRCH and TRLC; "the Service was chloroformed ... ," Richberg, *Tents of the Mighty,* pp. 50–51. Garland's views are given in Hamlin Garland to T.R., April 9 [1913], TRLC; correspondence between O. K. Davis and the New York City party headquarters details the history of the *Bulletin* and the Washington office, Progressive National Committee Files, TRCH; figures on party spending are from Frances A. Kellor to Elon H. Hooker, January 27, 1914, and account sheets, Progressive National Committee Files, TRCH. On the split between the social educators and the political organizers, and the last days of the Progressive Service, see Richberg, *My Hero,* pp. 53–55; Richberg, *Tents of the Mighty,* pp. 48–53; Vadney, pp. 24–25; George W. Perkins to Frances A. Kellor, December 14, 1914, Progressive National Committee Files, TRCH; T.R. to George W. Perkins, December 16, 1914. T.R. to Frances A. Kellor, December 17, 1914, T.R. to George W. Perkins, December 19, 1914, TRLC.

Pages 188–192: Perkins as a "drag" on the party, Medill McCormick to T.R., November 18, 1912, TRLC; Amos Pinchot's letter to Joseph M. Dixon, May 22, 1914, quoted in Amos Pinchot, p. 54; "I believe ... ," George W. Perkins to William E. Borah, February 27, 1914, Progressive National Committee Files, TRCH; "trouble maker," Raymond Robins to T.R., August 3, 1914; "treason in the ranks," Beveridge quoted in Braeman, *Beveridge,* pp. 233–234; "it seems to me ... ," Robert Ruhl to T.R., June 25, 1914, TRLC; "right-hand man," taken from the title of John Garraty's biography of Perkins; "when they read Perkins out ... ," and "no man has ... ," T.R. quoted by *New York World,* June 26, 1914. On the Borah-Perkins controversy, see George W. Perkins to William E. Borah, February 27, 1914 and March 1, 1914, two letters, George W. Perkins to Edwin M. Lee, March 3, 1914, Progressive National Committee Files, TRCH. For the articles praising Harvester and Standard Oil, see *Progressive Bulletin,* issues of June and July, 1913, respectively, TRCH. On the Jones controversy, see "Statement by George W. Perkins" [June, 1914], Progressive National Committee Files, TRCH; Link, *Wilson: The New Freedom,* pp. 449–457. On the controversy over Perkins's leadership, see Fausold, pp. 167–170; Garraty, pp. 282–283; Mowry, pp. 296–299; Amos Pinchot, pp. 37–59, 212–213; B. F. Harris to Amos Pinchot, June 12, 1914, Medill McCormick to George W. Perkins, June 12, 1914, Medill McCormick to T.R., June 22, 1914, Robert Ruhl to T.R., June 25, 1914, Alexander H. Revell to T.R., June 27, 1914, William Flinn to George W. Perkins, July 2, 1914, Medill McCormick to George W. Perkins, July 14, 1914, Raymond Robins to T.R., August 3, 1914, Hiram W. Johnson to T.R., August 20, 1914, TRLC. Perkins's loans and contributions to the party are noted in M. Kihm to Elon H. Hooker, October 17, 1913, M. Kihm to J. M. Stricker, May 15, 1914, George W. Perkins to Elon H. Hooker, July 3, 1914, George W. Perkins to Elon H. Hooker, February 6, 1915, Progressive National Committee Files, TRCH. On Perkins and the "trust triplets," see Richberg, *Tents of the Mighty,* p. 43.

Page 192: "It was my last chance to be a boy," quoted in Stefan Lorant, *The Life and Times of Theodore Roosevelt* (Garden City, N.Y., 1959), p. 590; "I am now an old man," T.R. to Leonard Wood, June 26, 1914, TRLC.

Page 193: T.R. quoted on Sulzer's impeachment from drafts of T.R. to William Sulzer, July 24, 1914, TRLC; "...my dear Hamilton," T.R. to Hamilton Fish, Jr., August 25, 1914, TRLC; "...I have at present...," William H. Hotchkiss to T.R., July 7, 1914, TRLC; "...I do not think," Pearl Wight to Frank Harper, June 20, 1914, TRLC; "...names and prejudices...," T.R. to Hiram W. Johnson, July 30, 1914, *Letters,* VII, pp. 784–790.

Page 194: "So conclusive of the lack...," C. S. Duell, Jr. to T.R., telegram, July 28, 1914, TRLC.

Pages 194-195: "In this campaign...," "Statement of Colonel Roosevelt," July 22, 1914, Progressive National Committee Files, TRCH, and see *New York Times,* July 23, 1914; "the question of governor...," George W. Perkins to Progressive national committeemen and state chairmen, July 22, 1914, Progressive National Committee Files, TRCH; "while it is true...," John J. O'Connell to Regis H. Post, August 19, 1914, TRLC; Chauncey J. Hamlin to T.R., July 16, 1914, TRLC.

Page 196: "There is a determined effort...," Moses E. Clapp to George W. Perkins, August 1, 1914, TRLC; "befog the minds...," George M. Leopold to T.R., August 3, 1914, TRLC; "it is hard...," Charles Sumner Bird to T.R., July 24, 1914, TRLC; Beveridge quoted from Bowers, pp. 451–452; "I have just read...," Victor Murdock to George W. Perkins, July 23, 1914, Progressive National Committee Files, TRCH; "idolatry of names," T.R. to Hiram W. Johnson, July 30, 1914, *Letters,* VII, pp. 784–790; "while running...," T.R. to Dwight B. Heard, July 31, 1914, TRLC; "we appeal...," "Statement Issued by Colonel Roosevelt, July 31, 1914," and T.R. to Halbert P. Gardner, July 31, 1914, Progressive National Committee Files, TRCH.

Pages 197-198: "New York is not...," and "we have got to give...," T.R. to Raymond Robins, August 12, 1914, *Letters,* VII, pp. 796–802; T.R. quoted on "anti-boss campaign" and economic and social issues from T.R. to William Draper Lewis, July 10, 1914, *Letters,* VII, pp. 776–777.

Pages 192-198: On the "fusion" question in New York State, see "New Alignments at Armageddon," *Literary Digest,* August 8, 1914, pp. 219–220. On Sulzer's candidacy, see William Sulzer to T.R., July 20, 1914, August 25, 1914, and August 29, 1914, three letters, Hamilton Fish, Jr. to T.R., August 24, 1914, TRLC, and letters cited previously. Letters from New York Progressives urging T.R. to run for governor include Walter M. Chandler to T.R., June 25, 1914, Frederick M. Davenport to T.R., July 3, 1914, and William Hamlin Childs to T.R., July 7, 1914, TRLC; on Beveridge urging T.R. to run, see Hagedorn, *Roosevelt Family of Sagamore Hill,* pp. 339–340. Letters from Progressives urging Roosevelt not to run include William H. Hinebaugh to T.R., June 5, 1914, Hiram W. Johnson to T.R., June 17, 1914, James R. Garfield to T.R., June 22, 1914, Miles Poindexter to T.R., June 29, 1914, TRLC. On the Whitman candidacy, see *New York Times,* July 29, 1914; C. S. Duell, Jr. to Jerome B. Cooper, June 13, 1914, C. S. Duell, Jr. to Orson J. Weimert, June 13, 1914, Royal W. France to T.R., July 18, 1914, C. S. Duell, Jr. to T.R., telegram, July 28, 1914, TRLC; T.R. to Royal W. France, July 25, 1914, *Letters,* VII, p. 781. Praise for T.R.'s backing of Hinman is in *New York Times* and *New York Tribune,* both July 29, 1914. Letters from New York Progressives endorsing Hinman include Frederick M. Davenport to T.R., July 3, 1914, Henry Salant to T.R., July 23, 1914, Carlos C. Alden to T.R., August 1, 1914, TRLC. Letters opposing Hinman candidacy, in addition to those cited previously, include Medill McCormick to T.R., July 21, 1914, Raymond Robins to T.R., August 3, 1914, Bainbridge Colby to T.R., August 7, 1914, Edward P. Costigan to T.R., August 10, 1914, TRLC.

Pages 198-199: "Yielded to Colonel Roosevelt's...," George W. Perkins to the Progressive national committeemen and state chairmen, August 22, 1914, Progressive National Committee Files, TRCH; "fast slipping...," William L. Ransom to T.R., August 10, 1914, TRLC; "I am and shall continue...," Hinman quoted from Francis G. Wickware, editor, *The American Yearbook: A Record of Events and Progress, 1914* (New York, 1915), pp. 48–49, which has a concise account of New York politics in 1914; "...the Hinman movement . . . ," T.R. to Henry M. Wallace, August 24, 1914, TRLC; "the time is not opportune . . . ," "Platform Adopted by New York State Progressive Committee at Utica, August 27, 1914," Progressive National Committee Files, TRCH. On New York developments in August, 1914, also see Samuel A. Carlson to T.R., August 4, 1914, T.R. to Harvey D. Hinman, August 5, 1914, TRLC; T.R. to Frederick M. Davenport, August 12, 1914, *Letters,* VII, pp. 802-803; T.R. to John Callan O'Laughlin, August 27, 1914, *Letters,* VII, 813-815. For the figures in the New York State primary of 1914, see *World Almanac: 1915* (New York, 1915), p. 791. The vote in the Progressive primary was Davenport 18,643 and Sulzer 14,366; Bainbridge Colby was unopposed. The TRCH has a complete file of the publications of Sulzer's American Party. For further information on the New York State political scene in 1914, see additional sources cited in Gable, dissertation, pp. 530-536; and see Fred L. Israel, "Bainbridge Colby and the Progressive Party, 1914-1916," *New York History,* XL (1959), pp. 33-46.

Page 199: Requests received by Roosevelt asking for endorsement of Republican candidates include Congressman Hunter H. Moss of West Virginia, on behalf of his candidacy, to T.R., July 14, 1914, R. B. Howell, Republican candidate for governor of Nebraska on behalf of his candidacy, to T.R., July 23, 1914, and former Governor William E. Glasscock of West Virginia, on behalf of his state's Republican ticket, October 13, 1914, TRLC. Roosevelt turned a deaf ear to such pleas. On the candidacy of Prouty and Vermont politics in 1914, see "Minutes of the National Progressive State Convention of Vermont, September 17, 1914, Burlington, Vermont," typed ms., Fraser Metzger to T.R., July 9, 1914, Charles A. Prouty to March M. Wilson, July 13, 1914, March M. Wilson to Charles A. Prouty, July 15, 1914, TRLC. On South Dakota, see Thomas Thorson to T.R., July 20, 1914, and on Wisconsin, Charles McCarthy to T.R., October 27, 1914, TRLC. On Utah, see "Democratic Platform [of Utah] " and "Progressive Platform [of Utah] ," TRLC.

Pages 199-200: "The forces making for evil . . . ," Lewis quoted by Fausold, p. 180; ". . . when there is so-called fusion . . . ," H. D. W. English to T.R., October 6, 1914, TRLC. On the political situation in Pennsylvania in 1914, see Fausold, pp. 141-182; William Flinn to T.R., July 14, 1914, Melvin P. Miller to T.R., September 10, 1914, William Draper Lewis to T.R., September 15, 1914, R. R. Quay to T.R., September 17, 1914, Charles N. Brumm to Vance C. McCormick, September 30, 1914, H. D. W. English to William Draper Lewis, September 30, 1914, A. Nevin Detrich to T.R., October 2, 1914, Robert L. Owen to T.R., October 7, 1914, R. R. Quay to T.R., October 29, 1914, Thomas Robins to T.R., November 27, 1914, TRLC. On Palmer, see Stanley Coben, *A. Mitchell Palmer: Politician* (New York, 1963). On the Pennsylvania political situation, also see M. Nelson McGeary, "Gifford Pinchot's 1914 Campaign," *Pennsylvania Magazine of History and Biography,* LXXXI (1957), pp. 303-318.

Page 201: The North Dakota situation is discussed in A. Y. More to T.R., June 29, 1914, and C. G. Boise to George W. Perkins, TRLC. On the Washington primaries, see Ole Hanson to T.R., telegram, September 3, 1914, J. A. Falconer to T.R., telegram, September 4, 1914, T.R. to Victor Murdock, telegram, September 5, 1914, W. K. Sheldon to T.R., telegram, September 5, 1914, J. A. Falconer to T.R., September 12, 1914, TR to J. A. Falconer, September 15, 1914, L. Roy Slater to T.R., October 26, 1914, TRLC. For the Oregon situation, see Blakenship, pp. 271-310. The contest between Rowell and Heney is discussed in Meyer Lissner to George W. Perkins, June 20, 1914, Chester H. Rowell to T.R., June 27, 1914, Francis J. Heney to T.R., July 6, 1914, Meyer Lissner to T.R., August 10, 1914, Francis J. Heney to Hiram W. Johnson, August 29, 1914, Hiram W. Johnson to Francis J. Heney, August 31, 1914, Hiram W. Johnson to Francis J. Heney, September 1, 1914, Francis J. Heney to T.R., September 4, 1914, and September 26, 1914, two letters, TRLC.

Page 202: "I am firm . . . ," William H. Hinebaugh to T.R., June 5, 1914, TRLC; "Progressive candidates are not . . . ," Henry L. Stoddard to T.R., July 13, 1914, TRLC; *Baltimore Sun* quoted in "Mr. Roosevelt and Republican Fusion," *Literary Digest,* June 13, 1914, p. 1422; "I do not agree . . . ," T.R. to Alexander P. Moore, July 10, 1914, TRLC.

Pages 202-203: On the record of the Wilson administration, see particularly Link, *Wilson: The New Freedom;* the fight over the women's suffrage amendment is discussed in Arthur N.

Holcombe, "Popular Government and Current Politics," *American Yearbook: 1914,* pp. 59–61; the depression of 1913-1914 is examined in S. S. Huebner, "Economic Conditions and the Conduct of Business," *American Yearbook: 1914,* pp. 318–342; T.R. condemned the proposed Colombian treaty, which was not passed during the Wilson administration, in T.R. to Senator William J. Stone, July 11, 1914, *Letters,* VII, pp. 777–779; T.R.'s opinions on the Mexican situation are expressed in T.R. to Henry Cabot Lodge, December 8, 1914, *Letters,* VIII, pp. 861–863.

Pages 203-205: "I am going out . . . ," Garford quoted by Warner, p. 473; "the temperance men . . . ," James R. Garfield to T.R., October 15, 1914; TRLC; ". . . as part of the new nationalism . . . ," "Progressive State Platform of Nebraska, adopted July 28, 1914," typed ms., TRLC; "in order that the people . . . ," "Minutes of the National Progressive State Convention of Vermont"; "the right and righteous side," Joseph Walker quoted from "Statement of Joseph Walker, to be released November 7, 1914," typed ms., TRLC; "I cannot back up National Prohibition," T.R. to Joseph Walker, October 21, 1914, TRLC; "as for prohibition . . . ," T.R. to William Allen White, July 6, 1914, *Letters,* VII, p. 773; "of course I am entirely . . . ," Arthur Dehon Hill to T.R., October 8, 1914, TRLC; "a terrible and bloodthirsty parlor Anarchist," Hiram W. Johnson to T.R., August 20, 1914, TRLC; for Heney's "peace plank," see "Platform of Francis J. Heney," *San Francisco Bulletin,* September 26, 1914; Walker quoted on the "two great moral and social reforms" from *Boston Post,* October 7, 1914. Sentiment for prohibition and for the Sheppard-Hobson amendment is discussed in *American Year Book: 1914,* pp. 46, 399–400. For a comprehensive discussion of the relationship between prohibition and progressivism, see James H. Timberlake, *Prohibition and the Progressive Movement, 1900-1920* (Cambridge, 1963). On the Massachusetts Progressive convention and platform in 1914, see *Boston Post.* October 7, 1914; *Boston Transcript,* October 7, 1914; Joseph Walker to T.R., October 8, 1914, and October 24, 1914, two letters, TRLC. On Michigan, see "State Platform of the National Progressive Party in Michigan 1914," typed ms., TRLC; *Detroit Free Press,* October 2, 1914. On Ohio, see Warner, pp. 472–473. On Nebraska, "Progressive State Platform of Nebraska"; F. P. Corrick to T.R., September 7, 1914. On Vermont, "Minutes of National Progressive State Convention;" on Arizona, Dwight B. Heard to T.R., October 3, 1914, TRLC; the Colorado platform is printed in *The Deadly Parallel* (Denver, 1914), pamphlet, TRLC; the Georgia platform is printed in the *Georgia Progressive,* October 25, 1914, copy in TRLC; on Utah, "Progressive Platform [of Utah];" on Maine, Ring, pp. 36–40. Portions of the Progressive state platforms of Indiana, Iowa, Kansas, Ohio, Pennsylvania, and other states are printed in *World Almanac: 1915,* pp. 748–749. On Record's New Jersey faction, see George W. Perkins to Progressive national committeemen and state chairmen, April 10, 1914, Progressive National Committee Files, TRCH; on Record's and Amos Pinchot's fight for government ownership, see Fausold, pp. 151–160; for Heney's views, see "Platform of Francis J. Heney."

9. "THEY WILL NOT ENDURE SOUND DOCTRINE"
The Campaign and Elections of 1914

Page 207: II Timothy 4:3–4 (King James Version), see p. 226; these verses constituted T.R.'s statement to the press on the results of the 1914 elections.

Page 208: "We, the Progressives . . . ," "Platform Adopted by New York Progressive State Committee;" "we hereby indorse . . . ," Connecticut Progressive platform quoted from *World Almanac: 1915,* pp. 748–749; "idolatry of names," T.R. to Hiram W. Johnson, July 30, 1914, *Letters,* VII, pp. 784–790.

Pages 208-211: The Colorado Progressive and Republican platforms are quoted from *Deadly Parallel,* which contains the 1914 Colorado state platforms of the Democratic, Progressive, and Republican parties; the Colorado Progressive platform is also in Goodykoontz, pp. 292–301; "fifteen years ago . . . ," T.R. quoted from "Colonel Roosevelt to Lead Colorado Fight," *Rocky Mountain News,* June 6, 1914, in Goodykoontz, p. 265; "it seems to me that not since the creation of the Progressive Party . . . ," T.R. to Edward P. Costigan, August 15, 1914, *Letters,* VII, pp. 804–809. On the U.M.W. strike,

Costigan work for the miners, and Colorado in 1914, see Carl Abbott, *Colorado: A History of the Centennial State* (Boulder, Colo., 1976); Goodykoontz, pp. 247–317; Link, *Wilson: The New Freedom*, pp. 457–459; George S. McGovern and Leonard Guttridge, *The Great Coal Field War* (Boston, 1972). The Colorado Progressive ticket of 1914 is given in Goodykoontz, pp. 281–283. On the 1914 Colorado campaign, see Edward P. Costigan, "Law, Order, and Justice to All," speech, Denver, June 8, 1914, Goodykoontz, pp. 262–276; O. K. Davis to T.R., July 13, 1914, Archibald A. Lee to T.R., August 6, 1914, J. S. Temple to T.R., August 11, 1914, Daniel D. Casement to T.R., September 24, 1914, Ben B. Lindsey to William Allen White, October 17, 1914, Daniel D. Casement to T.R., October 25, 1914, TRLC; O. K. Davis to George W. Perkins, June 27, 1914, Progressive National Committee Files, TRCH; Edward P. Costigan to R. M. McClintock, March 16, 1914, Goodykoontz, pp. 281–283; T.R. to Walter Weyl, August 6, 1914, *Letters*, VII, pp. 793–794; T.R. to John Callan O'Laughlin, August 27, 1914, *Letters*, VII, pp. 813–815; T.R. to William Allen White, September 14, 1914, *Letters*, VII, pp. 818–819; T.R. to Hiram W. Johnson, February 22, 1915, *Letters*, VII, pp. 894–896; T.R. to J. S. Temple, July 28, 1914, TRLC.

Pages 211–213: Roosevelt quotations from T.R., "Speech of Honorable Theodore Roosevelt, Pennsylvania Progressive Conference [Pittsburgh, Pa.], June 30, 1914," typed ms., TRCH; T.R.'s Pittsburgh speech was printed in *New York Times*, July 1, 1914; a summary of Roosevelt's seven principles on antitrust policy was published in the *Outlook*, July 11, 1914, pp. 572–573; "what the Progressive Party plan seeks. . . . ," Arthur L. Garford, "Address of A. L. Garford," Progressive banquet, Lima, Ohio, February 12, 1914, typed ms., TRCH. The Progressive position on the tariff was cogently summarized in the Colorado state platform, Goodykoontz, pp. 292–301. On the Wilson administration's antitrust policies, see Link, *Wilson: The New Freedom*, pp. 417–444; the visit of the women's delegation to the White House is reported in *New York Times*, July 1, 1914. Roosevelt in 1914 also expressed support for women's rights in T.R., "Women and the New York Constitutional Convention," *Outlook*, August 1, 1914, pp. 796–798; and for direct democracy in T.R., "The Right of the People to Review Judge-Made Law," *Outlook*, August 8, 1914, pp. 843–856.

Page 214: "Without saying . . . ," *New York Times*, July 1, 1914; "I hold that . . . ," T.R. to Halbert P. Gardner, July 31, 1914, Progressive National Committee Files, TRCH; "now, my dear Cal," T.R. to John Callan O'Laughlin, August 27, 1914, *Letters*, VII, pp. 813–815. On Roosevelt's June 30 Pittsburgh address, also see Mowry, pp. 300–302; *Nation*, July 9, 1914, p. 33; *Outlook*, July 11, 1914, pp. 572–573; John W. Batdorf to T.R., July 1, 1914, William Flinn to George W. Perkins, July 2, 1914, James N. Williamson, Jr. to T.R., July 2, 1914, Medill McCormick to T.R., July 3, 1914, TRLC.

Pages 214–215: "The Progressive Party focused . . . ," "Speech of Colonel Roosevelt at Boston, August 17 [1914]," typed ms., TRCH; appeal to "conscience and common sense" for "sane radicalism," "Speech of Colonel Roosevelt, Lewiston, Maine, August 18 [1914]," typed ms., TRCH. Also see "Speech of Colonel Roosevelt at Hartford, Connecticut, August 15 [1914]," typed ms., TRCH. On Croly, Lippmann, and Weyl, see Forcey.

Page 216: "If any party . . . ," *Nation*, July 9, 1914, p. 33. Roosevelt's 1915 speech on unemployment is T.R., "The Problem of Unemployment," address, New York City, January 26, 1915, *NWTR*, XVI, pp. 456–463.

Pages 217–218: Gubernatorial and senatorial candidates in 1914 are listed in *World Almanac: 1916* (New York, 1916), pp. 729–772. On the 1914 political situation and campaign in Connecticut, see Janick; in Illinois, George Fitch, "Politics in Illinois," *Collier's*, October 24, 1914, pp. 21–22, 29, Medill McCormick to T.R., July 10, 1914, August 3, 1914, September 10, 1914, October 8, 1914, four letters, TRLC; in Indiana, Bowers, pp. 449–454, Braeman, *Beveridge*, pp. 227–239; in Kansas, Hinshaw, pp. 136–139, LaForte, pp. 229–246, Sageser, pp. 143–153, White, pp. 503–504; in Maine, Ring, pp. 36–40, Irving E. Vernon to T.R., July 15, 1914, Halbert P. Gardner to T.R., September 26, 1914, TRLC; in Maryland, Charles J. Bonaparte to T.R., August 20, 1914, August 29, 1914, September 2, 1914, three letters, TRLC; in Massachusetts, Sherman, and Charles Sumner Bird to T.R.,

July 15, 1914, James P. Magenis to T.R., July 17, 1914, Richard Washburn Child to T.R., July 17, 1914, July 30, 1914, two letters, TRLC; in Michigan, *Detroit Free Press,* October 2, 1914, Chase S. Osborn to T.R., July 13, 1914, Charles F. Hoffman to John W. McGrath, August 29, 1914, TRLC; in Montana, Karlin, pp. 204-207; in New Hampshire, Henry D. Allison to T.R., August 22, 1914, Robert Perkins Bass to T.R., August 21, 1914, September 17, 1914, two letters, TRLC; in Ohio, Warner, pp. 467-495; in Oregon, Blankenship, pp. 271-310; in Vermont, Flint, pp. 61-73; in Washington, Allen, pp. 289-305; in Wisconsin, *LaFollette's Weekly,* October 10, 1914, Charles McCarthy to T.R., October 27, 1914, Frances E. McGovern to T.R., November 19, 1914, John J. Blaine to T.R., November 20, 1914, TRLC. On the Progressive candidates and the 1914 elections, also see Gable, dissertation, pp. 495-612; and biographical information on individual candidates in *BDAC, DAB, NCAB, WWW.*

Pages 218-219: Robins "ought to be supported . . . ," endorsement of Beveridge, and praise for Davenport, *Collier's,* issues September 19, 1914, pp. 16-17, October 17, 1914, p. 14, October 31, 1914, pp. 1-2; "go to the support of Francis J. Heney . . . ," and endorsements of Prouty and Robins, *LaFollette's Weekly,* issues October 3, 1914, p. 1. October 24, 1914, p. 2, October 31, 1914, pp. 1-2; endorsements of Costigan, Davenport, Heney, Pinchot, and Smith, *Harper's,* issues July 18, 1914, pp. 50, 59, October 10, 1914, p. 338, October 31, 1914, pp. 409-410; "the real issue . . . ," Robert L. Owen to Raymond Robins, October 5, 1914, TRLC; "Raymond Robins Democratic League," see George C. Sikes, *For the Honor of Illinois* (n.p., n.d.), pamphlet in TRLC. On the 1914 political situation and campaign in California, see Mowry, *California Progressives,* pp. 199-224, Olin, pp. 99-103; in Illinois, Peter Clark MacFarlane, "Is Roger Sullivan a Boss?" *Collier's,* August 8, 1914, pp. 5-6, 29-30; in Pennsylvania, Fausold, pp. 172-173, 182.

Page 219: "Especial emphasis . . . ," O. K. Davis to Progressive leaders, August 17, 1914, Progressive National Committee Files, TRCH; "a political revolution is on . . . ," Hinebaugh quoted in *American Review of Reviews,* July, 1914, p. 17. On the Delta County, Michigan ticket, see Cheever Buckbee to T.R., with enclosure, October 13, 1914, TRLC. Landon's work in Kansas is described in Donald R. McCoy, *Landon of Kansas* (Lincoln, Nebraska, 1966), pp. 14-19; Schall's campaign is described in great detail in William T. Coe to T.R., November 11, 1914, TRLC; 1914 candidates for the U.S. House are listed by state and district in *World Almanac: 1916,* pp. 729-772; biographical information from *BDAC, NCAB, WWW.*

Pages 219-220: For the 1914 Progressive campaign in Georgia, see James A. Metcalf to C. W. McClure, September 23, 1914, C. W. McClure to T.R., October 2, 1914, October 7, 1914, November 12, 1914, three letters, TRLC; *Georgia Progressive,* October 25, 1914. For the 1914 Progressive campaign in Louisiana and T.R.'s trip to the state, see Collin; *New York Sun,* July 9, 1914; *New York Times,* September 8-9, 1914; "Statement Made by John M. Parker" [June 28, 1914?], Progressive National Committee Files, TRCH; John M. Parker to T.R., November 6, 1914, Pearl Wight to T.R., November 10, 1914, TRLC; biographical information on Martin, *BDAC.*

Pages 220-222: "Oh, Lord, I wish . . . ," T.R. to William Allen White, September 14, 1914, *Letters,* VIII, pp. 818-819. Roosevelt's speaking schedule in 1914 is given in "Chronology," *Letters,* VIII, pp. 1484-1486. The report on the Troy, N.Y. speech is from *Troy Times,* October 7, 1914. Predictions of victory in 1914 by Progressives: Medill McCormick to T.R., August 3, 1914, Albert J. Beveridge to T.R., September 1, 1914, James R. Garfield to T.R., October 15, 1914, Francis J. Heney to T.R., telegram, October 26, 1914, TRLC; Victor Murdock to George W. Perkins, August 15, 1914, Progressive National Committee Files, TRCH; Fausold, pp. 185-186. On the Clayton Act, Federal Trade Commission Act, and the Wilson administration, see Link, *Wilson: The New Freedom,* pp. 241-243, 254-276, 417-471; George Rublee, "The Original Plan and Early History of the Federal Trade Commission," *Proceedings of the Academy of Political Science,* XI (1926), pp. 114-120; and Urofsky.

Pages 222-223: Judge Lindsey on the Colorado campaign and the "whip-saw" of the old parties, Ben B. Lindsey to William Allen White, October 17, 1914, TRLC; the Penrose "Full Dinner Pail" poster is reproduced in Kenneth M. Pray, "The Siege of Penrose," *Harper's,* October 17, 1914, pp. 375-376; "Penrose's only plea . . . ," Alexander P. Moore to T.R., June 26, 1914, TRLC; "the people who . . . ," T.R.'s speech at the First Regiment Armory, Philadelphia, October 1, 1914, quoted in *New York Times,* October 2, 1914; "be sovereigns of your own souls," T.R.'s speech in Troy, N.Y., October 6, 1914, quoted in *Troy Times,* October 7, 1914; ". . . be true to yourselves," "Speech of Colonel Theodore Roosevelt Delivered in the Lyceum, Monticello, New York, Friday Evening, October 23, 1914," typed ms., TRLC; "if we can only get the rubbish off . . . ," "Speech of Colonel Roosevelt, Lewiston, Maine, August 18 [1914]"; "Progressive Party will make such . . . ." T.R. to George L. Record, August 12, 1914, TRCH; also see T.R., *On the Way to 1916 and the Rule of the People* (n.d., n.p.), speech in Bay City, Michigan, September 30, 1914, pamphlet in TRCH. On Alice Carpenter's New York labor league, see Alice Carpenter to George W. Perkins, July 28, 1914, George W. Perkins to Alice Carpenter, July 29, 1914, Alice Carpenter to George W. Perkins, September 18, 1914, and other letters in Progressive National Committee Files, TRCH. For Roosevelt's private views on the hopelessness of the Progressive fight in 1914, see T.R. to R. H. M. Ferguson, October 5, 1914, TRLC.

Pages 223-224: "The Progressive Party has come a cropper," T.R. to Charles J. Bonaparte, November 7, 1914, in Bishop, II, pp. 353-354; "the two bright spots . . . ," and "east of Indiana . . . ," T.R. to Hiram W. Johnson, November 6, 1914, *Letters,* VII, pp. 832-833;" victory for Hiram Johnson . . . ," Meyer Lissner to T.R., November 5, 1914, TRLC; "as for the Republican Party . . . ," "revulsion" against reformers, and workers "felt the pinch . . . ," T.R. to William Allen White, November 7, 1914, *Letters,* VIII, pp. 834-840; "sick of reformers," T.R. to Meyer Lissner, November 16, 1914, *Letters,* VIII, pp. 843-845; "even although it is done . . . ," T.R. to Arthur Dehon Hill, November 9, 1914, TRLC. The 1914 election returns are given in *World Almanac: 1916,* pp. 729-772, and partisan divisions in Congress, pp. 490-499; on the election results also see *American Year Book: 1914,* pp. 47-55.

Page 225: "We cannot pay . . . ," T.R., "Progressive Democracy," *Outlook,* November 18, 1914, in *NWTR,* XII, pp. 232-239; this essay was a review of *Progressive Democracy* by Herbert Croly and *Drift and Mastery* by Walter Lippmann; for a discussion of the "social surplus" and progressive views of the economy, see Forcey, pp. 162, 178-217, 296.

Page 226: "The fact is . . . ," J. A. Falconer to T.R., November 19, 1914, TRLC; Progressives "way ahead," T.R. to Ethel Roosevelt Derby, November 4, 1914, *Letters,* VIII, pp. 831-832; "the fault is not . . . ," T.R. to Francis J. Heney, November 7, 1914, TRLC; "the trouble with . . . ," T.R. to Willis J. Hulings, November 28, 1914, TRLC; II Timothy 4:3-4, printed in *New York Times,* November 5, 1914; "well! we surely . . . ," Charles Sumner Bird, to T.R., November 19, 1914, TRLC; "the country still favors . . . ," Davenport quoted from unidentified newspaper clipping of *circa* November 5, 1914 in Frederick M. Davenport Papers, Syracuse University; "Teddy votes," William Allen White to T.R., September 24, 1913, *Letters of William Allen White,* pp. 144-146; "this was not the Republican party born over . . . ," T.R. to Arthur Dehon Hill, November 9, 1914, TRLC.

Pages 227-228: "Your anti-Wilson speeches . . . ," Henry L. Stoddard to T.R., July 13, 1914, TRLC; "if any party . . . ," *Nation,* July 9, 1914, p. 33; "paralyzing psychology," Ben B. Lindsey to William Allen White, October 17, 1914, TRLC; "perhaps they were right," Charles Sumner Bird to T.R., November 19, 1914, TRLC. For 1912 election returns in Maine, Michigan, and New York, see *World Almanac: 1913,* respectively pp. 737, 739-740, 748-751; for 1914 election returns in Maine, Michigan, and New York, see *World Almanac: 1916,* respectively pp. 742, 743-744, 751-756. For comments on the 1914 election, see Alexander P. Moore to T.R., November 4, 1914, John M. Parker to T.R., November 6, 1914, T.R. to Henry J. Allen, November 7, 1914, T.R. to Alexander P. Moore, November 7, 1914, T.R. to James R. Garfield, November 7, 1914, T.R. to Victor Murdock, November 9, 1914, Edmund B. Osborne to T.R., November 13, 1914, Walter F. Brown to T.R., November 19, 1914, Bainbridge Colby to T.R., November 20, 1914, James R. Garfield to T.R., November 20, 1914, TRLC.

10. THE ARMAGEDDON OF WORLD WAR
The Last Days of the Progressive Party

Page 229: "It is impossible . . . ," T.R. to the Progressive National Committee, June 22, 1916, *Letters,* VIII, pp. 1067–1074. The return of Davenport and Robinson to the Republicans is reported in *Standard,* Watertown, N.Y., October 18, 1915; McCormick's return is mentioned in T.R. to Hiram W. Johnson, February 22. 1915, *Letters,* VIII, pp. 894–896; on Toner, see Braeman, *Beveridge,* p. 243.

Page 230: "Very gravely in doubt . . . ," T.R. to Henry F. Cochems, November 7, 1914, TRLC; "as a party we should . . . ," T.R. to Charles J. Bonaparte, November 19, 1914, TRCH; ". . . we should hold on . . . ," T.R. to N. Winslow Williams, November 30, 1914, TRLC; "I will keep you posted . . . ," T.R. to John M. Parker, November 12, 1914, TRLC; "I know that . . . ," T.R. to Archibald B. Roosevelt, December 7, 1914, TRCH.

Pages 230-232: For Amos Pinchot's "radical" program and his views on the 1914 defeat, see Amos Pinchot, pp. 58–59; Record's "radical" plans are outlined in an undated "Paper," Progressive National Committee Files, TRCH; "into taking a position . . . ," T.R. to Everett Colby, November 28, 1914, TRLC; "sir: when I spoke . . . ," T.R. to Amos Pinchot, November 3, 1916, *Letters,* VIII, p. 1122; "all that should be done . . . ," and "as a matter of fact . . . ," T. R. to E. A. Van Valkenburg, November 23, 1914, *Letters,* VIII, pp. 848–849; "the industrial depression . . . ," "Minutes of the Meeting of the Executive Committee of the Progressive National Committee Held December 2nd, 1914," typed ms., copies in TRCH and TRLC; ". . . I was struck . . . ," William Allen White to T.R., December 15, 1914, *Letters of William Allen White,* pp. 157–160. For the November 2 New York City meeting, see "Minutes of the Meeting of Executive Committee of the National Committee of the Progressive Party, held November 6th, 1914," typed ms., copies in TRCH and TRLC. On Amos Pinchot and George Record, see T.R. to E. A. Van Valkenburg, November 23, 1914, *Letters,* VIII, pp. 848–849; T.R. to Meyer Lissner, December 11, 1914, *Letters,* VIII, pp. 863–865; T.R. to Chester H. Rowell, December 17, 1914, *Letters,* VIII, pp. 866–867. On the Chicago conference, see T.R. to Hiram W. Johnson, November 16, 1914, *Letters,* VIII, pp. 845–847; George W. Perkins to William Allen White, November 12, 1914, James R. Garfield to T.R., November 20, 1914, Everett Colby to T.R., November 24, 1914, Oscar S. Straus to T.R., November 25, 1914, Hiram W. Johnson to T.R., November 30, 1914, T.R. to Victor Murdock, December 9, 1914, TRLC; William Allen White to T.R., November 20, 1914, November 21, 1914, and November 30, 1914, three letters, TRCH; George W. Perkins to Progressive leaders, December 7, 1914, Progressive National Committee Files, TRCH. On T.R.'s views that someone other than Perkins should represent the party in public, see T.R. to Meyer Lissner, December 11, 1914, *Letters,* VIII, pp. 863–865; T.R. to Chester H. Rowell, December 17, 1914, *Letters,* VIII, pp. 866–867.

Pages 232-233: "Equality of right," T.R. to Ethel Eyre Valentine Dreier, October 15, 1915, *Letters,* VIII, pp. 974–975; the Ivins-Root exchange quoted from Bishop, II, p. 366; Ivins in the courtroom quoted from Wagenknecht, p. 9. For Roosevelt in 1915 on unemployment, T.R., "The Problem of Unemployment;" on proposals for New York constitution, T.R. to the New York Short Ballot Organization, January 19, 1915, *Letters,* VIII, pp. 875–876; against compulsory Bible reading in public schools, T.R. to Michael A. Schaap, February 22, 1915, *Letters,* VIII, pp. 893–894. The official proceedings of the Barnes trial were published as *William Barnes Against Theodore Roosevelt, Supreme Court of the State of New York, Appellate Division, Fourth Department* (4 vols.: Walton, N.Y., 1917). On the Barnes trial also see Bishop, II, pp. 365–369; Pringle, pp. 575–577; Wagenknecht, pp. 4, 9, 125, 198, 212–213, 223–224.

Pages 233-234: Hermann Hagedorn, *The Bugle That Woke America: The Saga of Theodore Roosevelt's Last Battle for His Country* (New York, 1940), a general account of T.R. in the war years by a friend and follower; Wilson and Daniels quoted by Link, *Wilson and the Progressive Era,* p. 177; Bryan quoted and the Roosevelt quotation on Bryan from T.R., *America and the World War* (1915), *NWTR,* XVIII, pp. 182–183. On the beginning of the preparedness controversy, the findings of the naval board, Stimson's views, the policy of the Wilson administration, and the state of American defense, see Link, *Wilson and the Progressive Era*, pp. 174-196; Arthur S. Link, *Wilson: The Struggle for Neutrality, 1914-1915* (Princeton, 1960); Elting E. Morison, *Turmoil and Tradition: A Study of the Life and Times of Henry L. Stimson* (New York, 1960), pp. 187-195; T.R., *America and the World War.*

Pages 234-235: Gifford Pinchot quoted by Fausold, p. 197; "very early I learned . . . ," T.R., "How I Became a Progressive," *Outlook*, October 12, 1912, in *NWTR*, XVII, pp. 315-319, quotation, p. 318. For the views of Progressive Party members on preparedness and the war, see Edmund B. Osborne to T.R., November 13, 1914, TRLC; Victor Murdock to G. O. Van Meter, September 25, 1915, Progressive National Committee Files, TRCH; Raymond Robins's speech to the 1916 Progressive convention, *New York Times*, June 8, 1916; Allen, pp. 289-305; Fausold, pp. 194-250; Harold L. Ickes, *Autobiography;* Frances Kellor, *Straight America* (New York, 1916); *Meeting of the Progressive National Committee, Chicago, January 11-12, 1916* (New York, 1916), pamphlet in TRCH; George W. Perkins, "We Are As Unprepared for Peace As We Are for War," address, Bankers' Club, Indianapolis, October, 1915, typed ms., Progressive National Committee Files, TRCH; Richberg, *Tents of the Mighty*, pp. 63-100, Vadney, pp. 28-29; White, pp. 512-519. On Roosevelt's work for preparedness, and on the preparedness movement in general, see Bishop, II, pp. 370-403; Hagedorn, *The Bugle That Woke America;* Hermann Hagedorn, *Leonard Wood: A Biography* (2 vols.: New York, 1931); Harbaugh, pp. 466-497; Kellor, *Straight America;* Link, *Wilson and the Progressive Era*, pp. 174-196; Earle Looker, *Colonel Roosevelt: Private Citizen* (New York, 1932); Cleveland Moffet, *The Conquest of America* (New York, 1916), a novel expressing preparedness views; Pringle, pp. 572-604; and see numerous letters on the preparedness movement in *Letters*, VIII, and TRLC. On the progressive movement and preparedness and the war, see particularly Howard W. Allen, "Republican Reformers and Foreign Policy, 1913-1917," *Mid-America*, 44 (1962), pp. 222-229; Charles Hirschfeld, "Nationalist Progressivism and World War I," *Mid-America*, 45 (1963), pp. 139-156; Walter I. Trattner, "Progressivism and World War I: A Re-Appraisal," *Mid-America*, 44 (1962), pp. 131-145. For a review of the extensive literature on the issues involved in American participation in World War I, see Daniel M. Smith, "National Interest and American Intervention, 1917," *Journal of American History*, LII (1965), pp. 5-24.

Pages 236-238: "I feel that . . . ," T.R., "How I Became a Progressive," *NWTR*, XVII, p. 319; "universal service . . . ," T.R., *America and the World War*, *NWTR*, XVIII, p. 175, and see pp. 87-104, 174-175; Roosevelt on the pacifist song quoted from T.R., *Fear God and Take Your Own Part* (1916), *NWTR*, XVIII, p. 306; "actually Roosevelt was . . . ," Beale, pp. 48-49; for Roosevelt's American Sociological Congress paper, see T.R., "Warlike Power—The Prerequisite for the Preservation of Social Values," American Sociological Society, *Papers and Proceedings* (1916), in *NWTR*, XVIII, pp. 227-237; Roosevelt on the *Lusitania* quoted by Hagedorn, *The Bugle That Woke America*, pp. 68-69; "otherwise, if Europe fails," Rudyard Kipling to T.R., September 15, 1914, TRLC. For Croly's views on preparedness, see Croly, *Promise of American Life*, pp. 246-264. On the general subject of T.R. and war and peace, see Wagenknecht, pp. 247-287; for an analysis and account of T.R.'s arguments for preparedness and intervention, see Harbaugh, pp. 466-497. Also see Russell Buchanan, "Theodore Roosevelt and American Neutrality, 1914-1917," *American Historical Review*, XLIII (1938), pp. 775-790.

Pages 238-242: "Military and economic preparedness," Victor Murdock to G. O. Van Meter, September 25, 1915, Progressive National Committee Files, TRCH; "The Newer Nationalism," *New Republic*, January 29, 1916, pp. 319-321; for the Progressives at Chicago in January, 1916, see *Meeting of the Progressive National Committee, Chicago, January 11-12, 1916:* George W. Perkins's speech, pp. 7-13, Bainbridge Colby's speech, "Our Country," pp. 15-25, statement of the Progressive National Committee, pp. 26-29. On the United States and the war in the period 1915-1916, see Link, *Wilson: Confusions and Crises, 1915-1916* (Princeton, 1964); T.R., *Fear God and Take Your Own Part*, *NWTR*, XVIII. On Roosevelt and the Progressive Party in 1915-1916, see Mowry, pp. 304-344.

Pages 242-243: "So far as possible . . . ," "Minutes of the Meeting of the Executive Committee of the Progressive National Committee Held in New York City, November 30th, 1915," typed ms., copies in TRCH and TRLC; "I have had . . . ," T.R. to George E. Miller, November 8, 1912, TRLC; "it makes my blood boil . . . ," T.R. to John Callan O'Laughlin, May 6, 1915, *Letters,* VIII, pp. 921–922; "we do not want . . . ," T.R. to George von L. Meyer, March 29, 1916, *Letters,* VIII, pp. 1024–1026; "politician's movement," T.R. to William Noble, May 2, 1916, *Letters,* VIII, pp. 1035–1036; "my own judgement . . . ," T.R. to Charles Grenfill Washburn, May 6, 1916, *Letters,* VIII, pp. 1037–1038; "I do not believe . . . ," T.R. to Arthur Hamilton Lee, June 7, 1916, *Letters,* VIII, pp. 1052–1056. On Progressive plans for 1916, also see George W. Perkins to Progressive leaders, November 30, 1915, "Statement Issued After the Executive Committee Meeting May 10, 1916," typed ms., Progressive National Committee Files, TRCH; "Minutes of the Meeting of the Executive Committee of the Progressive National Committee Held May 10th, 1916," typed ms., copies in TRCH and TRLC. For Roosevelt's views on his own possible candidacy and on other potential candidates for 1916, see T.R. to William Allen White, September 29, 1913, T.R. to Charles J. Bonaparte, July 22, 1914, T.R. to Medill McCormick, August 14, 1914, TRLC; T.R. to Victor Murdock, September 30, 1913, *Letters,* VII, pp. 750–752; T.R. to John Callan O'Laughlin, August 27, 1914, *Letters,* VII, pp. 813–815; T.R. to Hiram W. Johnson, November 6, 1914, *Letters,* VIII, pp. 832–833; T.R. to William Dudley Foulke, December 12, 1914, *Letters,* VIII, pp. 865–866; T.R. to Gifford Pinchot, June 1, 1915, *Letters,* VIII, pp. 925–926; T.R. to Hiram W. Johnson, April 3, 1916, *Letters,* VIII, pp. 1026–1029. On Beveridge and 1916, see Braeman, *Beveridge,* p. 244. For T.R.'s views that from the standpoint of foreign affairs even the conservative bosses were better than Wilson, see T.R. to Henry Cabot Lodge, December 8, 1914, *Letters,* VIII, pp. 861–863; T.R. to Henry Cabot Lodge, February 18, 1915, *Letters,* VIII, pp. 892–893; T.R. to Henry Cabot Lodge, November 27, 1915, *Letters,* VIII, pp. 991–992. For Roosevelt's views on Hughes, also see T.R. to Henry Cabot Lodge, December 7, 1915, *Letters,* VIII, pp. 995–996. On Hughes, see Merlo J. Pusey, *Charles Evans Hughes* (2 vols.: New York, 1951).

Pages 243-245: "No relations whatsoever . . . ," George von L. Meyer to Judge Kibbey, May 25, 1916, and telegram to Arkansas banker, George von L. Meyer to F. E. Patrick, telegram, May 25, 1916, both in 1916 Roosevelt Republican Committee Papers, TRCH; ". . . the Progressive Party advertised . . . ," Richberg, *Tents of the Mighty,* p. 72; "that it would be a mistake . . . ," T.R., "The Heroic Mood," statement to the press at Port of Spain, Trinidad, March 9, 1916, *NWTR,* XVII, pp. 410–413. For Lissner's activities, an account of the effort made for Roosevelt's nomination, and T.R.'s speeches in pacifist country, see Mowry, pp. 320–346. The 1916 Roosevelt Republican Committee Papers in TRCH contain letters, telegrams, clippings, campaign materials, and card files of the Meyer group. On the Roosevelt Republican Committee, T. R. Non-Partisan League, and Women's Roosevelt League, see T.R. to George von L. Meyer, May 10, 1916, *Letters,* VIII, p. 1039; T.R. to Guy Emerson, May 11, 1916, *Letters,* VIII, pp. 1039–1041; T.R. to Thomas A. Edison, May 13, 1916, *Letters,* VIII, pp. 1041–1042; T.R. to Guy Emerson, May 16, 1916, *Letters,* VIII, pp. 1042–1043; T.R. to Carrie Chapman Catt, June 6, 1916, *Letters,* VIII, pp. 1051–1052. On Progressive help for the Roosevelt Republican group, see William Loeb, Jr. (?) to George F. Porter, May 24, 1916, Emmet Morris to George von L. Meyer, telegram, May 22, 1916, George von L. Meyer to Emmet Morris, telegram, May 22, 1916, Roosevelt Republican Committee Papers, TRCH. Washburn's biography was Charles G. Washburn, *Theodore Roosevelt: The Logic of His Career* (Boston, 1916); and see Julian Street, *The Most Interesting American* (New York, 1915). On the attempt to secure the Republican nomination for T.R., also see Curry, p. 281; Karlin, pp. 208–227; Walter Merriam Pratt, *Seven Generations: A Story of Prattville and Chelsea* (privately printed, 1930), pp. 330–336; Stoddard, pp. 426–433.

Pages 246-248: "We'll take . . . ," Smoot quoted in Stoddard, p. 435; Roosevelt "was evading," Stoddard, p. 436; T.R.'s conditional refusal of the Progressive nomination, T.R. to the Progressive National Convention, June 10, 1916, *Letters,* VIII, pp. 1062–1063; "for a moment . . . ," White, pp. 526–527; resolution to fill vacancies on the Progressive ticket, "Resolution Adopted By the Progressive National Convention, June 10, 1916," *The Progressive Party: Its Record from January to July, 1916* (New York, 1916), p. 95.

The Progressive Party: Its Record, from January to July 2, 1916 (New York, 1916), p. 95.
The Progressive Party: Its Record, copy TRCH, was published by the Progressive National
Committee and includes many important documents of the last months of the party's
history, including the Progressive platform of 1916, pp. 91–94. John A. Garraty, editor,
"T.R. on the Telephone," *American Heritage,* IX (1957), pp. 98–108, gives part of the
transcript of Roosevelt's conversations over the private wire connecting Sagamore Hill
with George W. Perkins's rooms in the Blackstone Hotel, Chicago. The members of the
Progressive conference committee were Hiram W. Johnson, George W. Perkins, Horace S.
Wilkinson, John M. Parker, and Charles J. Bonaparte. The members of the Republican
conference committee were W. Murray Crane, Reed Smoot, William E. Borah, A. R.
Johnson, and Nicholas Murray Butler. Roosevelt wrote three messages for use at the con-
ventions in explaining his views on the issues and the necessity for a joint nomination:
T.R. to Charles J. Bonaparte, May 29, 1916, *Letters,* VIII, p. 1049; T.R. to William Purnell
Jackson, telegram, June 8, 1916, *Letters,* VIII, pp. 1058–1060; T.R. to the Conferees of the
Progressive Party, telegram, June 10, 1916, *Letters,* VIII, pp. 1060–1062, in which as a
final gesture T.R. suggested Lodge. The record of the Republican convention is *Official
Report of the Proceedings of the Sixteenth Republican National Convention* (New York,
1916). On Parker's position, see T.R. to Whitmell Pugh Martin, June 23, 1916, *Letters,*
VIII, pp. 1077–1078; on Missouri Progressives, *New York Times,* June 10–11, June 26–27,
1916; on Indiana Progressives, Painter. For accounts of the Progressive convention of 1916,
see *New York Times,* June 8–12, 1916; *American Review of Reviews,* July, 1916, pp.
4–12; Garraty, *Perkins,* pp. 327–352; Harbaugh, pp. 486–492; Harold L. Ickes, "Who Killed
the Progressive Party," *American Historical Review,* XLVI (1941), pp. 306–337; Amos
Pinchot, pp. 219–225; Mowry, pp. 345–358; Stoddard, pp. 434–437; White, pp. 520–527.

Pages 248–249: "The rest of the story . . . ," Garraty, "T.R. on the Telephone," p. 108.
On the June 26 meeting of the Progressive National Committee, see *New York Times,*
June 26–27, 1916; *The Progressive Party, Its Record,* pp. 96–132; T.R. to the Progressive
National Committee, June 22, 1916, *Letters,* VIII, pp. 1067–1074. On the antifusionist
Progressive conclave in Indianapolis, see *New York Times,* August 3–4, 1916; Mowry,
pp. 359–360. Since Parker returned to the Democratic Party, the plan to wage a national
Progressive campaign came to nothing. Progressive electors, however, remained on the ballot
in some states and received some votes. On the Progressives who joined the Republicans
and those who joined the Democrats in 1916, see Link, *Wilson and the Progressive Era,*
pp. 239–240; Mowry, pp. 358–367. On the 1916 campaign and election, see Arthur S.
Link and William M. Leary, Jr., "Election of 1916," in Schlesinger and Israel, editors,
History of American Presidential Elections, III, pp. 2245–2345. For discussion of Wilson's
Bull Moose support and analysis of the 1916 vote, see La Forte, pp. 256, 295; Arthur S.
Link, *Wilson: Campaigns for Progressivism and Peace* (Princeton, 1965), pp. 124–164;
Link, *Wilson and the Progressive Era,* pp. 223–251.

EPILOGUE: THE DIASPORA

Page 250: "Firm in the conviction . . . ," statement of progressive Republicans quoted
from *Letters,* VIII, p. 1128; and see T.R. to William Allen White, December 2, 1916,
Letters, VIII, pp. 1128–1131. On the Committee of 48, see Amos Pinchot, pp. 72–76.
Another remnant of the Progressives, led by Victor Murdock and Matthew Hale, met at
St. Louis in April. 1917, and merged with the Prohibition Party. See Mowry, p. 367. The
vast majority of Progressive leaders, however, found homes in one of the old parties. For
Roosevelt's plans for 1920, see T.R. to William Allen White, April 4, 1918, *Letters,*
VIII, pp. 1305–1307; Hermann Hagedorn and Sidney Wallach, editor, *A Theodore
Roosevelt Round-Up* (New York, 1958), pp. 51–52, 155–160; Hinshaw, pp. 114–119;
Leary, pp. 1–10. Republican National Committeeman John T. King of Connecticut was
scheduled to be T.R.'s campaign manager, and the mining magnate William Boyce
Thompson, who subsequently became the first president of the Roosevelt Memorial
Association (now the Theodore Roosevelt Association), had promised to provide
campaign funds.

Pages 251–252: "Looking back . . . ," White, p. 627. The careers and beliefs of Bull Moose
and other progressives after 1920 are thoroughly studied in Otis L. Graham, Jr., *An Encore*

for Reform: The Old Progressives and the New Deal (New York, 1967); also see Alan R. Havig, "A Disputed Legacy: Roosevelt Progressives and the Last La Follette Campaign of 1924," *Mid-America,* 53 (1971), pp. 44-64. Biographical information from *BDAC, DAB, NCAB, WWW.* Bainbridge Colby was Secretary of State under Woodrow Wilson 1920-1921. Other former Progressives who held cabinet posts through the years include Walter F. Brown, Postmaster General 1929-1933; Harold L. Ickes, Secretary of the Interior 1933-1945; and Frank Knox, Secretary of the Navy 1940-1944. John Franklin Fort of New Jersey served on the Federal Trade Commission 1917-1919; Victor Murdock was on the F.T.C. 1917-1924, and chairman 1919-1923. Edward P. Costigan was on the Tariff Commission 1917-1928 before being elected to the Senate as a Democrat from Colorado in 1930. Frederick M. Davenport was in the U.S. House as a Republican 1925-1933, before becoming president of the National Institute of Public Affairs. Several Progressives, including Alexander P. Moore and Miles Poindexter, held ambassadorial posts. Moore of Pennyslvania was ambassador to Spain, Peru, and Poland. Other Progressives, such as former Congressman Charles M. Thomson of Illinois and Francis J. Heney of California, became judges. Numerous former Progressives, including Stanley M. Isaacs, Alfred M. Landon, and John G. Winant, who had served in the ranks 1912-1916 or worked for the party in minor positions later rose to prominence in public life. Many Progressives were active in charity and civic affairs. Everett Colby's many posts included chairmanship of the National World Court Committee; James R. Garfield was president of the Roosevelt Memorial Association and the Cleveland Welfare Federation; Joel E. Spingarn was treasurer and president of the N.A.A.C.P. Former Progressives who became governors include Henry J. Allen, Republican governor of Kansas 1919-1923; John M. Parker, Democratic governor of Louisiana 1920-1924; Joseph M. Dixon, Republican governor of Montana 1921-1925; and Gifford Pinchot, elected governor of Pennsylvania on the Republican ticket in 1922 and again in 1930. Former Progressives who served in the U.S. Senate include Hiram W. Johnson of California, Medill McCormick of Illinois, Robert Carey of Wyoming, Thomas D. Schall of Minnesota, Bronson Cutting of New Mexico, Allen of Kansas, and Costigan of Colorado, all of whom except Costigan were Republicans. The list of former Progressives who served in the U.S. House after 1916 includes M. Clyde Kelley, Henry Willson Temple, and Willis J. Hulings of Pennsylvania; Walter M. Chandler, Hamilton Fish, Herbert C. Pell, Bourke Cockran, and Davenport of New York; Roy O. Woodruff of Michigan, who served 1913-1915 and 1921-1953; Whitmell Pugh Martin of Louisiana; Frank H. Funk of Illinois; Schall of Minnesota; and Joseph I. Nolan and John A. Elston of California. Pell, Cockran, and Martin were Democrats; the rest were Republicans.

INDEX